MAKING IT LIKE A MAN

Cultural Studies Series

Cultural Studies is the multi- and inter-disciplinary study of culture, defined anthropologically as a "way of life," performatively as symbolic practice, and ideologically as the collective product of varied media and cultural industries. Although Cultural Studies is a relative newcomer to the humanities and social sciences, in less than half a century it has taken interdisciplinary scholarship to a new level of sophistication, reinvigorating the liberal arts curriculum with new theories, topics, and forms of intellectual partnership.

Wilfrid Laurier University Press invites submissions of manuscripts concerned with critical discussions on power relations concerning gender, class, sexual preference, ethnicity, and other macro and micro sites of political struggle.

For more information, please contact:

Lisa Quinn
Acquisitions Editor
Wilfrid Laurier University Press
75 University Avenue West
Waterloo, ON N2L 3C5
Canada
Phone: 519-884-0710 ext. 2843
Fax: 519-725-1399
Email: quinn@press.wlu.ca

MAKING IT LIKE A MAN
CANADIAN MASCULINITIES IN PRACTICE

Christine Ramsay, editor

WILFRID LAURIER
UNIVERSITY PRESS

This book has been published with the help of a grant from the Canadian Federation for the Humanities and Social Sciences, through the Aid to Scholarly Publications Programme, using funds provided by the Social Sciences and Humanities Research Council of Canada. We acknowledge the financial support of the Government of Canada through the Canada Book Fund for our publishing activities.

 Canada Council for the Arts   Conseil des Arts du Canada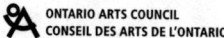

Library and Archives Canada Cataloguing in Publication

Making it like a man : Canadian masculinities in practice / Christine Ramsay, editor.

(Cultural studies series)
Includes bibliographical references and index.
Issued also in electronic formats.
ISBN 978-1-55458-327-0

1. Masculinity—Social aspects—Canada. 2. Masculinity—Canada. 3. Men—Canada—Identity. I. Ramsay, Christine, 1958– II. Series: Cultural studies series (Waterloo, Ont.)

HQ1090.7.C2M35 2011   305.310971   C2011-902983-9

Electronic resource.
Issued also in print format.
ISBN 978-1-55458-375-1 (PDF)

1. Masculinity—Social aspects—Canada. 2. Masculinity—Canada. 3. Men—Canada—Identity. I. Ramsay, Christine, 1958– II. Series: Cultural studies series (Waterloo, Ont.)

HQ1090.7.C2M35 2011a   305.310971   C2011-902984-7

© 2011 Wilfrid Laurier University Press
Waterloo, Ontario, Canada
www.wlupress.wlu.ca

Cover design by Martyn Schmoll. Cover photograph (top) by Afshin Matlabi, *On Technologies of Man's Sensuality* (1999), part of a project that comprises photo (24" x 36") with video projection and sound (artist vacuuming parking lot). Reproduced with the permission of the artist. Cover photograph (bottom) by Steve Cukrov/iStock. Text design by Catharine Bonas-Taylor. Layout by Daiva Villa, Chris Rowat Design.

This book is printed on FSC recycled paper and is certified Ecologo. It is made from 100% post-consumer fibre, processed chlorine free, and manufactured using biogas energy.

Printed in Canada

Every reasonable effort has been made to acquire permission for copyright material used in this publication and to acknowledge all such indebtedness accurately. Any errors and omissions called to the publisher's attention will be corrected in future printings.

No part of this publication may be reproduced, stored in a retrieval system or transmitted, in any form or by any means, without the prior written consent of the publisher or a licence from The Canadian Copyright Licensing Agency (Access Copyright). For an Access Copyright licence, visit www.accesscopyright.ca or call toll free to 1-800-893-5777.

CONTENTS

List of Illustrations / vii

Acknowledgments / ix

Introduction / xi
Christine Ramsay

I Identity, Agency, and Manliness in the Colonial and the National

1 Carnival and Masculinity in the Travel Fiction of James De Mille / 3
Ken Wilson

2 "No Money, but Muscle and Pluck": Cultivating Trans-Imperial Manliness for the Fields of Empire, 1870–1901 / 17
Jarett Henderson

3 Who's on the Home Front? Canadian Masculinity in the NFB's Second World War Series "Canada Carries On" / 39
Michael Brendan Baker

II Emotional Geographies of Anxiety, Eros, and Impairment

4 Making Art Like a Man! / 55
David Garneau

5 "Above Mere Men": The Heterogeneous Male in Attila Richard Lukacs / 79
Piet Defraeye

6 Stranger Than Paradise: Immigration and Impaired Masculinities / 101
Christina Stojanova

III The Minority Male

7 The "Hood" Reconfigured: Black Masculinity in *Rude* / 133
D.L. McGregor and Sheila Petty

8 "Keepin' It Real"? Masculinity, Indigeneity, and Media Representations of Gangsta Rap in Regina / 149
Charity Marsh

9 Fixing Stories "Is Sure a Lot of Work": Watching "the Men's Dance" in *Medicine River* and *Green Grass, Running Water* / 171
Peter Cumming

10 Masculinity in a Minority Setting: The Emblematic Body in Simone Chaput's *Le coulonneux* / 185
Nicole Côté

IV Capitalized, Corporatized, Compromised Men

11 The Politics of Marginalization at the Centre: Canadian Masculinities and Global Capitalism in Douglas Coupland's *Generation X* / 199
   Kit Dobson

12 Dangerous Homosexualities and Disturbing Masculinities: The Disabling Rhetoric of Difference in Barbara Gowdy's *Mister Sandman* / 215
   Sally Hayward

V Abject Masculinities

13 What Do Heterosexual Men Want? Or, "The (Wandering) Queer Eye on the (Straight) Guy" / 233
   Thomas Waugh

14 Boy to the Power of Three: Toronto's Drag Kings / 259
   Bobby Noble

15 Life Without Death? Space, Affect, and Masculine Identity in the Work of Frank Cole / 281
   Christine Ramsay

Bibliography / 297
Biographical Notes / 319
Index / 325

LIST OF ILLUSTRATIONS

Chapter 1
Fig. 1   "A Perplexed Senator," from *The Dodge Club* / 10
Fig. 2   "Senator and Donkey," from *The Dodge Club* / 11
Fig. 3   "Used Up," from *The Dodge Club* / 13

Chapter 2
Fig. 4   Blueprint from *Useful and Practical Hints for the Settler on Canadian Prairie Lands and for the Guidance of Intending British Emigrants* / 21
Fig. 5   "First Year in the Bush," from *Manitoba and the Great North West* / 24
Fig. 6   "Fifteen Years in the Bush," from *Manitoba and the Great North West* / 24
Fig. 7   "Thirty Years in the Bush," From *Manitoba and the Great North West* / 25
Fig. 8   "Ploughing on William Hamilton's Farm near Hamiota, Man., 1905–1909" / 27

Chapter 3
Fig. 9   Still from *Inside Fighting Canada* (1942) / 42
Fig. 10 Still from *Letter from Aldershot* (1940) / 43
Fig. 11 Still from *Letter from Overseas* (1943) / 48

Chapter 4
Fig. 12 Walter May, *Knockout* (2002) / 57
Fig. 13 Walter May, *Knockout*, detail (2002) / 57
Fig. 14 Dean Drever, *The only way it makes sense to you* (2003) / 59
Fig. 15 Craig Le Blanc, *I Don't Play* (2001) / 61
Fig. 16 Craig Le Blanc, *I Don't Play*, detail (2001) / 62
Fig. 17 Craig Le Blanc, *Slump* (2004) / 63
Fig. 18 Derek Dunlop, *Untitled* (n.d.) / 66
Fig. 19 Jeff Nachtigall, *Schwarzenegger Shrine*, detail (2004) / 68
Fig. 20 Jefferson Little, *Evo-Blaster 2000* (2002) / 70

Fig. 21 Kevin Friedrich, *Bass Acwards* (2001) / 71
Fig. 22 Daniel Fisher, *Wounded War Pony* (2002) / 73
Fig. 23 Blair Brennan, *Shirts and Skins*, front view (2004) / 74
Fig. 24 Blair Brennan, *Shirts and Skins*, back view (2004) / 75

Chapter 5
Fig. 25 Attila Richard Lukacs, *Wild Kingdom* (1992–93) / 87

Chapter 6
Fig. 26 Pierre reads to Momo in *La fabrication d'un meurtrier* / 110
Fig. 27 Atanas Katrapani in *Home* / 117
Fig. 28 Milena and Philippe in *Nos vies privées / Our Private Lives* / 123

Chapter 8
Fig. 29 "Arrested on Camera," article from *The Leader-Post* (18 August 2007) / 163
Fig. 30 Poster for *Dogz Lyfe: Burdens of a Gangster Rapper* (2008) / 164

Chapter 13
Fig. 31 *Bondage Television* (Stev'nn Hall, 1996) / 237
Fig. 32 *Touch* (Jeremy Podeswa, 2001) / 245
Fig. 33 Coach James and hockey player Kennedy in *The Sheldon Kennedy Story* (Norma Bailey, 1999) / 251
Fig. 34 Basement scene in *Léolo* (Jean-Claude Lauzon, 1992) / 254

Chapter 15
Fig. 35 Frank Cole, in a still from *Life Without Death* (2000) / 282
Fig. 36 Frank with camel, in a still from *Life Without Death* (2000) / 288

Acknowledgements

As we know, all books—whether single authored, co-written, or collections of individual essays—are the products of dialogue and collective effort. I would like to thank the contributors; my colleagues and friends Angela Stukator, Stephen McClatchie, and David Garneau for their earlier editorial contributions to this volume; and the constructive observations and cogent insights of the readers who critiqued the manuscript; as well as Lisa Quinn and her colleagues at Wilfrid Laurier University Press for their enthusiasm and patience. In addition, I would like to give special thanks to Thomas Waugh for his generous editorial feedback as well as for his friendship and inspiration to a generation of film studies, queer studies, and cultural studies scholars and students in Canada; and to Ken Wilson for his insights and encouragement throughout the preparation of this book.

Financial support for various phases of this project has been kindly provided by the SSHRC Standard Research Grant; the Canada Council for the Arts; the President's SSHRC, the Humanities Research Institute, and the Faculty of Fine Arts at the University of Regina; the MacKenzie Art Gallery; the City of Regina; the Saskatchewan Arts Board; and the Regina Public Library Film Theatre.

Introduction

CHRISTINE RAMSAY

Making It Like a Man: Canadian Masculinities in Practice is a collection of essays on the practice of masculinities in Canadian arts and cultures. In this anthology we are interested in mapping some of the uniquely Canadian spaces—contemporary and historical—in the international field of masculinity studies for an academic and culturally informed audience. The throughline of the book is Canadian masculinities in action across a diverse range of geo-physical settings—from the fields of empire to the sands of the Sahara; past the dance floors of First Nations and post-queer gender relations and the four walls of the exhibition gallery; around the urban 'hood, the churchyard, and the ice rinks of the NHL—and an aggregate sphere of more psychosocial dimensions—from the exclusionary margins of the forces of global capital, the screen mythologies of the heterosexual nuclear family and its homosocial 'other,' and the queer politics of the artist's canvas; to the fractured subjectivities of immigrants, minorities, and exiles. In our collective thinking, to "make it like a man" is to participate in the multiplicity of sites and scenes where masculinities have been "practised"—by which we mean variously constructed, staged, performed, contrived, experienced, enacted, engaged, exercised, carried on, tried on, put on, thrown off, and/or negotiated across the very broad landscape of Canadian gender identity in a global context—whether within the confines of traditional national boundaries, outside them in the transnational sphere, or somewhere in between. All but one of the chapters are original,[1] having been written specifically for publication in this volume, in which the purpose is to present a collective dialogue on the rich spectrum of current academic work on masculinities in our art, literature, film, cultural history, and sport to those students, teachers, and general readers interested in new transdisciplinary research in Canadian cultural studies—but research envisioned, in the first instance, through the lens of *gender*. *Making It Like a Man* situates itself in the theoretical context of what the contributors understand as the cultural, sociological, and historical *fluidity* of masculine expressions, representations, and power relations in Canada, gathered here through the five focused themes: colonialism/nationalism, emotional geographies, ethnic minorities, corporate capitalism/domestic politics, and otherness.

CONTEXTS

Sociologist R.W. Connell is one of the leading figures in the international field of masculinity studies. In the second edition of his foundational book *Masculinities* (2005), he traces its developments and shifts since its activist beginnings in the late 1960s with the rise of the second wave of feminism to the rich and varied academic research, public debates, and policy making on masculinities that have taken place around the globe in the past decade. Since 2000, many important monographs, readers, handbooks, and anthologies have also appeared, advancing theoretical interest, scholarship, and teaching in the field. While a comprehensive international listing is obviously impossible, works that have been particularly influential for the contributors to *Making It Like a Man* have included John Beynon's *Masculinities and Culture* (2002); Rachel Adams and David Savran's *The Masculinity Studies Reader* (2002); Stephen Whitehead's *Men and Masculinities: Key Themes and New Directions* (2002); Judith Kegan Gardiner's *Masculinity Studies and Feminist Theory: New Directions* (2002); Radhika Chopra's *South Asian Masculinities: Context of Change, Sites of Continuity* (2004); Michael S. Kimmel's *Handbook of Studies on Men and Masculinities* (2005); Bettina van Hoven's *Spaces of Masculinities* (2005); *Cultures of Masculinity* (2006) by Tim Edwards; and *Masculinity in the Modern West: Gender, Civilization, and the Body* (2008) by Christopher Forth.

Research into the history and historiography of masculinities is also burgeoning alongside sociological and theoretical perspectives, accounting for what is generally understood among scholars—including Connell himself—as the fundamentally historical nature of international masculinities and their ever-present and ever-changing construction and reconstruction in historical contexts. Here, John Tosh has been an influential figure, beginning with *Manful Assertions: Masculinities in Britain since 1800* (1991), *Masculinities in Politics and War: Gendering Modern History* (with Stefan Dudink, 2004), and *Manliness and Masculinities in Nineteenth-Century Britain: Essays on Gender, Family, and Empire* (2005). This kind of pioneering historically specific model for the study of British masculinities has been taken up and continues apace in Canada with the "Studies in Gender and History" series at the University of Toronto Press, which covers extensive terrain in terms of cultural, class-based, regional, and ethnic histories of gender, femininity, and masculinity, and which now numbers seventy volumes. Also trendsetting in scope is *American Masculinities: A Historical Encyclopedia* (2003), edited by Bret Carroll.

In addition, excellent discipline-specific analyses of masculinities as a function of culture, representation, and nation proliferate, such as *Masculinity: Bodies, Movies, Culture* (2001) by Peter Lehman; *Boys Don't Cry? Rethinking Narratives of Masculinity and Emotion in the U.S.* (2002) by Milette Shamir; *The Trouble with Men: Masculinities in European and Hollywood Cinema* (2004) by Phil Powrie; Patricia Vettel-Becker's *Shooting from the Hip: Photography, Masculinity and Postwar America* (2005); *The Romance of Transgression in Canada: Queering Sexualities, Nations, Cinemas* (2006) by Thomas Waugh; *Northern Love: An Exploration of Canadian Masculinity* (2008) by Paul Nonnekes; and *When Men Dance: Choreographing Masculinities Across Borders* (2009) by Jennifer Fisher. It is here, in the realm of critical analyses of cultural representations of masculinities in Canada, that *Making It Like a Man* is perhaps best located.

CULTURES OF MASCULINITY

In *Cultures of Masculinity*, Tim Edwards uses a cultural studies approach to survey the social, cultural, historical, and theoretical issues that have evolved in the critical study of masculinities. He identifies the three phases of masculinity studies that have been adopted from the "wave" model used by feminism to chart its own history. In the 1960s, the second wave of feminism ushered in the important theoretical shift from talking about "women" (women's histories, women and the image) to talking about "gender" as the primary subject of concern.[2] This shift enabled "men" and "masculinity" to become legitimate topics of inquiry in terms of their place in the sex–gender system, whereas before they had passed as transparent, normative, and natural. Thus, in the 1970s, the first wave of masculinity studies was born of the second wave of feminism. Women and men both began talking about masculinity as a social construction that relies on "socialization, sex role learning and social control" and documenting how the male sex role can be physically, psychologically, and emotionally damaging to both sexes.[3] A men's liberation movement emerged that mounted pro-feminist critiques of patriarchal masculinity, misogyny, and homophobia. But, as Connell observes, while this first wave "gave rise to interesting political discussions about men, power, and change," it did not offer insight into *practice*—"what men and boys actually do"—and it left the concept of gender confused and untheorized.[4]

As one would expect, the second wave of masculinity studies arose in response to the first wave. On the one hand, the mythopoetic men's movement took shape around Robert Bly's *Iron John*, which called for groups of (heterosexual) men to escape to nature, spirituality, and male bonding through wilderness retreats that could restore their "essential" masculine power and so retrieve the dominance guaranteed by their sex role—a supposed antidote to the "emasculating" forces of feminism.[5] On the other hand, this popular backlash was met with great strides by academic women and men in terms of (1) the deepening of gender theory and the expansion of empirical research into gender practices, and (2) gender as a social structure of power and inequality privileging men. For Edwards, this tangent of the second wave is generally accepted as having created the field of masculinity studies proper based in (1) a rejection of the sex-role paradigm and its assumption of a "level playing field" between the two sexes as equal but different, and (2) a rejection of the universalizing model of white, Western, middle-class masculinity in favour of a new portrait of how plural masculinities are socially constructed, produced, and reproduced in various discursive and historical contexts.[6] Foucault's *History of Sexuality* was influential in showing how gender categories are culturally produced by the sciences of sexuality and social control.[7] So was Connell's work, which used Gramsci to understand the struggles between hegemonic masculinity and oppressed masculinities across the fields of race, class, and sexuality; Eve Kosofsky Sedgwick's thinking on the homosocial continuum;[8] and the evolution of queer theory. While some feminists and queer theorists were nervous about the legitimacy of "men in feminism," and concerned about the dangers in returning attention, energy, and scarce resources to (straight) men and their anxieties, many began to see the importance of this new field of research in its pro-feminist forms, and to experience the productive alliances happening among masculinity studies, feminism, and queer studies.

Edwards observes that with the turn to inter- and trans-disciplinarity in the 1990s linked to post-structuralist and post-colonial theory, and with the interest generated by Judith Butler in questions of normativity, artifice, and gender as performance in analyzing and queering cultural texts of all kinds,[9] the third wave of masculinity studies has come to the realization that, "as is also the case with feminism," its terrain is now "less easy to define, often slipping across interdisciplinary lines and invoking literary, cultural and media studies alongside the work of social scientists. A common theme, however, is the importance of representation and its connection with wider questions of change and continuity in both contemporary, and in some more historical, masculinities and identities."[10]

So, as Connell suggests, "studies of masculinities and men's gender practices" are now a "comprehensible field of knowledge"[11]—or, as Edwards describes it, a "vast" canon, yet one that in his opinion is fast becoming an increasingly fragmented "array of Petri dishes growing cultures of masculinity" in crisis.[12] For Edwards, the talk of a "crisis of masculinity" has become so ubiquitous in popular and academic circles since the rise of the third wave of masculinity studies that the term has become almost meaningless.

Thus, part of the work he sets out for himself in *Cultures of Masculinity* is to clarify how this crisis is being defined; to document specific evidence of it across concrete issues such as work, education, crime, the family, sexuality, health, and representation; and to analyze its significance for the theory and practice of sexual politics.[13] In any case, the point is well taken that as the field proliferates, the need for meaningful focus rooted in cultural specificity is crucial. *Making It Like a Man* takes this cue, focusing on *the representation of men's gender practices in specifically Canadian arts and cultures.*

MASCULINITIES IN CANADIAN ARTS AND CULTURES

In their introduction to the *Handbook of Studies on Men and Masculinities*, R.W. Connell, Jeff Hearn, and Michael S. Kimmel argue that masculinity is variable across time (history) and space (culture) within particular societies and through the course of individual lives.[14] "Postcolonial theory," they write, "has shown that it matters whether the analysis of men is being conducted from within the West, the global South, the former Soviet territories, the Middle East, or elsewhere. In that way, history, geography, and global politics matter in epistemologies and ontologies in studying men."[15] Joanne P. Sharp concurs. In "Gendering Nationhood: A Feminist Engagement with National Identity," she observes that nation and gender are clearly central aspects of contemporary subjectivity that converge in the performance of identity in everyday life, but that we must be careful not to lose sight of the very real significance and uniqueness of individual nations in the current climate of globalization: "Despite intellectual narratives that describe the increasing internationalization or globalization of life, *realpolitik* would seem to suggest that nation-states continue to be significant actors in the constitution of international society. National self-determination has been a prevalent source of legitimation in many political struggles and national statehood is a requirement for representation in many global bodies."[16] Following Judith Butler's argument that "gender is constituted not by 'a founding act but rather a regulated pattern or repetition,'" Sharp sees nations as created not by "an originary moment or culturally distinct essence" but rather through repeated local/regional symbols and ritual practices that are *gendered*.[17] Hence Nancy Duncan's insistence in her introductory and concluding remarks in *Body Space: Destabilizing Geographies of Gender and Sexuality* (the collection in which Sharp's essay appears) that in our transnational global context we need to be advancing ideas about gender and sexuality through a "repoliticized geographical imagination"—a new epistemological and ontological viewpoint based on knowledge as "embodied, engendered and embedded in the material context of place and space."[18] In the case of masculinity studies, Kimmel, Hearn, and Connell note that since the 1990s and the third wave, such a geographical reconfiguration has emerged, producing sophisticated international research of increasing spatial, cultural, and historical specificity: "The analysis of masculinities, men, and men's place in the gender order has thus become a worldwide undertaking, with many local differences of analysis"[19]—analyses based in clearly contextualized and situated national social relations.[20] For example, there have been studies on masculinity in the military schools of settlement colonies such as New Zealand and Natal; studies on the relationship between boys and men across the issues of education, family dynamics, and men's changing identities, but with quite different national foci in Australia and the United States; studies of white-collar middle-class masculinity in Japan; studies of men and gender equity policies in Scandinavia; studies of race relations and male violence in South Africa; studies of masculinity, modernization, and Islam in the Eastern Mediterranean and Southwest Asia; and studies of the roots of machismo in colonialism and its effect on men's development and sexual behaviour in the context of HIV/AIDS in Latin America and Mexico.[21]

Accordingly, masculinity also matters in Canada as part of the "scripting of the gendered subject into the narrative of national community," and beyond, into the international realm.[22] In fact, masculinity has mattered in the national discourse since Margaret Atwood's influential book *Survival: A Thematic Guide to Canadian Literature* emerged in 1972. A student of Northrop Frye and his thinking in *The Bush Garden*, Atwood contended that the Canadian national identity rests on a preoccupation with survival—personal and cultural. Moreover, she argued, in the face of the utopian American dream and the "will to win" that fuels it, the scarcely surviving colony we call Canada has developed a despairing "will to lose"; and according to Atwood, this negativity has manifested itself through gender in the way we construct and represent heroes as crippled "victims" and "losers."[23] So, whereas an important element of the scripting of masculinity in Latin America and Mexico has been into a national narrative of machismo, Atwood observed that a key element of the scripting of men in Canada has been into a national narrative of melancholy and masochism, and her thinking gained purchase in Canadian Studies circles throughout the 1970s and 1980s.

For example, in my own discipline of film studies, Robert Fothergill adapted Atwood's concept to Canadian cinema in his article "Coward, Bully, or Clown: The Dream Life of a Younger Brother," and thus the characters of Pete and Joey in Don Shebib's *Goin' Down the Road* (1972) became poster boys for the ubiquitous figure of the "male loser" in English Canadian film and popular culture.[24] The parody of Pete and Joey that appeared on Second City TV in the early 1980s is now a classic moment in the Canadian imaginary, as Geoff Pevere writes in *Mondo Canuck: A Canadian Pop Culture Odyssey*.[25] With the entrenchment of film studies programs at the undergraduate and graduate levels in Canadian academia, and the rise of the third wave of masculinity studies, the 1990s saw a burgeoning of interest in masculinities in

Canadian cinemas, evidenced in Thomas Waugh's Martin Walsh Memorial Lecture to the Film Studies Association of Canada on the topic "Cinemas, Nations, Masculinities" in 1998, which inspired a special issue of the *Canadian Journal of Film Studies* under the same title edited by Angela Stukator in 1999.[26]

However, in addition to the masculinities scene in Canadian film culture, groundbreaking work on the practice and representation of masculinities in other disciplines has exploded in Canada in Atwood's wake and in the context of the rise of masculinity studies proper—in disciplines such as literature, the fine arts, sociology, history, communications studies, sport, popular culture, philosophy, women's studies, and men's studies. Complementing the hundreds of articles and theses on such topics as masculinity and fatherhood, hockey violence, school bullying, film festival culture, and labour history, to name only a few, important series, anthologies, and monographs have emerged, such as Studies in Gender and History from University of Toronto Press (mentioned above); *Gender and History in Canada* (1996) by Joy Parr; *Masculine Migrations: Reading the Postcolonial Male in New Canadian Narratives* (1998) by Daniel Coleman; *Here Is Queer: Nationalisms, Sexualities, and the Literatures of Canada* (1999) by Peter Dickinson; Gendered *Pasts: Historical Essays in Femininity and Masculinity in Canada* (1999) by Kathryn McPherson; *Ways of Being Male: Representing Masculinities in Children's Literature* (2002) by John Stephens; *Who da Man? Black Masculinities and Sporting Cultures* (2005) by Gamal Abdel-Shehid; and The *Manly Modern: Masculinity in Postwar Canada* (2007) by Chris Dummitt. Making It Like a Man takes its place here, as the first scholarly volume in Canada to bring fine arts, humanities, and social science researchers together across disciplines to share ideas on the practice of masculinities in historical and contomporary Canadian arts and cultures.

MAKING IT LIKE A MAN: SPACES AND PLACES OF CANADIAN MASCULINITIES IN PRACTICE

The goal of *Making It Like a Man* is to offer the international field of masculinity studies what Duncan has called for in terms of "situated knowledge"[27]— the most recent research on the cultural, geographical, and historical specificity of Canadian masculinities in practice. Asking "what it means to be a man" of a diverse range of Canadian arts and cultural activities, it stages a forum in which masculinities can be investigated in several contexts—across disciplines (film, music, literature, history, sociology, sports, popular culture, and everyday life); across cultures (from the traditional "two solitudes" of the Canadian linguistic "centres" to the margins of class, First Nations cultures, ethnicity, sexual minorities, regions, and other minority expressions); as well as transnationally.

This anthology deliberately positions itself to advance the dialogue on masculinities on two fronts: the international and the national. From the international perspective, it takes enthusiastic part in the "new directions" in masculinities research that Stephen Whitehead calls for—directions that are leading us away from the "crisis vocabulary" mentioned above toward broad transdisciplinary and transnational discourse-based analysis. He outlines four reasons why the "crisis of masculinity" paradigm does not convince in the new millennium:

> The reasons for this are complex, but they come down to understanding that men are not a predictable, homogenous group, needing to control women and others in order to be "masculine"; a natural state that, if knocked back, inevitably results in some sort of profound sense of rejection and existential crisis for males. Men are much more complicated than that. First, we should recognize the multiple ways of being a man and the multiple masculinities now available to men in this, the postmodern, age. There can be no prevailing, singular masculinity in crisis. Second, this crisis of masculinity thesis can be used by some to inform a backlash against feminism and women's interests. One outcome of such antifeminist feeling is that it stops many men from coming to recognize that perhaps their traditional, blinkered ways of seeing the world are no longer tenable. Third...men, as individuals, are riven with contesting pressures and variables, particularly in respect of class, culture, ethnicity, economics, education, nationhood and sexuality. Finally, men (particularly white, heterosexual, Anglo-Saxon men) control, directly or indirectly, most of the world's resources, capital, media, political parties and corporations. It is difficult to imagine this group in crisis.[28]

So, while the crisis paradigm has proven to be too monologic and essentialist in the third wave context of the now globalized field of masculinity studies, the same is true of the paradigm of the loser figure in Canadian studies.

For example, in the case of film studies, a debate emerged in the 1990s in the wake of Peter Morris's important critique of the trope of the male victim/loser as a form of all too simplistic thematic criticism—a mode of interpretation that was produced, understandably, in the early 1970s at a particular cultural moment that had set itself the crucial task of canon formation for fledgling Canadian arts and cultures, but one that quickly "degenerated into a rote formula."[29] In "In Our Own Eyes: The Canonizing of Canadian Film," he writes:

> It is perhaps hardly surprising that thematic criticism of Canadian cinema should have been so prevalent in this period, given its inter-

national popularity in English language film criticism. What is surprising in retrospect is that such criticism should have been dominated by a single theme: that Canadian cinema is a negative cinema focused on victims and losers...For example, in a recent essay on four Canadian features of the late eighties, all four are forced into the "loser" model...This seems not only somewhat contemptuous of each films [sic] uniqueness, as criticism it verges on the tautological.[30]

Regarding Atwood's discussion of literary texts, and Fothergill's modelling of that discussion for cinema, he suggests that the problem is largely a lack of critical sophistication and analytical subtlety:

Atwood uses the terms "victims" and "losers" interchangeably, even though one can clearly be one without the other. Fothergill concentrates on the weakness of male protagonists, assuming that they are necessarily the central characters around whom the narratives revolve; a different emphasis might have led to a different interpretation of the function of men in the narrative structure...Finally, both Atwood and Fothergill assume that the thematic structures they identify are precisely based in a socio-political colonial mentality, with Canada as either "collective victim" (Atwood) or envious "younger brother" (Fothergill).[31]

"It is significant," Morris concludes, that "Canadian film critics have not challenged the negative connotations of these influential thematic analyses." This leads him to call for "fresh critical approaches to the canon."[32] Accordingly, in "Canadian Narrative Cinema from the Margins: The Nation and Masculinity in *Goin' Down the Road*," I have attempted to offer a fresh approach to Canadian cinematic masculinity by focusing not on the characters' generalized status as victims and losers in crisis, but on the disparities of region (they are Maritimers) and class (they are uneducated cannery workers trying to make it in white-collar Toronto) that are specific to Pete and Joey's marginalized situation and how these underwrite their masculinity in crucial ways.[33]

This embryonic focus on the specificities of geo-physical place and social space proved useful in advancing and deepening the discourse on masculinities in Canadian cinema in the 1990s,[34] and fifteen years later the authors included in this volume are concerned to do the same for *the practice of masculinities across disciplines in Canadian arts and cultures*. In their introduction to *Spaces of Masculinities*, Bettina van Hoven and Kathrin Hörschelmann talk about "the recent emergence of research on the geographies of masculinities"—research that shows how "gender identities are lived and constructed in different cultural settings. Space has been shown to be gendered in many ways, while gender itself is seen to be constructed through spatial relations and geographical imaginations."[35] The point is that while masculinities are constructed "in and through space," particular places also become "gendered as masculine."[36] *Making It Like a Man* subscribes to this very fluid, spatial conception of the construction of Canadian masculinities—this sense that masculinities "can attach to bodies, objects, places and spaces well beyond the apparent confines of biology and sex."[37]

Thus, for our collective purposes, and simply put, we borrow from Kimmel, Hearn, and Connell to define masculinities as "patterns of practice," and gender identity not as a "psychological property" of an individual person but as "a constant process, always being reinvented and rearticulated in every setting, micro or macro. Gender identity is the codified aggregation of gendered interactions; its coherence depends on our understanding of those interactions."[38] So, as John Beynon writes in *Masculinities and Culture*, while all people have a sexed body, "there are numerous forms and expressions of gender, of 'being masculine'"[39]—of practising gender—of making it like or as a man. Moreover, those practices are "always interpolated by cultural, historical and geographical location"—they are "enacted" in and across the specificities of cultures and their various categories of class, subculture, age, ethnicity, education, status, regional hierarchy, national identity, and so on, and so are inherently "diverse," "mobile," and "unstable" (trans)national constructions.[40]

Accordingly, the individual authors in *Making It Like a Man* have come together to advance ideas about the practice of masculinities through a *specifically Canadian geographical imagination, interrogating how our local/regional/national/transnational symbols and practices are gendered "masculine."* Some writers' investigations traverse the distinct physical regions of Canada and beyond—from the prairies (Cumming, Garneau, Henderson, Marsh) and Quebec and the North (Baker, Côté, Stojanova) to urban Ontario (McGregor and Petty), Italy (Wilson), and the Sahara Desert (Ramsay). Others are concerned with more abstract social and political spaces, such as the war front and the home front (Baker), the nuclear family (Hayward), the dark spaces of sexual abuse in the church and the national sport (Waugh), or the subversive subcultures of punk (Defraeye) and queer/post-queer desire (Noble). Moreover, in editing this volume, I have become aware of several striking thematic threads that weave among the authors' diverse approaches, creating interesting and productive geospatial metaphors in this geography of Canadian masculinities in practice—metaphors such as colonial–national spaces; psycho-emotional spaces; spaces of ethnicity and minoritization; spaces of public and private marginalization, from the global economy to the nuclear family; and spaces of otherness and abjection. Consequently, the chapters have been grouped to take up these spatial themes.

In Section I, "Identity, Agency, and Manliness in the Colonial and the National," Ken Wilson, Jarrett Henderson, and Mike Baker take us back in time, to the nineteenth and mid-twentieth centuries, to chart practices of masculinity in Canada's colonial and national contexts. Wilson takes us travelling—to 1850s Italy, in fact—with the carnival of masculinity that characterizes the comic popular fiction of late-nineteenth-century Halifax writer James De Mille. Located on the margins of Canada's literary canon, De Mille's work is interesting for its surprising self-consciousness in turning traditional notions of Victorian masculinity upside down. Informed by Judith Adler's work on travel as "performed art," Wilson argues that travel to other national spaces and places "lends itself to dramatic play with the boundaries of selfhood," such that De Mille's characters are carnivalized in the Bakhtinian sense, performing what he calls "new and sometimes extravagant identities": female masculinities, drag kings, young women masquerading as boys with whom middle-aged men fall in love—these are the focus of De Mille's characters' serial sex romps through Europe. Wilson offers a close reading of *The Dodge Club; Or, Italy in 1859* (1869), De Mille's first and most successful travel novel, in which a group of Canadian male tourists join together with a hyperbolic American senator for some riotous misadventures at Mount Vesuvius, in Naples, and at the Italian Royal Opera House. Their transnational buffoonery reveals De Mille's savvy, parodic, and ironic treatment of different models of masculinity, ultimately complicating our perception of the boundaries of gender representation in nineteenth-century Canadian literature.

However, while De Mille's comic characters were swanning around the continent with abandon and wreaking havoc with traditional gender identities, an entirely different, hetero-normative masculinity was being modelled for the Canadian North West through the popular non-fiction form of the immigration handbook. Jarett Henderson's chapter takes up the power of such handbooks to advertise to eastern Canadians and new immigrants the open prairie as a "site of Empire" where any man with proper "muscle and pluck" could aspire to "trans-imperial manliness." Henderson describes how the values of a healthy climate, an agrarian lifestyle, and homeownership were harnessed in these manuals, such as Thomas Spence's *Useful and Practical Hints for the Settler* (1878), to create the promise of independent, manly agency in a new Canadian space—in a "white settler geography" that would ideally have the power to transform both British and European foreigners into men as they "fertilized" the great North West and broke its "virgin soil" in the practice of a proud and dynamic "domestic patriarchy."

This theme Henderson raises of how historical forms of Canadian domestic patriarchy and ideal masculinity operated through promotional discourse returns sixty years later, but in a different cultural context, with Michael Brendan Baker's analysis of the representation of men on the "home front" in the National Film Board of Canada's World War II series Canada Carries On. Baker examines how, under the direction of the NFB's founding commissioner John Grierson, the films in this prestigious and internationally renowned series created a binary of dominant stereotypes of Canadian masculinity based in strident heterosexuality while silencing other ways of being a man. He examines *Inside Fighting Canada* (1942) as a key example of the representation of this Griersonian binary between the manly "protectors" on the one hand (the soldiers bravely fighting and dying on the war front)—and the equally manly "producers" or domestic patriarchs on the other hand (the fishermen, farmers, loggers, and factory labourers keeping the war effort going on the home front). However, he is less concerned with these binaries themselves than with the gender insecurity they suggest and, so, the kind of masculinity they ignore and exclude from representation: the intelligentsia (the judges, clergy, professors, and teachers)—the "war-exempted," who are stereotypically aligned with "cowardice," whose contributions to the war effort remain unrecognized, and whose stories go untold. Ironically, for Baker, it is what the Canada Carries On series "did not say"—its Foucauldian "exclusionary practices" in defining Canadian manly agency—that define the spaces within which marginalized Canadian males contributed to the war effort.

David Garneau opens Section II, "Emotional Geographies of Anxiety, Eros and Impairment," which brings questions of affect to bear on the experiences of straight Canadian men under a changing patriarchal order, unfettered homosocial desire, and immigrant subjectivity. His chapter is his curatorial account and interpretation of the work of the twelve prairie-based male visual artists represented in the Making It Like a Man! exhibition held at the MacKenzie Art Gallery in Regina, Saskatchewan, in the summer of 2004. Interested primarily in opening a visual space for straight men's and Aboriginal men's experiences alongside those of women and gay men in the interrogation of Canadian masculinities, he focuses on those artists who are using their practice to re-evaluate gender construction and the supposed "superiority" of men and boys over women and girls as the legacy of the patriarchal tradition. He writes that he was surprised to have found no evidence of artists producing images of "iconic" or "celebratory" masculinity, discovering instead a common feeling of anxiety permeating their paintings, sculptures, and installations. All in some way "ironic, deconstructive, wounded, reflective, perplexed, or otherwise troubled," these artists are all at the same time incredibly *moving* in their creation of situated knowledge about the anxieties characteristic of their predominantly hetero-masculinities.

In contrast, Piet Defraeye shifts the discussion of the anxieties of masculinity as reflected in Canadian artists' practice from the prairies to the transnational realm, from the shared social space of the four walls of the "gallery show" to the depths of the individual artist's canvas, and from hetero- to homo-masculinities. His chapter offers a close psychosocial and political reading of an important work by the internationally renowned Calgary artist Attila Richard Lukacs: the triptych *Wild Kingdom*, from the E-Werk series. Defraeye situates Lukacs in the transnational space of his postmodern, bohemian, queer lifestyle. Informed by Georges Bataille's theory of "excessive expenditure," Defraeye reads *Wild Kingdom* as Lukacs' erotic metacommentary on his own performative and figurative painting practice—as a wild canvas by a wild prairie expatriate in "envy" and "awe" of the bold, savage, homoerotic abandon of an exclusively masculine skinhead world. Thus, Defraeye's chapter moves us from the highly personal social anxieties of Garneau's straight prairie masculinities toward transnational flights of epic homosocial and homosexual desire without any moral compass—into Lukacs's "wild kingdom"—a hypermasculine, transcendent fantasy space of Eros beyond productive social activity.

Christina Stojanova's interest in emotional geographies turns to examining cinematic representations of masculinity and immigration in contemporary Quebec, where the subject cannot simply escape but rather is forced by the globalizing geopolitical circumstances of what Zygmunt Bauman calls our "liquid modern world" to wade into that province's notoriously fraught socio-political milieu. It is one in which, she argues, the three conflicting discourses of a multicultural Canadian nation—the separatist agenda of the Bloc Québécois; rural francophone racism; and xenophobia—cluster to create profound anxiety for male immigrants. Focusing on a group of pre- and post-referendum feature fiction films, she uses Bauman, Fredric Jameson, Julia Kristeva, and Slavoj Žižek to offer a psychoanalytically informed analysis of pre-Oedipal, Oedipal, and post-Oedipal tendencies in Quebec's immigrant masculinities—masculinities that are ultimately impaired in their emotional relationships by the "spectre of redundancy" as the forces of globalization "reshuffle people," "play havoc with their social identities," and turn their "labours and relations" to cultural and human waste.

The next four chapters are concerned with questions of ethnicity and minoritization. In Section III, "The Minority Male," the spaces, places, and practices of Canadian masculinities are examined in the context of "minority settings"—whether the urban 'hood of the Afro-Caribbean Canadian diaspora in Toronto's Regent Park, or the Aboriginal hip-hop scene in Regina's North Central; Alberta's Aboriginal reserves; or the abstract itinerancy of escape from the provincial delimitations of Franco-Manitoban identity into the oblivion of the open roads of North America. In their discussion of Clement Virgo's *Rude* (1995) as a Canadian reconfiguration of the Hollywood "black action" or "gangsta rap" genre, D.L. McGregor and Sheila Petty suggest that black Canadian masculinity is as "fraught with indefinition" as Canada itself. Like the intelligentsia whom Michael Baker describes in the Canada Carries On documentary series, Canadian blackness is a kind of "absented presence" in Canadian feature film. Informed by the work of

Rinaldo Walcott and bell hooks, McGregor and Petty argue that due to the "polycultural make-up" of the black community in Canada, a North American history of hostile and racist economic environments for black men, and the dominance of American representations of black male gangster behaviour in our popular culture, black Canadians are forced to negotiate many competing imperatives. This means that opening up a space to establish a coherent and positive black male Canadian identity—whether for the larger community or individually—is extremely difficult. *Rude*'s redefinition of black masculinity against iconic symbols of African Zulu, Caribbean Rastafarian, and Mohawk cultures in the Toronto ghetto thus constructs an "imaginary geography" that vacillates between national boundaries and urban diasporic desires, ambitions, and disappointments. *Rude*'s achievement, for McGregor and Petty, is in charting a complex black minority space that is "simultaneously Canadian and global in scope."

Charity Marsh also takes up the question of Canadian gangsta rap cultures and minoritization in the urban 'hood, but with a particular focus on non-fictional media representations of Aboriginal rapper Robin Favel (a.k.a. Burden) in the context of Regina's notorious ghetto, North Central, which was recently branded by *Maclean's* as "Canada's worst neighbourhood." Borrowing from Murray Forman and Andy Bennett's work on how young people's experience of the city is made "audible" and "authentic" by youth cultures around the world, Marsh explores how *local* Aboriginal Canadian masculinity is constructed through the practice of the global genre of rap music via hip-hop culture's "intimate ties to the city and particularly to the racialized spaces of its inner city neighbourhoods." Marsh's chapter thus also situates Canadian masculinity in a complex and racialized minority space—that of the marginalized city of Regina, where we witness the burden of the urban Aboriginal warrior as he struggles to resist white oppression while caught in the blind intersections of colonialism, capitalism, and patriarchy.

In his chapter comparing two key novels of Cherokee/Greek/American/Canadian author Thomas King—*Medicine River* (1989) and *Green Grass, Running Water* (1993)—Peter Cumming examines the viability of masculinity in Aboriginal minority cultures. He argues that both of King's narratives are concerned with "fixing" the destructive stories that some Aboriginal men live by steering them away from dominant Western traditions of individual male heroism toward valorization of Native community relations. This is symbolized by the "men's dance" that King's characters practise and by the leather jackets that represent hegemonic masculinities they must shed. Influenced by Theresa de Lauretis's method of reading across "several axes of difference," Cumming reads the intersections of race, ethnicity, narrative structure, and gender in King's comedic fiction in order to recognize both its "radical subversions" and its "potential limitations."

For Nicole Côté, the spaces of identity that linguistic minorities inhabit in a globalized world are extremely complex, necessarily hybrid, and often fraught as they oscillate between what Francois Paré calls "an acute and painful consciousness of their marginal status" and "oblivion." Her chapter deals with the minority male in a Franco-Canadian literary context—specifically, in Simone Chaput's *Le coulonneux* (1998), a novel set in the Franco-Manitoban milieu of St. Boniface, a marginalized place that seventeen-year-old high school dropout Gabriel Tardiff longs to escape for life on the road. As such, he exemplifies how minorities use "oblivion" as a survival strategy to deal with their feelings of alienation and paralysis. Côté reads Gabriel through his adoption of this "oblivion strategy" but is particularly interested in the way masculinity intersects with the character's itinerancy and his gendered relationship to the body—his own and those of the women he encounters, rejects, and *ab*jects on his sojourn across North America. Ultimately, his is a "vectored" Canadian masculinity—one of self-discovery and transcendence, yes, but one, Côté argues, that still exorcises its minority condition of erasure on the bodies of women.

Section IV, "Capitalized, Corporatized, Compromised Men," explores the gendered spaces of the public versus private realm, examining masculinities in the contexts of the transnational forces of global corporate capital, on the one hand, and of the interpersonal forces of domestic family politics, on the other. Like Côté, Kit Dobson offers a generational focus, in this case set in the context of the disenfranchising effects of the decentring forces of corporate capitalism on mainstream (white, heterosexual, Anglo) Canadian men. His aim is to problematize how dominant/privileged groups use and appropriate the language of marginality to express disagreement with the ways in which the new global economic system has marginalized them. He does this through an analysis of Douglas Coupland's *Generation X* (1991)—a novel that had "major sociological impact" in defining a generation of North Americans. Dobson uses Fredric Jameson, Jacques Derrida, Michael Hardt, Antonio Negri, David Harvey, and Arjun Appadurai, among others, to understand the destabilizing forces of the new "Empire of capital" as it operates across the Canadian–American and American–Mexican borders. *Generation X* tells the story of three "victims" of this scenario of destabilization whose "rebellion," Dobson concludes, is more narcissistic and hollow nostalgia for their position of lost hegemony than principled, let alone informed, dissidence. His critical reading of Coupland's hip and ironic but confused characters comes to rest on Andrew's compromised search for a utopic space outside the flows of corporate capital; despite his jaded political awareness, he metaphorically retains his white and gendered privilege as a hip Gen-X Canadian male still comparatively firmly anchored in the driver's seat of mobile corporate capital.

Sally Hayward's chapter shifts the discourse from contemporary global economics to historical domestic politics with her focus on questions of compulsory heterosexuality and compulsory able-bodiedness in the Canadian nuclear family. Informed by the work of Adrienne Rich and Robert McRuer on the "naturalization" of dominant identities, Hayward offers a close reading of Barbara Gowdy's ironic and subversive novel *Mister Sandman* (1995) as it imagines a "counter-narrative" to the "Wonder Bread" image projected by the Canadian patriarchal family structure of the 1950s and early 1960s. A far cry from the "normal" image that they project to the world, the Canary family is disturbed by "forbidden desires" and "secrets" of epic proportions. The disabled mother, Doris, is bisexual and a flagrant liar while the father, Gordon, is a closeted homosexual in love with neighbour Al Yothers. Together they have produced a family plagued by false dichotomies ("healthy versus unhealthy marriages; well-behaved versus misbehaving children; straight versus gay sexualities; able-bodied versus deviant disabled bodies"). The fact that Gordon eventually comes out to Doris, but to no one else, means he will continue to practise and publicly pretend a normalized heterosexuality at the head of the nuclear family—a compromised masculinity that Hayward critiques, along with the continued closeting of Joan and her disabled body, as emblematic of this troubling novel's productive contradictions and its incisive critique of the compulsory heterosexuality of the Canadian family.

Section V turns on the question of "Abject Masculinities" involving representations of Canadian men and boys—from hockey heroes and drag kings to artists-in-exile—who are tragically "othered" or who ironically or self-reflexively "other" themselves. Thomas Waugh's chapter is an overview of the "child abuse" narratives produced by the National Film Board of Canada, CTV, and the CBC over the past fifty years, as well as an incisive critique of the hyperbolic hetero-masculinity and homophobia that characterize them. Waugh founds his argument on Judith Butler's understanding of heterosexuality as a "compulsive and compulsory repetition" of itself as the idealized "origin and ground"—or "degree zero"—of sexual identity. He analyzes several films and videos, paying particular attention to *The Boys of St. Vincent* (1998) and *The Sheldon Kennedy Story* (1999), in which the tragic pain, humiliation, and shame for both heterosexual and homosexual masculinities as practised in our homosocial, homoerotic, and homophobic national game figure in important ways. Thus, Waugh exposes the abject contradictions of male desire, sexual response, and agency—and their obfuscation—as they inhabit the porous "border zone" between "so-called queer" and "so-called straight" Canadian masculinities.

Bobby Noble shifts the discourse from "hockey kings" at centre ice to "drag kings" on centre stage and in so doing performs a radical twist on our framing of Canadian masculinity and abjection. Noble's focus is on what he calls the "transformations" through three different "waves" of drag kinging in Toronto's urban centre and how each of these distinct historical moments maps its own unique "social, historical, and epistemological context" and is obviously dependent on ironic and performative constructions of masculinity for its "conditions of possibility." The third and current wave Noble describes as a "No Man's Land" of multiple "boi" cultures (lesbian, gay, FtM) in which "discernible gender identifications and affiliations are all but rendered incoherent" and hetero-normativity *itself* is abjected. Gender identity and its performance are now flying off in all directions, he argues, using Bakhtin to describe the "inherently dialogic" nature of post-queer identities and drag king performances and their ability to trouble the idea that reality is reducible to gender appearances. For Noble, the deliciously polymorphous practice of drag kinging reminds us, after Bakhtin, that there is not one word, but many words—a multiplicity of ways of making it like a man—making Canadian masculinity a truly "free floating signifier."

Helping us close the volume is Mikhail Bakhtin, whose thinking has been influential in several chapters of *Making It Like a Man*. My chapter uses Bakhtin's understanding of subjectivity as *inter*subjectivity, Lawrence Grossberg and Christopher Faulkner's thinking on affective identities, and Margaret Wertheim's interest in the relationship between our sense of identity and spatial schemes to interpret the abject life and work of an obscure but fascinating and important Canadian documentary filmmaker, Frank Cole. Cole's emotional obsession with death and immortality took him on not one, but two gruelling solo treks of the Sahara Desert, where he wished to "confront death by experiencing the absolute limits of life"—while documenting it. His compulsion to self-reflexively "beat death" by surviving this self-imposed existential exile represents what Noble would agree is yet another kind and degree of Canadian "No Man's Land" hinged on a hypermasculine regime of bodybuilding, vitamins, a strict diet, and crushing solitude. After Wertheim, who suggests that "our conception of ourselves is indelibly linked to our conception of space," and that "conceptions of space and conceptions of self mirror one another," I suggest that the Sahara can be understood as this Canadian artist's idiosyncratic and increasingly pathological transnational quest for "a place to put his soul." Cole's practice is the work of an artist attempting to live on the threshold of existence and speak his *soul* at the same time as it represents the limits of personal and social identity for an atomistic, agonistic, narcissistic, and nihilistic masculine subjectivity. In his obsessive quest for immortality, his melancholic solipsism rendered him unable to see and accept what Bakhtin would call the value of limits in our spatial schemes and in the spatialized social situations in which we find ourselves—the limits of the self in relation to others, and the limits of life itself in relation to death.

CONCLUSION

By way of a brief summation, Frank Cole and his self-reflexive "othering" through his highly idiosyncratic art brings us back full circle to the very threshold of the culture of masculinity, cultural geographies, and the gendering of space where we began this volume on Canadian masculinities in practice: our cover image by Montreal-based Iranian Canadian photographer and installation artist Afshin Matlabi. As suggested so well by Matlabi's equally self-reflexive "othering" through his self-portrait with vacuum cleaner titled "On Technologies of Man's Sensuality," to make it like a man in Canada is a highly complex social and personal gesture articulating the cultural, sociological, and historical *fluidity* of masculine expressions, representations, and power relations in our nation. Race, gender, masculinity, femininity, domesticity, art and cultural history, power—all are harnessed together in this hilarious but highly insightful and in-your-face twenty-first-century Canadian orientalist *Playgirl/Playboy* male centrefold. Whereas Cole's cinematic representation seems to suggest a kind of tragic closure on a particular way of practising Canadian masculine subjectivity, Matlabi's photographic representation seems to invite a kind of radical aperture, or opening up, of what it means to make it like a Canadian man.

Together, the contributors to *Making It Like a Man* hope to have opened a dialogue that will offer the national/international/transnational field of masculinity studies a distinctive taste of the specificities of masculinities in Canadian arts and cultures as truly diverse "patterns of practice" in geophysical space and time, and a revealing portrait of gender identity as a "constant process" that, as Kimmel, Hearn, and Connell indicate, is indeed "always being reinvented and rearticulated in every setting, micro or macro"[41] as it crosses the multiple and converging lines of sex, gender, history, psychology, class, work, leisure, religion, subcultures, sport, race, ethnicity, regions, and nations in our contemporary globalized world.

NOTES

1. Bobby Noble's chapter on Toronto's drag kings appears in its entirety in *Sons of the Movement: FtMs Risking Incoherence on a Post-Queer Cultural Landscape* (Toronto: Women's Press, 2006), 53–75; and is reproduced here by permission. Donna-Lynne McGregor and Sheila Petty's chapter expands in new ways on ideas that originally appeared in *Contact Zones: Memory, Origin, and Discourse in Black Diasporic Cinema* (Detroit: Wayne State University Press, 2008).
2. Rachel Adams and David Savran, eds., *The Masculinity Studies Reader* (Oxford: Blackwell, 2002), 4.
3. Tim Edwards, *Cultures of Masculinity* (London and New York: Routledge, 2006), 2.
4. R.W. Connell, *Masculinities,* 2nd ed. (Berkeley and Los Angeles: University of California Press, 2005), xii.
5. See Robert Bly, *Iron John: A Book about Men* (Reading: Addison-Wesley, 1990).

6 Edwards, *Cultures of Masculinity*, 6.
7 See Michel Foucault, *The History of Sexualilty* (Harmondsworth: Penguin, 1978).
8 See Eve Kosofsky Sedgwick, *Between Men: English Literature and Male Homosexual Desire* (New York: Columbia University Press, 1985).
9 See Judith Butler, *Gender Trouble: Feminism and the Subversion of Identity* (London: Routledge, 1990).
10 Edwards, *Cultures of Masculinity*, 3.
11 Connell, *Masculinities*, xiii.
12 Edwards, *Cultures of Masculinity*, 1.
13 Ibid., 7.
14 Michael S. Kimmel, Jeff Hearn, and R.W. Connell, eds., *Handbook of Studies on Men and Masculinities* (Thousand Oaks: Sage, 2005), 3.
15 Ibid., 4.
16 Joanne P. Sharp, "Gendering Nationhood: A Feminist Engagement with National Identity," in *Body Space: Destabilizing Geographies of Gender and Sexuality*, ed. Nancy Duncan (London and New York: Routledge, 1996), 97.
17 Ibid., 98.
18 Nancy Duncan, ed., "Introduction" and "Conclusion," in *Body Space: Destabilizing Geographies of Gender and Sexuality* (London and New York: Routledge, 1996), 1–10 and 245–47.
19 Kimmel, Hearn, and Connell, *Handbook of Studies*, 6.
20 Duncan, "Introduction," in *Body Space*, 1.
21 Kimmel, Hearn, and Connell, *Handbook of Studies*, 6.
22 Sharp, "Gendering Nationhood," 105.
23 Margaret Atwood, *Survival: A Thematic Guide to Canadian Literature* (Toronto: Anansi, 1972), 34–35. See also Northrop Frye, *The Bush Garden: Essays on the Canadian Imagination* (Toronto: Anansi, 1971).
24 Robert Fothergill, "Coward, Bully, or Clown: The Dream Life of a Younger Brother," in *Canadian Film Reader*, ed. Seth Feldman and Joyce Nelson (Toronto: Peter Martin, 1977), 234–51.
25 See Geoff Pevere and Greg Dymond, *Mondo Canuck: A Canadian Pop Culture Odyssey* (Toronto: Prentice-Hall, 1996).
26 See Angela Stukator, ed., "Cinemas, Nations, Masculinities: The Martin Walsh Memorial Lecture (1998)," *Canadian Journal of Film Studies* 8, no. 1 (Spring 1999): 8–44.
27 Duncan, "Introduction," in *Body Space*, 3.
28 Stephen Whitehead, *Men and Masculinities: Key Themes and New Directions* (Cambridge: Polity, 2002), 3.
29 Peter Morris, "In Our Own Eyes: The Canonizing of Canadian Film," *Canadian Journal of Film Studies* 3, no. 1 (Spring 1994): 27–44 at 37.
30 Ibid., 36–37.
31 Ibid., 37.
32 Ibid., 37, 38.
33 Christine Ramsay, "Canadian Narrative Cinema from the Margins: The Nation and Masculinity in *Goin' Down the Road*," *Canadian Journal of Film Studies* 2, nos. 2–3 (1993): 27–49.
34 For two excellent examples, see Lee Parpart, "Pit(iful) Male Bodies: Colonial Masculinity, Class, and Folk Innocence in *Margaret's Museum*," and Brenda Longfellow, "Hyperbolic Masculinity and the Ironic Gaze in *Project Grizzly*," *Canadian Journal of Film Studies* 8, no. 1 (Spring 1999): 63–86 and 87–101.
35 Bettina van Hoven and Kathrin Hörschelmann, eds., *Spaces of Masculinities* (London and New York: Routledge, 2005), 1, 5.

36 Ibid., 11.
37 Ibid., 10.
38 Kimmel, Hearn, and Connell, *Handbook of Studies*, 5, 7.
39 John Beynon, *Masculinities and Culture* (Buckingham: Open University Press, 2002), 1.
40 Ibid., 1, 2.
41 Kimmel, Hearn, and Connell, *Handbook of Studies*, 5, 7.

I: IDENTITY, AGENCY, AND MANLINESS IN THE COLONIAL AND THE NATIONAL

CHAPTER I

Carnival and Masculinity in the Travel Fiction of James De Mille

KEN WILSON

Scholars in the humanities and social sciences tend to accept the premise that gender is a social construction rather than an innate biological phenomenon. Moreover, such constructions are the product of complex social and cultural negotiations, as Stephen M. Whitehead suggests:

> The more we delve into men and masculinities, the more is revealed of the complex dynamics of difference, subjectivity, power and identity, weaving their way across the social web. These processes are never fixed and never settled. They are under constant revision, negotiation and movement; in which case the idea that a core masculinity lies deep in man's inner biological state, to be rendered into the social through men's natural propensities, is just not tenable.[1]

If this description of masculinity is true for contemporary cultures, it must also be true of cultures that existed in the past. To claim that the constructions of gender in other centuries, or the political landscape in which they existed, were any less complex than such constructions in our own time, would be to ignore the historical record.

And in fact, those who have examined the past in the light of recent theoretical work on gender have discovered just how complex historical constructions of gender were. In his book on masculinity in nineteenth-century Britain, for example, John Tosh examines the complexity of the dominant construction of masculinity, manliness, in Victorian society. Manliness, Tosh suggests, "embraced moral or cultural as well as physical facets of being a man: courage as well as virility (or 'vigour'), for example."[2] Closer to home, the essays collected in *Gendered Pasts: Historical Essays in Femininity and Masculinity in*

Canada seek to explore "the multiple identities of gender, sexuality, class, ethnicity, and race, as well as those such as age, religion, and nation, that might well coalesce or compete in any specific historical moment."[3] The range of historical moments where the essays collected in *Gendered Pasts* discover evidence of the importance of constructions of gender—from political discourse in the 1820s to labour relations in the 1960s—suggests that questions about gender can be asked of almost any event in Canadian history, and that the answers will illuminate these events in new and unforeseen ways. If that is true of historical events, it is also true of cultural artifacts and literary texts: they contain traces of the way gender was constructed when they were produced. One body of literary texts where traces of the complex ways that masculinity, nation, and ethnicity were constructed and practised in late-Victorian Canada can be found is the fiction of James De Mille.

In the 1860s and 1870s, while he was teaching at Wolfville College (now Acadia University) and Dalhousie College (now Dalhousie University), De Mille became well known in both Canada and the United States as a writer of popular historical and comic fiction for both adult and youth audiences. As a university professor and popular writer, he straddled two very different discursive communities in his writing (and perhaps in his life as well). He was a prolific author; aside from works of poetry, rhetoric, and history, De Mille published twenty-five novels between 1861 and his untimely death in 1880 at the age of forty-six; three more were published posthumously. One of these, *A Strange Manuscript Found in a Copper Cylinder*, is his only novel for adults that remains in print in Canada (a children's book, *The Martyr of the Catacombs*, is also available in the United States). Other than specialists in Canadian literature, few people have heard of De Mille; he sits on the margins of Canada's literary canon. However, his writing deserves more attention, particularly because De Mille's novels about North American tourists make explicit use of the phenomenon that the Russian polymath Mikhail Bakhtin describes as "carnival" in his influential book on Rabelais. In De Mille's travel fiction, the experience of European travel becomes a kind of carnival, in which, among other things, gender becomes (however briefly) fluid and polysemic and traditional notions of masculinity are turned upside down. And while it's true that the narrative closure in these novels brings an end to the carnival—they typically end in marriage and the conclusion of their characters' European tour—their carnivalized treatment of masculinity and gender is unusual and something we might not expect in nineteenth-century Canadian writing. This chapter will begin by discussing the role that carnival plays in these texts, before shifting to an examination of the way they use carnival to play with constructions and practices of gender. Finally, it will focus on *The Dodge Club*, De Mille's first travel novel and his biggest critical and commercial success.

Carnival in De Mille's Fiction

Richard Cavell was the first to read De Mille's fiction through Bakhtin. To support his argument, Cavell quotes an entire chapter of De Mille's novel, *The Dodge Club*, in which a list appears of objects that travellers may view from (and on) Rome's Pincian Hill. The narrator invites the reader to "contemplate" this list, which he claims is "narrated and detailed not columnarily but exhaustively, and after the manner of Rabelais."[4] Clearly De Mille was aware of his text's Rabelaisian antecedents—his literary self-consciousness is one of the typical markers of his fiction. Cavell suggests that in this list, "all of culture is presented...as a collection of ruins contained in one vast museum."[5] This "museum," however, consists of Roman sights and artifacts ("The Tiber, The Campagna, The Aqueducts, Trajan's Column"), the tourists who have come to view them ("Michiganders," "Men from Bosting"), idealized notions of the tourist's experience of Roman monuments ("Memories," "The Dust of Ages"), and objects associated with the daily life of the tourists themselves and the tourism industry that serves them ("the Hurdy-Gurdys," "Pale Ale," "The Stands for Roast Chestnuts," and "Harper's Guide Book").[6] One sees De Mille's interest in (and love of) language here in the way the passage plays with vocabularies and accents. Moreover, the distinction between spectator and sight is nearly obliterated, and the result is less a museum than a semiotic rubbish heap—Victorian Canadians would have understood the double meaning contained within the phrase, "The Dust of Ages"—in which Saint Peter's Basilica and The Vatican are emptied of their cultural importance and become mere signs, the equivalents of any other objects on the list, in what Bakhtin describes as "*joyful relativity.*"[7]

However, in De Mille's fiction it is clear that for North American tourists simply being in Europe is an experience that can only be understood as carnival. Take, for example, this excerpt from a description of Naples, also from *The Dodge Club*:

> On for miles through interminable streets of houses that bordered the circular shore, through crowds of sheep, droves of cattle, dense masses of human beings, through which innumerable caleches darted like meteors amid the stars of heaven...Long lines of macaroni-cooks doing an enormous business; armies of dealers in anisette; crowds of water-carriers; throngs of fishermen, carrying nets and singing merry songs...For crowds, noise, tumult, dash, hurry-skurry, gayety, life, laughter, joyance, and all that incites to mirth, and all that stirs the soul, even New York couldn't hold a candle to Naples.[8]

Again we can see the narrator's unwillingness or inability to arrange the scene except as a list of people, objects, and activities. It is as if the scene's chaos and excess have overpowered his attempts at description. At the end of the passage, the narrator concludes, "Rabelais ought to have been a Neapolitan."[9] Once again, De Mille pays his respects to his master.

Complicating the carnival quality of these texts is the fact that De Mille's tourists find themselves in Europe during times of revolution and war: the revolutions of 1848; the Italian *Risorgimento* of the 1860s; the Franco-Prussian War, the siege of Paris and the Commune in 1870 and 1871; and the Carlist War of 1872–76 in Spain. De Mille's tourists completely misunderstand the political events around them. This is no surprise, since they usually have little knowledge of Europe other than what's contained within the covers of a tourist guidebook. In these novels, moreover, revolution is represented as a carnival. For example, told that Rome is in the throes of a republican revolution, one of the characters in *The Babes in the Wood* responds, "It's nothing of the kind...It's some Carnival—of some new sort, without masks."[10] However, the relationship between tourists, politics and carnival in these texts can be much more complex. In *The Cryptogram*, for example, an American tourist whose homonymic name, Obed Chute, indicates he always carries a revolver, arranges a yachting excursion around the Bay of Naples just after the Battle of Solferino in 1859, which marked the beginning of the process of Italian unification. It was a time when, De Mille's narrator explains, "throughout the Neapolitan dominions the population were filled with strange vague desires" and "one magic word"—"Garibaldi"—had become "the symbol of some great change by which all were to be benefited."[11] The excursion party dresses in "red flannel shirts and broad-brimmed hats," and are surprised and confused when they are surrounded by "the whole population of Salerno" when they disembark. The crowd follows the group to their hotel, where it hails them with cries of "Viva la Republica!" and "Viva Garibaldi!"[12] Later, the tourists figure out what has happened: somehow they "had been mistaken for Garibaldini," and Chute "accepted as Garibaldi himself."[13] The reason for the confusion is clear, except to the members of the excursion party: red shirts were the uniform of Garibaldi's troops.

Carnival, Tourism, and the Practice of Gender
The red shirts worn by Chute and his party had been adopted as a joke—one that is clearly part of a performance of a temporary identity, licensed by the fact that the tourists are away from home. Judith Adler has suggested that "travel lends itself to dramatic play with the boundaries of selfhood,"[14] and in De Mille's travel fiction, characters acquire and perform new and sometimes extravagant identities, however temporarily. The acquisition and performance of these new identities also involves a carnivalization of gender roles, a blurring of the boundaries of gender through inversion, cross-dressing, and masquerade. Drawing perhaps from Shakespeare's comedies, De Mille's fictions are filled with young women who disguise themselves as men—nineteenth-century versions of drag kings, perhaps. In *Old Garth*, for

example, the eponymous hero falls in love with a young woman who has disguised herself to look "like a handsome Sicilian lad of about fifteen."[15] Garth tells his companion, in a voice "hoarse and tremulous with emotion,"

> There's not a woman in all the world that I care a straw for. As for you, I want you to know that you are always welcome; I want to have you always with me; I want you, and no one else. I can't have too much of you. I can't have enough of you. Boy, I love you better than I ever loved any human being. When you are away I hunger and thirst after you.[16]

Garth is confused by these emotions: "This is the land of Damon and Pythias," he says; "there must be something in the air of the place, or why should I have grown so fond of you?"[17] Garth also compares their relationship to another famous example of male friendship, the Biblical story of David and Jonathan. Clearly part of what confuses Garth is the apparently homosexual nature of his love for Paul—it is a love that cannot speak its name because Garth doesn't seem to know what it would be called. When "the boy Paul" is finally revealed to be a young woman named Pauline, however, Garth's confusion increases, and he must reason himself into transferring his affections from a young man to a young woman. It's not an automatic process or even a reassuring one for Old Garth; instead, it's difficult intellectual work (perhaps because Garth, like many of De Mille's characters, is none too bright). There's a strange confusion in the novel between reason and emotion. At the end of the text, after the wedding of Garth and Pauline, the narrator states that Pauline "never lost in after life that sweet charm which had once made Garth feel all his nature go forth in unextinguishable love for 'the boy, Paul.'"[18] Despite the effects of narrative closure, it seems that the text's carnivalization of gender identities continues. Perhaps it's not surprising that De Mille was unable to publish this book while he was alive, and after his death his family was only able to place it with a cheap paperback publisher instead of the more established publishers (such as Harper Brothers) that published his other books.

A similar play with gender takes place in *A Castle in Spain:* a young woman named Miss Sydney Talbot dresses as a priest to avoid capture by revolutionaries, and she and her male companion decide to call each other by their surnames, as men do. "Talbot" comes to enjoy this situation:

> I love to have you call me "Talbot," for it sounds as though you have confidence in poor me; but best of all, I love to hear you say "Talbot, lad"; for it seems as though you look on me as your equal. Your tone is that of a brave man addressing his comrade, and the very sound of your voice seems to drive all my fear away.[19]

Her companion, a young man named Brooke (note the gender ambiguity of the pair's names), responds to this statement with the words, "Good boy!"[20] Indeed, though he knows Talbot's gender identity, Brooke still expresses his feelings for her as though she were a man: he calls her his "younger brother"; he also compares their relationship to that of David and Jonathan (a standard comparison).[21] Talbot continues to carry out this masquerade throughout the novel; even when there is no longer any need for the disguise, Brooke implores her to continue wearing it, because in this costume she saved his life[22]—a reversal of the damsel-in-distress trope. There is a narrative motivation for this behaviour—Brooke and Talbot are engaged to marry other people, and their play with gender roles is partly motivated by a conflict between honour (or social convention) and desire—but it nonetheless suggests the importance of the connections among gender, travel, and carnival in De Mille's fiction.

Carnival and Male Gender Tourism in *The Dodge Club*

De Mille's first and most successful travel novel, *The Dodge Club; Or Italy in 1859*, was published serially in 1867 and in book form two years later. *The Dodge Club* tells the story of a group of male tourists who band together in order to "dodge all humbugs and swindles" to which tourists in Europe are subject.[23] At the outset, the club's membership consists of two young men— Buttons, a resourceful fellow with a grasp of most European languages; and Dick, a somewhat younger and less experienced individual—and two older men, neither of whom speak any European languages at all: a Doctor Snakeroot, of Philadelphia, and a Senator Jones, of Massachusetts. Despite their age, both the Doctor and the Senator depend on their younger companions, particularly Buttons, to navigate their way through France and Italy. The novel tells the story of the Club's various comic adventures.

As in *Old Garth* and *A Castle in Spain*, masquerade is important in *The Dodge Club*, particularly women dressing as men. For example, Buttons is attracted to Dolores, the daughter of the club's Neapolitan innkeeper. One evening, he finds the innkeeper "chatting familiarly" with a stranger who was "dressed like a cavalry officer" and "the most astounding fop" Buttons had ever seen. The stranger

> paced up and down, head erect, chest thrown out, sabre clanking, spurs jingling, eyes sparkling, ineffable smile. He strode up to the two youths, spun around on one heel, bowed to the ground, waved his hand patronizingly, and welcomed them in.[24]

Buttons reacts "coldly" to the stranger, because of his foppishness—his excessive and unsettling femininity—and his patronizing behaviour. However, once the cavalry officer's true gender is revealed—he is Dolores—Buttons begins to enjoy the performance. "Bellissima! Bellissima!" he cries, "in unfeigned admiration."[25] It's worth noting that earlier the narrator indicated that "Bellissima!" is Dolores's favourite word. The reader is left wondering whether Buttons is responding to Dolores's performance of masculine behaviour, to her inviting appearance in male costume, to her inviting appearance in her usual dress, or to all three. Later, the travellers attend a masquerade at the Royal Opera House, where Buttons discover Dolores in a second costume, this time dressed as a woman. Once again, Buttons is completely fooled by her appearance. He tries to pick the strange woman up—his search for sexual or romantic adventure is one of his typically masculine traits—and is pleasantly surprised when her true identity is revealed.

Much of the text focuses on the Senator's conflicted masculinity. He is described as "a very large and muscular man, with iron-gray hair, and features that were very strongly marked and very strongly American."[26] In fact, his body seems to grow in size as the novel proceeds; he is repeatedly described as "colossal" and "a giant." The Senator fights heroically during three separate battles with bandits: once near Mount Vesuvius, again on the road north of Rome, and finally outside Florence. During one of these battles, his strength is described as "enormous—absorbed as it had been from the granite cliffs of the old Granite State";[27] during another, "his giant form" is seen "towering up amidst the mêlée, his muscular arms wielding the enormous iron bar, his astonishing strength increased tenfold by the excitement of the fight."[28] So, on the one hand the Senator is large, powerful, violent, and hard; he wields a phallic weapon, a crowbar; and he rescues his companions from danger. In this way, the Senator is manly, according to the normative codes of nineteenth-century masculinity (and a lot of work has been done to describe these codes, particularly in the context of nineteenth-century imperialism, as Tosh's work suggests). However, despite his strength and stereotypically heterosexual masculine power, the Senator has two unusual weaknesses. First, he attracts sexual attention from women and has no idea of how to respond. He's clearly a fighter, not a lover. Second, he often draws the attention of crowds of Italians, becoming an object of spectacle. In John Berger's formulation, he both acts and appears, but when he becomes the object of others' gazes he doesn't know how to react. His response to both situations is typically flight—which merely brings more attention to him. Despite his manly physical prowess, then, sexual attention and being an object of the gaze of others completely defeat or "unman" the Senator.

For example, in Rome he tries to ask his attractive landlady where he can find a laundress (he has run out of underwear). Of course, as the narrator explains, "the landlady had always shown a great admiration for the manly, not to say gigantic charms of the Senator."[29] He is embarrassed to talk about "soiled linen" to such a beautiful woman, and she mistakes his confusion for sexual desire. Her own desire further confuses the Senator: "She glanced at

A PERPLEXED SENATOR.

Figure 1 "A Perplexed Senator," an illustration from *The Dodge Club* (1869).

the manly figure of the Senator with a tender admiration in her eye which she could not repress, and which was so intelligible to the Senator that he blushed more violently than ever, and looked helplessly around him."[30] Neither can speak the other's language, and the confusion feeds on itself until the landlady flings herself into the Senator's arms. The narrator conveys the Senator's response in a lengthy list of emotional reactions: he is

> thunderstruck, confounded, bewildered, shattered, overcome, crushed, stupefied, blasted, overwhelmed, horror-stricken, wonder-smitten, annihilated, amazed, horrified, shocked, frightened, terrified, nonplused, wilted, awe-struck, shivered, astounded, dumbfounded. He did not even struggle. He was paralyzed.[31]

Once again, the narrator is unable or unwilling to describe what is happening except in terms of a list of words suggesting the Senator's complete inability to respond (my favourite is "wilted," which suggests the Senator may not be as phallic as he appears). The number of terms included in the list suggests the intensity of the Senator's reaction—it's once again almost sublime,

Figure 2 "Senator and Donkey," an illustration from *The Dodge Club* (1869).

in the sense of being beyond description. He is once again rescued by Buttons, and flees from both Rome and his inamorata. Flight is the only way the Senator can deal with sexual attention from women—he has no other response.

When the Senator receives sexual attention from women, he often ends up becoming a spectacle for the enjoyment of crowds of Italians. One example occurs after the Senator finds himself the object of the attention of a "bevy of masked beauties" at the masquerade in Naples, who "were attracted by the colossal form of the Senator."[32] The Senator is more than confused: "To say that he was bewildered would express his sensations but faintly."[33] Four of the women ask him to dance—either with each of them in turn, or with all of them at once; it matters little to them. (He's like an unwilling Victorian Hugh Hefner.) The women argue among themselves, and each tries to draw the Senator away; the activity draws the attention of a "crowd of idlers," who "gathered grinningly around."[34] The Senator's response is confusion and outrage. He notes his position at home and the fact that he is "the father of a family," and he begins to try to defend himself, loudly and in broken English (unable to speak Italian, he believes that volume and fractured grammar and syntax are useful substitutes). However, this behaviour merely increases the number of onlookers until there are nearly 1,000 people standing around watching. The Senator does not know what to do. "Covered with shame and perspiration," he spots Buttons and cries out for help: "These confounded *I*-talian wimmin! Take them away. Tell them to leave me be. Tell them I don't know them—don't want to have them hanging round me. Tell them *I'm your father!*"[35]

However, this recourse to patriarchal authority (both real and imaginary) is insufficient. Being a father, a Senator, a Presbyterian church elder, or the president of a temperance society is simply beside the point. None of these things matter. The women do not cease their attentions, and Buttons's advice is to run for it. His escape becomes a carnival spectacle that simply draws more attention from the onlookers:

> Away they started. It was a full run. A shout arose. So arises the shout in Rome along the bellowing Corso when the horses are starting for the Carnival races. It was a long, loud shout, gathering and growing and deepening as it rose, till it burst on high in one grand thunder-clap of sound.
> Away went the Senator like the wind...Crowds cheered him as he passed. Behind him the passage-way closed up, and a long trail of screaming maskers pressed after him. The louder they shouted the faster the Senator ran.[36]

The Senator ends up hiding in the Opera House's topmost box. Typically, his only recourse to sexual attention from women, or to the attention of a curious crowd, is flight and concealment. His strength and violence—his manliness—are useless in these situations. He is handicapped by his limited repertoire of responses—a repertoire whose limitations are defined by nineteenth-century codes of manliness.

Finally, *The Dodge Club* juxtaposes two different models of masculinity—the Italian or Latin, and the English or American—in a way that turns cultural stereotypes around to the disadvantage of the travellers. For example, at the masquerade in Naples, despite the fact that the Club members are wearing masks, "every body knew that they were English or American, which is just the same; for Englishmen and Americans are universally recognizable by the rigidity of their muscles."[37] The apparent fluidity of Italian men seems to be privileged here over the "rigidity" of the Americans. Later, Dick meets an old friend in Milan, an Italian Count who had lived in exile in Boston during the 1850s. Their encounter is an emotional one:

> The Count came rushing into the room, flushed and trembling, and without a word threw himself into Dick's arms, embraced him, and kissed him. It was a trying moment for Dick. Nothing is so frightful to a man of the Anglo-Saxon race as to be hugged and kissed by a man.[38]

"However," the narrator continues, "Dick felt deeply touched at the emotion of his friend and his grateful remembrance of himself."[39] Dick's homophobic reaction to his friend's emotion is countered to some extent by his awareness of cultural difference and his understanding of his friend's emotions. Given the ethnocentrism of nineteenth-century Canada—think of Susanna

Figure 3 "Used Up," an illustration from *The Dodge Club* (1869).

Moodie's comments about Irish emigrants—De Mille's understanding that different cultures have different models and practices of masculinity is most unusual.

CONCLUSION

All good things must end, however, and in De Mille's travel fictions, narrative closure marks the end of the carnival and a consequent normalizing of identities and social positions—a normalizing that, perhaps unsurprisingly, takes on conservative political resonances. For example, in *Old Garth*, the main character abandons his somewhat Byronic attempt to foment a republican revolution in Sicily and returns to England to take possession of an inherited estate and the title of "Lord Landsdowne."[40] And, as in many forms of comedy, these texts end in marriage (usually multiple marriages in De Mille's fiction), which further marks the end of the carnival and the normalization of gender identities. In many ways, De Mille's fiction is not dissimilar to other forms of comedy, from Aristophanes to Shakespeare to Howard Hawks: comic, carnivalesque disorder creates a plethora of potential identities, which narrative closure must shut down. Nevertheless, the importance of carnival in De Mille's fiction may perhaps surprise us and complicate to some extent our perceptions of nineteenth-century Canadian writing and its representations of masculinity.

NOTES

1 Stephen M. Whitehead, *Men and Masculinities* (Cambridge: Polity, 2002), 5.
2 John Tosh, *Manliness and Masculinities in Nineteenth-Century Britain: Essays on Gender, Family, and Empire* (Harlow: Pearson Longman, 2005), 72–73.
3 Kathryn McPherson, Cecilia Morgan, and Nancy M. Forestell, *Gendered Pasts: Historical Essays in Feminity and Masculinity in Canada* (Toronto: Oxford University Press, 1999), 6.
4 James De Mille, *The Dodge Club; or, Italy in MDCCCLIX* (New York: Harper and Brothers, 1869), 60. See also Mikhail Bakhtin, *Rabelais and His World*, trans. Helene Iswolsky (Bloomington: Indiana University Press, 1984).
5 Richard Cavell, "Bakhtin Reads De Mille: Canadian Literature, Postmodernism, and the Theory of Dialogism," in *Future Indicative: Literary Theory and Canadian Literature,* ed. John Moss (Ottawa: University of Ottawa Press, 1987), 205–11 at 208.
6 De Mille, *The Dodge Club,* 60.
7 Mikhail Bakhtin, *Problems of Dostoevsky's Poetics,* ed. and trans. Caryl Emerson (Minneapolis: University of Minnesota Press, 1984), 124.
8 De Mille, *The Dodge Club,* 60, 29.
9 Ibid., 29.
10 James De Mille, *The Babes in the Wood* (Boston: W.F. Gill, 1875), 103.
11 James De Mille, *The Cryptogram: A Novel* (New York: Harper and Brothers, 1871, reprinted by University of Toronto Press, 1980), 141.
12 Ibid., 141–43.
13 Ibid., 145.
14 Judith Adler, "Travel as Performed Art," *American Journal of Sociology* 94, no. 6 (1989): 1366–91 at 1385.
15 James De Mille, *Old Garth: A Story of Sicily* (Seaside Library 75.1512) (New York: George Munro, 1883), 32.
16 Ibid., 38.
17 Ibid., 38.
18 Ibid., 52.
19 James De Mille, *A Castle in Spain: A Novel* (New York: Harper and Brothers, 1883), 73.
20 Ibid., 73.
21 Ibid., 91.

22 Ibid., 157.
23 James De Mille, *The Dodge Club*, 6.
24 Ibid., 21.
25 Ibid., 21.
26 Ibid., 7.
27 Ibid., 93.
28 Ibid., 114.
29 Ibid., 85.
30 Ibid., 86.
31 Ibid., 87.
32 Ibid., 22.
33 Ibid., 22.
34 Ibid., 22.
35 Ibid., 23.
36 Ibid., 23–24.
37 Ibid., 22.
38 Ibid., 128.
39 Ibid., 128.
40 James De Mille, *Old Garth*, 51.

CHAPTER 2

"No Money, but Muscle and Pluck": Cultivating Trans-Imperial Manliness for the Fields of Empire, 1870–1901

JARETT HENDERSON

In 1878, Thomas Spence, immigration handbook author and a clerk in the Legislative Assembly of Manitoba, encouraged "any man, whatever his station in life may be, who is able and willing to work and has any adaptability for agricultural pursuits" to immigrate to the Canadian prairies.[1] Twenty-two years after Spence published his handbook, *Useful and Practical Hints for the Settler,* Prime Minister Wilfrid Laurier endorsed similar sentiments as he defended his government's immigration scheme in the House of Commons. "It is not the policy of this government to bring out paupers," explained Laurier, "but I know of no restriction against able-bodied men who are willing to work and can work."[2] In an effort to discern the central tenets of what I call trans-imperial manliness, this chapter investigates Canadian immigration handbooks designed to encourage immigration from the imperial metropole to the Canadian North West in the waning decades of the nineteenth century. These handbooks provided intending immigrants with a variety of services: they reproduced for those in the metropole a particular imagining of the social world of the North West; they located this settler geography within the broader British world; and consequently they situated it within the messy histories of British imperialism and colonization. Furthermore, to interrogate the language of immigration handbooks reveals that they also sought to educate would-be farmers and nation builders about how to properly perform and practise manliness on Canada's colonial frontier.

By linking colonialism to immigration history, and Canadian history more generally, this chapter conceives of immigration as an imperial act. By doing so it contributes to an expanding body of literature that comprehends the British Empire as a connected yet always shifting and changing entity.[3] Furthermore, it uses gender as a primary framework of analysis to interrogate the empire as a sphere of physical manliness. It seeks to complement the literature on immigration and imperialism that has focused predominately on the diverse experiences of white female migrants who were ambiguously complicit throughout the empire as colonizers and colonized.[4] But empire, as John Tosh notes, framed the lives not only of women but also of men: "the colonies were a man's world, and manhood might be secured by becoming a colonist."[5] My interest, then, is in interrogating this masculine aspect of empire in an effort to discern how immigration handbooks constructed trans-imperial manliness.[6] I argue that the brand of manliness advertised in the pages of Canadian immigration handbooks was "trans-imperial" because it was designed to appeal to the imperial imaginations of men in the metropole *and* to guide their gendered performances as the masculine colonizers of the Canadian North West once they had arrived.

As the title of Thomas Spence's handbook suggests, the primary purpose of immigration handbooks was to provide intending immigrants with "useful and practical hints." Immigration handbooks were written for and by men. Their language was designed to appeal to the imperial imaginations of male British subjects in Canada and the United Kingdom. The hints these handbooks provided settlers, colonists, and intending immigrants (individuals always identified as male) suggest one of the ways that Canadian immigration promoters – who were often themselves recent ex-settlers – blended manliness with British imperial ideals in the late nineteenth century. Whether this trans-imperial manliness was encountered by intending immigrants in the metropole at emigration offices, or by settlers in the Canadian North West, this ideal was composed of three central factors: the healthy climate of the North West, a successful agricultural life, and the ownership of a home. In their appeals to metropolitan men, handbooks constantly reiterated that such things made imperial men. Moreover, as Canadian immigration officials argued, these markers of masculinity could only be found in the "more tolerable" colony of "the Great North West." Handbooks, and the government agents who distributed them, advertised the Canadian North West as a settler geography where intending British immigrants could, with "no money, but muscle and pluck," attain this trans-imperial ideal.

"A POUND OR TWO IN HIS POCKET"

In 1896, a handbook issued by the Canadian Department of the Interior listed "Persons with Capital" as the most desirable class of settler. "The first great demand is for practical men with some capital at their disposal," advertised this handbook, "for which class there are unlimited openings." However, it quickly reassured those intending immigrants who had little capital that even their fellow settlers *with* capital "often desire[d] to enter upon agricultural pursuits."[7] This fusion of agriculture, manliness, and character with the ambiguity about the amount of capital required permeated the pages of immigration handbooks published in the last three decades of the nineteenth century. In fact, handbooks rarely published parameters to regulate migration and did not prohibit intending immigrants with little to invest from entering Canada. Instead, they often advertised that the intending immigrant with only a "pound or two in his pocket," who was full of pluck and muscle, and who desired independence, was superior to the immigrant with an abundance of capital and an undesirable character.[8] The "less irksome social restrictions imposed by society" in the Canadian North West, commented one handbook, provided British subjects from the metropole with an opportunity to overcome the rigid class hierarchy that limited their ability to possess a home and land in Great Britain.[9]

One handbook from 1898 deployed the method of publishing what it called "Settlers' Opinions of the Country." Such letters were no doubt carefully selected and even doctored to promote a desirable image of Canada to the metropole.[10] Thus, they reveal what Canadian immigration promoters considered the essential threads of trans-imperial manliness. One male settler testified that he had "every confidence in recommending Canada to the notice of all classes of British agriculturists, but especially to young, strong men, with or without capital, who are blessed with habits of sobriety, industry, and perseverance."[11] William Riddle, reported to have recently settled in the North West, observed that "comfort and prosperity" awaited any man "with patience, pluck, and perseverance...No man need be afraid of making a good thing of [immigrating to Canada]."[12]

The proper balance of character, capital, and brawn was consistently left open by immigration handbooks. *Western Canada,* a handbook that was reissued annually by the Department of the Interior in the late 1890s, contended that "it [was] difficult to lay down a hard and fast rule as to the amount of capital necessary to start farming."[13] When the North Atlantic Trading Company was established in 1897, it required that the head of each family arrive in Canada with at least $100.00 in hand.[14] Immigration handbooks published between 1870 and 1900 all advertised that intending immigrants who wanted to be "successful" should arrive in the North West with somewhere between $400 and $1,000. Like numerous other handbooks, *Western Canada* reiterated that success within the colonial space of the North West was not intimately connected to social status; rather, the successful performance of trans-imperial manliness "depend[ed] upon the energy, experience, judgement and the enterprise of the person concerned."[15]

Yet intending immigrants needed information about costs, and handbooks sought to provide it. A table included in the 1878 handbook *Information for Immigrants,* published by the Province of Manitoba, outlined the amount of capital that was required if intending immigrants were to attain a "comfortable start" in the North West. The table reproduced below was accompanied with a detailed description that separated intending immigrants into two classes. The first was branded as capable of "a comfortable start" and commenced at $465.

A Comfortable start:
One yoke of oxen	$120.00
One Wagon	$80.00
Plough and Harrow	$25.00
Chains, Axes, Shovels, etc.	$30.00
Stoves, Beds, etc.	$60.00
House and Stable, say	$150.00
Total	**$465.00**

According to the handbook, the second tier—"large scale farming"—required that intending immigrants arrive with a capital of $800 to $1,000.[16] This extra capital was said to enable the settler to secure additional land and commence more sizeable agricultural endeavours faster in the North West, yet the handbooks took great care to insist that finances did not trump character.

Though immigration handbooks provided financial information for intending immigrants, they continued to advertise that the "energetic man" who "looked cheerfully" upon his future in the North West could overcome the setback of having little capital. "Many such men have taken up the free grants," noted a handbook printed by the British Colonial Office in 1880, "and have then hired themselves out to labour, cultivating their own land during spare time, and employing a man at harvest when necessary. By this means they are able to stock and cultivate their farms in a few years with the results of their own labour and profits of their harvests, and there are many men in Canada now in positions of independence."[17] That same year, G.H. Wyatt penned a handbook for the Government of Canada that reinforced this testimony of the Colonial Office. "With land secured, a small house erected," observed Wyatt, "a few farming tools and livestock, oxen, cows, hogs and poultry, in a country of fertile soil and genial climate, a man is thenceforth independent.[18] Colonial societies held out economic opportunities that were attractive to settlers in the material sense.[19] They promised settlers independence, but they also offered – as Kirsten McKenzie has demonstrated for Sydney and Cape Town – an opportunity for colonists to invent new identities.[20] Immigration handbooks advertised the North West as a colonial society wherein intending immigrants from the metropole could overcome their status, achieve independence, and successfully perform trans-imperial manliness. For as the handbook *Western Canada* and others have suggested, in the North West there were numerous "openings [for] the poor man if he will work and exercise economy, for after a year or two of hard work he finds himself in possession of a home, all his own, and free from the harnessing conditions of a rented or mortgaged farm."[21]

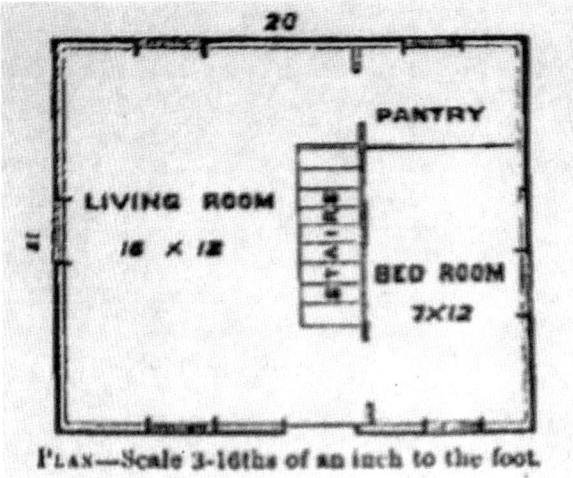

Figure 4 Blueprints such as this one included in Thomas Spence's 1882 handbook, "Blueprint," *Useful and Practical Hints for the Settler on Canadian Prairie Lands and for the Guidance of Intending British Emigrants*, outlined for male settlers what a properly structured colonial home should look like. Source: Library and Archives Canada/ AMICUS 2603826.

"BY FAR THE PRETTIEST AND BEST HOUSE"

Immigration handbooks advertised a form of trans-imperial manliness to intending immigrants in the metropole and hoped that it would then guide their gendered performances in the Canadian North West. A thorough examination of these handbooks has yielded a brand of manliness that included clearing the land, building a home, and starting a family. These symbols of middle-class masculinity were, as John Tosh has observed, often beyond the grasp of imperial subjects in the metropole. Consequently those men who sought to emulate this ideal looked to the empire to acquire land and practise domestic patriarchy.[22] Kathryn McPherson's exploration of immigration handbooks published in the early twentieth century reveals that handbooks restricted white female settlers to the home, the front porch, or garden, while they situated male settlers in the fields, next to barns, or lingering by the forests.[23] McPherson concludes that the home framed images of settler femininity in the Canadian West, and rightly so. Yet settler masculinity, as advertised in the pages of immigration handbooks, was equally associated with the colonial household as that of the settler femininity.

In their influential work, *Family Fortunes: Men and Women of the English Middle Class, 1780–1850,* Leonore Davidoff and Catherine Hall have shown how studying the properly ordered household can illustrate the positions that men *and* women occupied within. According to Davidoff and Hall, the home was "as much a social construct and state of mind as a reality of bricks and mortar."[24] Though immigration handbooks do not reflect the lived domestic relations deemed appropriate within the ideal British home – or in the case of the Canadian North West, colonial home – they do suggest how the normative ideas of "family" and "home" operated within the imperial world as highly gendered symbols. For as Catherine Hall has observed elsewhere, "true manliness [encompassed] the capacity to establish a home, protect it, provide for it and control it: all of these were part of a man's good standing."[25] That domesticity was integral to trans-imperial manliness is underscored in an 1879 handbook titled *North Western Canada*. In this handbook, settler Frank Middleton testified that any man "who wishes to secure a home for himself [ought] not to be influenced by the lingo of those chicken-hearted fellows who turn back at the first mud-hole they come to, or can be chased by a mosquito...Any man with ordinary intelligence and a little pluck cannot fail to make himself a comfortable home in a few years by coming to the Great North West."[26]

Another settler, when asked to reflect on his experience in the North West, further demonstrated how he understood the links among manliness, independence, and the home. He informed the Department of the Interior that the North West was "a country that any young man [could] make himself a house and be independent and comfortable by home and industry."[27] G.H. Wyatt in the handbook *Dominion of Canada* posed a question to intending immigrants that further connected manliness and the home. Wyatt inquired of settlers: "Who does not wish for a home of his own?"[28] Wyatt's question illustrates how the coupling of manliness and the home operated as a valuable tool in navigating the terrain between colonial and metropolitan spaces; for according to Wyatt, there existed a "universal yearning" among the classes of mechanics and workers in Britain to obtain their own home and farm in Canada. It was this yearning that Wyatt identified as the "home instinct"—for "a man who labours with this end in view is a happier man, a better husband, a kinder father, and a more valuable citizen."[29]

The home has been seen as a generative social force that affects a variety of experiences that include both gender and familial identities. Within the British imperial context, as Adele Perry asserts, the home was perceived as something of a mirror: it was "a powerful reflector of people's character."[30] The written testimonies of male settlers demonstrate how they themselves reacted to the trans-imperial manliness that immigration handbooks advertised. Thomas E. Jackson illustrated for metropolitan and Canadian readers how he had improved his lot since resettling in the Canadian North West. Upon his arrival, Jackson recalled, "I built a shack about as small as it was possible, but I had to make it do for a time, then I built a second house...and last year I built a brick house which has cost $3000."[31] J.B. Clapp, who settled in the Melita region of Manitoba, similarly used his extra income to improve his home. "The first season's crop when threshed and marketed, realized enough to pay all my bills," stated Clapp. With his remaining income, Clapp declared, he "finish[ed] and paint[ed] [his] house."[32] The publication of letters in which settler men paid attention to improving their homes, both structurally and visually, not only indicates the importance of the home as a public reflector of character, but also as central to their performances of trans-imperial manliness.[33]

Yet not all attempts at cultivating this trans-imperial manliness in the Canadian North West were successful. The gender and racial categories created in the colonies, suggests Ann Laura Stoler, are best understood as "homespun handiworks" that manufactured differences between prescription and practices as well as between metropoles and colonies.[34] Moreover, as recent studies of colonialism have suggested, the largely homosocial character of settler societies across the empire fostered alternative sites and expressions of both masculinity and domesticity.[35] At the core of these societies was the all-male household. These spaces were key components in the maintenance of a homosocial culture that legitimized everyday performances of masculinity.[36] Among the British middle classes, the creation of homes without white women signalled what John Tosh calls a "revolt against domesticity." Whether in the metropole, or in the settler geography of the North West, where male settlers significantly outnumbered female ones, the all-male household presented a challenge to the increasingly hegemonic concepts of gender and family. By the end of the nineteenth century, domesticity and manliness within the British Empire were taking on new constructions that were increasingly centred on the relationship between men and the home.[37] Perhaps it is somewhat ironic, then, that immigration and imperial expansion provided young British men with the opportunity to distance themselves from the trans-imperial manliness that immigration handbooks advertised as well as to react against this gendered ideal.

Cecelia Danysk's work on bachelor identity in the prairie West further suggests that the process of Western resettlement revealed a "contradiction between present realities and future potentials" and that for those men involved in settling the North West, the experience was anything but "a paradise."[38] As a form of propaganda, immigration handbooks were intended to produce an attractive image of the Canadian North West for intending immigrants in the metropole. Negative images of the territory would have done little to entice metropolitan men. Handbook authors, government agents, and Members of Parliament *spun* settler testimonies to the best of their ability in their efforts to attract potential settlers, foster immigration, and as this chapter suggests, guide the gendered performances of settler men. To further entice intending immigrants, immigration handbooks constructed the North West as a white, settler geography rather than the racially plural society it was. A careful reading of these handbooks indicates the fragility of this gender ideal,

Figure 5 "First Year in the Bush," from *Manitoba and the Great North West: The Field for Investment; The Home of the Emigrant*, 1883. Source: Library and Archives Canada/AMICUS 12066631.

Figure 6 "Fifteen Years in the Bush," from *Manitoba and the Great North West: The Field for Investment; The Home of the Emigrant*, 1883. Source: Library and Archives Canada/AMICUS 12066631.

Figure 7 "Thirty Years in the Bush," from *Manitoba and the Great North West: The Field for Investment; The Home of the Emigrant*, 1883. Source: Library and Archives Canada/AMICUS 12066631.

while revealing some of the ways that settler men negotiated their gendered performances in this predominantly homosocial space.

The testimony of a young English settler, reproduced in *North Western Canada*, demonstrates one of the many hurdles that men faced in their efforts to perform the manliness that handbooks advertised: the all-male household. In an emotional account of the house he shared with his brother, this young settler illustrates how men living in an all-male household could revise the trans-imperial manliness advertised in handbooks to accommodate their own experiences of empire:

> I have got my own house now, and am keeping bachelors' hall along with my younger brother... If I get a chance next year to get it photographed I will have it taken and then send you [the Department of Agriculture] one. It is pronounced by the people around to be by far the prettiest and best house in this part of the country, which gives me much pleasure, considering that I was my own architect and worked at it myself from the time we took the timber out of the bush till we moved into it.[39]

The manliness of this settler was filtered through the alternative site of the all-male household. Even so, he continued to subscribe to the man–house relationship that immigration handbooks advertised as central to this trans-imperial ideal. The pleasure this settler alleged he experienced when describing the home that he and his brother built and shared, enabled him to proudly hold up their homosocial home as a trophy of their manly endeavours. The publication of this young settler's testimony illustrated to metropolitan readers that life in the peripheries was not a simple transcript of life at "home." In this outpost of the British Empire, the relationship between men and the home persisted, even if it took on novel and innovative forms in its construction.

"A MAN IS A MAN IF HE IS WILLING TO TILL THE SOIL"

The requests made by immigration handbooks for tillers of the soil, tenant farmers, and farm labourers not only identify the class of settler that Canada wanted, but also suggest how entwined land, agriculture, and manliness were in the late-nineteenth-century imperial world. In *Important Information for Immigrants,* Nicholas Ennis reminded readers that "it should be borne in mind that all the houses in this country are occupied not by tenants, dependants, or serfs as in many parts of Europe, but by industrious and intelligent farmers and mechanics, the bone and sinew of the land, who own the ground upon which they stand, build their houses for their own use, and arrange them to satisfy their own *peculiar* wants and gratify their own tastes."[40] Ennis revealed in this statement the many tenets of trans-imperial manliness—independence, homeownership, and the cultivation of the land—while recognizing the peculiarities of gender in the Canadian North West. Immigration agent John W. Down noted in 1877 that "those who have free arms, and free aspirations, and who wish to emancipate themselves from the iron bonds of poverty, which unfortunately encircle the agricultural population of [Great Britain]" should immigrate to the Canadian North West. In a subsequent section of the handbook, Down further fused trans-imperial manliness with control of the land: "it is watered by streams of crystal purity, and indeed, nothing is wanting but the labour of a man to turn this beautiful prairie into a land of fertility and promise."[41]

That prevailing over the land was a masculine pursuit has been demonstrated in relation to numerous historical circumstances. In her examination of British fur traders' journals and diaries, Elizabeth Vibert demonstrates that on the Columbia Plateau, traders articulated appropriate performances of manliness as including both the domination of the land and the building of a home.[42] In the Okanagan region of British Columbia, as Jason Patrick Bennett recognizes, immigration handbooks did more than encourage the growing of fruit. Immigration handbooks, whether advocating fruit farming in the Okanagan Valley or wheat growing in the Canadian North West, radiated what Bennett identifies as "a significant sexual element in [their] invitation for men to tend the fertile earth."[43] Consider Thomas Spence's flirtatious and sexualized description of the Canadian North West, designed to arouse the

Figure 8 "Ploughing on William Hamilton's Farm near Hamiota, Man., 1905–1909." Source: Library and Archives Canada / Credit: Endre J. Cleven / Department of the Interior fonds / PA-021561.

male settler's interest in immigration. The settler, "feeling himself every inch a man, as he gazes upon the unclaimed acres which shall reward his toil... breathes a freer air, his bosom swells with prouder purpose, and his strong arms achieve unwonted results."[44] Sexualized descriptions of the land such as this one articulated by Spence not only enabled immigration handbooks to associate proper displays of trans-imperial manliness with male authority and heterosexuality, but also encouraged settler men to *feel* this manliness.

The seductive images of the North Western landscape as female, fused with descriptions of colonization as the penetration of male settlers into virgin territories, made immigration handbooks highly sexualized texts. That Canadian immigration handbooks were sexually charged share parallels with other colonial contexts: for as Ann Laura Stoler reminds us, "probably no subject is discussed more than sex in colonial literature."[45] Immigration handbooks were no exception. They advised settlers of the "remarkable ease" with which the "virgin prairies" could be brought "under cultivation."[46] When the Province of Manitoba issued a handbook in 1879, it gave a very suggestive description of how to "break" the virgin soils of the Canadian North West. "Before the prairie is broken, the sod is very tough and requires great force to break it, but after it has once been turned, the subsequent ploughings are very easy."[47] The union of earth and farmer intimately linked trans-imperial manliness with heterosexuality and endeavoured to make such gendered performances the ideal for both the "new nation" and this outpost of empire.[48]

This explicit heterosexuality did not, however, run unchecked throughout the pages of immigration handbooks. As Patrick A. Dunae observes, some very vulgar statements made by settlers to handbook authors and immigration officials were not included in handbooks because of their crudeness.

When immigration handbook author Alexander Begg was interrogating settlers about their experiences in the North West for a handbook he was writing, he stumbled upon a few undesirable responses. Begg wanted to know from settlers, in their experience, when was the best time to break the virgin soil? The following response did not appear in Begg's eventual publication, *Free Homes for All in Manitoba*.[49] Yet it masterfully illustrates, albeit in graphic terms, not only how one Dublin settler conceived the "virgin soil" of the prairies, but also the connection between land and heterosexuality.

> *Begg*: Which is the best time for breaking the virgin soil?
> *Dublin settler*: In my opinion, night is the best time to break a virgin, but if opportunity favoured, anytime would do: I would not be particular.[50]

The sexualized invitations that handbooks made indicated to heterosexual men that these erotic and virgin lands could gratify their sexual desires, while perhaps offering homosexual men equal satisfaction in the predominantly homosocial and masculine Canadian North West.[51]

Agriculture did not offer the opportunity to aspire to late-nineteenth-century ideals of trans-imperial manliness to British men alone, however. The North West could be as transformative of ethnic identity as it was of class. A handbook printed in 1893 remarked that any "man is a man if he is willing to till the soil."[52] Another claimed that the "unsuccessful immigrant in Canada [was] the man who [would] not work. Those who [would] stay on the land, and work, [could] not help getting on."[53] When, in the late 1890s, the Department of the Interior's campaigns to attract "foreign" immigrants from northern Europe finally began to show positive results, handbooks extended their brand of trans-imperial manliness to these settlers likely because of their shared whiteness. In its depiction of Manitoba, the 1899 issue of *Western Canada* suggested that

> any part of the Province that is desired to visit, will give sufficient evidence to satisfy all that those who have followed farming as a pursuit and given it anything like ordinary attention have made it a success. This not only applies to English-speaking people, and those who have hitherto been farmers, [but] to foreigners and to those who have gone out into the country without any previous experience in farming.[54]

The agricultural lifestyle seemingly had, as Sarah Carter rightly observes, "a mystical power to it."[55] Moreover, as the testimony of Mr. Jackson suggests, there was no better place than in the North West to achieve the trans-imperial manliness that handbooks advertised. "I think," recollected Jackson, "that this is fair showing that we have a good country for farming, and any man that is a farmer cannot help but prosper."[56] By the end of the nineteenth century, immigration handbooks, in tandem with the federal government's official immigration policy, were advertising the North West as a settler geography that could transform both intending immigrants from the United Kingdom and "foreign" immigrants from northern Europe. The fusion of ideas of whiteness, sexuality, and agriculture in the pages of immigration handbooks made the gendered ideals they depicted simultaneously encompassing, limited, and hybrid.

That this trans-imperial manliness was hybrid is further suggested in the way it was imposed on the Aboriginal populations of the North West. Very rarely did the Aboriginal people occupying the lands over which settlers claimed ownership appear in the pages of immigration handbooks. In 1874 the Province of Manitoba published one of the few handbooks to advertise that Aboriginal people lived in the North West, and it posed a question believed important for intending immigrants to consider: "Are there many Indians, and are they peacefully inclined?" To this question, it replied with the assertion that the "Indians" were both "quiet" and "inoffensive" and were "well satisfied" with the annuity of three dollars provided them by the Government of Canada. The handbook also explained that the "Indians [have] hunting grounds for themselves *far back* in the North-West."[57] After the ratification of the Indian Act in 1876, the portrayal of Aboriginal people in handbooks took on another dimension. Aboriginals were no longer depicted as actual bodies inhabiting the North West; instead, they were vanishing from the landscape, or—more important to this discussion—they were being converted to a sedentary, agricultural, and *civilized* life.

In 1882 a handbook proclaimed that "the Indians have now vanished from their old hunting grounds."[58] *Free Homes,* a pamphlet published by the Canadian Pacific Railway in 1886, noted that "the prairie is fast becoming a thing of the past. In that respect it is following the herds of buffalo and the poor Indians who are receding before the face of the white man."[59] By 1899, *Western Canada* was describing the North West without any mention of Aboriginal occupancy: "There was a time when this vast region was supposed to be fit only for the habitation of the beaver, the buffalo, and the bear: but that day is past, as since the movement of immigration westward it has been demonstrated that this region contains the finest wheat and grazing lands in the world."[60] This image of the "vanishing Indian" predominated throughout the British Empire across the late nineteenth and early twentieth centuries. It was an ideology that appealed to immigration promoters because it removed Aboriginals—the perceived obstacles to the creation of a white, settler society—from Canada's North West.[61]

Immigration handbooks sometimes commented on how agriculture could offer Aboriginals access to a *civilized* existence. In 1886, when Canadian government officials visited the region, they reported seeing "signs of culture" emerging in the form of "homesteads" and "fields under cultivation."[62] Four years earlier, in 1882, handbook author Nicholas Ennis had illustrated for intending immigrants how the agricultural life had been "adopted" by Aboriginals living in the North West:

> Where the Indian so recently maintained a precarious existence there are populous villages, fast merging into towns, the clink of the hammer is heard in the forge and the rush of the stream from the milldam tells of agriculture and commerce... The Indians themselves have become labourers, they have been removed to large reserves, and have been raised to the dignity of cultivators... Many of them have houses in place of wigwams, they have schools and churches, they have in short, been adopted into the great family of civilized man.[63]

Ennis thus confirmed for the white male settlers of the North West (whether British or "foreign") that they *could* become civilized men and dignified cultivators: an ideal that Aboriginal farmers could only hope to "adopt."

Yet Ennis's message was much more pointed. As he suggested, the "adoption" of Aboriginals into the white family of empire through agricultural labour confirms what Sarah Carter identifies in *Lost Harvests*: that agriculture was believed to be the "solution" that could end the Indian's nomadic ways. Carter shows how the scientific community and Canadian government officials alike viewed agriculture as a key step in man's evolutionary process: it marked progress from "savagery" to barbarism to civilization. As a result, the Indian farm was identified as a training ground for civilization and citizenship.[64] Handbooks advertised that agriculture could foster virtue, independence, and hard work in both British and "foreign" settlers, but the presence of Aboriginal people in the North West made this a more complicated venture. So immigration handbooks were forced to deal with the issue, but they did so ambiguously. Yet these moments forced immigration handbooks to confront and reckon with the realities of empire—in particular, the hybridity of settler society in the North West that limited this trans-imperial ideal.

"THE HEALTHIEST CLIMATE UNDER THE SUN"

The final aspect of the Canadian North West that immigration handbooks associated with trans-imperial manliness was its healthy climate. In the late nineteenth century the British world believed that the climate could affect, positively or negatively, the morality and health of an individual. Immigration handbooks manipulated this concern for the healthy body, advertising that the climate of the North West improved physical health and stimulated robustness—indeed, it was unsurpassable; it was, as one handbook claimed, "the healthiest climate under the sun." That the climate was central to handbooks' construction of trans-imperial manliness was suggested by the Department of the Interior in 1897. The handbook *Manitoba and the North-West Territories* stated that the first question any "sensible man" asked when considering immigration was: "What is [Canada's] climate?"[65] Yet despite the healthy promotion of the Canadian climate in immigration handbooks, relatively few historical studies consider the climate as a significant factor affecting gendered performances.[66]

Carl Berger noted over forty years ago that the importance of the Canadian climate was not merely that it sustained "the hardy character of the stronger races, but that it also constituted, in Darwinian terms, 'a persistent process of natural selection.'"[67] When advertising the healthiness of the climate of the North West, immigration handbooks often relied on the expert testimony of church officials, soldiers, and doctors to legitimize the notion that the climate was an agent of masculinization. That "the climate is a good one for the development of a man," explained Dr. James Paterson, Chief Officer of Health of Manitoba in 1899, "is shown by the fact that those who have come here during the last 20 years have not deteriorated, but stand today as the equal of any other man in mental or physical vigour, independent in thought and action."[68] After spending seven years in Canada practising medicine, Dr. Harvey J. Philpot validated his diagnosis of the exceptional healthiness of the Canadian climate in true scientific fashion: "As a race, the Canadians are fine, tall, handsome, powerful men, well built, active, tough as pine knot, and bearded like pards. The good food, upon which they have been brought up, with the invigorating climate, appears to develop them to the fullest proportions of the *genus homo*."[69]

By exploiting turn-of-the-century discourses of degeneration, immigration handbooks were in effect declaring that even if immigrants entering Canada were perceived as impure or unhealthy by contemporaries, the Canadian climate could transform them and their offspring into healthier citizens.[70] In 1872, a handbook issued by the Department of Agriculture illustrated how the climate of the North West could transform the male settler: "a man in changing his country should have some ambition, [he] should feel that it is his duty, to plant his family in a climate, where they may become a vigorous and healthy race; and such races are found pre-eminently in the zones of wheat and grasses."[71] Thomas Spence's handbook, *Useful and Practical Hints for the Settler*, claimed that "there are hundreds of robust men in Manitoba today who came here physical wrecks, who now bear grateful testimony to the salubrity of the climate, the purity of the atmosphere and the presence of other conditions that make this Province one of the healthiest places in the world."[72]

Neither the metropole nor the more tropical colonies in the empire could compete with the restorative qualities of the North West. Spence noted that there is no country under the sun where unaided muscle, with a plucky purpose, reaps greater rewards than under the bright skies and helpful atmosphere of this fair land, the settler's countenance in the pure, dry, electric air, will be as fresh as the morning. His muscles will be iron, his nerves steel. Vigour will characterize his every action; for climate gives quality to the blood, strength to the muscles, power to the brain...Indolence is characteristic of people living in the tropics, and energy of those living in the temperate zones.[73]

As Ann Laura Stoler has argued, it was believed that a gamut of maladies could plague settlers if they stayed "too long" in the tropics. Male and female settlers in those regions were thought to suffer from fatigue and physical breakdown, but it was racial degeneration that worried imperialists most. As Stoler observes, the ability of white women to reproduce the "white race" could be called into question in the tropics.[74] Similarly, Anne McClintock notes that the imperial metropole, with its slums and crowds, was a site of empire where gender and race had degenerated—an understanding that Canadian immigration handbooks often used to their benefit.[75] In 1899 the Department of the Interior maintained that the transformative capabilities of the Canadian climate could only be comprehended when compared with the climate of England. The handbook reproduced the testimony of a young settler who had just returned to the prairies after a visit "home." This young settler commented that "it was only when [he] visited England that [he] began to appreciate the [Canadian] climate." He testified that the pure air and healthy winters were "physical restorers" and that the climate "made [his] blood circulate." The North West, he boasted, enabled him to acquire both "vim and energy."[76]

An 1886 handbook produced by the Canadian Pacific Railway reprinted the "testimony of actual settlers" to illustrate for those considering immigration the wealth, resources, and prospects of the North West. According to this handbook, the most crucial question when considering immigration was, "Are you satisfied with the country, the climate, and the prospects ahead of you?"[77] It reprinted more than 200 settlers' responses, of which 84 simply replied "Yes" to the question. However, some settlers provided additional comments. G. McGill declared: "So far as climate, it is more desirable than Great Britain or Ireland on the whole. Winter is clear, dry, and healthy; no need of umbrella, mud-boots or top coat round home." John Kemp simply scribbled that both the climate and country "are first class."[78] Glaringly absent from these testimonies, however, were the snow and the blistering cold of winters in the North West. Nonetheless, when considered alongside handbooks' descriptions of independence, an agricultural life, and homeownership, the climate was a vital determinant of health and character in the making of healthy, strong, manly, imperial bodies in the North West.

CONCLUSION

The immigration handbooks analyzed here advertised the Canadian North West as a site of empire where British immigrants, northern Europeans, and (to a lesser degree) Aboriginal people could practise and aspire to the central tenets of trans-imperial manliness. These handbooks repeatedly identified masculine roles, traits, and behaviours that those in the metropole and the peripheries of the British Empire would have recognized and considered appropriate displays of gender for men. Moreover, handbooks offered the North West as the *only* theatre of empire wherein such a gendered performance could be enacted. Though the main purpose of Canadian immigration handbooks was to encourage the resettlement of what is now western Canada, they were not so one-dimensional. Rather, immigration handbooks reflected and at the same time constituted the broader social worlds of the metropole, the outposts of empire they were designed to represent, and the imperial imaginations that fashioned them.[79] Handbooks identified an array of manly characteristics that settlers and Aboriginal people had to practise and exhibit if they had any hope of becoming bona fide settlers, respectable Canadian citizens, and ideal imperial men. These handbooks idyllically advertised that in the Canadian North West, neither class nor race would inhibit one's ability to aspire to these advertised images of trans-imperial manliness. The owning of a home and the independence it brought, combined with successful agricultural ventures, the breaking of virgin soils, and living in the regenerative climate of the North West were all offered as ingredients that would produce a new and vigorous manliness in this outpost of the British Empire. Undoubtedly these visions of trans-imperial manhood as advertised in the pages of Canadian immigration handbooks were more imagined than lived. And as such, they serve to remind us, as does Ann Laura Stoler, that gendered and raced practices on the ground often diverged from overarching discourses of imperialism.[80] Nonetheless, these virtues served as the guide rails for male settlers en route to independence and prosperity, while indicating for these aspiring imperial men the direction to ideal manliness.

NOTES

This chapter has benefited from the advice and support of many friends and conference participants. In particular I would like to thank Kristine Alexander, Stacey Alexopoulos, and Sarah Glassford for their comments on earlier versions of this chapter, and Mike Wilton for his constant encouragement. Both Adele Perry and Bettina Bradbury have graciously helped me hone my arguments. My students in History 2500 at York University asked great questions that aided me in the editing process. The Department of History at the University of Manitoba provided financial assistance that made it possible for me to present this paper at the Making It Like a Man! conference at the University of Regina; for this I am grateful.

1 Thomas Spence, *Useful and Practical Hints for the Settler on Canadian Prairie Lands and for the Guidance of Intending British Emigrants to Manitoba and the North-West of Canada* (Manitoba: 1878), 8.
2 *Debates*, House of Commons, Canada (1900), 10187.
3 Philippa Levine, *The British Empire: Sunrise to Sunset* (London: Pearson, 2007); Angela Woollacott, *Gender and Empire* (Houndsmills: Palgrave, 2006); Tony Ballantyne, *Orientalism and Race: Aryanism in the British Empire* (Houndsmills: Palgrave, 2001); Alan Lester, *Imperial Networks: Creating Identities in Nineteenth-Century South Africa and Britain* (London: Routledge, 2001); and Elizabeth Elbourne, "The Sin of the Settler: The 1835–36 Select committee on Aborigines and Debates over Virtue and Conquest in the Early-Nineteenth-Century British White Settler Empire," *Journal of Colonialism and Colonial History* 4, no. 3 (2003), http://muse.jhu.edu/journals/cch.
4 Anne McClintock, *Imperial Leather: Race, Gender, and Sexuality in the Colonial Conquest* (London: Routledge, 1995); Rita S. Kranidis, ed., *Imperial Objects: Essays on Victorian Women's Emigration and the Unauthorized Imperial Experience* (London: Twayne: 1998); Angela Woollacott, *To Try Her Fortune in London: Australian Women, Colonialism, and Modernity* (London: Oxford University Press, 2001); Jan Gothard, *Blue China: Single Female Emigration to Colonial Australia* (Melbourne: Melbourne University Press, 2001); and Lisa Chilton, *Agents of Empire: British Female Migration to Canada and Australia, 1860s–1930* (Toronto: University of Toronto Press, 2007).
5 John Tosh, *Manliness and Masculinities in Nineteenth-Century Britain: Essays on Gender, Family, and Empire* (London: Longman, 2005), 186.
6 For a discussion of "trans-imperialism," see Alan Lester and David Lambert's introduction to *Colonial Lives Across the British Empire: Imperial Careering in the Long Nineteenth Century* (Cambridge: Cambridge University Press, 2006); and Ann Curthoys and Marilyn Lake, eds., *Connected Worlds: History in Transnational Perspective* (Canberra: Australian National University Press, 2005).
7 Minister of the Interior, *Letters from Settlers in Canada: Official and Other Information for Intending Settlers in Manitoba, the North-West Territories, British Columbia, and the Other Provinces of Canada* (Euston: McCorquodale and Co., 1896), 45.
8 Jarett Henderson, "'Grumblers, Complainers, Cranks, and Slanders are NOT invited': Immigration Handbooks, Agents, and Empire in Western Canada, 1870–1900," paper presented at the British World Conference, University of Auckland, July 2005.
9 Government of Manitoba, *Manitoba, Official Information for Investors and Settlers* (Winnipeg: 1893), 21–22.
10 Patrick Dunae, "Promoting the Dominion: Records and the Canadian Immigration Campaign," *Archivaria* 19 (1984–85), 73–93.
11 Department of the Interior, *Canada: As a Home for the Scotch Agriculturist* (Ottawa: 1898), 21.
12 G.H. Wyatt, *Dominion of Canada. Manitoba, The Canadian North-West and Ontario* (Toronto: 1880), 12.
13 Minister of the Interior, *Western Canada: Manitoba, Assiniboia, Alberta, Saskatchewan, and Northern Ontario* (Ottawa: 1899), 32.
14 Valerie Knowles, *Strangers at Our Gates: Canadian Immigration and Immigration Policy, 1540–1990* (Toronto: Dundurn Press, 1992), 65.
15 Minister of the Interior, *Western Canada*, 32.
16 Department of Agriculture, *Province of Manitoba and North-West Territory of the Dominion of Canada: Information for Immigrants* (Ottawa: 1878), 57.

17 British Colonial Office, *Information for Immigrants* (1880), 7.
18 Wyatt, *Dominion of Canada*, 6.
19 Tosh, *Manliness and Masculinities*, 177.
20 Kirsten McKenzie, *Scandal in the Colonies: Sydney and Cape Town, 1820–1850* (Melbourne: Melbourne University Press, 2004); and *A Swindler's Progress: Nobles and Convicts in the Age of Liberty* (Cambridge, MA: Harvard University Press, 2010).
21 Minister of the Interior, *Western Canada*, 47–49.
22 Tosh, *Manliness and Masculinities*, 182.
23 Kathryn McPherson, "Domesticity and Disease: Disciplining Healthy Bodies in the Colonization of the Canadian West," unpublished paper presented at Germs, Selves, Rules: The Gendered Body, State, and Colonialism in Western and Northern Canada, Canada Research Chair in Western Canadian Social History Colloquium, University of Manitoba, 21 November 2003.
24 Leonore Davidoff and Catherine Hall, *Family Fortunes: Men and Women of the English Middle Class, 1780–1850* (London: Hutchison Education, 1987), 358.
25 Catherine Hall, *Civilising Subjects: Metropole and Colony in the English Imagination, 1830–1867* (Chicago: University of Chicago Press, 2002), 27.
26 Department of Agriculture, *Dominion of Canada: The Province of Manitoba and the North-West Territory, Information for Intending Immigrants* (Ottawa: 1879), 38.
27 Minister of the Interior, *Western Canada*, Testimonies.
28 Wyatt, *Dominion of Canada*, 5.
29 Ibid., 6.
30 Adele Perry, "From 'The Hot-Bed of Vice" to the 'Good and Well-Ordered Christian Home': First Nations Housing and Reform in Nineteenth-Century British Columbia," *Ethnohistory* 50, no. 4 (Fall 2003): 593.
31 Minister of the Interior, *Western Canada*, 28.
32 Canadian Pacific Railway, *What Farmers Say: The Experience of Farmers Cultivating the Land of Manitoba, Assiniboia, Alberta, and the Saskatchewan* (1892), 6.
33 Jessica Dempster, "'Aye, Daughter, and My Boys Too!': An Examination of English-Canadian Iconography of the South African War, 1899–1901," Master's research paper, McGill University, 2005.
34 Ann Laura Stoler, "Making Empire Respectable: The Politics of Race and Sexual Morality in 20th Century Colonial Cultures," *American Ethnologist* 16, no. 3 (1989): 634–60; and Frederick Cooper and Ann Laura Stoler, eds., *Tensions of Empire: Colonial Cultures in a Bourgeois World* (Berkeley: University of California Press, 1997).
35 Robert Alrich, *Colonialism and Homosexuality* (London: Routledge, 2002); and Jessica Harland-Jacobs, *Builders of Empire; Freemasons and British Imperialism, 1717–1927* (Chapel Hill: University of North Carolina Press, 2007).
36 Bettina Bradbury, "Colonial Comparisons: Rethinking Marriage, Civilization, and Nation in the Nineteenth-Century White Settler Societies," in *Rediscovering the British World*, ed. P. Buckner and R.D. Francis (Calgary: University of Calgary Press, 2005); Adele Perry, *On the Edge of Empire: Gender, Race, and the Making of British Columbia, 1849–1871* (Toronto: University of Toronto Press, 2001); and Cecilia Danysk, "'A Bachelor's Paradise': Homesteaders, Hired Hands, and the Construction of Masculinity, 1880–1930," in *Making Western Canada: Essays on European Colonization and Settlement*, ed. Catherine Cavanaugh and Jeremy Mouat (Toronto: Garamond Press, 1996), 154–85.
37 John Tosh, "Domesticity and Manliness in the Victorian Middle Class: The Family of Edward White Benson," in *Manful Assertions: Masculinities in Britain since 1800*, ed. Michael Roper and John Tosh (London: Routledge, 1991), 67–69.

38 Danysk, "'A Bachelor's Paradise.'"
39 Department of Agriculture, *Dominion of Canada* (1879), 38.
40 Nicholas Devereux Ennis, *Important Information for Intending Settlers in Manitoba: Respecting a Quarter of a Million Acres of Select Farming and Stock-Raising Land in the County of Minnedosa, Little Saskatchewan* (Liverpool: Turner and Dunnett Printers, 1882), 22.
41 J.W. Down, *The Manitoban and Great North West Colony: Explanations of Its Advantages and Objects* (Bristol: Jeffries and Sons Printers, 1877), 6.
42 Elizabeth Vibert, *Traders Tales: Narratives of Cultural Encounters on the Columbia Plateau* (Norman: University of Oklahoma Press, 1997), 107.
43 Jason Patrick Bennett, "Apple of the Empire: Landscape and Imperial Identity in the Turn-of-the-Century British Columbia," *Journal of the Canadian Historical Association*, New Series, 9 (1998): 72.
44 Spence, *Useful and Practical Hints* (1878), 19–20.
45 Stoler, "Making Empire Respectable," 635.
46 Government of Canada, *Manitoba the Home of Agriculturalists* (Ottawa: 1890), 19.
47 Province of Manitoba, *Dominion of Canada* (1879), 18.
48 Bennett, "Apple of the Empire," 72. See also Sarah Carter, *The Importance of Being Monogamous: Marriage and Nation Building in Western Canada to 1915* (Edmonton: University of Alberta Press, 2008).
49 Canadian Pacific Railway, *Free Homes for All in Manitoba and the Canadian North West* (Winnipeg: 1886).
50 Dunae, "Promoting the Dominion," 86.
51 Lyle Dick, "Same-Sex Intersections of the Prairie Settlement Era: The 1895 Case of Regina's Oscar Wilde," *Histoire sociale / Social History* 42, no. 83 (2009): 107–45; Terry Chapman, "Male Homosexuality: Legal Restraints and Social Attitudes in Western Canada, 1890–1920," in *Law and Justice in a New Land: Essays in Western Canadian Legal History*, ed. L. Knafla (Toronto: Carswell, 1986); and Terry Chapman, "'An Oscar Wilde Type': 'The Abominable Crime of Buggery' in Western Canada, 1890–1920," *Criminal Justice History* 4 (1983): 97–118.
52 Minister of the Interior, *Letters from Settlers in Canada: Official and Other Information for Intending Settlers in Manitoba, the North-West Territories, British Columbia, and the Other Provinces of Canada* (Euston: McCorquodale and Co., 1896), 45; and Government of Manitoba, *Manitoba: Official Information for Investors and Settlers* (Winnipeg, 1893), 21.
53 Mrs. George Cran, *A Woman in Canada* (London: John Mile, 1910), 98.
54 Minister of the Interior, *Western Canada*, 43.
55 Sarah Carter, *Lost Harvests: Prairie Indian Reserve Farmers and Government Policy* (Kingston and Montreal: McGill–Queen's University Press, 1990), 20.
56 Minister of the Interior, *Western Canada*, 28.
57 Department of Agriculture, *Information for Intending Emigrant* (1874), 44. My italics.
58 Ennis, *Important Information* (1882) 6.
59 Canadian Pacific Railway, *Free Homes*, 6.
60 Minister of the Interior, *Western Canada*, 5.
61 Penelope Edmonds, *Urbanizing Frontiers: Indigenous Peoples and Settlers in 19th-Century Pacific Rim Cities* (Vancouver: UBC Press, 2010); Daniel Francis, *The Imaginary Indian: The Image of the Indian in Canadian Culture* (Vancouver: Arsenal Pulp Press, 1992).
62 Canadian Pacific Railway, *Free Homes*, 5–6.
63 Ennis, *Important Information*, 6.
64 Carter, *Lost Harvests*, 18–20.

65 Department of the Interior, *Manitoba and the North-West Territories, Assiniboia, Alberta, Saskatchewan in Which Are Included the Newly Discovered Gold Fields of the Yukon* (Ottawa: 1897), 6.
66 Myra Rutherdale, "'If Only We Had Some Sort of Communal Wash and Bathhouse': Southern Nurses and Northern Bodies, 1945–1970"; Mona Gleason, "Small Bodies of Knowledge: Building the 'Healthy Child' in 20th Century Canada"; and Kathryn McPherson, "Domesticity and Disease: Disciplining Healthy Bodies in the Colonization of the Canadian West"; papers presented at Germs, Selves, Rules: The Gendered Body, State, and Colonialism in Western and Northern Canada, Canada Research Chair in Western Canadian Social History Colloquium, University of Manitoba, 21 November 2003.
67 Carl Berger, "The True North Strong and Free," in *Nationalism in Canada* (Toronto: University of Toronto Press, 1966), 9.
68 Minister of the Interior, *Western Canada*, 9.
69 Acton Burrows, *North Western Canada, Its Climate, Soil Productions, with a Sketch of Its Natural Features and Social Condition* (Winnipeg: 1880), 12.
70 Mariana Valverde, *The Age of Light, Soap, and Water: Moral Reform in English Canada, 1885–1925* (Toronto: McClelland and Stewart, 1991), 116.
71 Department of Agriculture, *Dominion of Canada: Information for Emigrants* (Ottawa, 1872), 8.
72 Spence, *Useful and Practical Hints* (1878), 8.
73 Ibid., 6.
74 Stoler, *Carnal Knowledge and Imperial Power*, 72–73.
75 McClintock, *Imperial Leather*, 43–48.
76 Minister of the Interior, *Western Canada*, 12.
77 Canadian Pacific Railway, *Plain Facts about the Canadian West* (Ottawa: 1884), 42–46.
78 Ibid., 42–46.
79 Jarett Henderson, "'Most of Our Country Is Wild and Unspoiled': Advertising Gender, Race, and Empire for Western Canada, 1867–1911," M.A. thesis, University of Manitoba, 2004.
80 Stoler, *Carnal Knowledge and Imperial Power*.

CHAPTER 3

Who's on the Home Front? Canadian Masculinity in the NFB's Second World War Series "Canada Carries On"

MICHAEL BRENDAN BAKER

It is widely accepted, and rightfully so, that the prestige of Canada's documentary tradition is wedded to the success of its Second World War–era film series, Canada Carries On. John Grierson, founding commissioner of the National Film Board of Canada, and Stuart Legg, the executive producer of the series (and a British documentarian who had worked with Grierson at the General Post Office Film Unit during the 1930s), shaped Canada Carries On in such a way that it became the signpost for Canadian documentaries of the war and immediate postwar eras. Films produced as part of Canada Carries On were not exclusively war-themed, but the series was the cornerstone of the NFB's wartime production schedule. The series was intended by Grierson to introduce and explain domestic and international events to Canadian citizens, and the short subjects that comprised the series sought to demonstrate Canada's role in the war effort in the domestic *and* international spheres.[1] As I will argue, the series also clearly demonstrates, in its ways of portraying "who was on the home front," the assumed cultural values about identity, agency, and manliness in the NFB's Canadian nation-building project.

MEN ON THE HOME FRONT

Several films from the Canada Carries On series were produced specifically to address the situation on the home front, in direct relation both to events in Europe and to domestic issues related to events overseas. Curiously, an index of the appearance of male figures in those films specifically committed to illustrating wartime (if not war-related) activity on the home front produces a list of characters comprised almost exclusively of men directly involved in the machinery of war. The representations of men in these texts serve to engender a highly constructed and delimited notion of masculinity. This masculine character is put on display not at the expense of representations of women on the home front—whose contributions to the war effort are ultimately secured within the NFB filmography in Canada Carries On films such as Jane Marsh's *Wings on Her Shoulder* and *Proudly She Marches* (1943)—but at the cost of male characters who exist outside the margins of this overdetermined cinematic space. In the broader context of the destabilization of traditional gender relations by the recruitment of women into the workforce and the uprooting of entire demographic swaths of young men from their traditional patterns of socialization, images of masculinity produced and endorsed by an agency of the federal government—images that engineer a specific type of Canadian male citizen in the young nation's social imaginary at the expense of others—demand our attention.

The exact degree to which Grierson (as commissioner) crafted the NFB's version of masculinity is debatable, but his central role in the production of these films is not. With this in mind, it is an interesting exercise to examine representations of male characters in NFB films circa World War Two in terms of the commissioner's authoritative and authorial role in the production of the films for the Canada Carries On series. The legend of John Grierson has been writ large in numerous texts, and the impact of his personal politics and ideologies on documentary practice in general (and in the Canadian context specifically) is regularly reviewed.[2] My task is to place close readings of selected films in dialogue with production documents from the era and the historical record as it concerns conscription in Canada in an effort to gauge to what degree the images of masculinity were influenced by the commissioner and to what extent any exclusionary practices impacted on representations of Canadian masculinity in the postwar era of the NFB.

THE CANADIAN MALE CARRIES ON: PROTECTORS AND PRODUCERS

Relative to the Canada Carries On productions concerned with Canada's presence on the war front, films focusing on the home front are quite limited in number. Only a half dozen of the over fifty specifically war-themed series entries address domestic activities. *Letter from Aldershot* (Stuart Legg, 1940), *Quebec Path of Conquest* (Raymond Spottiswoode, F.R. Crawley, 1942), *Inside Fighting Canada* (Jane Marsh, 1942), and *Letter from Overseas* (1943) are the primary sources for the domestic imagery under examination. Each of these films acknowledges the domestic sphere of Canada's war effort. However, the limited amount of material addressing the home front necessitates a consideration of several key war front texts in order to appreciate the dynamic nature of the representation of masculinity in the series.

In the Canada Carries On series, indexing the male characters establishes a clear dichotomy in terms of the roles these characters play—roles henceforth labelled *protectors* and *producers*. Given the context of the production of these films, male characters in the series are primarily soldiers—that is, protectors. On the home front, however, men are depicted working furiously to sustain the war effort, and the result is a small selection of domestic films that underscore the significant role played by merchant sailors, farmers, loggers, and general labourers, as well as the entry of women into the workforce—that is, by producers. The latter classification can be broken down further along the lines of the type of production—industrial, agricultural, mineral extraction. Further reading of these films through this particular lens has clear class-based implications in terms of what type of male character occupies any given producer role. Canadian masculinity as defined by the protector/producer dichotomy in effect excludes those male characters who do not easily fit one of these moulds. Apart from producers, the vast expanse of geographical space between Vancouver and the Atlantic presented in Canada Carries On is inhabited mainly by carefree youth, dedicated housewives, or otherwise entirely faceless Canadian citizens.

Inside Fighting Canada is the most representative film of the aforementioned sample, with its stereotypical depictions of fishermen on the east coast, farmers in the prairies, and loggers in British Columbia. It strives to portray Canada as a nation well equipped (in terms of both human and natural resources) to play a prominent role in the Allied war effort. The voice-over commentary in each of these films—performed by series narrator Lorne Greene—invokes Canada's founding myth, citing it as a country "created by men who are not afraid to harness the overwhelming forces of the landscape." Action verbs and Greene's booming baritone demonstrate a power and assuredness that defines the quintessential Canadian man as one fit to conquer nature and enemies alike.[3] The film uses a geographical sweep from one coast to the other to structure a narrative that addresses the ways in which Canada's natural resources assist in the war effort. Without much subtlety, this narrative metaphorically links the power of Canadian men in dominating their environment to the strength of Canada as an Allied nation. This formulaic deployment of the man-overcoming-nature allegory characterizes each film in the series concerned with the home front. *Letter from Aldershot* and *Letter from Overseas* are the anomalies in this group, as the content of each of these films does not consist of domestic imagery but rather training footage, barracks life, social nights and—in the case of the latter—the planning and execution of the Dieppe Raid. In each of these films, however, the framing narrative features the family of a young soldier receiving and reading a letter from overseas in the comfort of their quaint Canadian residence. This simple device bridges the spatial divide between home and abroad and effectively separates the domestic experience of the Second World War from the machinery of war at home and abroad.

Inside Fighting Canada was the source of some controversy on its release, for reasons that speak directly to the issue of subjective reporting as it relates

Figure 9 Still from *Inside Fighting Canada* (1942). The film was the source of some controversy for its subjective reporting and charges of factual inaccuracy.

to the representation of masculinity in Second World War–era Canadian cinema. Ontario Premier Mitchell Hepburn, with the aid of his appointed civil servants on the Ontario Board of Censors, fought an unsuccessful battle all the way to the Supreme Court of Canada to have *Inside Fighting Canada* suspended from exhibition for reasons of political partisanship and factual inaccuracy as it related to voluntary service in Canada.[4] The story made provincial headlines in December 1942 with a front-page story on Christmas Day in Canada's national newspaper, the *Globe and Mail*, and the release of an official statement by John Grierson after the issue became fodder for editorials in *Globe,* the *Toronto Star,* and the *Winnipeg Free Press*.[5] The statement chiefly concerned the history of the production (it was solicited by the U.S. government) and explained away the inaccuracies as mistakes and as not politically motivated; today, it also serves as evidence of the authorial control that Grierson exercised over Canada Carries On productions.

Official documents and personal memos to film units archived at the NFB illustrate how strongly Grierson shaped the material gathered for the series. Grierson sent highly detailed telegrams to his photographers outlining the images he wanted to include in the Canada Carries On films. His directions, however, often resulted in the misrepresentation of soldiers' experiences. Moreover, the war-themed films of the Canada Carries On series

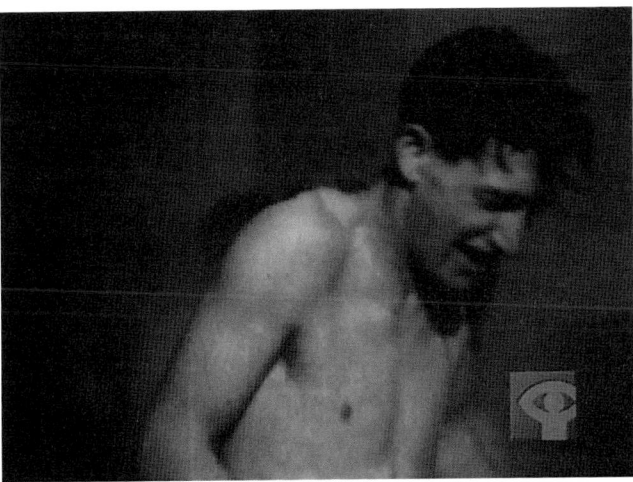

Figure 10 Still from *Letter from Aldershot* (1940). The shower scene is used as archival evidence in Jose Torrealba's *Open Secrets* (2003), a film examining homosexuality in the Canadian military during the Second World War.

defined Canadian masculinity in very specific terms that favoured direct involvement with the war effort, essentially excluding examples of male characters who remained at home. With regard to the social aspects of military service, Grierson was clear about his expectations of the soldiers' behaviour, telling an NFB representative in England that he required shots of Canadian soldiers "talking with girls in London parks" and giving their opinion on "English food, beer, cigarettes, weather...music halls, [and] girls."[6] The commissioner also expected to get laughs out of "soldiers darning socks and other domestic problems."[7] In a telegram dated 18 January 1940, Grierson outlined his demands for the material required to produce *Privates' Lives (A Film of the First Canadian Division in Britain)*, a proposal that would ultimately become *Letter from Aldershot*:

> National Film Board want for earliest possible exhibition in Canada film showing how Canadian troops are getting on. Stop. Wanted personal human film showing individuals from all districts of/in Canada what they are doing in their spare time in barracks and on leave what towns they are near if the censors all what they do in London what girls they go out with etcetera. Stop.[8]

One could argue that Grierson, by giving photographers such rigid guidelines concerning what was noteworthy and of interest to Canadians with regard to the lives of soldiers, intentionally or not was fabricating a masculine character that would have negative connotations when revisited by contemporary viewers. His stereotypically girl-crazy, bar-hopping soldiers narrowly defined both the military lifestyle and the behaviour expected of new recruits in an effort to consolidate the function of these films as propagandistic tools of enlistment and social education.

In *The Colonized Eye,* Joyce Nelson outlines Grierson's mandate for NFB productions as one intended to eschew nationalistic pride in favour of a collectivist view that emphasized ambivalence toward Canada's goals as a young nation.[9] Nelson contends that Grierson's "editorial internationalism"—the use of footage from a broad range of international film bureaus and news agencies in the Canada Carries On and World in Action series obscured any clear view of Canada.[10] Personalized and localized views were avoided in the wartime films. That being so, what impact did such a mandate have on a citizenry represented as strictly homogenous and compliant?

EXCLUDED MASCULINITIES IN ENVISIONING CANADIAN NATIONAL IDENTITY

"Where is here?"—Nelson invokes this famous Canadian aphorism coined by Northrop Frye during an examination of the dislocating effect that editorial internationalism has on Canada as a nation and on Canadians as both filmmakers and viewers. If we, like Nelson, consider Frye's question of Canadian national identity in relation to this practice of editorial internationalism and retroactively (perhaps playfully) construct a link between the dislocating effect this compilation practice had on Canadian geography and cultural constructions of masculinity, Frye's "confused nowhere"—representing "boundaryless and restless absences of place"—could metaphorically represent a confused or destabilized Canadian masculinity as authorized only by overdetermined cinematic representations.[11] The exclusion of marginal figures—specifically non-protecting and non-producing male characters—is justified by a rigidly controlled representational scheme such as the protector–producer paradigm. In the case of the home front films of the Canada Carries On series, this exclusion is so complete that the few images of men in domestic spaces are not men at all, but preschoolers depicted with their mothers as they shop on Main Street, Canada (presumably doing their part to keep the wartime economy chugging along). However, Canada's Conscription Act—a document with a great deal of authority in terms of the impact it had on shaping the nation's demography during times of war—serves as evidence that the producer–protector dichotomy misrepresented the identity of male characters who remained at home yet who played equally significant roles in maintaining Canada's wartime quality of life and development as a young nation.

Conscription in Canada provided exemptions for a limited number of non-medical categories, from judges and clergymen to university professors, schoolteachers, and the only sons of widows.[12] All but the last group could be labelled intelligentsia—a category often associated with cowardice during this era and that heightened suspicions about men exempted on the basis on these fields of employment. The existence of these exemptions (and common sense) confirms that male characters outside the restrictive limits of the producer–protector dichotomy remained in the domestic sphere for the producers of the Canada Carries On to present to the Canadian public in the context of the series mandate. Yet none of the war-themed films expressly acknowledge the contributions made by male characters working in these fields during wartime. Again, only those individuals directly involved in the manufacture of military equipment or the broader infrastructure of war receive attention. Apart from timid figures in lab coats calibrating equipment in munitions plants, adult males aligned with the intelligentsia are invisible. This suggests that men remaining on the home front whose roles did not conform to the conception of masculinity embodied by producers and protectors were excluded in lieu of images that advanced a notion of Canadian masculinity built upon strength, collective spirit, and—obviously enough—unambiguous heterosexuality.

As war-time documents intended to mobilize support for government action (by making concrete the issues—as defined by the Allies—deemed central to winning both the physical and the ideological war, and by serving as tools of public education), the Canada Carries On series could not risk any sort of ambiguity, be it in regard to the Allied position on the war or the character of the men committed to fighting that war. Working backwards from Tom Waugh's analysis of the cultural reflection of geopolitical insecurities in Canadian cinema of the 1950s, the Canada Carries On series can be understood as initiating a project of securing gender through processes of representation that denied the existence of male figures outside the predefined roles of protector and producer. Accepting the binary construction of masculinity introduced here—either a soldier on the warfront or a labourer at home—the image of Canadian masculinity presented in Canada Carries On is quickly supplanted by the Cold War's iconic businessman-consumer. Interestingly, the only non-uniformed, non-labouring male characters over the age of twenty from *Inside Fighting Canada* are several businessmen trapped in a sea of soldiers parading down an overcrowded city street. The only other images of male characters of any age existing outside the protector–producer paradigm are two young boys playing in a sandbox under their mothers' supervision. If it is the Cold War that ultimately shakes gender roles from their secured positions with the return of men to a workforce that has been "infiltrated" by women, we can look to the NFB's wartime series to understand how these roles were secured in the first place, through a process of denial—not necessarily of the feminine, but perhaps a denial of the effeminate.

These anxieties fully manifest themselves in the NFB's postwar corpus of psychosocial "issue films" such as *Is It a Woman's World?* (Don Haldane,

1956) and *Howard* (Don Haldane, 1957), films that Waugh discusses at length in his recent work, *The Romance of Transgression in Canada: Queering Sexualities, Nations, Cinemas*. And it is the denial and the silence surrounding these marginalized masculinities that exist outside of the protector–producer paradigm in the war era that connects them to a postwar manifestation. Waugh invokes Michel Foucault when declaring that "silences in cultural imaginaries are a familiar problem."[13] Foucault argues:

> Silence itself—the things one declines to say, or is forbidden to name, the discretion that is required between different speakers—is less the absolute limit of discourse, the other side from which it is separated by a strict boundary, than an element that functions alongside the things said, with them and in relation to them within overall strategies. There is no division to be made between what one says and what one does not say; we must try to determine the different ways of not saying such things.[14]

Adopting Foucault's interpretation of silence and absence in cultural histories, we should consider that it is what Canada Carries On *does not say* about those male characters remaining on the home front during the Second World War that determined the space within which marginalized male figures established themselves in the Canadian imaginary and contributed to Canada's wartime socio-economic and cultural life.

Gender hegemony through queer exclusion is at the heart of the matter Waugh investigates, but it is the more basic issue of exclusion at the expense of male characters outside the producer–protector dichotomy that undermines the NFB's wartime representation of masculinity. There was, it seems, a prohibition on the depiction of exempted males in the war-themed entries of Canada Carries On, and it is precisely the absence of male characters on the Canadian home front in these films and the silence that surrounds this absence that should become an issue for examination. Does the fey male librarian bachelor appear from nowhere in a postwar Canada and its cinematic imaginary, or can we safely assume that he existed on the home front, albeit off-screen and excluded from view? Grierson and company's propaganda damages the Canadian self-image through a one-sided, idealized portrayal of masculinity. But if war and national identity are entwined, it is foolish to think that any perceived vulnerabilities would be left on display for discriminating eyes.

Images of homosocial behaviour in the Canada Carries On films serve to challenge the NFB's notion of wartime Canadian masculinity. Loosely defined, homosocial spaces are aligned with the sympathetic identification of male protagonists and crypto homoeroticism by way of a "nostalgic longing for all-male public spheres."[15] Conversely, these spheres are depicted as the conduit for "infection"—that is, for marital break-up, addiction, and promiscuity. While nothing so graphic is captured in Canada Carries On, the reliance on male-dominated spaces of social interaction to establish and portray the good life of young Canadian soldiers invites such subversive readings. A shower scene in *Letter from Aldershot* features a platoon of naked men rushing toward the camera—all while narrator Lorne Greene takes on the character of a young soldier and declares in the first person that it is "the best moment of the day." It is a deliriously camp moment, to be sure, and read against the grain of the film's overarching message, it retroactively suggests that queer representation in the war-era films is not entirely hidden from view. Jose Torrealba's 2003 NFB-produced film *Open Secrets* (2003) examines homosexuality in the Canadian military during the Second World War and thus formally initiates the on-screen revelation of this hitherto unacknowledged socio-sexual realm of Canadian masculinity.

Ironically enough, it is precisely this homosocial sphere of downtime on the war front that constitutes the central thrust of *Letter from Aldershot*'s function as a recruitment tool. While it was the mandate of the NFB to explain Canada to Canadians, the war series had another function that was, for a time, far more significant. Films concerning the lives of soldiers abroad were employed as recruiting films for those at home. The military was keenly aware that you could never turn a regular citizen into a soldier with the thirty-day recruitment program used by the Canadian Armed Forces at the time, so they would instead sell young men on the *idea* of life as a soldier to ensure they remained committed to training.[16] The target of this appeal was "the young proletarian and farm-boy cannon-fodder that [will be] lured by group showers and the nightlife in London."[17] If the films reviewed here are any indication, it was the assurance that the conveniences of domestic life would not be sacrificed abroad (accompanied by the perks of being far away from home) that proved to be the favoured strategy of recruiters at the Non-Permanent Active Militia (NPAM—known as the Canada Army Reserve after 1940), the group responsible for enlisting young men in advance of Mackenzie King's plebiscite on the conscription issue.

Images of domesticity appear within a rigorously structured framework that is careful to balance the shadowy realities of military service with the perks that make enrolment appear to be a few steps shy of a relaxing vacation abroad. The result is a recurring rhetorical trope that paints the motivation for Grierson's telegraphed demands with a shadowy hue: the infantilization of the young recruit for the purpose of leveraging the appeal of life in the military. This device is also visible in recruitment films from outside the Canada Carries On series, often produced expressly for the Canadian Army. Among these commissioned films, *13th Platoon* (Julian Roffman, 1942) is noteworthy for the way that class difference and the infantilization of young recruits and officers alike are represented in spaces coded as homosocial.[18]

Figure 11 Still from *Letter from Overseas* (1943). Scenes of domesticity distinguish barracks life from fighting on the front.

The aforementioned shower sequence in *Letter from Aldershot* is mirrored by a similar segment in *Letter from Overseas*. In it, soldiers are found splashing playfully in a pond while another serviceman, laundering uniforms in a specialized facility nearby, executes his duties while the narrator Greene waxes enthusiastically about the conveniences of modern living as it exists on the battlefield (in fact, he boasts that many of the home appliance technologies far exceed anything "mom" is using back home). Similar scenes play themselves out in dining halls and social clubs in this and other films, almost completely in denial of the grim realities of the front line. In fact, in each of these films there seems to be a deliberate buffer between the viewer and war imagery—these sequences of domestic life on the war front are formulaically inserted so as to play themselves out with a relaxed air in advance of the brief shock of the battle scenes, which disappear from the narrative just as quickly as they arrive.

But any reconsideration of Canada Carries On is not about the absence or sidelong presence of queer masculinity in the NFB's wartime productions. In returning to this material, I seek to understand the implications and ramifications of these representations of masculinity in films intended for public education by a federal institution. While we need not go so far as to say that the NFB's construction of masculinity in Canada Carries On was the mandate of Grierson and Grierson alone, Nelson's central thesis contends that these films smack of a conservatism rooted in one man's individual vision. Drawing upon Bruce Elder's examination of Grierson's project as one that demanded that documentary be "socially effective" and contain "realistic imagery"—the emphasis here should be on the word *realistic*—far more problematic than the commissioner's ideological zeal is what these images of reality say about a male citizenry that is only allowed to assert itself on the battlefield.[19] Proto-feminist views that arose during the Cold War, however, would quickly redefine masculinity along terms of sensitivity, expressiveness, creativity, and tenderness—the character of the modern "sissy" emerges, to use Waugh's shorthand.[20]

PROTO-FEMINIST CANADIAN MASCULINITY AND THE POETIC TURN

In the Canada Carries On series, several decidedly non-war-themed films illustrate how exempted males are conceived of and represented within the cinematic space of the NFB. The Québécois ethnography film *Alexis Tremblay: Habitant* (Jane Marsh, 1943) and selections from the series on fine art and agriculture are particularly germane to the present discussion and represent opportunities for further consideration of the producer–protector dichotomy in the whole of the Canada Carries On series. In the art and agriculture films, the sensitivity, expressiveness, creativity, and tenderness considered to be signs of weakness in the war-themed films are offered as central to a uniquely Canadian identity. *Canadian Landscape* (F.R. Crawley, 1941), *Iceland on the Prairies* (F.R. Crawley, 1941), *Painters of Quebec* (F.R. Crawley, 1944), and *West Wind* (Graham McInnes, 1944) are the strongest illustrations of the art films, while *Battle of the Harvests* (James Beveridge, 1942) and *Hands for the Harvest* (Stanley Jackson, 1944) address how men of all ages are involved in the agricultural domain of wartime Canada. There is a poetic quality to these works that echoes the humanism of Humphrey Jennings's films for the GPO (films that Grierson openly disliked) and that foreshadows the humanist tone that the postwar NFB would establish in the Perspective and Candid Eye series, thereby gaining international recognition.[21] This postwar corpus also a marks a decisive shift from the macho posturing institutionalized by the NFB via Lorne Greene's trademark bellow as Stanley Jackson's mellifluous tone becomes the standard for the Board's voice-over commentary. Overall, it is the art series, select agricultural films, and the work of female directors such as Gudrun Bjerring Parker (*Before They Are Six*, 1943) that point toward the postwar manifestation of destabilized Canadian masculinities in productions of the NFB. Canada Carries On, under the direction of Grierson, offers a version of Canadian masculinity in practice that could be said to have died with the end of the war and Grierson's subsequent departure. At the very least, the series is a fascinating repository of images charting a young nation's negotiation of its own identity, a self-image dependent on a clearly delineated brand of masculinity intended to reinforce the notion that Canada is able to fulfill its responsibility to the Allied effort.

NOTES

1 The success of Canada Carries On prompted the reassignment of several films to a companion program, World in Action, which United Artists distributed on an international scale. World in Action concerned itself with subjects that demonstrated Canada's role in the war on broader, international terms and in turn explained international issues and policies to Canadians. For this reason, these films featured less of a uniquely Canadian character and spoke in terms that were more general. A complete listing of films produced for both series is available in Peter Morris, ed., *The National Film Board of Canada: The War Years* (Ottawa: Canadian Film Archives, 1965), 20–23, 27–28. For a close reading of the successful Canada Carries On / World in Action film *Churchill's Island* (Stuart Legg, 1941), see Michael Brendan Baker, "Churchill's Island," in *24 Frames: The Cinema of Canada*, ed. Jerry White (London: Wallflower Press, 2006), 23–32.
2 For example, Peter Morris, "Re-thinking Grierson: The Ideology of John Grierson," in *History on/and/in Film*, ed. T. O'Regan and B. Shoesmith (Perth: History and Film Association of Australia, 1987), 20–30; and Brian Winston, *Claiming the Real: The Griersonian Documentary and Its Legitimations* (London: British Film Institute, 1995).
3 For a brief consideration of the structure of these voice-over commentaries in relation to image, see Ernst Borneman, "Documentary Films: World War II," in *Canadian Film Reader*, ed. Seth Feldman and Joyce Nelson (Toronto: Peter Martin Associates, 1977), 48–57.
4 For a brief summary of Hepburn's efforts and a history of this era of film exhibition in Ontario, see Wyndham Wise, "History of Ontario's Film Industry, 1896 to 1985," *Take One* 9, no. 28 (Summer 2000): 20.
5 "Statement on *Inside Fighting Canada* by John Grierson, Government Film Commissioner, in answer to a statement by the Treasurer of the Province of Ontario," National Film Board of Canada Archives, file no. 304-1-33 (13 April 2004).
6 Grierson outlined his expectations for the material in a telegram addressed to "Golightly" dated 24 January 1940. NFB Archives, file no. 0122 (13 April 2004).
7 Ibid.
8 Ibid.
9 Joyce Nelson, *The Colonized Eye: Rethinking the Grierson Legend* (Toronto: Between the Lines, 1988), 69–70.
10 The term "editorial internationalism," used by Nelson in *The Colonized Eye*, is a recurring reference, among other histories of Grierson's NFB, to the previously cited Borneman text in which he explains a compilation process involving footage from film bureaux around the word. Ibid., 54–55.
11 Ibid., 72.
12 J.L. Granatstein and J. Mackay Hitsman, *Broken Promises: A History of Conscription in Canada* (Toronto: Oxford University Press, 1977), 146–47.
13 Thomas Waugh, *The Romance of Transgression: Queering Sexualities, Nations, Cinemas* (Montreal and Kingston: McGill–Queen's University Press, 2006), 41.
14 Michel Foucault, *The History of Sexuality* (New York: Vintage Books, [1976]1990), 27.

15 Waugh, *The Romance of Transgression*, 37.
16 Granatstein and Hitsman discuss the role of the National Resources Mobilization Act (NRMA) and the recruitment of NPAM. Granatstein and Hitsman, *Broken Promises*, 142–47.
17 I must thank Tom Waugh for this succinct (and saucy) analysis of the film's ideal audience. Personal communication with the author, 23 August 2008.
18 In *13th Platoon*, a young officer attempts to win over the hardened, working-class men of his platoon. Moulded in the fashion of his British-born and university-educated superiors, the baby-faced officer—referred to as "just another ninety day wonder" by the soldiers—tries to win over his men on a personal level in an attempt to overcome the stereotype that he is a "pussy-footer" suited only to "fight in a truck, not on his feet."
19 Bruce Elder, *Image and Identity: Reflections on Canadian Film and Culture* (Waterloo: Wilfrid Laurier University Press, 1989), 89.
20 Waugh, *The Romance of Transgression*, 28–47.
21 For a brief illustration of this lineage, see Peter Harcourt, "The Innocent Eye," in *Canadian Film Reader*, ed. Seth Feldman and Joyce Nelson (Toronto: Peter Martin Associates, 1977), 86–94.

II: EMOTIONAL GEOGRAPHIES OF ANXIETY, EROS, AND IMPAIRMENT

CHAPTER 4

Making Art Like a Man!

DAVID GARNEAU

Making It Like a Man! is the exhibition I curated for the MacKenzie Art Gallery (Regina, Saskatchewan) to accompany the conference and film series of the same name that took place in Regina in the summer of 2004. This chapter of *Making It Like a Man: Canadian Masculinities in Practice*, titled "Making Art Like a Man," represents a condensed revision of the exhibition essay and my curatorial impressions or readings, not to mention experiences, of the kinds of insights on masculinity and gender embodied in these varied works.[1] These paintings, sculptures, photographs, and prints by a dozen Canadian male artists were selected from eighty submissions and forty studio visits in six provinces. No exhibition of contemporary Canadian masculinities can be exhaustive, only provocative. My intent was to survey the scene as deeply as time and budget allowed and present a critical sampling. The more than eighty works ranged from self-conscious interrogations of masculinity to more performative expressions of what it means to "make it like a man" in Canadian men's contemporary art practices.

To *be a man* in the (hetero-normative) culture of everyday life is to conform to social expectations assigned to male bodies. These requirements vary across cultures and over time, but there are some consistent characteristics. Traditional gender differentiation is founded on the concept that men should not behave like women. If this premise is accepted, then all sorts of ideas and behaviours seem to follow "naturally." If women act one way, then men must act contrarily. If women are passive, then men must be aggressive. Men who are not aggressive must then be "like" women. Perhaps they are gay. Well, if not gay, they certainly are not-quite-men. And so the "logic" goes. This division of qualities makes some practical sense. Binary thinking simplifies the management of social relations. However, maintaining a uniform hetero-masculinity can cause personal discomfort if not outright anxiety, because, as most men know from experience, being oneself and being a man are not identical. Tensions arise, for example, when a male is required to *act like a man* or *take it like a man* when those behaviours contradict their personal feelings, preferences, ethics, basic logic, or instinct for self-preservation.

Gender division, as the foundation of patriarchy, favours "masculine" traits. And "naturally," those with preferred qualities should rule and receive more goods.[2] Boys in the patriarchal tradition are raised to have an (unearned) sense of superiority over girls, and even women. However, attitudes are slowly changing in the everyday life of Canadian society. Faced with evidence of the inaccuracy of this patriarchal doctrine, many boys and men are re-evaluating gender construction. I found repeated evidence of this shift in my curatorial research: I did not find any artists producing images of iconic or celebratory masculinity; interestingly, all the works were characterized by ironic, deconstructive, wounded, reflective, perplexed, or otherwise troubled attitudes toward "being a man," and this anxious state of the Canadian masculine "nation" is reflected in my readings, and my experience, of them.

FRANCIS B. SIM GALLERY[3]

Walter May

Walter May's *Knockout* is a row of 105 hammers hung by their claws on a 2-x-4 beam set high on the wall. The worn steel heads face forward; the handles hang in various lengths. Flames have blackened the wooden handles. Some are scorched; others are deeply charred, twisted, and broken. The phallic queue evokes the experience of being measured and compared. These metaphoric tools appear exposed, humiliated, they have endured trial by fire. They remind me of men in a lineup: worn out soldiers, prisoners, athletes? Are they waiting to be chosen, for a firing squad, for employment? The title suggests a violent contest in which, one by one, combatants are eliminated.

May's sculpture is the progeny of Duchampian readymades, *Arte Provera*, and other art practices that resuscitate abject things. Is this a masculine quality? I don't know. But I do know a lot of men who compulsively rescue and fix derelict things. My grandfathers were legendary for their home workshops, which were stuffed with recovering appliances and with parts becoming useful wholes. This activity has grown to hyperbolic proportions for my recently retired uncle. It seems that these men have a need to rescue and also to be useful in a specific way: to have meaning with others through things.

There is an expression of longing in *Knockout* for an authentic relationship to tools and craft. Many Western, urban men are estranged from manual labour yet still see their masculinity dovetailed with making and repairing. They often keep well-stocked home workshops. Even if little actual work goes on in there, it is a token of masculinity.

Figure 12 *Knockout* (105 scorched hammers). Walter May, 2002.

Figure 13 *Knockout* (105 scorched hammers), detail. Walter May, 2002.

There are mere tools and then there are tools with personalities and history. A wooden handle yields to a habitual grip and is patinated by its owner's sweat. In *Being and Time*, Martin Heidegger explains that we realize the full nature of a hammer only when it breaks.[4] When they work, tools are invisible. They conform to their function as part of an (almost) unconscious action. A broken tool is not its self, and its new nature is not easy to determine. We have to examine the thing, turn it over in our hands. We rehearse the tool in its old ways to determine not only the nature of the damage but also the nature of the tool itself. This rehearsal requires us to "get our hands dirty," to interrupt work and relate to the object both intellectually and sensually as it is and how it ought to be.

On the one hand, *Knockout* reminds us of the fragility of flesh. Even the most virile body eventually falls apart. We all return to carbon. The sculpture evokes distressed bodies damaged by external forces—hammered, knocked out. These broken bodies bear witness and demand address. On the other hand, *Knockout* also critiques the construction of men as tools, which are objects defined by their use. For me, May, the most senior artist of the group, seems to be expressing anxiety about post-employment identity. If a man identifies himself with his work, who is he when he is unemployed or retires?

Dean Drever

I am both fascinated and repelled by Dean Drever's *Instructional Bat Series #2*. He seduces us with shiny luxury goods and then smacks us with the fine print. The stainless steel bats are engraved with "witty" cracks. Some are movie tough-guy lines: "Gather up what is left of your teeth and leave." A few hint at homoerotic panic: "We cannot continue to meet under these circumstances"; "If you can understand this you are too goddamn close." But my skin crawls when I read lines that could come from a real, domestic abuser: "The only thing you have ever been able to understand"; "The only way it makes sense to you"; "You've never been very good at listening"; "You have not left me any other choices."

There is a sinister creative intelligence behind the design of a *stainless* steel baseball bat meant for beating people. A weapon designed for criminal acts that is *stain*less yet retains fingerprints is the very embodiment of an ambivalent object and perhaps reflects an ambivalent ethical position.

The *Instructional Bats* imply a perverted imaginary that everywhere seeks malignant possibilities, either for defence or offence. These cynical objects embody a basic distrust of the world and oneself. They present civilization as a thin veneer over our true, aggressive natures. Perhaps Drever views this perspective of violence as neither optimistic nor pessimistic, but realistic.

There is something cathartic and instructive about exposing private language: dark comedy can voice unspeakable experience. But Drever is not a reformer; he is an instructor who shares street knowledge like Chuck D., Kanye West, or Rex Smallboy. His ambivalence toward violence is chillier than his chrome-plated knuckle-dusters. When he says, in his artist statement, that society is hypocritical when it deems state-sanctioned cruelty acceptable while condemning similar tactics used by street gangs, I have the feeling that he is not arguing for less violence, just less hypocrisy.

For those not living with the imminent threat of violence, the *Instructional Bats* may offer a vicarious thrill. Like gangsta rap, they present a polished taste of the thug's life without the broken bones, and the psychological scars caused by betrayal and the grinding stress of anticipation. But, also like gangsta rap, the bats offer young men in violent (under)worlds a practical guide to their codes and dangers. Drever plays Virgil; he is here to describe hell, not reform it.

Figure 14 *The only way it makes sense to you, Instructional Bat Series* #2. Engraved stainless steel. Dean Drever, 2003.

Mark Dudiak

Mark Dudiak's photograph, *Dudiak CAN (After the Alkaholiks)*, is a tableau of the artist and his friends drinking and breaking beer bottles over their heads in imitation of the cover of The Alkaholiks' 1997 album *Likwidation*. The artist explains:

> Growing up in Saskatoon during the 90s, my friends and I followed the trend of young white men who chose to express teenage angst through product association, particularly with the image of black, urban rap musicians. We of course were not marginalized in any true sense of the word, but we found a message, which seemed to condone our general lack of ambition, and adolescent pre-occupation with fighting, partying, and minor, generally destructive crime. I can remember sitting in cold parking lots during the winter, on coffee breaks from some minimum wage job, smoking a joint and listening to groups such as the *Alkaholiks*, and honestly believing that what they said was true and that it was a representation of my life and possible future. There was seldom much reflection upon the odd scenario of a bunch of white, middle class, prairie kids believing that we were in the same position as poor, legitimately angry black men from Los Angeles.
>
> This pre-packaged cultural set of aspirations, produced far away in a very different cultural environment came to form an aspect of my young identity, and is still present today. I think that the self-reflection encouraged by contemporary art has helped me to recognize that I may not be as completely of my own making as I might like to believe. Feminism is one of the routes that I turn to better understand my identity. This might seem like a paradox or a play to appear as a "sensitive" (read more desirable) man, but I'm specifically drawing on the critical feminism, which emerged in the mid seventies. Far from man bashing, I think that this form of academic inquiry and social action was more concerned with examining social relations, not only between men and women but subjective internal relations. Its concern with discovering why certain beliefs might be held, determining whether social behaviour was inborn or learned, and if negative, divisionist beliefs could be changed, has contributed a great deal to our understanding of self.[5]

Craig Le Blanc

Men watch broadcast sports, in part, for allegories of masculinity. These impressive images derive their power by pairing noble traits with baser drives

Figure 15 *I Don't Play* (mixed media). Craig Le Blanc, 2001.

within archetypal narratives in a compressed time and compact, theatrical space. The stories simplify life into binary contests, win/lose matches constructed to build and release tension in a regulated format. Add the mass, men-with-men ritual, and you have a very successful form of masculine modelling. Sports are the democratic men's lodge of the media age. Sports narratives compose masculinity as heroic, vital, competitive, and aggressive. The dominant themes are the tensions between comradeship and individuality, violence and pain, victory and loss, the love of the game and money. The great taboos of these homosocial narratives are homosexuality and women. Few media spectacles reinforce the dominant capitalistic, homophobic, and sexist agenda as effectively as do sports media. For a man to choose not to participate in this circuit is to jeopardize his status as a *real* man.

Craig Le Blanc's installation, *I Don't Play,* is a display of sports equipment—hockey pucks, ball caps, sweatbands, golf towels, and badges. Each is impressed with the slogan *I Don't Play*, rendering the items ironic and impotent. If you use the puck, for example, then you *do* play—but then it is no longer an *objet d'art*. If you don't play with it, it may be a work of art, but it is disabled as sports equipment. It is a wounded proposition. Le Blanc's game reifies sport as a ubiquitous presence and inscribes alternatives as absence. That is, in his display, *playing* is a positive attribute signified by the presence of sports objects. *Not-playing* is signalled by the text, but no alternatives are named. The work places sports at the centre of attention even

Figure 16 *I Don't Play* (mixed media), detail. Craig Le Blanc, 2001.

while rejecting it; ironically, this reinforces the idea that sport is what counts. If being a man means playing, or at least watching, *I Don't Play* does not hint of what a guy *does* do if not sports, or what he may be if he refuses this way of being a man.[6]

Art that endeavours to critique a dominant discourse can, paradoxically, end up supporting it. If the gesture is strictly formed as an alternative, the connection to what is being rejected might not be made. But if the mode rejected is stated — and especially if it is imitated, as it is here — then the artwork is caught within the dominant mode's signifying field. In other words, someone who wears the *I Don't Play* clothing line is a *player* in the sports commodity circuit. Even if the message is a rejection of that discourse, it *calls up* that mode and affirms its power (only the powerful are worthy of such satire).

My temptation is to read Le Blanc's work as a rejection of sports as a positive masculine mode. But, in fact, there is a more melancholic tone. He is not rejecting sports; after all, he *did* play:

> Hockey, baseball, wrestling, and volleyball. I was a goalie, a pitcher/back catcher and a setter in volleyball. All the positions that are somewhat solo. I guess I liked the clutch positions, either being the hero or the goat. I am somewhat of a non-team player now, working solo and barely liking assistance. I quit at 18–19 because I had to get a job, and it would never have been a profession. Baseball was my best chance, and I blew my arm.

Figure 17 *Slump* (altered baseball bat). Craig Le Blanc, 2004.

Perhaps *I Don't Play* is more of a statement of resignation: "I don't play; but I used to."

Please Use Me is a hockey stick with those words carved into the blade. Le Blanc reads his work as symbolic of "the commodification of the athlete; the use of the athlete as an object and tool for big business. The objects of sport become irrelevant, even though they are objectifying sport." It's another tool made impotent. If you were to make a single slap shot, the thing would be ruined. The words resemble the thoughts every boy has while waiting to be chosen for a team. It is also a sense many men have of themselves—as tools defined by their utility.[7] This idea is summed up in the unforgettable *Slump*, a Dali-esque wooden bat mounted perpendicular to the wall, but instead of jutting out it suddenly droops downward. *Slump* emphasizes the relations between masculinity, sexuality, and power/impotence.

NORTHERN CANADIAN OILS GALLERY

Andrew Szatmari

An unnamed young white male poses for Andrew Szatmari, and us. He has short hair and, except for lean sideburns, is clean-shaven. A thin metal chain rings his neck. Below his bare chest the thick band of his Joe Boxer underwear peeks out over low-riders. The instant camera's crude flash creates a hotspot that recedes toward the edges of the picture. The man was in the dark is briefly illuminated and then returns to the night.

He displays his body to attract sexual attention, but the gender codes are blended. His lean yet muscular build is obviously male, but his lack of body hair, coyly tilted head, and slightly puckered mouth suggest stereotypes of 'femininity.' He looks at the camera/photographer/viewer with a slightly averted face, as if to invite assessment. Some of Szatmari's other portraits in *Street Hustlers* are more confrontational. All send out subtle codes that intimate preferences, specialties, receptivity, and limits.

There is an implied violence and a certain risk in these photographs and their acquisition. Men wandering the streets at night—the wrong look could lead to an attack. There is a tension in the poses between availability and readiness for defence or assault. Szatmari says that he uses an instant, disposable camera in part "for protection against expensive equipment being stolen, my being mugged, harmed."

Szatmari sees his work as a participatory performance, a fair exchange. He approaches his subjects, explains his project, and gives them "just enough money for them to say yes." Photographers pay models all the time. But when a man pays a hustler, it signals more than an aesthetic relationship. Szatmari is not a disinterested observer and does not see his art as a just a recording of one person by another: "I don't consider the work documentary. I don't believe that documentary exists within the context of art-photography." He says that he is "fascinated by hustlers," how they "view our interaction and my activity, how they interpret what I'm doing." This exchange is captured and passed to the viewer, who becomes wound up in this relationship.

Staring at young male bodies might feel exploitative. It may make you wonder: Isn't this young guy familiar with being lied to by older men with cameras? What is the artist's real interest? Is this voyeurism, a hunting licence granted by the title *artist*? The photographs give the straight male viewer a taste of what it is like to look at another man with sexual interest, and to be seen sexually by a man. In this sense, these are not only pictures of *Street Hustlers*, but also, perhaps, aspects of ourselves.

Derek Dunlop

From the centre of the small, untitled, black-and-white digital print, an eight-year-old boy grins. He looks up into a camera, which, judging from the angle, is held by an adult. Superimposed on the boy's white shirt is a text from a mid-twentieth-century primary school textbook. The lines include:

> Are you a boy or a girl?
> Is "Mary" a girl's name or a boy's name?
> Was your brother a girl when he was little?
> Was your mother a boy when she was little?
> Was your father's mother a girl or a boy?

These queries would have been innocuous to most people a few generations ago. On one level, the test was not about gender but was designed to test logic and comprehension. The correct answers were supposed to be unambiguous. But today this interrogation looks like an almost comically obvious effort to reinforce the traditional nuclear family and heterosexual norms. At a time when it is conceivable that your mother *could* have once been a boy, the answers to these questions are less stable than they once were. Dunlop's artist's statement reads:

> The photograph was taken at my grandparent's house at some family gathering. With one arm behind my back I am hiding something, while at the same time I am pushing one hip forward. In this unstable gesture, I stare directly into the camera and smile unselfconsciously. It is the type of candid posturing that the camera would *never* catch me in today. It was taken before a gendered physicality had been socialized into my body; it is the easy smile before my discovery of shame and guilt.

Young Derek looks genuinely happy and at ease. He has composed himself into an expected representation, but one that does not seem to conflict with his self-image—a happy boy! However, seen twenty years later, and with the addition of the questions and the artist's statement, we might find a subtle twist in this re-presentation. The boy's *contrapposto* pose and hidden right arm hint of a coyness. By concealing some *thing* behind his back, the young Derek demonstrates self-consciousness; he knows that the *thing*, whatever it is, is not appropriate to this picturing. Even at that age, he performs an awareness that some things should be concealed, repressed, hidden from the family's gaze and from the historical record (a family album). What *it* was is probably not important. Now, as a family snapshot remade into a work of art, the hidden thing is a metaphor, a preterition that stands for "a gendered physicality... socialized into my body" and "my discovery of shame and guilt."

Not accidentally, there are two boys in the background. The younger one plays on the floor. The older boy is looking into a full-length mirror on

Figure 18 *Untitled* (digital print). Derek Dunlop, n.d.

the hall wall. These figures may refer to a moment of transition that the young Derek is passing through, from pre-gender formation (unselfconscious play) to a more self-conscious inscription (reading self-image in the mirror). Interestingly, the secret hidden from the camera and us is available to them.

Afshin Matlabi

When I first glanced at Afshin Matlabi's self-portrait, *On Technologies of Man's Sensuality*, which also serves as the cover image of *Making It Like a Man*, I saw a grim-faced naked man reclining against a Persian rug that lies on the floor and runs up a wall. Strangely, a machine gun is strategically angled across his body. *That* photograph is a disturbing blend of macho sexuality and sinister gun culture. However, a second look reveals that the object is not a machine gun but a vacuum cleaner! Racist associations are deeply ingrained. I assumed that this artwork had to be, first, about race. I could not see it as, first, a play on gender.

On Technologies of Man's Sensuality is a hilarious send-up of Western art history and gender expectations. Matlabi mixes a nineteenth-century orientalist fantasy with a *Playgirl* centrefold circa 1975. Unlike Ingres's languorous, pale, and shaved harem girls, Matlabi is alert, uncomfortable, dark, and male. His gaze is penetrative rather than receptive. It is an "are you talkin' to me" look that challenges the viewer. Even though he is in a 'feminized' position, he manages to cloak himself in "masculine" authority. It is the physical attitude of a man making a boudoir photograph, but one worried about it falling into the wrong hands (i.e., being seen by another man). Matlabi, for several years a househusband, explains:

> As I was vacuuming, I could feel the absurdity of the act. Sophisticated technologies created this machine to enable the other sex to clean the house. It is a strange reciprocation. I discovered the love affair, the obsession, between making and improving this machine and objectifying its use. Maybe that is how men express their sensuality. What needs saying, expressing, translates into a design, a power to suck, or ability to clean efficiently. Man's expression of sensuality is technology and the vacuum cleaner is his common thread of understanding with the domestic world.

PEGGY WAKELING GALLERY

Jeff Nachtigall

Jeff Nachtigall's sprawling, six-panel *Schwarzenegger Shrine* is a cacophonous reminiscence of his youthful worship of that paragon of late-twentieth-century celluloid masculinity. While there is some irony in the assemblage, it is primarily an *homage* to the iconic power of the can-do muscleman and his impact on the artist and his peers. Each panel is named after a Schwarzenegger movie—*Pumping Iron* (George Butler and Robert Fiore, 1977), *Conan the Barbarian* (John Milius, 1982), *Commando* (Mark Lester, 1985), *The Terminator* (James Cameron, 1984), *Predator* (John McTiernan, 1987), and *Running Man* (Paul Michael Glaser, 1987)—spanning Nachtigall's youth.

Nachtigall paints on an old sign, a dismantled kitchen cupboard, cardboard and wood scraps, chipboard and metal siding. There are stained sections; areas with dripped and slathered house paint; layers of handwritten text in acrylic; fine, painterly passages; scratches and violent gouges. From the tangle of lines and marks, accident and incident, cryptic word fragments emerge: "no more, no less"; "true story"; "looking for the silver lining"; "somewhere somehow, someone's going to pay"; "all white people look alike"; "sucked like me"; "no good"; "sucker"... Some are movie tag lines. Others are insults or internalized rebukes. Figures also emerge. Self-made men untangle themselves from the marks and emerge into form. They are funny: hieroglyphic profiles with phallic noses; overblown and misshapen bodies. Veins, or nerves, pulse across their flesh as child's approximations rather than as illustrations of anatomic fact. It is a rogue's gallery of buffoon he-men trying to retain their dignity.

Figure 19 *Schwarzenegger Shrine*, detail (six mixed-media paintings). Jeff Nachtigall, 2004.

Nachtigall may be using derelict materials to suggest that the masculine styles he is portraying are outmoded. But it is more likely that his project is resuscitative—that it is "looking for the silver lining" in these macho types. He still seems to admire Arnold, but he is more aware of the consequences for young men who emulate him. Arnold once seemed above the fray, a mortal who earned his pumped meat the old-fashioned way. Recent admissions that he, too, used steroids might be a discouragement to wannabes, or a prescription. Nachtigall seems to be sending an "approach with caution" message.

Arnold and Nachtigall appear together in *Pumping Iron*. A muscleman poses on an Olympic platform. At the bottom right, a boy pokes his head into the composition. He looks wide-eyed at the engorged body. Nachtigall writes:

In Grade 11 [*Pumping Iron*] changed my life. After seeing it, I ran to the gym to work out. Muscles meant money, fame, power and girls. My friends and I would wake up at 5 am and work out for three hours before school and return to the gym after school for another two hours. We were obsessed with body image. We were taking all sorts of supplements: amino acids, weight gain powder, carbohydrates, and lactic acid inhibitors. Many of my friends were taking steroids like candy. Some were even taking human growth hormone! This obsession for the perfect body was a frightening experience. Stupid kids doing stupid things at an age when they believe they are immortal.

We only see the boy's head. It is as if he only signifies when he views. Perhaps this man-in-formation is not worthy of a fuller representation until he imitates the body on display.

Jefferson Little

Jefferson Little's *Evo-Blaster 2000* is a giant pull-toy. Mounted on a cart with heavy-duty wheels is a wood, plastic, and metal structure that features the lower part of a *Tyrannosaurus rex*, two targets, and a huge ray gun with a row of four soldiers that bob up and down when the toy is pulled. Little's sculptures and paintings are fun. They are not critical essays; rather, they are appealing but disturbing confections. His toys seem to be the expressions of an extended adolescence.

Few contemporary Canadian men have had a signal experience that marked them as men. Traditional cultures mark the transition from boyhood to manhood through elaborate ceremonies. A result of this lack in contemporary Western cultures is that the boy-to-man transition can be protracted over many years; in some cases, old boys may never feel that they have been accepted into the company of men. Many young men do not know how and when to put away the toys of childhood and assume the tools of adulthood—masculinity becomes a perpetual and unresolved contest.

The sources for Little's works are hypertrophic comic book superheroes and weapons—popular masculinity, but an older version. The references are to childhoods from ten to sixty years ago. The artist even distresses *Evo-Blaster 2000* with dulling stains to make it appear antique. He seems to want to construct a generalized and nostalgic male childhood. In my research, I have come across many male artists who use archaic sources of broadcast masculinity—sometimes from their own childhood, but often from their fathers' or grandfathers' youths. It is as if they are conducting an archeological dig to find the legitimate roots of maleness, or the source of where things went wrong.

Figure 20 *Evo-Blaster 2000* (mixed-media sculpture). Jefferson Little, 2002.

A common theme in Little's work is aggression. The artist acts like the evil Sid in *Toy Story* (John Lasseter, 1995). Both break and reassemble toys into cannibalistic hybrids that are more disturbing than funny. Sid's play is not only a symptom of his personal rage but also an elaboration of the script written into boys' playthings. The reassembled toys are just hyperbolic expressions of that latent message.

However, Little may not be critiquing stereotyped masculinity but trying to inhabit and understand it symbolically. If some play is a means to apprehend social roles, then these constructions may be an effort to gain control over masculinity or just express what it feels like. The targets on *Evo-Blaster 2000*, and the darts pinning a figure in one of the paintings, are interesting because while most toys and video games position the player as a shooter, many boys' nightmares and lived experiences are of being a target.

The *Evo-Blaster 2000* is artificially aged to suggest that the viewer is in the future looking at an antique. Written across the target is: "It's Apoc-o-licious!" Little may be offering this toy as a humorous artifact of the turn of the millennium that will be as absurd to the future as Cold War duck-and-cover films are to us. However, the reference to the biblical end-of-days tied to the extinct dinosaur, the soldiers and ray gun, may be hinting that our continued socialization of boys into a culture of violence may end in extinction.

Figure 21 *Bass Acwards* (oil on relief sculpture, with taxidermy and found objects). Kevin Friedrich, 2001.

Kevin Freidrich

A naked angel gazes out over her right shoulder from the polychrome relief sculpture, *Bass Acwards*. She tugs on a red ribbon attached to a poorly taxidermied pike that hangs from a branch at the centre of the composition. A taut line runs from the fish to a hook held gingerly by a tanned man who reclines on the right. He wears a John Deere hat and sunglasses. A cigarette juts from his lips. The setting is bucolic, in the Prairie Gothic mode. The mid-ground is bright with straw and chickens. The background is dark — perhaps a storm is rolling in. The wings, ribbon, fish, line, hooks, sunglasses, and cigarette are all real objects.

Kevin Friedrich explains: "*Bass Acwards* is an allegory of 'fishing' and the ying/yang between men and women, romantic and tactile. Both characters are attempting to help the fish; one pulling the stitches shut, the other wanting to release the fish, ironically opening the wound. Neither is making anything any better but both are content with their endeavours. PS: I was quite bitter about relationships at the time."

In this allegory of romantic love, the fish represents the relationship as an objectified thing *between* lovers rather than as a relation. Instead of the conventional lovers trysting in the woods, this couple is incompatible and distant: she looks at us, while sunglasses shield his gaze. The root of this strained relationship may be in the way genders are figured. The woman is an unconvincing angel; she looks like an ordinary mortal with homemade wings. Perhaps the man has tried to elevate her to celestial status only to be disappointed by her humanness. He holds the hook but the fish has the line, reversing the usual scenario; it's *Bass Acwards*! Perhaps he is anxious about being *hooked* by a relationship; he wants to keep *fishing*. I really can't help but see phalluses everywhere in this show. Is the pike a wounded phallus / masculinity that the man wants to repair but the woman just wants to let go?

As Freidrich explains, the lovers are "content with their endeavours," with their own way of doing things, but they aren't doing the fish/relationship any good. While they both want to save the fish/relationship, they can't get together on the best method. The differences in how they perform their compassion seem stereotypically gendered. He takes heroic, medical measures; she tries to relieve the immediate pain. While some may wonder why they cannot just get together and work this thing out, the artist seems more interested in inscribing a chasm between men and women as a "just so" story. When women are constructed as angels and men as Huck Finns, how can you be anything but fatalistic about their being able to form a mature relationship?

Daniel Fisher

Daniel Fisher's *Wounded War Pony* is a dilapidated boys' bicycle salvaged by the artist and transformed into a mechanical horse. It is more showpiece than functioning vehicle: the bike is missing a pedal, chain, front tire, and rear wheel. It has, nevertheless, been outfitted with a horsehair tail and mane, and decorated with feathers, brightly coloured beads, and leather tassels. The saddle is wrapped in rabbit fur. Screwed into the red frame are new metal parts that suggest a head, back, flanks, and thighs. Striped paint on the nose and thighs, and other markings, indicate that the steed is prepared for battle.

On the one hand, *Wounded War Pony* draws a continuity between urban First Nations boys on two-wheelers and their ancestors on horses. The bike becomes a stallion, the boy a warrior. It is a sculpture about cultural survival. This vehicle has been adopted and adapted by Fisher just as his ancestors adopted and adapted the horse from the first colonizers. On the other hand, the resuscitation is melancholic. Despite his creative efforts, the transformation is incomplete. The horse/bike is missing vital parts, and an arrow pierces its side.

Fisher reminds us that Aboriginal youth have both a proud and a tragic history. This legacy is written on their bodies and continues to influence their actions and sense of self. *Wounded War Pony* teeters between optimism and pessimism. The sculpture could be read as a first step on a healing journey: the body is salvaged, the repairs begun, but there is still much to do. However, these initial treatments seem cosmetic. Time and money have been spent on decorating rather than on taking care of basic repairs. The result is a wounded body/soul decked in regalia.

This object embodies an ongoing crisis. How do contemporary Aboriginal boys and men compose themselves? Do they try to revive something of

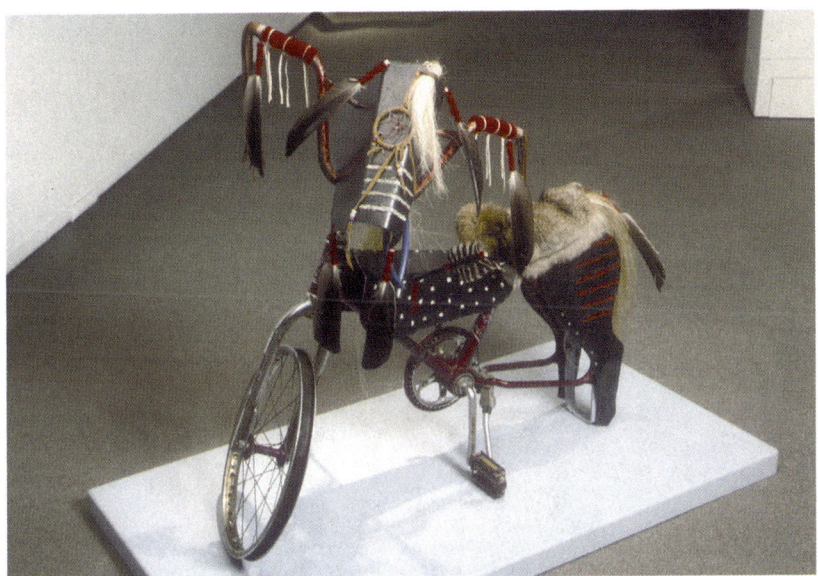

Figure 22 *Wounded War Pony* (bicycle, hide, feathers, metal). Daniel Fisher, 2002.

what has been actively discouraged, banned, and beaten out of so many generations? Do they adapt, even assimilate into the dominant culture? It isn't really an either/or debate, but there is a struggle on both personal and social levels between maintaining traditional ways and swimming in the mainstream. Many devise ingenious ways to perform, adapt, and balance both. Others remain wounded and unsure which way to turn.

Blair Brennan

The Making It Like a Man! exhibition had its origins in *Men in Relation*, an exhibition curated by Robert Milthorp and Monte Greenshields for two Saskatoon artist-run centres (A.K.A. and the Photographer's Gallery) in 1993. I had a peripheral involvement with that event as a writer.[8] Blair Brennan was in that exhibition and it is fitting that he is in this one too. His present contribution is an installation of things collected and gently altered. Those things include a belt, shirt, and leather jacket, a large Boy Scout cap, three army cots, a ring toss game, steer horns, two propane tanks, and three branding irons: all that leather, old canvas, and metal—definitely masculine territory. The embroidered shirt, the hat, and the cots—which might hint of feminine labour—are actually done by machine. The branding iron, with its mark, is Brennan's obsession. It has a flexible power. I see it as a profound symbol for the mark-of-the-father. The long, firm, hot rod with the ability to imprint itself numerous times is a fine phallic and male fertility symbol. It is also, he

Figure 23 *Shirts and Skins*, front view (painted and branded leather jacket and embroidered cotton shirt). Blair Brennan, 2004.

explains, a painful marker of territory and property. It is a sign of masculine patrimony, an inheritance that is a privilege as well as a burden, making much of Brennan's work a sign of pain and the possibility of redemption.

"Shirts and Skins": the title alone sends shivers of humiliation up my spine. The words drag me back to junior and senior high school gym class. For some perverse reason, boys were divided into teams who wore *shirts* and those who were shirtless. "It always takes women longer to get the *shirts and skins* reference. I was one of those unfit, overweight boys (now an unfit, overweight man) praying to be a *shirt*." "Shirts and Skins" is a white T-shirt embroidered with the word "shirt." Draped over top is a leather jacket branded "skins."

Words can sear youthful flesh with indelible meanings like a brand. Or, more hopefully, some words burn less deeply and can (like our clothes) be outgrown. They may still be in the closet as a reminder, but they don't have

Figure 24 *Shirts and Skins*, back view (painted and branded leather jacket and embroidered cotton shirt). Blair Brennan, 2004.

the same power. "Shirts and Skins"' branded leather jacket may be a proxy for human flesh. Does it suggest that men have to develop a thick skin to endure the taunts designed to *make men* of us?

Supplemental to the exhibition, I created a space for comments. On a large, low table in a separate room were a suitcase, paper, envelopes, and pens. Participants were invited to write "Impossible Letters," notes to men who had made positive or negative impacts on their lives. The envelopes were not sealed, so anyone could read them and respond. Most were filled with messages of love, some of anger; many more expressed regret for missed opportunities to express themselves to men in their lives. The second supplement was a tool shed that was placed just outside the exhibition space. It was outfitted with a video camera and monitor. Participants were asked to talk about men in their lives. The often poignant results were edited and played back during the exhibition.

CONCLUSION

It is, of course, as I suggested above, not possible to construct an exhibition that exhausts the possibilities of current Canadian masculinities. There are more masculinities than there are men and boys. And why exclude women and girls from an expansive future project? The curation of contemporary art is not a profession but a subjective, creative, and intuitive practice informed by specific bodies and temperaments. There are, in this selection, clear traces of my identity positions as a heterosexual male, husband and father, Métis, prairie Canadian, artist...the list goes on. But, of course, the Making It Like a Man! exhibition is not a display of masculinities as such. These are works of art, and works of art are not propositional. They have no truths to impart. Their meanings are made by viewers who experience rather than read them. Perhaps they might be better understood as symptoms, as subjective accounts of how, in this case, masculinity feels. And, in conjunction with the viewer's experience, these suggestive objects can unfold to encompass a greater range of experience than can mere propositions.

Given the interestedness of curators and the non-propositional nature of art, little that curators or artists say about their work can be trusted. Nevertheless, patterns do emerge. Contemplating masculinity is anathema to the masculine condition. Such public inquiries threaten the phallic position. So it is interesting that such work is being made across Canada and that such an exhibition, and now an academic anthology, should emerge. As mentioned above, none of the artists whose studios I visited were building non-ironic or untroubled representations. All present being male as a question, as an anxious, uncertain, and contested state. The current national and international interest in studying masculinity may be symptomatic of a spreading condition—the uncertainty that such a category exists.

NOTES

1. The exhibition "Making It Like a Man!" ran from June 5 to August 22, 2004. Making It Like a Man! Masculinities in Canadian Arts and Cultures, the conference, ran 10 to 12 June at the University of Regina; the Film Series took place from 3 to 6 and from 10 to 12 June at the Regina Public Library Film Theatre. I would like to thank my curatorial assistant Sharon Pelletier; the funders (the Humanities Institute, the Office of the President, the Dean and Faculty of Fine Arts, and the Visual Arts Department, all at the University of Regina; the Canada Council for the Arts; the Saskatchewan Arts Board; the MacKenzie Art Gallery [Kate Davis, Timothy Long, and Patricia Deadman, and the many others who installed the show, created the educational programs, etc.]); and especially my conference co-organizers, Stephen McClatchie, Christine Ramsay, and Angela Stukator.
2. Dale Spender, *Man Made Language* (London: Routledge and Kegan Paul, 1980).
3. The artworks discussed in this essay are grouped according to the various named galleries within the MacKenzie Art Gallery in which they were installed: the

Francis B. Sim Gallery, the Northern Canadian Oils Gallery, and the Peggy Wakeling Gallery.
4 Martin Heidegger, *Being and Time* [1926], trans. John Macquarrie and Edward Robinson (New York: Harper and Row, 1962), 405–6.
5 All uncited quotations are from artist statements and interviews with the artists named in the section where the quotation appears.
6 This problem arises when any hegemonic discourse is challenged and is itself a challenge of feminism and masculinities studies. We cleverly deconstruct problematic masculinities but are shy about positing better ways of being men. Few are willing to point out positive role models who are not just *troubling* masculine stereotypes. Championing particular men as good examples is always liable to generate disappointment. But until academics step up to the plate (so to speak) with credible alternatives, we will be left in our metatextual armchairs, critics not coaches.
7 The positive and negative aspects of this concept are well documented in Susan Faludi's "Utility Men," in *Stiffed: The Betrayal of the American Man* (New York: Harper Perennial, 1999).
8 David Garneau, "Other Men," *BlackFlash* 4, no. 12 (Winter 1994): 21–22.

CHAPTER 5

"Above Mere Men": The Heterogeneous Male in Attila Richard Lukacs

PIET DEFRAEYE

> *I was very astonished at having unknowingly substituted an image devoid of any sexual implication with a wholly obscene vision.*
> —GEORGES BATAILLE, *L'HISTOIRE DE L'OEIL*

Vancouver-based painter Attila Richard Lukacs continues to draw critical focus on his original work and modern-day bohemian lifestyle. The recent documentary film *Drawing Out the Demons*[1] traces back two decades of the artist's challenging circular journey from Calgary, via Vancouver, to Berlin and New York, and back to Calgary and Vancouver. While it is tricky and unproductive to catalogue Lukacs's work as typically Canadian, his obsessive foregrounding of the able-bodied male may well be construed as the product of a Canadian Western-based imagination, which posits a straightforward and unrefined masculinity—the bunkhouse lumberjack—as a normative image or fantasy of what *a man* is all about. In this respect, it is worthwhile to note that the Spring 1990 issue of the cultural quarterly *The Massachusetts Review* sported the Lukacs painting *Requirements of Monumentality* (1987) on its cover for a volume that explored the untraditional Canadianness of different Canadas. The painting of a young hunk dressed in a gold-coloured kilt clearly implies a different kind of Canada than what is stereotypically projected as a *northern beyond*. Its irony lies in the fact that the icon-like painting was completed while Lukacs was living in Berlin's Kreuzberg district, then a teaming urban landscape of students, artists, squatters, and political activists, far removed from the middle-class suburbia of his native Calgary and from the nearby rugged Badlands with its oil rigs, woodlots, and redneck males. In their selection of this particular painting as the cover for a volume on alternative Canadianness, the editors clearly recognized Lukacs's central position in the framing of Canadian artistic practice in which, typically, the raw, muscular hunk is placed in a cultural context of decoration and urban exchange. Not the undomesticated of Canada's vast natural expanse—surely the more typical German perception of Lukacs' Canadian origins at the time, but rather the urban space of the teeming metropolis, becomes Lukacs's favourite background as a place of encounter for his almost exclusively masculine world.

Lukacs worked and lived in Berlin between 1986 and 1997, straddling the tail end of the divided city's Cold War period and a new era of Berlin's united and booming economy, which fizzled out toward the mid-1990s. The period also marked a radical departure in Canadian politics with the election of the first Reform candidate in 1989 for a newly launched rightist party; this eventually led to a new conservative revival with the amalgamation of two conservative parties a decade later and the subsequent electoral successes of the political right. The early 1990s, however, also marked a decisive turn in Lukacs's work. While a fascination with the male body continued to characterize and dominate his art, feeding into an establishment of the male mystique, that art also acquired a remarkable political resonance. Robin Major credits Lukacs's move to Berlin with heralding a "new level of social commentary,"[2] one not present in his earlier paintings, which are often described as savage sexual fantasies. Not all critics take this politicking seriously. Blake Gopnik, for one, suggests it is nothing more than "puerile rebellion," and "very tame."[3]

The Berlin paintings that drew the most criticism for their supposedly reactionary politics are bundled under the title E-Werk, a collection of six canvasses in which Berlin's inner cityscape functions as a dramatic setting for the hyperbolic performances that unfold before the viewer.[4] These canvasses have enormous dimensions; they could serve magnificently to embellish airports or some of the few urban neoclassical railway stations left in Canada. Their impact is intensified by their vibrant and often screaming colours. Their size and use of colour as well as their iconographic syntax remind us of some of the gigantic paintings of German artists Norbert Tadeusz or Neo Rauch.

In an earlier book chapter, I have written on the performance of masculinity that can be observed in these six paintings, with special emphasis on the nightmarish canvas *Glamour Crew*.[5] Lukacs's paintings are fascinating cultural objects whose implied politics pose tough problems for any critic or viewer who confronts them. They are often called "reactionary" or even "fascist"—a response that bears witness to a provocative imagery that flirts with Nazi and fascist propaganda. When we look at these paintings, we find ourselves in an uncomfortable position of both attraction and repulsion. The aggressive settings and menacing dispositions of his characters, frequently portrayed with swastikas and other politically charged symbols, contrast sharply with the youthful innocence of many of Lukacs's characters, implying a romantic yearning for some or other utopia. The impact and effect of these paintings on the viewer is one of transgression, contestation, and recognition. This is an aesthetic–ideological conundrum similar to the one presented by the heterologies of French philosopher-sociologist Georges Bataille (1897–1962). In this chapter I incorporate some of the concepts and notions of Bataille to shed light on the complexity of Lukacs's highly eroticized and politicized world as it is evoked in E-Werk, with a particular focus on the triptych *Wild Kingdom*.

THE HETEROGENEOUS, EXPENDITURE, AND DESIRE

Reading Georges Bataille can be a risky business, similar to viewing the paintings of Attila Richard Lukacs. Jonathan Dollimore cautions against the troublesome prevarications of Bataille's writing—"How far do we follow before turning back?"—and adds, for good measure, that "to read it and not turn back, is to have not read it properly."[6] Dollimore's warning is an apt caveat for any critical study of Lukacs's canvases. To closely read *Wild Kingdom* is in many ways to probe into an excessive visionary world, a discursive fisting during which we always wonder, "How far do we go?" and "When do we turn back?"

The point of departure, then, is Bataille's notion of the heterogeneous: a field of heterological socio-political dissent within a society that continually enforces a homogeneic structuring of the behaviour, actions, and ideas of its members. The heterogeneous is that which threatens the organization and balance of the homogeneous whole. Bataille's examples of heterogeneous forces include the prostitute, the fool, the workman of the lowest class, the outcast or untouchable; but he also invokes the leader, the soldier, and the master as moments or opportunities of heterogeneous endeavour or accomplishment. Lukacs's subjects in E-Werk fit remarkably into these paradigms. Strapping labourers, servile slaves or pseudo-slaves, and displaced youth mingle with nude smelter workers, overbearing superiors, and brawny thugs. The hierarchies within this performance are laid out and supported by means of costuming, props, and a strategic posturing and blocking on the canvas.

It is important to remember that there is no moral dilemma in Bataille's notion of a structured, commensurable, and normative homogeneity versus the nonconforming, transformative, and potentially subversive practice of heterogeneity. In fact, rarely does the issue of morality enter into the aspirations to break with or escape from or disrupt homogeneity. There is a striking parallel here with one's appraisal of Lukacs's E-Werk. Clearly, the effect of Lukacs's paintings is greatly impacted by a remarkable absence of morality as a discerning or hierarchical criterion in the extravagant narratives displayed on his canvas. Whatever ideology reigns in the world of these pictures, it is not infused with our familiar moral codes. Bataille reminds us (as does

Lacan later) that ideology always and necessarily depends on a gap or emptiness, which is then replaced by a space of projection the immediate impact of which is a structuring of desire and actions.[7] Lukacs's paintings—even those, like *Glamour Crew*, that are filled with a spectacle of visual excess, or spectacular *visions of excess*—are equally characterized by an emptiness, which is then occluded and filled with fantasy and/or utopian anticipation. These works are eerily reminiscent of Giovanni Piranesi's prison fantasies, *Carceri d'Innenzione*. Like Lukacs, this seventeenth-century artist had a knack for performative, dramatic architectural layouts, clearly aimed at drawing in an outside spectator. They are also reflections of a fantastic world that is governed by ruthless hierarchies and that reflects a yearning imagination in which physical desire seems a prime mover. *Wild Kingdom* goes a step further in this fantastic genesis. Just as the *Carceri d'Innenzione* may well be the reflection of a wandering but imprisoned mind, perversely enjoying its own ensnarement, Lukacs's triptych and its syncopated, performative narrative can be read as a metacommentary on his own performative and figurative painting practice.

Lukacs's central theme, clearly, is desire—more particularly, the social and historical constructions of that desire and the actions that surround it.[8] That this desire is located within a male–male framework is not only important but also unapologetically obvious. To declare, as just about every newspaper or art journal review does, that Lukacs's works are homoerotic or "represent masculinity"[9] may not be all that helpful in our search for meaning. After all, calling Peter Paul Rubens's *Venus and Adonis* a *hetero-erotic* painting is not particularly insightful. The inherent danger is that a signifier or label like homoerotic will dull the paintings' impact and make their affect more palatable, and therefore harmless. These paintings are far from harmless or innocuous. On the contrary, to watch and read them is to enter a hazardous exploration of desire, removed from any moralistic analysis. As Jonathan Dollimore points out in his study of sexual dissidence: "All desire bears its histories, the desires of the exploited and the repressed no less than the desires of those who exploit and repress."[10] Exploitation and repression not only govern desire but also reflect the very experience of it, and Lukacs's iconographies reflect these structures of exploitation and repression abundantly in their imaginative narratives.

In the footsteps of Freud, Georges Bataille wrote extensively on the erotics of desire, focusing on our attraction to the forbidden. His notion that we are inevitably and irresistibly attracted to the forbidden may also be a good explanation of the attention that Lukacs's paintings have drawn. More important, however, is that one of these forbidden realms has to do with aversion or sexual disgust. Critical work on the abject[11] has shown that attraction and disgust operate in areas that are extremely proximate. And because of the machinations of repression and exploitation, both the expression of desire and the expression of disgust are loaded with cultural significance. Bataille's erotic novel *Histoire de l'oeil* is an apt example, its different chapters functioning like Lukacs's triptychs and diptychs. Both artists force us to *see* into a fantastic and excessive world of flesh, desire, and expenditure. Bataille's narrative is graphic and tactile, while Lukacs's graphics are epic and discursive. As it happens, the motif of seeing or watching is the prime mover for both artists. While the stories that unfold suggest an extremely private and intimate nature, they are brought into a public realm, locking us into a voyeuristic gaze. These are stories of and for the eye.

As we zoom in on the lugubrious details, we discover recurring motifs and obsessions, and during our journey become aware of moments of repulsion and disgust. Bataille's fascination with orifice—and with eyes and eggs—matches Lukacs's crude anality and fixation on genitalia. In our response to both novel and canvas, disgust and attraction are remarkably close. Lukacs plays with their proximity on many levels. The monumental backgrounds of his paintings expose a historical framework that gives them status and, consequently, an alluring quality. Yet they have an awesome impact in their rigidity and geometric architecture. The skinheads portrayed on the canvas cause aversion and reproach, but at the same time they allow Lukacs to create, in Thomas Sokolowski's words, a concrete image of the abstract notion of "the beautiful and the noble" or the Homeric *kalos kagathos*.[12] We look at these powerful, suntanned, conquering athletes with envy and awe. The contiguity of this beauty and nobleness with the abject and coarse, which is prevalent in narratives of Lukacs as well as Bataille, brings about two competing but ultimately complementary emotions: euphoria and annihilation. This antithetical outcome reminds us of a basic tenet of Bataille's outlook on life, expressed in his essay "The Labyrinth."[13] In his view, life is not a harmonious structure into which one is plunged, like a fish into water, in order to completely realize oneself. On the contrary, the principal structure governing life is expenditure, a compulsive need that hovers between insufficiency and its ontological opposite, which is waste. At the basis of all life, life that comes and life that goes, lie insufficiency and waste: "life is an energy which is never conserved but perpetually squandered and wasted."[14] The global story, then, is "a tale of scarcity and oppression, not success" or, in the world of Adorno's negative dialectics, a narrative of "permanent catastrophe."[15]

Lukacs's paintings too are informed by insufficiency and waste. Apart from the quasi-exclusively male environments he creates, a clear example is the painter's omnipresent use of graffiti, an expression characterized by a thorough sense of lack and, at the same time, superfluity. The latter is stressed by means of a literal crossing out or covering up of these graffiti in his paintings. Their negation, of course, makes them paradoxically more present and engaging in their signification of lack and redundancy.

The need for expenditure that is at the core of this sense of lack and waste appears to be a crucial component of Lukacs's paintings. Most prominent is the implied sexual yearning of all this ravishing, primal flesh—a desire that, within the stillness of the paintings, seems mostly unfulfilled. However, Lukacs's unrelenting insistence on this sexual desire as a central focus in his paintings suggests a more fundamental urge to break with cultural limitation or restraint in favour of what Bataille calls the natural urge of expenditure. The libidinousness performed in E-Werk exhibits a predatory disposition, ready to pounce at any opportunity. Together with the implicit/explicit homosexual nature of this concupiscence, the emphatic foregrounding of its perverseness—and therefore its unproductiveness—constitutes a shattering of cultural prohibition. Lukacs's art is, after all, often called "scandalous," and the E-Werk cycle was certainly taboo-breaking, especially at the time of its first exhibition in the early 1990s. While some critics have labelled his provocative imagery proof of an "adolescent" imagination at work,[16] others have deconstructed him as a romantic soul with a melancholic yearning for lost innocence.[17] This romantic disposition is surely evident in the way Lukacs fetishizes manual labour;[18] it is also clearly present in the naive but parodic idyllicism of his contemporaneous Garden of Eden series.[19] However, the more complex paradoxes that prevail in E-Werk imply a fundamental—though fetishized—conflict between nature and culture, and it is in this conflict that the effect of disgust must be situated.

Disgust is a cultured response to certain elements, products, or cultural expressions that we are trained and conditioned to censor, particularly in certain circumstances, most often governed by social conventions. Disgust, therefore, necessarily flags a transgressive opportunity, be it one that usually is not embraced, or, on the contrary, one that is emphatically denied in the discourse that accompanies it. As such, expressions of disgust reiterate a cultural dynamic that, in Bataille's words, implies the disavowal of the abhorrence of nature. There is, however, a primal attraction to this uncensored and unregulated rawness: it allows us to revolt, at least in theory, against the cultural prohibitions we have constructed around us as a protective screen. Disgust, therefore, has an indexical function, because it reminds us of the constructions that we set up around us in order to create protection from the very things to which we are attracted as opportunities to shed our artificial cloak and to participate in dissoluting expenditure. While disgust responds to that "nauseous, rank and heaving matter, frightful to look upon, a ferment of life, teeming with worms, grubs and eggs," it also "keeps alive in some indirect fashion at least the consciousness that the terrifying faces of death, its stinking putrefaction, are to be identified with the sickening primary condition of life."[20]

The tableaux in E-Werk straddle a dyadic world: a homogeneous economy of organization and conservation is at loggerheads with the heterogeneous urge to expend, consume, and waste. While the former implies a movement of appropriation, the latter implies secretion. In a painting like *In My Father's*

House, these secretions are pointedly present on the canvas. A group of naked men surround another youth underneath the spouting stream of a barrel: water, semen, and urine are liquids that, in Bataille's vocabulary, are sacred excess or profane waste. Considering and experiencing these through the medium of another liquid—paint now congealed—allows us, the viewers, to participate in another transgressive experience, which is called *art*. For Bataille, art allows for an ideal opportunity to transcend the homogeneous and prohibitive pressures of productive social activity and to indulge in what he calls "holiday" or *unproductive* activity. The remarkable parallel here between regular homogeneous, economically driven activity and art is that the latter also yields objects—not always tangible, but most definitely so in the case of Lukacs's paintings. (The fact that they in turn acquire a face value, expressed in monetary terms, testifies to the ferociousness of the homogenous to reclaim every inch of territory that is temporarily yielded to *holiday*, back in the marketplace.) While sometimes these objects may serve practical functions, they exist mainly—and this is surely so in the case of Lukacs's E-Werk— for their own sake and in defiance of a myriad of homogenous pressures and prohibitions that shelter our quotidian world from all kinds of disturbances. Bataille, in the footsteps of Freud, isolates death and sexuality as the two principal disruptions that threaten the homogeneous. He describes this mechanism in his fascinating study of the prehistoric paintings of Lascaux, works that in terms of technique bear in many ways a striking resemblance to some of Lukacs's paintings.[21] Bataille's observation could well serve as a preamble to Lukacs: "the enduring animality in us forever introduces raw life and nature into the community: prohibitions exist to quell these uprisings and spread oil on the sea of insurgent animal passion and unruliness."[22] Lukacs's E-Werk is in clear defiance of this suppression of animality: the oil is flaming on the canvas.

It has become fashionable nowadays, especially in cultural studies of masculinity, to translate Bataille's "enduring animality" into notions of "desire" or "longing." As implied earlier, desire is certainly a pertinent term of operation in critical response to Lukacs. However, we must be careful, again, not to trivialize or expurgate the radical nature of these paintings with critical categories of the sort that seem to make them perfectly containable and hermeneutically negotiable. Analogical to the absence of morality, Bataille's heterological approach to desire posits it as neither positive nor negative. For Bataille, desire is not something that stems from an awareness of lack (as it does for philosophers like Lacan), nor is it purely an affirmative and constructive urge and opportunity for further self-realization (as in Gilles Deleuze's conception) or genetic promulgation (as in Darwinistic conceptions of desire). While for Bataille, there is a clear connection between desire and expenditure—desire also means an *au-delà* of expenditure and a movement toward or brushing with the sacred. Desire is one of the crucial ways in which we transcend the homogeneity to which we are condemned as social human beings, and, in consequence, experience the heterogeneous other. Desire, for Bataille, is not about lack, but about desire itself, which wants nothing less than "the emancipation of human lives."[23] Anthony O'Shea's comment on Bataille is particularly useful for our understanding of Lukacs's paintings: "We do not become more than human through desire. Desire reveals that we are humans because we are insufficient to contain desire."[24] Indeed, as O'Shea concludes on the same page: "All we can...do is experience desire and attempt to communicate the experience." Lukacs's *Wild Kingdom* is such an attempt at the exploration and communication of desire.

WILD KINGDOM

Wild Kingdom[25] is a triptych, whose three parts measure more than 12 metres in length and 4 metres in height. It is an imposing ensemble that one doesn't easily avoid. The tableaux depicted have a similar impact. The background is the obvious uniting force: Berlin's Brandenburg Gate is spread out over the three parts, seen from three different distances. The left portion shows two youth sitting in a public square playing a game of cards, undisturbed by a dramatic scene unfolding right behind them. Two older, naked men hold a blanket as a protective measure for another, well-built nude hovering above them, abducted in the claws of an oversized dark eagle. The centrepiece has no obvious correlation and seems itself a compilation of three or four different parts or narratives. Against the Lukacsian background of Berlin's monumental but scaffolded Brandenburger Tor, our eyes lock in on a preposterous posse of donkey-headed, uniformed men with enormous erect penises hanging from their pants. Apart from their heads, they come across as a group of mods, the better-healed predecessors of the skinhead movement. Two winged naked boys seem undisturbed in their preoccupation with each other and the translucent piece of pillar they hold on to. A Taurus-headed figure on the left overwhelms a scantily clad, shaggy woman, gagged, her breasts exposed, clasping a painter's palette. A group of unfinished male silhouettes carrying red flags cross this multiple stage. The right portion of the triptych would seem completely incongruous from the other two were it not for the repetition of the (now scaffolded) façade of the left portion. A blind wall stretches from one side to the other; against it is a broom on a paved sidewalk, edging up against a strip of graffiti with the bottom half cut off.

The opaque mythological and political references, the diachronic setting, and the narrative character of the composition give *Wild Kingdom* an overtly allegorical quality.[26] The viewer of the painting is looking for a legend to decode the specifics of this allegory, as in *une peinture à clef*, though at the same time we are very much aware of the parodic nature of most of the imagery. For Bataille, parody is a universal mode of operation: "It is clear

Figure 25 Attila Richard Lukacs, *Wild Kingdom*, 1992–93 (oil, enamel, and tar on canvas; 400.7 × 1259.8 cm). Collection of The Nickle Arts Museum, University of Calgary. Gift of Daryl K. Seaman, Donald R. Seaman, and Bernard Coady. Image courtesy of The Nickle Arts Museum.

that the world is purely parodic, in other words, that each thing seen is the parody of another," he writes in his famously titled essay "The Solar Anus." And it is with the aid of a *"copula"* that each sentence is parodically tied to one thing or another: "all things would be visibly connected if one could discover at a glance and in its totality the tracings of an Ariadne's thread leading thought into its own labyrinth."[27] As it happens, and uncharacteristically, Lukacs may have been less preoccupied with anuses, but all the more with copulation during the creative process of the triptych. Ariadne may well have been on his mind too, though she did not quite make it to the final canvas. Surely we are looking for the copulating thread that appositions an accumulation of hysterical figures in a fascinating stage *décor*. And a theatrical *décor* it is, for the emphasis is on the tableau's histrionics, as is often the case with Lukacs.[28] The *repoussoir* effect of the drawn curtain in the left part of the triptych and the prompter's box and orchestra pit in the central canvas create an obvious theatrical framing. The violoncello or double bass bow, which is visible in the centre, gives the composition not only an operatic setting but also a clear sense of inside versus outside. There is a strong resonance of Edgar Degas's painting *L'Orchestre de l'opéra* (1868),[29] with its similar *repoussoir* effect of the double-bass bow. Both Degas and Lukacs foreground the performativity of their subjects. However, in contrast to Degas, Lukacs clearly breaks the continuous perspective. Performance is a heterogenous activity because it allows a transference—a *différance*—that in quotidian, homogeneous life is normally not possible. Antonin Artaud reminds us that "theatre is a passionate overflowing, a frightful transfer of forces from body to body." While the theatre's obvious advantage in this unique transference is in the use of the bodily presence of both performers and audience, theatre is also a short-lived experience. The medium of painting lacks bodily presence but replaces this with a more overt and therefore more manipulable simulacrum. Moreover, it does not need to deal with the ephemeral moment, nor does it need to reckon its effect on a present audience, at least not immediately. *Wild Kingdom*, then, is a pictorial and two-dimensional theatre of cruelty, an aporetic opera in multiple acts.[30] The series' title E-Werk itself evokes the huge dimensions of opera, with its connotation of electrical or power plants.[31] The title also resonates with the musical term, *E-Musik (ernste Musik)*, which stands for serious music, versus *U-Musik* for *Unterhaltungsmusik* or musak.[32] While Lukacs himself is usually flippant about any critical underpinnings of his work, the startling imagery, compositions, and signs of these paintings invite us for a more inquisitive journey into the canvas and the spectator's position.

Lukacs's stage, like postmodern theatre, presents a fragmented world of dissonance and dissolution as well as a composite world of collage, in which any semblance of homogeneity with the world as we know it is under assault. The composition presents an incoherent trajectory into a world of dissolution. The restless universe of *Wild Kingdom* is essentially heterogeneous, and Bataille's definition seems strikingly applicable to its multiple scenes and their effects, rather like a theatre of cruelty: "*Heterogeneous* reality is that of a force or shock. It presents itself as a charge, as a value, passing from one object to another in a more or less abstract fashion, almost as if the change were taking place not in the world of objects but only in the judgments of the subject."[33]

What seems important in *Wild Kingdom* is the spectacle of its visual excess, and not the theme, message, or narrative it wants to convey. Any narrative, as productive argumentation, is sacrificed in favour of unproductive expenditure. In Bataille's words, this consists of everything rejected by *homogenous* society as waste or as superior transcendent value. Included are the waste products of the human body and certain analogous matter (trash, vermin, etc.); body parts; persons, words, or acts having a suggestive erotic value; the various unconscious processes such as dreams or neuroses; the numerous elements or social forms that *homogeneous* society is powerless to assimilate: mobs, the warrior, aristocratic and impoverished classes, different types of violent individuals or at least those who refuse the rule (madmen, leaders, poets, etc.).[34] The world of *Wild Kingdom* shows this expenditure amply in its visual excess. Its spectacle as a whole, in all its parataxis, fragmentation, and dislocation, is one of utter disarray, perhaps not in its geometric composition, but all the more so in its eclectic and appositional imagery. Here is a force at work "that disrupts the regular course of things, the peaceful but fastidious homogeneity powerless to maintain itself."[35]

WILD KINGDOM AS POLITICAL ALLEGORY

We are familiar with the forces and events that are alluded to in the painting. In 1989, a few years before the painting was finished in 1993, the Berlin Wall, which ran within metres of the Brandenburg gate—the painting's apparent *locus*—had come crashing down under the heterogeneous pressures of a restless East German populace and the huge economic homogeneous pressures of an equally eager Western business conglomerate. The resulting upheaval was one in which unbridled potential went hand-in-hand with disillusions, locally, nationally, and internationally. The procession of unfinished men walking across the scenic stage with red flags alludes to those thousands of workers whose steadfast livelihoods were endangered by the new market economy, after the *Wende*.

The dauntless overnight absorption on 3 October 1990 of a crumbling economy, with its 17 million state-employed workers, proved too enormous a project to pull off without pain. Even today, in spite of huge state funding, the former East Germany has the highest unemployment in the country, with a daunting 17 percent of workers without a job and thousands of jobs being scaled down in pay because of perceived inequalities in "ossie" training and qualifications. An initial real estate boom was quickly followed by a prolonged slump, and the new federal government saw its debt rising to crippling proportions. Frustrations are deep in former East as well as in the former West, visible in the fact that one of the biggest electoral forces in greater Berlin is the party that replaced the old East German Socialist Party (SED). In its train, from the opposite end of the political spectrum, the neo-fascist National Democratic Party (NPD) has acquired an impressive following. Media reports zoom in on frustrated youth who have joined the neo-Nazi movement. "Tough times need tough guys" seems to be the luring call for young males to manifest themselves, to find identity and break through their isolation, as they aspire for a future that will bring back a sense of victory and control.

Lukacs's use of fascist imagery in *Wild Kingdom* is troubling, perhaps more so than in any of the E-Werk cycle. One skin-ass sports the term "skin army" on his sleeve. (Characteristic for Lukacs's use of slide projection during painting, and somewhat as a giveaway, the term is visible in mirror image.) Swastikas are visible in the right side of the central panel and in the crossbeams of the scaffolding. While the uniform and homogeneic appearance of the ass-heads brings a strong homogeneous element into the painting, the parodic impact of this imagery resonates overwhelmingly, and the parody operates on multiple levels.

There is, first, a mischievous reference to Lukacs's well-known voyeuristic fascination with skinheads (as in skin boys; skin girls never make it to his canvas). The painting was completed at a time when his interest in the skinhead look started petering out; he gave up on the image, for a while, as the preferred outlook for himself: "Maybe I've been tanking it," he declared in 1993. "I don't want to become an imitation of myself. That gets pathetic."[36] It was also painted at a time when the skinhead stigma was increasingly associated with the rising neo-Nazi following in the Berlin capital. The history of violent gangs of Nazi skinheads that attacked refugee hostels and that firebombed boarding houses for immigrants in and around Berlin in the early 1990s—a history still fresh in people's minds—was one of the reasons for the troubling reception of Lukacs's E-Werk. It was a period of intense rivalry and violent street clashes among various groups of skinheads and mods on either side of the political spectrum. SHARPs (Skinheads Against Racial Prejudice) clashed with Blut und Ehre Skins (Pure Blood and Pride); Ska-Skins barred Hammerskins from their music gatherings; yet others took up post near Nollendorfplatz for a good bit of gay-bashing.[37] The popular media and powerful German tabloid press soaked up the whole scene, not making any differentiation between the different breeds, and accompanying their stories with generous pictures of SS and Swastika ensigns. The image of the donkey—a recurrent motif in contemporaneous work of Lukacs—is drawn directly from iconographic imagery that accompanied the discourse of right-wing politics. During a demonstration, one Nazi revisionist carried an unforgiving but naively ironic statement that clearly rang home in the painter's imagination: "I am an ass. I still believe that Jews were gassed in German Concentration Camps. I am an Ass."[38] Lukacs later literalized the metaphor by concretizing the image of the donkey.

For the painter, meanwhile, the skinheads' politics were less exciting than their looks and accessories, though Lukacs himself seems mindful of the various codes and their differences. Similar to the media, he uses the fascist symbols liberally—mostly, it seems, to generate an impulsive response from his viewers and critics. By the time *Wild Kingdom* was completed in 1993, every skinhead on the streets of Berlin was a potential firebomber and nostalgic Nazi sympathizer in the minds of the respectable, museum-visiting denizens of Germany's new capital. No wonder, then, that people in Germany as well as Canada responded with great suspicion to the indulgent and excessive scenes depicted in E-Werk.

"Boots, the bomber jackets, the jeans tight in the crotch and in the ass" (Lukacs's own words) are still the wardrobe of choice for the *metteur en scène* of *Wild Kingdom,* but Lukacs has given them a new mask with their short-cropped donkey heads. The two leaders of the gang, in camouflage coveralls over white shirts and ties and overlaying suspenders, look even more stupid than the rest, particularly in their funnel hats, which point up between their long donkey ears. Their huge phalluses protruding from their crotches, each with its own distinctive foreskin, make the image outrageous. It is disturbing and hilarious at the same time. The forceful masculinity of these uniformed ithyphallic men stands in great contrast with the powerlessness of the woman. However, it is a masculinity that is so full of parody that we don't take it seriously anymore, and this is where the allegory acquires a political impact. Similar to the paradox of revolt and consuetude in the appearance of the skinhead, the group of ass-men present themselves as a homogeneous group; but at the same time, in their disfiguration and their violent threat, they represent a heterogeneous force. It is their *otherness*, in spite of their uniformity, that gives them an aura of threat and aggression in spite of their outrageous ridiculousness.

Bataille's fascination with fascist leaders like Mussolini and Hitler is well known. For the French sociologist, it was "impossible to ignore the *force* that situates them above men, parties, and even laws: a *force* that disrupts the regular course of things, the peaceful but fastidious homogeneity powerless to maintain itself."[39] So too do these *ass-skins* threaten all that is around them; their superiority designates them as masters whose authority is justified in their nature "as something other, without being able to account for it rationally."[40] Lukacs foregrounds this army of beastly men as an incarnation of what Bataille calls an exalted, glorious, but negative force. In fact, they may well be on their way to a later Lukacs painting. *That's It* (2000) is a particularly disturbing work in which a mob of nude skinheads, equally muscular and strapping as his gang of skin-asses in *Wild Kingdom,* are mercilessly clobbering a stricken male with baseball bats. While it is less violent, *Wild Kingdom* is also, paradoxically, less prudish, though the artist's exhibitionist intervention is one of parody. He reins in this army of skinheads with a few strokes of a brush, leaving their spears hanging rather miserably in the cold. Parody always brings about a certain reversal, astutely forecast by Bataille in his comment on perceptions of class and status: "Communist workers appear to the bourgeois to be as ugly and dirty as hairy sexual organs, or lower parts; sooner or later there will be a scandalous eruption in the course of which the asexual noble heads of the bourgeois will be chopped off."[41] Though no beheading occurs in this painting, in contrast to for instance *Glamour Crew,* noble heads are played with nonetheless. The *dirty communist worker* acquires a still and mute but dignified presence in the background, while the two leading ass-men in the front may well represent, say, the CEOs of Sony, Daimler, or Deutsche Bank, who reside in their shiny head office edifices on nearby Potsdamer Platz. These men, clearly, represent a whole different sort of *kalos kagathos*. Looking at it from a G.W. Bush / Bin Laden era, multiple other connotations come to mind in this homosocial world, caught in a manic imbalance of power and powerlessness. Parody, being a "queer mode of narrative,"[42] always maintains the footprints of the original denotation of an image in its redeployment. In the mythological world of *Wild Kingdom,* the satyrs have changed cloaks and headgear but maintain their indisputable mark.

Wild Kingdom may well be *une peinture à clef;* however, there are many different keys required, and for various doors. If the throng of ass-men represent the violent negation of homogeneic structure, they also incarnate, in their identical heads, uniforms, and footwear, the principle of order, productive and profitable behaviour, and the homogeneic principle of commensurability. Their sizable phalluses and foreskins offer particular measures of homogeneic masculinity. The solid wall in the right-hand panel, from which they seem to emerge, is an index of both, as was the Berlin Wall: it is an enclosure and thus a homogenizing constraint, but it also represents the potential for rupture and subversion. In fact, the painter, in a quasi-metamove, leaves the semi-visible graffiti ambiguous. While its morphology— VERRECK! or VERRECKT (Die!/Damn You! or Damned)—is an easy guess, it is not clear whether the scrawl is intruding or being phased out. The wall, in all its ambivalence of in or out, or entry or exit—a motif that is repeated in the encasing affect of the scaffolding—indicates a more fundamental ambiguity of the central panel's performance narrative: with the exception of the woman and the Taurus couple, it is hard to tell whether any of the other characters are on their way out or on their way in.

There is less ambiguity in the left panel. The eagle, most likely, is flying off with his prey, and there is little doubt that this fragment is a (slightly altered) quotation of Michelangelo's *Rape of Ganymede*.[43] The reference to the young Trojan prince, who was abducted by Zeus and bestowed with the gift of immortality, is parodied with the two men anxiously following the lift with a rescue blanket, and also with the aggrandizement of the scene with the velvet blue curtain on the side. It comes across as a wishful move, to be hoisted to another world, away from the confusion and abjection of the central panel, leaving the wall—old and new—for what it is. It is a heterogeneous intervention, a transgression that is marked by a desire for expenditure; it is a shedding of the "careworn mien,"[44] so evident in the central panel. In its mythical origins and proportions, the transgression that unfolds in the painting has religious connotations, but it also of the flesh: it is a yearning for the sacred, where all desire wants to be. Bataille reminds us that it "is the state of transgression that prompts the desire, the need for a more profound, a richer, a marvelous world, the need, in a word, for a sacred world."[45] And Anthony O'Shea, in his comment on desire and the sacred in Bataille, may well have had *Wild Kingdom* in front of him: "What is expended *by* desire is an Icarus, burnt by the Sun, found wanting by it, wanting to return *to* it even whilst knowing that it is insufficient to contain the very experience of desire and the sacred."[46] Desire takes us to the sacred, but it also, clearly, expels us from the sacred. The middle panel is at opposite ends of the sacred; yet the quotidian card players—half in, half out of the left panel—are undisturbed by what unfolds above them, or next to them, and seem firmly settled in their solipsistic twosome world, which is reminiscent of the naive but placid self-absorption in Pieter Breughel's *Fall of Icarus*. Unperturbed, the two card players go about their idle game, in the middle of all this strife and confusion. It is a disposition also reflected in the lovestruck angelic muscleboys at the very centre of the triptych. This pairing is one of the few occasions in Lukacs's paintings where the gaze is not directed outward but instead becomes a more personal looking-into-each-other's-eyes. Here is the start, perhaps, of a sacred bliss. The two are about to fly off and make their nest; or perhaps they are on a salvaging mission with the piece of (unfinished/transluscent) column they try to carry off.

Apart from the two crowd scenes, pairing is certainly one of the main structuring elements in the blocking of *Wild Kingdom*. Two ass-skin leaders, two card players, an eagle with his prey, two doting rescuers, two angel boys, and the Taurus figure with the woman are the obvious pairs that populate this dyadic world. Supported by the *stage lighting*, the Taurus/woman pair is in the strongest position on this stage in terms of focus, though there's tough competition for focus from the two or three overendowed donkey skinheads in the very centre. It is a rare occasion to see a female figure in Lukacs's paintings,[47] and this one in particular is special since, in his own words, it is his "first painting of a woman."[48] Anemic-looking with her waxy, pallid skin, straggly hair, and sagging breasts, gagged and utterly disempowered, the woman—or whatever is left of her—stands in great contrast with all the plays on masculine power and physicality in the rest of the painting. The woman seems to be at the centre of an exchange, utterly objectified and utterly abject. The classical draping of the tatters of her garb cannot recover the image of a deeply wounded woman. Freud's designation of female clothing as a symbolic indication of psychic wound, with all its misogynistic implications, comes to mind. These clothes, then, cover genital deficiency, or a "woman's 'genital wound' (à la Freud),"[49] and the stigmatic shame this brings about stands in great contrast to the genital pride of the oncoming donkey skinheads. While traditionally, in the footsteps of Freud, the woman's lack is correlated to a fear for castration,[50] in this painting it clearly leads to an excess of phallic pride and conquest. The affect of the opposition between male and female is warped with political discomfort and potential misogyny, so we are quick to grasp the allegorical implications of the Taurus/woman figure.

Europa's abduction by Zeus, the ruler of the Olympian gods, marks the violent and transgressive beginning of a continent whose history has been mired in inequity and expenditure. The painter's provocative use of some of the most flagrant symbols of Europe's violent past, especially the wall and the image of the Swastika, are forceful emblems of the discord. Lukacs's *mise-en-scène* also preserves some of the mythological aspects of the story, and it may well be inspired by one of the many classical representations of the myth. Rubens's *Abduction of Europa*[51] with its cherubic boys in full flight in pursuit of a distressed Europa on the back of Zeus, incarnated by a white bull, lurks strongly in the background of *Wild Kingdom*. In Lukacs's painting, however, the bull is no longer the handsome, affable, irresistible bull, but instead an apocalyptic omen, a skeletal mask of death. Zeus not only is paired with the abject, impotent Europa but is also paired with himself, the stalwart eagle in the left-hand panel, who flies off with the sturdy-limbed Ganymede. Here are politics at work; we are witness to "a complex politicization of the erotic, and an eroticisation of the political."[52] *Wild Kingdom* gives us an artist's snapshot of Europe at the crossroads of a new millennium.

While the pair of leading donkey-skinheads is in strong competition with the Taurus/woman pair for central focus of the painting, a small isolated butterfly is, in fact, the *very* centre of the triptych. It is a highly incongruous image in its singleness, its isolation, its fragility, its bright yellow colour, and its purity. Whatever symbolic meaning it acquires, its chances for survival in this bombastic world of stone and steel, aggression and disintegration, with not a flower or blade of grass in sight, are close to nil. In the composition, it seems dangerously close to being swatted by the Nazi salute of the skinhead in a lime-green bomber jacket, just below it. Its bright colour pairs with the orange-yellow flesh of the pumpkin-like orchestra shell in the foreground of the painting. Both are organic, feminine presences between the commensurate and conquering world of the penile organs and the abject existence of a gagged and vanquished woman. Or, on the other hand, in a more romantic reading, the butterfly may be taunting the skinhead's threatening salute; in its pristine innocence, it is unreachable, however ineffective it may be. Lukacs himself seems to choose the more sinister outcome, especially where he paints the shadow of the double bass bow on the orchestra shell as a reflection of one of the giant penis heads hanging above.

The fall of the Berlin Wall and, resulting from it, the promised reunification of an old, battered, and wounded continent gave rise to excessive hope and new dreams of freedom, prosperity, and democracy, not just for the citizens of East (and West) Berlin but for all of Europe and a triumphant North America. *Wild Kingdom*, then, is a response to the paralyzing predicament in which democracy finds itself. As Georges Bataille reminds us in one of his "Propositions": "Democracy, which rests on a precarious equilibrium between classes, is perhaps only a transitory form; it brings with it not only the grandeur but the petтиness of decomposition."[53] Lukacs, not surprisingly, seems to situate this pettiness primarily on a heterosexual level, starting with his re-evocation of the mythological (heterosexual) origin of the continent, and, even more so, with the obvious binary opposition in the central part of the painting between the wounded woman and the minatory ithyphallic men. Against the background of Berlin's reunification and reconstruction, this visionary evocation of Berlin's Pariser Platz presents a dystopian mythology, one in which the sole promise of salvation lies not in the pathetic central butterfly, but rather in a series of dyadic configurations: the two angelic youth in the central painting, the two dispassionate card players in the left triptych, and the evasive/salvaging move of the eagle with his Ganymede. The promise, clearly, is in a same-sex monadic twosome-ness. In the gay nineties, this kind of sexual retreat was an ideology that was often embraced or put forward—especially in feminist theory—as the only possible answer to the horrible history of masculinist heterosexual organization of desire, of self, and of community. The painting seems to present a gay male version of this response, though it does so, somewhat tongue in cheek, as a nightmarish pastiche, in spite of its remorseless totalization. It is not too far-fetched, then, to extend the mythological reading of the triptych and see the two angelic youth as representing the two lovers Harmodius and Aristogeiton, the legendary saviours of Athenian democracy during the reign of Tyrant Hippias in the sixth century BC.[54] In between the dystopian representation of Europa and the advancing fascist posse, the two angelic youth represent a naive and utopian world of archeological safeguarding, redemption, and survival, situated explicitly within male–male sexuality.

Wild Kingdom presents a queer allegorical response to Europe's momentous geopolitical transformation in the early 1990s as a result of the collapse of the Iron Curtain, an event that led some critics to conclude that we had arrived at the end of history. *Wild Kingdom,* in its oracular vision, presents an altogether different scenario. Here we are, quite literally, at a juncture in history. The scene that unfolds in front of us takes place on Berlin's Pariser Platz, since, from the position of the two side buildings in the left and right panels, we can conclude with certainty that we are looking at the Brandenburg Gate from the East, toward the West. There is also little doubt that the wall structure in the right panel is in fact misplaced. There was never any wall on the east side of that building. Quite likely, we are dealing with a newly erected wall, hence the broom (a quotation from his own painting *This Town*), which the bricklayers have left behind after packing up. The triptych probably is best read from right to left, with the curtain on the left ready to fall on the completed play.

With its exclusive real estate and select chic, Pariser Platz may be an unlikely location for the scene. Its choice, however, is strategic. Left virtually untouched since the Allied bombardments of 1945, the square became a hotly contested area of urban renovation and planning in 1989. While literally a *terra prohibita* until the collapse of the Berlin Wall, the square was the geographical heart of its fall and has since been the scene and subject of numerous rowdy protests and confrontations. National and international business interests and diplomatic powerhouses wanted it restored to its former glory as the pulse of Berlin's high-society life before the Second World War. German cultural powerhouses wanted to see their headquarters on the square, while community and left-leaning political groups claimed it as a people's place that would bear witness to the forces of resistance that had brought down a totalitarian government. Ultimately, while the space has maintained its function as a public square, banks, exclusive hotels, and embassies (of France and the United States, no less) have conquered the perimeters of the Pariser Platz using the designs of renowned architects such as Frank Gehry, Josef Paul Kleihues, Christian de Portzamparc, and Moore Ruble Yudell for their façades. *Wild Kingdom,* with its outspoken focus on architecture past and present, can be read as a parable that explicates the opposing forces, not only in the rebuilding of Pariser Platz, or a unified Berlin, but also, and more fundamentally, of a new Europe that is struggling under the hegemonic weight of an atavistic American empire. In the decade that has passed since the making of the painting, what is most striking is the visionary and oracular impact of these three scenes as we look back on the economical and political developments of the turn of the century, both in Europe and in North America.

This painting signalled a significant departure for Lukacs himself. He left Berlin shortly after completing *Wild Kingdom* and the final painting in the E-Werk cycle, *Everybody Wants the Same Thing* (1993). His move to New York signalled the beginning of a new style of painting, one that became decidedly less figurative and less human-based. This development seems already announced in the word "IMITAT" on the palette held by the semi-nude woman. The German *Imitat* translates as "facsimile" or "replica" or "imitation" and has a negative resonance to it. Also, the prop of the palette in the woman's hand turns her into a muse of painters, and as such, Lukacs has included a metacommentary on his own art. Clearly, in view of the disempowered state of the woman, the comment is skeptical about the function and power of art—or, perhaps more precisely, about the kind of realistic figurative parodic art that Lukacs had been practising. It is a highly mimetic art, and, as in all mimesis, the process of representation always involves something that Mieke Bal calls "'absentification' of the represented object: the object is replaced."[55] Of course, because of the expository character of art, there is also a process of "presentification" of the object, which becomes the source of the experience of the work of art. In Lukacs's paintings, the highly visceral figures make for a complex interplay between an absent body and the exuberant suggestion of flesh alive with desire. Here too, Bataille's notion of expenditure as non-productive interaction with the world can be helpful. In line with mimetic absentification, artistic expenditure for Bataille always involves loss. Art generates "creation by means of loss." It is clear, then, that figurative art involves a greater loss of its physical or concrete underpinning of the imagery than non-figurative art; the latter brings about a greater freedom through its more radical heterogeneous intervention. Non-figurative art, then, is a more radical obliteration or annihilation of the homogeneic forces around us.

If *Wild Kingdom* is to be read from right to left, as earlier suggested, it culminates in a profound sense of loss and longing for the unattainable in the left part of the triptych—a nostalgia that informs the entire E-Werk cycle. Quite obviously, the imitated world of *Wild Kingdom*, with its excessive and monumental masculinity, is calculable, sizable, commensurable, and mimetic, a fact much less evident in *Everybody Wants the Same Thing*, a painting that permeates loss and expenditure while still clearly drawing on masculinity and masculine power. In his later Arbor Vitae (1999) and Flowers (2001) cycles, masculinity is still referred to in titles and phallic shapes, but what strikes us most is the quiet murmur of loss that comes to us in a more non-figurative language. Those later paintings no longer answer overtly to a male sexual economy in the way E-Werk does. The figure of the woman in tatters may well be an allegorical admonition to the painter that the attempt at transfiguration through imitation is troublesome and unsatisfactory and may only lead to a paradigm of continuous repetition. Duplication is a characteristic that many critics have identified as a problem in Lukacs's oeuvre. His more recent work has been an uncompromising return to the figurative male that landmarks E-Werk. His series, for instance, of a dozen or so surfboards serves as a serial canvas for the performative male body, positioned upside down against a Baroque, Hiëronymus Bosch-like infernal universe, against a background of vines, fruits, and cityscapes. As they sway in the draft of his studio, they become haunting and transfixing fetish objects reminiscent of the sado-masochistic world of *Glamour Crew,* another canvas in the E-Werk series. The male body of muscle and brawn remains a major fetish, fascination, and inspiration for the painter and continues to feature in his most recent allegorical-mystical canvasses. *Wild Kingdom,* then, is a transitional work that comments not only on male desire and its unattainable realization, but also on the political, cultural, and social expenditures of male economies. It also provides a metacommentary on its own masculine aesthetics of imitation and duplication. The apocalyptic vision of *Wild Kingdom* may well have emerged from a homosexual desire of survival and escape. Its outcome is an expenditure *au delà* and *in excess* of its own aesthetics of masculinity.[56]

NOTES

I would like to thank Marena Arndt, Diane Farris, Stephen Fouquet (+), Joan Greer, Joe Lukacs, Stephen McClatchie, Colleen Sharpe, Christine Sowiak, Lisa Tillotson, and Ruth Vanderwoude for their assistance in carrying out this study. Special thanks to my graduate research assistants, Heidi Bickis and David King. My research was facilitated by a study grant in Berlin from DAAD (New York) and by a travel grant from the University of Alberta's Support for the Advancement of Scholarship.

1 David Vaisbord, *Drawing Out the Demons* (Vancouver: Screen Siren Pictures, 2004).
2 Robin Major, *Attila Richard Lukacs—Recent Work 1990,* Exhibition Catalogue (Calgary: Alberta College of Art, 1991), 10.
3 Blake Gopnik, "Bad-Boy Aside, Attila Richard Lukacs Is Actually Bland and Softcore—the Ken Danby of the Avant-Garde," *Globe and Mail,* 17 October 1998.
4 *My Father's House* (1989), *This Town* (1990), *Tomorrow and Tomorrow and Tomorrow* (1991), *Wild Kingdom* (1992/93), *Glamour Crew* (1993), and *Everybody Wants the Same Thing* (1993) constitute the six paintings of *E-Werk* and are reproduced in Paulette Gagnon, *Attila Richard Lukacs, Exhibition Catalogue* (Montréal: Musée d'art contemporain, 1994).
5 Piet Defraeye, "Performances of Masculinity in Attila Richard Lukacs's *E-Werk,*" in *Queering the Canon: Defying Sights in German Literature and Culture,* ed. Chris Lorey and John Plews (Columbia: Camden House, 1998), 420–33.
6 Jonathan Dollimore, "Sexual Disgust," *Oxford Literary Review* 20, nos. 1–2 (1998): 69.
7 Fred Botting and Scott Wilson, *Bataille* (Houndmills: Palgrave, 2001), 199.
8 See also Defraeye, "Performances," 431.
9 Susan Douglas, "In the Field of Visibility: Cadieux, Houle, Lukacs," *University of Toronto Quarterly* 71, no. 3 (June 2002): 761.
10 Jonathan Dollimore, *Sexual Dissidence: Augustine to Wilde, Freud to Foucault* (Oxford: Clarendon, 1991), 325.
11 See, for instance, Mary Douglas, *Purity and Danger: An Analysis of the Concepts of Pollution and Taboo* (London: Routledge, 1966); and Jonathan Dollimore, "Sexual Disgust."

12 Thomas Sokolowsi, "Attila Richard Lukacs," *Attila Richard Lukacs* (Exhibition Catalogue) (New York: 49th Parallel, 1989), 2.
13 Georges Bataille, "The Labyrinth," in *Visions of Excess: Selected Writings, 1927–1939* (Minneapolis: University of Minnesota Press, 1985), 171–77.
14 Dollimore, "Sexual Disgust," 65.
15 Terry Eagleton, *The Significance of Theory* (Cambridge: Blackwell, 1990), 42.
16 See n3.
17 Jo-Anne Birnie Danzker, "Foreword," *Young Romantics* (Exhibition Catalogue) (Vancouver: Vancouver Art Gallery, 1985), 2.
18 See Piet Defraeye, "Kicking the Pricks: Attila Richard Lukacs's *E-Werk*," *Nashwaak Review* 5 (1998): 68–74.
19 See also the collection "Love in Art" in the painter's *Attila Richard Lukacs* (Exhibition Catalogue) (Vancouver: Diane Farris Gallery, 1992). In an interview, Lukacs himself uses the term "romantic" in reference to this cycle of paintings. See Attila Richard Lukacs, "Regendering the Garden: The Very Rich Painting of Attila Richard Lukacs," interview by Robert Enright, *Border Crossings* (Summer 1992), 22.
20 Georges Bataille, *Eroticism: Death and Sensuality* (San Francisco: City Light Books, 1986), 56–7. Also quoted in Dollimore, "Sexual Disgust," 66.
21 There are striking parallels between the haunting paintings of *E-Werk* and these marvellous cave pictures. The use of black as a prominent accent in combination with flesh-coloured ochre is just one of the striking similarities. Lascaux's twisted perspective and the technique of superimposition is another one. The isolated animal figures of the cave paintings echo the insularity of Lukacs's figures, paratactically distributed on the rock or on the canvas. Lascaux's animals are mostly bulls, obsessively painted as prey before the hunt, and just like Lukacs's males, are the object of a desirous fantasy. The painting of the figures is a symbolic taking possession.
22 Georges Bataille, *Lascaux or the Birth of Art* (Lausanne: Skira, 1955), 37.
23 Georges Bataille, "The Psychological Structure of Fascism," in *Visions of Excess*, 159.
24 Anthony O'Shea, "Desiring Desire: How Desire Makes Us Human, All Too Human," *Sociology* 36, no 4 (2002): 939.
25 Attila Richard Lukacs, *Wild Kingdom* (Calgary: Nickle Arts Museum), 1992–93, oil, enamel and tar on canvas, 400.7 x 1,259.8 cm, 5 panels.
26 On the allegorical character of Lukacs's paintings, see also Eric Savoy, "Queer Apocalypse: Attila Richard Lukacs at the End," *Torquere* 3 (2001): 2–5.
27 Georges Bataille, "The Solar Anus," in *Visions of Excess*, 5.
28 On the histrionic aspects of Lukacs's paintings, see Defraeye, "Performances," 423–24.
29 Edgar Degas, *L'Orchestre de l'opéra* (Paris: Musée d'Orsay).
30 The operatic quality of Lukacs's Berlin paintings may well be connected with the fact that, since its reunification, no other city in the world has so much opera on offer as Berlin. The Deutsche Oper Berlin, the Komische Oper, the Staatsoper Unter den Linden, and the Staatsballett Berlin all offer a rare experience of close to one hundred original productions, with hundreds of soloists throughout the year.
31 For the meaning of *E-Werk*, see Defraeye, "Performances," 427.
32 Thanks to Stephen McClatchie for this note.
33 Georges Bataille, "Fascism," in *Visions of Excess*, 143.
34 Ibid., 142.
35 Ibid., 143.
36 Quoted in Bruce Headlam, "Attila Up Against the Wall," *Saturday Night*, December 1993, 87.

37 For an overview of the Skinhead movement in Berlin, see Murray Healy, *Gay Skins* (London: Cassell, 1996).
38 The original text runs: "Ich bin ein Esel. Ich glaube immer noch das im Deutschen K.Z.'s Juden vergased wurden. Ich bin ein Esel [sic]." The obvious (most likely unintentional) grammatical errors are part of a complex layer of irony at work here. Interview with A.R. Lukacs, Vancouver, 2 September 2005.
39 Bataille, "Fascism," in *Visions of Excess*, 143.
40 Ibid., 145.
41 Bataille, "The Solar Anus," in *Visions of Excess*, 8.
42 Savoy, "Queer Apocalypse," 5.
43 Michelangelo, *The Rape of Ganymede*, c. 1533, black chalk, 19 x 33 cm (Cambridge: Fogg Art Museum). Ganymede has been the source of countless artworks.
44 Bataille, *Lascaux*, 36.
45 Ibid., 38.
46 O'Shea, "Desiring Desire," 935.
47 See also Defraeye, "Perfomances," 423 and 431.
48 Lukacs in Headlam, "Attila," 86.
49 Kathryn Bond Stockton, "Cloth Wounds, or When Queers Are Martyred to Clothes: The Value of Clothing's Complex Debasements," *Women: A Cultural Review* 13, no. 3 (2002): 289–321 at 291.
50 See also Briony Fer, "Poussière/peinture. Bataille on Painting," in *Bataille: Writing the Sacred*, ed. Carolyn Bailey Gill (London: Routledge, 1995), 154–71.
51 Peter Paul Rubens, *The Abduction of Europa*, 1628–29 (Madrid: Prado Museum).
52 Savoy, "Queer Apocalypse," 18.
53 Bataille, "Propositions," in *Visions of Excess*, 198.
54 On the day of the Athenean festival Panathenea, in 514 BC, Harmodius and Aristogeiton murdered Hippias' brother Hipparchos but failed to kill Hippias—who took bloody revenge on the two lovers. Hippias was later expelled by the Athenians, who honoured the pair as martyrs of freedom.
55 Mieke Bal, "Mimesis and Genre Theory in Aristotle's *Poetics*," *Poetics Today* 3, no. 1 (1982): 172.
56 Georges Batailles, "The Notion of Expenditure," in *Visions of Excess, 120*.

CHAPTER 6

Stranger Than Paradise: Immigration and Impaired Masculinities

CHRISTINA STOJANOVA

A spectre hovers over the denizens of the liquid modern world and all their labours and creations: the spectre of redundancy.
— ZYGMUNT BAUMAN

Displaced persons hoping for another chance to "recycle their wasted lives," as the Polish-born social philosopher Zygmunt Bauman would have it, are gradually but surely evolving from exception to norm in our "liquid modern world."[1] Therefore, frictions between the welcoming populace and the newcomers—whether solicited by the "benign forces of globalization" or by undesirable side effects of their unpredictable impunity—are inevitably bound to get worse. The strangers at our door with their incessant clinging to material signs of once solid identities (burkhas, hijabs, yarmulkes, turbans) also painfully remind us of what our pleasure-seeking postmodern society has lightheartedly thrown aside along the way toward the dubious freedom of, as Bauman has it, "not being tied up by any legacies of the past, wearing one's current identity as one wears shirts that may be promptly replaced when they fall out of use or out of fashion."[2]

Despite the great significance of immigrants and immigration for both English Canada and Quebec, their representations on screen differ radically in tenor and mode across the cultural divide, obviously due to the clash between what Regine Robin calls the "trop plein / too full" (Québécois) identity, usually "manifested through the absolutization of differences of racism, nationalism, ethnic retreat, and religious fundamentalism" and the "trop vide / too empty," pulverized identity "represented by American mass culture" (and by extension, by the English Canadian one), by the "reign of the image, and the post-modern erasure of history."[3] Indeed, English Canadian culture offers seemingly less resistance to the solid cultural identities of foreigners vis-à-vis the elusive Canadian identity, which is vaguely defined by the pursuit of (material) happiness and respect for the law of the land (and, one feels eager to add, for the pre-eminence of the financial, political, and intellectual Anglo-Saxon elites). This explains why in English Canada films about immigrants are made mostly (if not singularly) by immigrants, and why most of them share an ironic approach, beautifully formulated by Julia Kristeva in her "Toccata and Fugue for the Foreigner": "Always elsewhere, the foreigner belongs nowhere...There are...those who [find themselves caught] in struggle between what no longer is and what will never be—the followers of neutrality...They are not necessarily defeatists, they often become the best of ironists."[4]

The fact that one of the most prominent Canadian directors, Atom Egoyan, has succeeded in consistently reflecting on his personal experience as an offspring of Armenian-Egyptian immigrants (*Family Viewing*, [1987]; *Calendar* [1993]), and in pondering the most tragic historic event in Armenian history, the genocide of 1915 (the million-dollar epic *Ararat* [2002]) challenges Bauman's criticism of the liquid promiscuity of (post)modern identities and cultures. In this sense, Egoyan, to quote Kristeva again, is one of the "foreigners...who transcend: living neither before nor now but beyond...[His] is a passion for another land, always a promised one." A "believer," she says, who is however most likely to "ripen into a sceptic."[5]

In contrast, I argue, films about immigrants in Quebec are made mostly by francophone filmmakers. In the context of the province's notoriously confused politics of diversity and its variously competing majority discourses of multiculturalism, separatist nationalism, and rural xenophobia, these works are interesting in the context of *Making It Like a Man: Canadian Masculinities in Practice* for their focus on a decidedly impaired vision of immigrant masculinities.

QUEBEC'S CULTURAL DILEMMA

It is difficult if not impossible to imagine CBC's *Little Mosque on the Prairie* being filmed in Quebec, where Bauman's global paradigm is played out in a particularly complex manner, and where Quebec's more "solid" identity is opposed not only to the English Canadian "liquid" one but also to the "full" identities of the newcomers, which seem to "solidify" in direct proportion to the reluctance of the host society to accommodate them, thus enhancing the endemic tendency toward cultural regression that is characteristic of the immigrant experience.

Cultural and social theorist Homi Bhabha has noted that in every discourse sanctioning diversity, the host society or dominant culture makes sure that the incorporation of new cultures or established sectors of difference agrees with its own normative system. However, on settling in Quebec (or in Montreal, the city of choice for most immigrants), the foreigner is expected to work her own way through the maze of not one but three dominant and often contradictory cultural discourses. The discourse she first familiarizes herself with is the inclusive multicultural politics of Canada as entrenched in the Charter of Rights and Freedoms. The federal discourse is promulgated, somewhat *sotto voce*, by the stance of the provincial Liberal Party and the federal Liberal caucus, but is usually upstaged by the much more intense second official discourse, that of Quebec nationalists and sovereigntists on both provincial (Parti Québécois) and federal (Bloc Québécois) levels, who are concerned exclusively with preserving the French language and the Québécois *pur laine* (dyed in the wool) or *de souche* (from the source) culture and much less with defining an inclusive Québécois identity. The revamping of the notion of the Québécois nation since the last referendum in 1995 is a case in point. As Daniel Salée writes in his highly engaging article "Quebec Sovereignty and the Challenge of Linguistic and Ethno-Cultural Minorities," the referendum has sent

> mixed signals to all those who, by virtue or the vagaries of history, do not readily share Quebec's Francophone, foundational, pre-political identity...This sentiment of exclusion, of erasure from *la nation quebecoise*, felt by non-francophones, is, in the end, quite normal. They are invited to partake in *la nation quebecoise*, but according to terms and parameters upon which they have little or no control. In other words, they can be *in* the nation, if they so wish; somehow, they will never really be *of* the nation.[6]

The chronic failure of the nationalist discourse to define the terms of inclusion for anglophones and especially for allophones is compounded by Ottawa's systematic—overt and covert—attempts to both contain and appease Quebec nationalism. This confusion is undoubtedly aggravated by a third, unofficial discourse percolating among the so-called silent, smalltown francophone majority—a discourse prompted by decades of fear mongering against the religious, ethnic, and metropolitan Other, initiated two centuries ago by the Catholic Church and later encouraged by sovereigntist rhetoric. Therefore it would be difficult not to see the intricate interrelatedness between Stephen Harper's equivocally unbinding declaration of Quebec as a nation, which he made recently, and the escalating public debate on "reasonable accommodation" that is taking place currently in Quebec.[7]

The political entanglement produced by these three majority discourses has had a direct effect on Quebec society and culture and certainly on gender and ethnic representations in Quebec cinema.[8] Against the backdrop of the drawn-out debate on multiculturalism between the two referendums (1980 and 1995), and the failure of the Meech Lake and Charlottetown Accords in the early 1990s, a number of documentaries and docudramas have been made that feature immigrants and immigration. They were funded mostly by government agencies, whose role is extremely intriguing with regard to Quebec's cultural complexity. It goes without saying that their policies reflect the major contradictions of the two official discourses. Obviously, federal institutions (such as the NFB) and federal agencies (such as the Canada Arts Council and Telefilm Canada) are expected to endorse the federal cultural discourse, whereas provincial agencies (such as SODEC[9] and the Quebec Arts Council)[10] would be more inclined to stimulate Quebec's nationalist discourse. The federal institutions, however, have rarely turned down projects with nationalist, even sovereigntist content,[11] and the NFB French unit has always enjoyed its own independent cultural policy.[12]

During the period in question, a number of films, corroborating the official discourse of inclusiveness and multiculturalism, were made at the NFB by Montrealers of both anglophone and francophone origin. John Smith's docudrama *Welcome to Canada* (1989) and Tom Cadieu's *Land of Hope* (1996) are representative of this trend. *Welcome to Canada* reconstructs the drama of the Sri Lankan boat people who were cast up at the mercy of the elements near Newfoundland and saved by Canadians. Its didactic narrative and expediently (even stereotypically) drawn characters, however, fail to grasp the human dimensions of this rare feat of human solidarity.[13] The miniseries *Land of Hope*, a homegrown Quebec product sharing the same message, was produced by Productions La Fête. It focuses on another historical event, the welcoming of famished and ailing Irish settlers who arrived by boat in Quebec in the mid-1800s. In tune with the Heritage Minutes pathos, *Land of Hope* is less concerned with historical and psychological accuracy than with creating a monument of sorts to values at the very core of the collective national identity. It energetically propounds the message that immigrants are an essential ingredient *of* the nation, though it remains a bit murky whether the "nation" is the Québécois or the Canadian one. Constructed as dramatizations of Canadian history texts, these films showcase Canadians (immigration officers, fishermen, housewives, rich and poor members of the populace) — what Kristeva calls "paternalists" — as overwhelmingly concerned to demonstrate "how they understand [immigrants], how they commiserate, how they appreciate our talents, provided they can show that they have 'more' — more pain, more knowledge, more power, including that of helping us to survive."[14]

Thanks to the NFB and its traditional openness to controversial social issues, a rather diverse bag of mostly low-budget documentaries, docudramas, and short fictions made by immigrant directors appeared in the late 1980s and early 1990s, facilitating the emergence of a specifically immigrant voice among the multitude of alternative Quebec discourses. These works question multicultural inclusiveness and realistically suggest that Quebec newcomers cannot hope to be more than merely allowed *in* the nation—not, however, before a prolonged and painful negotiation of their identities and expectations. *Les Voleurs de job* (1980) and *Haïti (Québec)* (1985), made by Tahani Rached, a Haitian Canadian, and *Les "Borges"* (1978) and *Chère Amérique* (1990), made by Marilu Malet, a Chilean Canadian, come to mind, as well as *Xenofolies* (1991), made by the French-born Michel Moreau. From the fierce competition on the volatile Montreal job market, through thinly disguised or brutally expressed xenophobic attitudes and racist tensions between the Québécois *de souche* and the newcomers, to incompatibility of political views, these works foreground tensions that have been threatening the fragile balance of the confused Quebec politics of diversity. Unfortunately, they suffer from an endemic lack of artistic merit, with characters featured at best as mouthpieces for important cultural, moral, or social stances.

The *real* drama of aliens' acceptance by the host society is played out in fiction films made during that period and featuring mostly male immigrants. As a Symbolic construct, I would argue, the male gender tends to be much more susceptible to the effects of immigration. I am fully aware of Tania Modleski's criticism of analytical approaches that foreground issues of masculinity, and my analysis takes into consideration her claim that the most effective discussion of masculinity is that which is concerned with the impact of changing masculinities on the female subject. I am also aware of her claim that "male power is consolidated through cycles of crisis and resolution... with men dealing with the threat of female power by incorporating it."[15] But the psychoanalytical discussion of screen representations of male, non-Western identities, and their painful transformation (or unravelling) vis-à-vis the dual challenges of Westernized Quebec society and nationalist culture, allows for a closer look at the gender and ethnic subjectivity of the filmmakers and reveals deep-seated psychological and cultural attitudes (and prejudices) otherwise hidden in their unconscious. Building on Fredric Jameson's definition of narrative film as a "socially symbolic act," that is, as a text "whereby real social contradictions, insurmountable in their own terms, find a purely formal resolution in the aesthetic realm,"[16] I will try to uncover the painful process of dis-integration and re-integration of immigrant masculinities in Quebec on film through a psychoanalytical examination of their slow movement from objects of narcissistic and projective identification, displacement, and transference, toward subjectivity. In this progression, three phases are discernible: pre-Oedipal, Oedipal, and post-Oedipal.

The pre-Oedipal male subject formation on screen involves works where immigrant presence is seen as a *fait accompli*. Represented as foreign to Quebec's society and culture, ethnic otherness is used as a depository of exotic images and sexualized sentiments of a sometimes unexpectedly conservative nature—a subject position otherwise marginalized or challenged by the mainstream Quebec cinema. This tendency to construct the immigrant as "l'autre intime / the intimate Other" is further defined by Sherry Simon in her celebrated study on the subject as "convey[ing] a simplistic view of Quebec's cultural Others, tending to convert differences into a...fantasmatic Otherness...which never really goes beyond fascinated curiosity."[17] Made mostly by francophone *de souche* directors, these films can be interpreted in light of Salée's argument as establishing the conditions under which immigrants would be allowed *in* the nation.

FRIENDS AND LOVERS

Kristeva defines "semiotic process" as rooted in the feminine as "a pre-Oedipal energy, which needs (symbolic) channelling for social cohesion."[18] The pre-Oedipal is characterized by narcissistic identification and other primary psychic processes, which in the realm of the films below translate into an amorphous, mostly non-verbal presence on the part of the characters in which "the speaking subject is divided, de-centered, and process-oriented."[19]

Michael Brault's paradigmatic work *Les Noces de papier (Paper Wedding*, 1989) delineates the ideological and artistic horizon of the pre-Oedipal films. Its premise is a love affair between a Montrealer and an alien. This (melo)dramatically charged situation substitutes old class divisions with new cultural tensions threatening the cohesion of Quebec society, and Brault sees their only resolution via heterosexual marriage. The unrealistic representation of the omnipresent immigration machine as the villain—showing its officials at first as menacing and later as easily outsmarted—supplies the plot with clandestine thrill and urgency. The principal personages are designed in a similarly facile manner. The female protagonist, Claire Rocheleau—a single, forty-something professor of literature, trapped in a dead-end relationship with a married colleague—falls under the dark spell of Latin American revolutionary Pablo Torres, a refugee, whom she marries to save from deportation. Brault's trademark observational style, however, gives his excellent actors Manuel Aranguiz (Pablo) and Quebec star Geneviève Bujold (Clair) enough breathing space to ensure the psychologically convincing evolution of their stereotypical roles. The camera lingers on Pablo's face, capturing his evocative silence as a "meaningful" lapse of "tenuous symbolic control"[20] at this particularly traumatic moment in his life. When the couple is forced by suspicious immigration officials to live together, Pablo gradually arouses Claire's sexual curiosity with his silent suffering, underscored by torture scars she discovers on his back. It is, however, not long before he wins her heart when, in a moment of uncharacteristic and brief animation, he takes her to a fiesta, organized by his Latino community, and lets the "semiotics of [its] rhythms, tones and movements"[21] express his feelings.[22]

Michel Brault's subsequent film *Shabbat Shalom* (1992) again features the "theme of the fantasized Other whose cultural difference exerts a powerful...attraction...anchored in the immigrant's vulnerability and social marginality."[23] Here, the interaction between Québécois and non-Québécois ethnicity (in this case Jewish) takes the shape of narcissistic identification meant to soften the experience of loss.[24] After the suicide of his wife, and encountering worsening relations with his son, the grieving mayor of a Montreal municipality longs for the family warmth of his neighbours, a large Hassidic family. Here, as Simon observes, "the Jew is portrayed as the exact opposite of the French Canadian, as the embodiment of all that contemporary Quebecois culture has rejected but may perhaps still desire."[25]

The Jewish connection brings together the estranged father and son, thus linking up with other Oedipal narratives of Quebec cinema where, to quote Bill Marshall's well-informed discussion on the "immigrant Other," the strangers are "filling the lack,[26] the *telos* being that of union or reconciliation with the father."[27] Or, as is the case with the most artistic work of them all, Jean-Claude Lauzon's *Léolo* (1992), where the eponymous hero "assimilates an aspect, property or attribute of the [Italian] Other and is transformed, wholly or partially, after the model provided,"[28] triggering a tragic but unavoidable rupture with the past, dominated by a series of what Christine Ramsay calls "inefficient father-figures."[29]

Micheline Lanctot's *Sonatine* (1982), Joanne Prégent's *Les Amoureuses* (1993), Isabelle Hayeur's *La Bête de foire* (1992), and Isabelle Poisant's *La Fabrication d'un meurtrier* (1996) are auteur films by *de souche* women directors. Apparently under the immediate influence of the fast-growing diversity of the Montreal film industry, these works display an intriguing metamorphosis of the pre-Oedipal trend, where the imagined alien masculinities invariably point back to their creators, who "each have the foreigner of their choice to the extent that they would invent him if he did not exist."[30] Yet these characters also move away from the static presence of *Paper Wedding's* Pablo toward a more active engagement on narrative and psychological levels.

Micheline Lanctot's *Sonatine* offers the earliest take on the non-verbal alien. It is a psychological drama about two lonely teenage girls[31] who, longing for understanding, end their lives in the subway as a very public protest against alienation. The foreigner of Lanctot's choice is a Bulgarian sailor (Kliment Denchev) from a ship moored in Montreal's harbour. He serves as an emotional and psychological counterpoint to the dramatic buildup, providing a much needed auspicious respite before the disastrous end. For a brief moment it seems as if the handsome sailor—a perfect father figure, complete with the romantic appearance of a seawolf—will resolve the unbearable tension by either sexually abusing or falling in love with the girls. However, his poor communication skills—a friendly babble in very broken English—render him charmingly childlike and asexual. The intertextual reference to the sailor's exotic origin (and to that of the actor)[32] contributes additionally to his enigmatically undifferentiated status of pre-Oedipal object, stuck in the Imaginary realm. Since little was known about Bulgaria at that time, it served well as some mysteriously intriguing foreign place—one where people were still genuinely compassionate.

This facile dramatic approach—to reach for *prêt-à-porter* masculine stereotypes in order to resolve a narrative issue—is taken further in Joanne Prégent's *Les Amoureuses* (*The Enamoured*), another psychological drama, where the image of the sexualized male Other is conjured up not for the sake of "secret and shameful jouissance,"[33] but as a pawn in the director's feminist line of reasoning, briefly formulated as the unresolvable clash between women's liberation and emotional attachment. Two mature, good-looking professional women and their relationships are therefore closely scrutinized. Lea (Louise Portal) is a theatre costume designer married to David (Kenneth Walsh), an intellectual and sexually insecure introvert who is undergoing a severe midlife crisis. As much as she loves him and values his intelligent company, his cold inability to respond to her passionate sexuality pushes her into the arms of a young actor and she eventually leaves her husband.

To prove her point, Prégent counterbalances Lea's situation by choosing a much younger and virile extrovert as a partner for her second protagonist, Marianne (Léa-Marie Cantin), a successful chiropractor in her late thirties. This logical proposition has found an ideal embodiment in the stereotyped Italian immigrant male, associated in the popular imagination with construction work, temperamental sexuality, and patriarchal family values, including marriage, which Marianne finds unacceptable. Unlike David, Nino is denied any agency, and in Marianne's confidential conversations with Lea he comes through mostly as amusing but not very bright. His few appearances are geared to her motherly condescension: uninhibited by formalities, Nino prances about the house with only a towel on and a moment later is heard singing Italian arias in the shower, which happens to be the longest verbal statement he ever makes. Needless to say, only an excellent actor of the calibre of Tony Nardi, with his unique sense of character (and humour), could bring to life such an expendable dramatic construct.

The two other films could be defined broadly as essays on identity transformation, where the narratives stand or fall on the psychological power of the stranger as either a subject or an object of projected desires and fears. Isabelle Hayeur's *La Bête de foire* (*Beast of the Fair*) is an ambitious effort to illustrate a textbook case of transference,[34] combined with projective identification and defence mechanisms.[35] The Russian immigrant Borkine's otherwise successful life and career in Montreal is marred by an obsessive memory (shown in exquisite flashbacks by Yves Beaudoin's camera) of a passionate love affair he has had in prison with a mysterious gypsy woman, Tanya, whom he killed out of jealousy before fleeing to Canada. Borkine is drawn to his young Québécois employee, the construction worker Grégoire (David La Haye), who looks like Tanya to the extent that Borkine transfers his repressed feelings of love and guilt onto him. In turn, Grégoire internalizes these projections and gradually identifies with Tanya until the day he feels that his own life is in danger.

Heyeur's aspirations to probe the elusive boundaries of reality and imagination, freedom and captivity, self and other fails, however, because the nebulous Russian stranger and his campy story remain isolated from the realistic part of the narrative, which is situated in Quebec. And while the sexual and emotional ambivalence of the Québécois projective object of desire is psychologically engaging, the Russian-speaking subject remains "divided and decentered"[36] by the need to embody the most confusing stereotype if ever there was one—that of the mysterious Russian soul. In spite of his enticing presence, the Ukrainian-born actor Gregori Hlady is unable to create an "ideal ego" from the bits of imaginary Russian masculinity (or masculinities) offered by the director-writer, and his Borkine, not unlike a Lacanian *corps morcelé*, crumbles into disparate fragments: a romantic Mafioso, passionate lover, sadistic murderer, reckless drinker, and caring friend. Hlady's histrionics and improvised Russian wail remain a far cry from the great Russian literary tradition with its sacred monsters dominated by the "triad of subversive forces: madness, holiness, and poetry," where the "semiotic overflows its boundaries."[37]

Isabelle Poisannt's *La Fabrication d'un meurtrier* (*The Fabrication of a Murderer*), based on her eponymous book, strains to bring credibility to the stranger's image. Her work marks the outer limits of the cinematic alien's prospect of pre-referendum subjectivity.[38] Here, the male stranger becomes a subject of projective identification, which eventually precipitates the protagonist's transformation.

After his Bulgarian wife has left him for another man, Pierre (Pierre Chagnon) embarks on a journey to find the truth about who she really is—or was—but ends up making unexpected revelations about himself. What he discovers is a far from exotic country and people engaged in a dreary day-to-day struggle for survival in the Communist aftermath. Shot candidly by the Bulgarian Canadian cameraman Ivan Gekoff, the film's representation of the distant land pays off by providing a solid contextual basis for his urgent need to face the beast within. In his wife's hometown, Pierre meets a small, dishevelled man, Momo (Denis Bouchard), who has suffered total amnesia and has no communication skills, but who reacts when spoken to in French. Pierre takes him back to Montreal, where, together with some survival skills, he inscribes onto Momo's *tabula rasa* of a mind a new personality through nightly readings from his secret diaries. The violent personality that Momo acquires as a result is but a projection of Pierre's repressed desire, lurking in the pages of those diaries, for bloody revenge ever since his wife left him.

Figure 26 Still from *La fabrication d'un meurtrier*. Pierre reads his diaries to Momo. Courtesy Amerique Film.

The composite image of the stranger conveyed so far is not unlike the objectified female presence in classical Hollywood cinema, analyzed by Laura Mulvey in her seminal article "Visual Pleasures and Narrative Cinema," but with a twist. While in *Paper Wedding, The Enamoured,* and *Stolen Glances,* male immigrants are construed as the "erotic object of the [female] gaze" or as the sexually fantasized Other,[39] they fail to offer that "more perfect, more complete, more powerful ideal [male] ego" that is supposed to emerge in the process of male viewers' identification with male protagonists on screen.[40] Isabelle Poissant's film exposes unequivocally the reasons for this failure by taking to their extreme the negative tendencies informing the representation of immigrant masculinity in the pre-referendum period: tightly controlled and dependent on a *de souche* protagonist (male or female), the male immigrant (albeit sometimes charismatic) is expected to be mostly silent and psychologically ambiguous.

In addition to its metaphorical function, the hampered verbal exchange of the immigrant could be described psychologically as a regressive process, set in motion by immigration-related identity trauma. To quote Steve Neale's remarks on the silent hero, "silence…absence of language can further be linked to narcissism and to the construction of ideal ego." But if "the acquisition of a language is a process profoundly challenging to the narcissism of early childhood" and as such is associated with "symbolic castration,"[41] then the *de rigueur* acquisition of a foreign language and other accoutrements of the new Symbolic order present an even greater threat of "symbolic castration," which pushes the male immigrant back into the silent narcissistic cocoon of the Imaginary. Kristeva has aptly captured this moment of symbolic linguistic castration: "No one listens to the immigrant...You never have the floor...Your accented speech is quickly erased by the more garrulous...talk of the community. Your speech has no past and...no power over the future of the group...You do not have enough status—'no social standing'—to make your speech useful."[42]

PERENNIAL OUTSIDERS

The outcome of the 1995 referendum brought to a head what Salée calls the "dialogue of the deaf" and revealed the unresolvable differences "between sovereigntists and their mainly immigrant opponents, denounced as the ethnic vote,"[43] thus creating "an impossible situation which largely inhibits consensus, accommodation or discovery of a common ground...at least in the short term." Salée explains this post-referendum dead end using Nietzsche's concept of *ressentiment*, where "saying 'no' to an outsider, to an other, a non-self, is the only creative act of the powerless...*Ressentiment* is about power—who holds it and who does not—and about exclusion—who is an integral part of society and who is not."[44] Such an atmosphere could hardly be fertile ground for representations of immigration-related issues, and the NFB documentaries and docudramas promoting or contesting the success of multiculturalism in Quebec were reduced to a trickle during the post-referendum decade.

The number of fiction films engaging immigrants has since remained consistently low even though the bulk of Quebec films are set and produced in Montreal, one the busiest (multi)cultural centres in North America. Even so, the immediate post-referendum years saw an intriguing shift in representations of immigrant masculinities, stemming from two major factors. First, the "white francophone Quebecois position," which "does not want to be named and is thus naturalized," has ceased to "constitute the exnominated horizon"[45] of these films, and other voices (anglophone and allophone) have begun to be heard. Second, the important films of the post-referendum decade feature immigrant male subjectivity as possible only *outside* the nation, not *of* it or *in* it. If saying "no" to the world of the others is the only creative act of the powerless, it seems to be also an important step toward acquiring subjectivity in a foreign land.

The notion of the immigrant as a perennial outsider was launched by *Les Clandestins* (*Stowaways*), the first film of *pur laine* director Denis Chouinard, made in 1997 in collaboration with the Swiss Nicolas Wadimoff and co-produced by Quebec, Switzerland, Belgium, and France. Along with Lea Pool's *Emporte-moi* (*Set Me Free*, 1999), it comes dangerously close to the Lacanian Real in revealing the messy immigrant experience, which in this case is literally isolated from the host society and "contained" in the claustrophobic

25 square metres of a cargo container. The laboratory purity of this psychological drama allows for an intense focus on the escalating frustration of six refugees (a Russian male, an Arab family of two, a mother and a daughter from Romania, and a teenage Gypsy boy)—a frustration that erupts into racial slurs and brutal violence when their Canada-bound cargo ship breaks down on the high seas and the meagre food and water supplies deplete. Marshall rightfully claims that this universal situation "threatens to unravel the national altogether"; since the "overspill of immigrant and ethnic themes into wider genres and co-productions" is bound to generate a "world text." The director, however, anchors the text by establishing the forces that inadvertently set the tragic chain of bigotry and anger in motion: the Canadian immigration bureaucracy with its policy of $5,000 fines per illegal immigrant brought into the country; and its proxy—the captain of the cargo ship, who will do anything to avoid such fines. In addition, Chouinard interprets this universal drama from the tangible perspective of psychological displacement and chain scapegoating.[46] "The domination/exclusion fantasy [is] characteristic of everyone," says Kristeva. "Just because one is a foreigner does not mean one is without one's own foreigner."[47] Thus Roman (Anton Kouznetzov), the Russian, demonstrates unabashed resentment for the Romanian woman (Simona Maicanescu) and for the Arab male Walid (Moussa Maaskri). Walid responds violently to Roman's challenge but later gangs up with Roman against the Gypsy boy, Sandu (Ovidiu Balan). To quote Kristeva: "As enclave of the other within the other, otherness becomes crystallized as pure ostracism: the foreigner excludes before being excluded, even more than he is being excluded."[48]

In spite of a certain flirtation with stereotypes (the Russian is unequivocally cynical and foul-mouthed, while the Arab is mild-spoken and a practising believer), and thanks to the actors, both Roman and Walid come through quite convincingly. Young Ovidiu Balan's Sandu, however, is the real discovery of the film, for he introduces a new type of immigrant masculinity. Being a Gypsy—arguably one of the poorest and most marginalized ethnic minorities in Central and Eastern Europe—he seems better equipped than the others to survive in a hostile environment. He is fiercely independent, shrugs off harassment, and is the only noble soul, readily sharing his scarce food with little Svetlana (Christelle Sabas). For all the macho rhetoric and knife brandishing of the adult males, it is Sandu who volunteers for the dangerous reconnaissance trips out of the container. Because of his ingenuity, he and Svetlana remain in hiding until the ship reaches Canada, while the four adults are sent to more or less certain death in an open boat. It is true that the survival of the children is a "promise of renewal,"[49] but the ending remains ambiguous regarding the future of Sandu's free spirit as he meets Canadian authorities.

FATHERS AND SONS

The Oedipal and post-Oedipal phases include works mostly by allophone directors, who offer a different spin on the immigrant drama through the family romance and the *masala* genre. Kristeva and the prolific cultural philosopher Slavoj Žižek, like most (post-)Lacanian scholars, generally agree on the basic distinction between the pre-Oedipal and the Oedipal as intertwined aspects of personality development. Thus for both scholars the pre-Oedipal is the order of the irrational Imaginary, the Oedipal that of the rationalized Symbolic. Also, the Symbolic (as an order superimposed on the Semiotic) is an Oedipalized system "regulated by the secondary processes and the Law of the Father... [i.e.] by paternal competition and identification."[50] However, as will become clear from the argument below, Žižek offers a discussion of the Oedipal and post-Oedipal that is more relevant to current social and cultural developments in Quebec and to the complex artistry of the films under scrutiny.

In Chouinard's second film, *L'Ange de goudron* (*Tar Angel*, 2001), scripted by him and shot by Guy Dufaux, one of Quebec's foremost cameramen, the director reflects on the complexity of the actual immigrant experience, foreshadowed by *Stowaways*. It should be noted that, with its naive pathos and weak dramatic structure, *Tar Angel* is less successful than its predecessor. The major redeeming factor is the character of Ahmed, a hard-working, law-abiding Algerian immigrant, who lives in a small Montreal apartment with his fluently francophone family: son, daughter, and pregnant wife (Hiam Abbass). In eager anticipation of the upcoming citizenship ceremony, Ahmed goes about his daily routine spreading tar on rooftops in the bitterly cold Montreal winter. In Quebec fiction cinema, he is arguably the first immigrant shown not in a state of existential angst or at leisure but at his workplace, which strengthens the realism of his character. The immigrant, says Kristeva, is the "one who works... You will recognize the foreigner in that he *still* considers work as a value."[51] In this, Ahmed is strongly reminiscent of the father from *Manuel le fils emprunté* (*Manuel, the Awkward Son,* 1990)—made by another *de souche* director, François Labonté[52] —who is seen briefly toiling in his bakery. Both fathers fit into the stereotype of the ideal immigrant male: a simple, hard-working guy and a family man, happily engaged in manual labour and without pretensions to upward mobility. Overwhelmed by the struggle for survival, however, such a father is doomed to remain outside the linguistic, moral, and political realities of the new Symbolic. Worse, he is doomed to remain outside the world of his own children, and therefore never to become a role model for his son. Not surprisingly, the sons in these films turn for guidance to a surrogate father figure with a tumultuous revolutionary past, who would sanction their radical split with the traditional Law of the Father. *Manuel, the Awkward Son* accentuates the positive development of its twelve-year-old hero from defiant ignorance to enlightened recognition of his complex identity (a Portuguese Canadian, living in Quebec) with the help of a former Spanish civil war guerrilla Alvarez (played by famous Spanish actor Francisco Rabal).

Paradoxically, in his failed attempt to symbolically unite his son Hafid's desires with the Law, Ahmed arrives at a defiant truth not much different from Hafid's, learned from his local mentor. Roberto (Raymond Cloutier), portrayed as a vague reminder of the *felquistes*,[53] gets Hafid involved in an act of electronic terrorism, destroying thousands of files of illegal immigrants in an attempt to prevent their deportation. This highly questionable act, presented with a pre-9/11 romanticism, becomes a turning point in the narrative, which drastically abandons its psychological and emotional rigour and turns intoa tale of an imaginary underground group, nostalgically reminiscent of the FLQ's early years. Its muddled agenda involves picturesque and even acrobatized (*à la* Cirque de Soleil) actiions, ranging from environmental activism to human rights protest. Hafid's girlfriend, Huguette (Catherine Trudeau), a tattoo artist, dabbles as a group leader in defiance of Roberto's radicalism. This implausible imaging of the Québécois is yet another failed attempt to "find a purely formal resolution in the aesthetic realm of real social contradictions." By reversing the pre-referendum paradigm of representation—now it is the *de souche* majority that is seen as mysterious and irrational—*Tar Angel* becomes a veritable cinematic metonym for what Salée calls "dialogue of the deaf" and what Marshall views as the "absence of Quebec national metadiscourse."[54]

The rejection of Ahmed's authority by his son Hafid serves as a catalyst for the father's movement toward a new subjectivity. He persuades Huguette to help him find Hafid, and their scenic trip deep into the Quebec North ends tragically when Hafid, at a secret airport base, is kicked to death by police officers when he attempts to sabotage the deportation of a group of aliens. The subversive activities of Hafid and his co-plotters, construed under the obvious influence of the French *Beur* films and their urban ghetto rebels,[55] reach their height with Hafid's gratuitous death as the only possible way out of the narrative impasse. Raba Aït Ouyahhia, as the rebellious son, is particularly unconvincing compared to Zinedine Soualem, the famous French actor of Arabic origin, who brings a taciturn credibility to Ahmed, a mild but strong man of very few words. His silence is ever changing: in the beginning it is the depressed muteness of a *pater familias* who feels emasculated—or symbolically castrated—by the inability to understand and control his growing children and to provide for his expectant wife. But during the search trip his growing silence is of a completely different kind, especially against the backdrop of Huguette's loud and somewhat tasteless eccentricity. On the surface, his silence is the logical outcome of his many troubles, but on a deeper level it is the result of the disturbing proximity of his son's sexy girlfriend, with whom he is forced to share a room. While she freely exposes her shapely body as she would in front of an older brother or a friend, it is doubtful whether the director has realized the unexpected dimension that his film acquires through this "explosive, incestuous danger, which always lurks beneath the surface of such a reliable desexualized relationship."[56] It is Ahmed's subtly implied ability to "stop before the precipice" of the taboo violation that shapes him as a "resigned and reconciled... figure of the reserved silent father... [who] is not the bearer of paternal authority, of the Symbolic Law, but something... more ambiguous and mysterious"—a non-paternal father, if there ever was one.[57]

Strangely enough, the final scene, meant as a sarcastic anti-climax, actually restores the balance. Ahmed, and his wife, daughter, and newborn son, at a dull ceremony, receive their Canadian citizenship with silent dignity. It remains doubtful, however, whether this new immigration status will affect Ahmed's self-imposed exile as a "non-paternal father" or a sage, residing outside the Symbolic of his new nation.

FATHERS AND DAUGHTERS

Two auteur films by female immigrant directors of Jewish origin, released almost simultaneously in 1999—Lea Pool's *Set Me Free* and Michka Saal's *La Position de l'escargot (The Snail Position)*—also construct their male protagonists' subjectivity outside of the nation. Both films resemble the Oedipal pursuits of *Léolo* but are closer to two of Mordecai Richler's semi-biographical *bildung* sagas: *The Apprenticeship of Duddy Kravitz* (filmed in 1974 by Ted Kotcheff, a Bulgarian Canadian) and *St. Urbain's Horseman* (turned into a television miniseries in 2007 by Peter Moss). Myriam, a Tunisian Jewish beauty (Mirella Tomassini), is Saal's transparent stand-in, and the fragile teenager Hana (Karine Vanasse) is Pool's alter ego. The two heroines rival Richler's young males in their painful but rewarding acceptance of their ethnic and religious otherness, sexuality, and intellectual yearnings, and especially in coming to terms with their fathers. They see this bond as an existential burden that they would like to cast aside (thus the title of Pool's film, "set me free") but that they nonetheless drag along, not unlike a snail its home, as the double meaning of Saal's film title suggests.

In the nostalgic world of *Set Me Free*, set in Quebec in the early 1960s, the drama of the immigrant father takes centre stage. David Cohen is a frustrated writer, a macho and a bully, but the director brings out the tragic dimensions of his personality, his palpable loneliness as a stranger and a misfit in a foreign land and even in his own family. His eagerness to find an excuse for his brutality in the wounds of the Holocaust rings hollow as his fragile and ill wife (Pascale Bussières) suffers in silence and supports the family. The commanding presence of the Yugoslav Miki Manojlovic, Emir Kusturica's fetish actor (*When Father Was Away on Business,* 1985; *Underground,* 1995) enhances David Cohen's hysterical personality. According to Lacan, "the biggest uncertainty, related to the hysterical subject is his/her sexual position, therefore the question 'Am I a woman?' and 'What is a woman?' is of equal importance to both male and female hysterics...The term 'woman' here refers not only to some biological essence, but to a position in the Symbolic order; it is synonymous with the term 'feminine position,'"[58] which amounts to symbolic castration. Like many frustrated immigrant males, David Cohen clings to bullying, which he believes will keep his masculinity intact and protect it from the threat of feminization brought about by his bread-winning wife.

The hysterical subject, Žižek says, is a "subject whose very existence involves radical doubt and questioning, his entire being is sustained by the uncertainty as to what he is for the other."[59] David Cohen's fear of having his professional and intellectual abilities doubted by persons of authority—his friends, his publisher, his wife's parents, and ultimately his timid wife all deny him the recognition he craves—ensnares his subjectivity between the ego-driven morass of the Imaginary and the ever-elusive Symbolic. Unexpectedly for both of them, it is his empathic daughter, mesmerized by his lavish poetic skills in more than one language, who emerges as his significant Other. Their candid rapport is, however, devoid of the explosive, incestuous danger that threatens the relationship between Ahmed and Huguette. Hanna's devotion to her father could hardly be explained by penis envy, which, according to Freudians, turns girls toward their fathers and away from their mothers, integrating them into the patriarchal social order. Clearly Hanna, who is just coming to terms with her budding lesbianism, would never be completely free from desiring her gentle and beautiful mother instead of her hysterical father. Thus the father's symbolic castration and the daughter's coming-out drama converge in a common right of passage as they painstakingly search for subjectivity in a world where, to quote Robin once again, the "*trop plein* / too full (Quebecois) identity...is manifested through the absolutization of differences." Curiously, *Set Me Free* suggests that the unsettling experience of the male immigrant-cum-outsider may have less to do with the social, cultural, and national(ist) policies of the day than with purely existential issues, related to deeper psychological and emotional layers, which can never be brought into the open or healed.

In Saal's film, the long absence of the father has emotionally crippled the daughter, and his re-emergence seems—in spite of the pain—to have a healing effect on her. Referring to Lacan, Žižek stresses the vital importance of the prohibition effect of the "paternal metaphor," which, "far from hindering... [the sexual] realization...guarantees its condition." "No wonder," continues Žižek, "that the retreat...of the Symbolic Law entails the...rise of sexual indifference...[In the post-Oedipal universe] the suspended paternal Law... returns in the Real in the guise of the multitude of 'undead' spectral appari-

Figure 27 Atanas Katrapani in *Home*. Coutesy Amazone Film.

tions which intervene in our daily lives."⁶⁰ Thus twenty years into their separation, Myriam's father Dédé (Victor Lanoux) is conjured up as a controversial symbol of stability or rather a counterbalance, one that is needed to catapult her out of her emotional entrapment between two lovers and into mature sexual realization. Dédé, however, remains one among many outward projections of Saal's anxieties or "undead" apparitions invoked—a long deceased mother, a garden with a fountain, the African Mediterranean shores, and so on—and this enhances the auto-therapeutic effect of Saal's only fiction film. It disperses the nostalgic anguish, which had blurred the boundaries between there and here, then and now, between the Imaginary and the Symbolic, in her earlier short cinematic essays *Loin d'où* (*Far from Where*, 1989) and *L'arbre qui dort rêve à ses raciness* (*A Sleeping Tree Dreams of Its Roots*, 1992).

The "paternal metaphor" re-emerges in the intimately confessional narratives of the young Montreal filmmaker Phyllis Katrapani as a synonym of the ever-illusive idea of home. Born in Montreal to a family of immigrant intellectuals, she has devoted all three of her films—*Ithaca* (1997), *Home* (2002), and *Within Reach* (2006)—to the ever-pressing need for stability and home, epitomized by her father Atanas Katrapani. The documentary *Ithaca* is a tribute to his Ulysses-like quest for a spiritual home somewhere between Canada and his native Greek islands, and in the docudramatic *Home* he appears in the role of the archetypal Poet, who helps the young artistic couple discover a virtual homestead in their creativity. Again, the masculinity of the immigrant father is actualized outside the nation, but this time he is not forced there by social and historical circumstances as in Pool's film; neither is he seen as a narrative foment of the daughter's intricate process of self-realization, as in Saal's. Not unlike David Cohen, Katrapani's father figure comes through as a narcissistic but inspiring outsider. Yet his idealized presence remains secluded in the domain of his daughter's creative Imaginary, far from the harsh and controversial realities of his actual existence.

Significantly, the angst-ridden narratives of Pool, Saal, and Katrapani, with their male protagonists condemned to linger as eternal outsiders, evoke sentiments strikingly similar to those of art films by *de souche* directors, who have, however, so far resisted featuring the immigrant Other as a psychologically and intellectually complex character.

FATHERS AND MOTHERS

The films of Pool, Saal, and Katrapani stand quite apart in tenor and mode from those made by their English Canadian counterparts, in which the clash of the "*trop plein* / too full" immigrant identities with the "*trop vide* / too empty" or pulverized identities of the locals often takes the form of a mosaic narrative pastiche of what I have defined as the *masala* genre,[61] and rarely that of a linear drama as in the films by the three Québécois directors, discussed above.[62] Prime examples of the *masala* aesthetics are the bittersweet irony of Hong Kong Canadian Mina Shum's *Double Happiness (*1994) and *Long Life, Happiness, and Prosperity* (2002); or the hilariously acerbic observations on the incongruity of Indian tradition and Canadian values that the characters negotiate in *Bollywood, Hollywood* (2002) by the Indian Canadian Deepa Mehta; or Srinivas Krishna's *Masala* (1991), a magic realist story by another Indian Canadian about the reconciliation of the main character with his Canadian-ness, the only identity he has been left with since the early death of his parents in the Air India bombing.

What Pool, Saal, Katrapani, Mehta, and Shum agree on is that the process of integration, of negotiation and renegotiation of male identities, shaped by the Symbolic order of the old country is invariably frustrated by the oftentimes unanswerable question of what it is to be male in the new country. They have also demonstrated that, under the pressures of sudden disempowerment brought on by immigration, both men and women tend to turn into formidable custodians of traditions. As Kristeva writes: "On foreign soil, the religion of the abandoned forebears is set up in its essential purity and one imagines that one preserves it better than do the parents who have stayed 'back home.'"[63]

The only Quebec film that comes close to the self-conscious stance of the *masala* genre is *Mambo Italiano* (2003). Émile Gaudreault's film, a comedy of manners based on the popular play by the Italian Canadian Steve Galluccio, offers another look at immigrants outside the heterosexual mainstream. As Tom Waugh has aptly put it in *The Romance of Transgression in Canada,* its "commercial success was due in part to the flashes of authenticity and over-the-top humour tapped from Galluccio's own experiences growing up and coming out in Montreal's Little Italy, and in part to timing...[as] distributors [were] eager for a repeat of the humungous 2002 G-rated ethnic sleeper *My Big Fat Greek Wedding.*"[64]

Following the familiar curve of the *masala* genre, *Mambo Italiano* focuses on the secret (homosexual) love affair between two second-generation Italian Canadians, Angelo Barberini (Luke Kirby) and Nino Paventi (Peter Miller), only to contrast it with their parents' shock when the truth comes out. Like Toula Portokalos's father in *My Big Greek Wedding,* Jade's parents in *Double Happiness,* or Rahul's grandmother and mother in *Bollywood/Hollywood,* the Barberinis (Ginette Reno and Paul Sorvino) and mamma Paventi (Mary Walsh) expect their sons to proceed in life like good (heterosexual) kids and get themselves (Italian) spouses and live happily ever after. Indeed, under the relentless pressure of his unassailable mother, Nino does bend and marry an Italian girl in a big church wedding.

As with the other *masala* films, the humour here originates in the incompatibility of the parents' conservative expectations, which is linked to the religious and social traditions of the old country, on the one hand, and the modern North American realities of their children's love lives, on the other. Curiously, in the romanticized universe of these films, the archetypal family arrangement has undergone a transformation from patriarchy to matriarchy: while the father is either dead (*Bollywood/Hollywood*), or silenced by the unintelligible English chatter of his daughters (*Double Happiness*), or reduced to a charmingly harmless whiner as in *Mambo Italiano* (but most notably in *My Big Fat Greek Wedding*), the mother is construed as "archaic" (in Kristeva's terms): the "mother-as-primordial abyss...the cannibalizing black hole from which life comes and to which all life returns,"[65] the one who literally makes or breaks her children's happiness. In spite of the overall light tone of the *masala* genre, there is hardly a redeeming quality to the Chinese mother's declaration that she would rather see her daughter dead than married outside her own (*Double Happiness*); or to the intended tragic effect of the grandmother's spells on Rahul's Caucasian girlfriend (*Bollywood/Hollywood*); or to the emotional blackmail that mamma Paventi applies to "straighten" her son's ways. Yet at the same time, both Toula and Angelo owe the freedom to be themselves to their good, fat, and understanding mothers.

The run-away success of Gaudreault's film is due in part to a steadily growing number of films that focus on the Italian immigrant experience in Quebec. As it is, most of these works are associated one way or another with the above-mentioned versatile Italian Canadian actor Tony Nardi. One of his first appearances on film is in *Caffe Italia Montréal* (1985), a feature-length documentary by Italian Canadian director Paul Tana, which reflects on the waves of Italian immigration to Montreal since the turn of the last century. Since then, Nardi has landed two major roles (among many others) as an Italian Canadian in mainstream TV series: in *Bonanno: A Godfather's Story* (1999), a Canadian *Godfather* cycle spinoff; and in *Il Duce canadese* (*The Canadian Duce*, 2004), the story of Italian Canadians in Montreal during the Second World War. He has also co-scripted and played the main part in Paul Tana's art film *La Sarrasine* (1992).[66]

Mambo Italiano has also benefited from the successful historical and social integration of Italians in Montreal and in Quebec—an integration that has ensured the success of *La Sarrasine*. Says Marshall: "The Italians are... [a] representative group in Quebec society, for they are proximate and adjacent to the Quebecois *de souche* through their Catholicism, Latin origins and narratives of modernization."[67] Clearly, Italian immigrants—and by extension, Italian Canadian filmmakers—have broken a hole in the rigid fence surrounding the "*trop plein / too full*" Québécois *de souche* identity, through which they can converse as equals over their absolutized differences.

However, the commercial success of *Mambo Italiano* is seen as a mixed blessing by Waugh since it seems to "cater mostly to the tastes of the outsiders...who found its caricatural humour...most hilarious"—unlike queers, who "recognized the moments of truth but found much of the gaps and excesses troubling, not the least of which was the downbeat ending...[having] Nino end up as...unrepentant and unproblematic paterfamilias."[68] Despite the film's shortcomings, its Italian pedigree and the homosexuality of its characters have defied the reign of straight francophone *de souche* heroes on the Quebec commercial screen, paving the way for the unprecedented popularity (especially in English Canada) of bold coming-out stories such as Jean-Marc Vallée's *C.R.A.Z.Y.* (2005).

BEYOND THE NATION?

Over the last decade or so, Quebec society has been shifting from an "enhancement of essentialized identities" toward a slow "recognition that identity is translational, hence fluid and mutable" and that it must take place within a "construction of a civic space acceptable to all."[69] However, this process has not been without setbacks, such as the current reasonable accommodation controversy, which could be seen simultaneously as a painful lapse and as an attempt to ward off a pending crisis.

Precious few works reflecting on the interaction between immigrants and locals have been made since the turn of the new millennium. In the light of Jameson's concept of film as a "socially symbolic act," the histrionics and sensationalism of their style could be interpreted as panic-stricken, even hysterical attempts to find "resolutions in the aesthetic realm of...insurmountable social contradictions." While *Tar Angel* basks in the mystifying representation of its *de souche* characters, Gabriel Pelletier's *Karmina I* (1996) and especially *Karmina II* (2001) relegate his vampire-immigrants to the Real of its mock-horror aesthetics. On the other hand, Robert Morin, with *Le Nèg* (*The Negro*) (2002),[70] drives the Québécois *de souche* majority into (self)flagellation in his over-the-top effort to exorcise the horrors of racism in rural Quebec.[71]

Catherine Annau's documentary *Just Watch Me: Trudeau and the 70s Generation* (*Frenchkiss – La génération du rêve Trudeau*, 1999) stumbles upon a possible explanation for this impasse. In their candid comments, her thirty-something "talking heads" from the hopeful Trudeau generation try to make sense of the divisive referendum outcome in light of Trudeau's legacy of bilingualism and multiculturalism, which they were raised to believe would remedy all social and cultural evils, including Quebec separatism. What transpires from the film is that the nationalist ideal still holds sway over the Québécois *pur laine* interlocutors but is just one of the layers constituting their postmodern, multiple, or fragmented identities (as Lacan would have it). In Žižek's terms, the post-Oedipal "disintegration of paternal authority" in general (and the crisis of Trudeau's nation-building ideas in Quebec in particular) has resulted in "*symbolic* prohibitive norms" being replaced by "*imaginary* ideals (of social success, of bodily fitness)." At the same time, "the lack of symbolic prohibition is supplemented by the re-emergence of ferocious superego figures," dominating a "subject who is becoming increasingly narcissistic," who "perceives everything as a potential threat to his precarious imaginary balance"—that is, to his/her personal well-being.[72] In this way the production of (capitalist, modern) national culture, built by Trudeau and "organized by renunciation and the Law-of-the-Father," is gradually replaced by the production of a postmodern one of "consumption, organized around a curious inversion of the superego," the paradox of which is a subject terrorized by the superego injunction to enjoy.[73] This postmodern moment is described by George Steiner as a "casino culture," one that no longer "feels like culture of accumulation and learning...[but] like a culture of *disengagement, discontinuity and forgetting*."[74]

The painful "emptying" or liquefying of Québécois *de souche* identity under the injunction to enjoy is linked to the emergence of a transnational, transcultural type of narcissistic personality, bent on "bio-political (self) control...excessive fear of harassment and...'self-realization'"[75]—a phenomenon that accounts for the tentative "fluidity and mutability" of other Quebec (immigrant, anglophone) identities in the spheres of biopolitics and pleasure-seeking "casino" cultural industries, in which instant gratification of any and all forms of lack is indiscriminately supplied by new technologies.

A powerful illustration of this volatile inconsequentiality of cultures and identities can be found in *Nos vies privées* (*Our Private Lives*, 2007). In his second film, Denis Côté, a young film critic turned director, isolates and observes two aliens with entomological precision and gracious engagement attainable only by those who, in Kristeva's view, "feel foreign to themselves":[76] "After Stoic cosmopolitanism, after religious universalist integration, Freud brings us the courage to call ourselves disintegrated in order not to integrate foreigners and even less so to hunt them down, but rather to welcome them to that uncanny strangeness, which is as much theirs as it is ours."[77]

Following a lengthy Internet affair, Milena (Anastasia Liutova), a middle-class *Montréalaise* of Bulgarian descent, and Philip (Penko Gospodinov), a fashionable photographer living in Sofia,[78] meet in a secluded chalet, tucked into the Quebec countryside. The obscurity of their Bulgarian origins (and that of the young actors) and their language (the film is subtitled) are, however, immaterial to the character development and serve as what Žižek calls the "Thing," a Hitchcockian McGuffin, "a piece of the Real...a guarantor of meaning in the Symbolic," which each viewer could "invest with his or her own scenario of desire."[79] As a "world text," the film "unravels the national altogether" but transcends the existentialist universalism of 1960s modernist cinema and lands in an emotional and spiritual desert, enunciated as rural Quebec. The film is shot in washed-out colours; its space is experienced as nurturing but threatening, not unlike the archaic pre-Oedipal *chora* (a Kristevian term borrowed from Plato), where the characters find precarious comfort in their passion. Under the pressing requirements to indulge, however, the couple's voracious erotic experiments soon subside into an unbearable boredom, compelling them to venture outside the chalet. Despite the new thrills, found briefly at the local fair, where Philippe flirts heavily with a local girl, the relationship sinks ever deeper into abject silence after Milena accidentally kills Guillaume, the neighbour (Jean-Charles Fonti), for making passes at her. Guillaume, whose ethnic identity is just as irrelevant—Milena notes that he speaks French with a (non-Québécois) accent—is the third character in the film, but survives barely long enough to utter some pedestrian remarks, including the crucial ones about her sexy figure and accent. Milena evidently experiences his unsolicited interest in her as a threat serious enough to justify the shocking outcome, which she chooses to keep secret. The ferocious superego figures threatening Philippe's narcissistic imaginary balance, however, originate in the world of nature, not in the world of culture. The startling forest noises he hears while taking pictures are endured as demonic—an impression enhanced by the old car dump, which is eerily reminiscent of the post-Oedipal wasteland in Andrei Tarkovsky's "zone" from *Stalker* (1979).

The rotting corpse, hidden deep in the forest, is returned to the Real—that is, it gets repressed in Milena's unconscious—while Philippe's undead spectral apparitions linger on, eliciting his growing inadequacy vis-à-vis Milena's intimidating beauty and increasingly enigmatic behaviour. Philippe's

Figure 28 Milena and Philippe in *Nos vies privées*. Courtesy Denis Cote.

emasculation mirrors the narrative jump into the realm of the demonic: after his macho self-confidence peaks at the fair, where the crowd cheers his victory over a slippery piglet in the muddy arena, loneliness and depression set in, and he gradually succumbs to drinking. The ending reflects the unravelling of characters and narrative.[80] Stuck in the chalet for another fortnight until Philippe's departure, with no desires left to indulge, the couple roam from one seedy joint to another like vampires seeking nourishment. During the final bar sequence, the camera gradually abandons Philippe's hapless figure and focuses on Milena's dance, which is reminiscent of an ancient sacrilegious ritual.

The demise of the couple is actually engraved into the matrix of their Internet relationship, defined by Bauman as "emotional skiving,"[81] a metonymic recognition of a fundamental inability or reluctance "to enter in spontaneous interaction with real people,"[82] prompted by extreme narcissism. Once the code of "skiving" is violated by "continuous proximity (dubbed 'presenteeism')," real life bursts in with its threats of "being rejected, stripped of what we are, being refused what we wish to be."[83] Paradoxically, the events that come to pass in this looming no man's land involve three people whose emotional numbness and fear of moral choice and commitment render them equally unsympathetic regardless of ethnic origin, age, or beauty.

Côté's vision of the liquid modern world is certainly chilling. Without advocating return to the "symbolic authority of the paternal Law as the only way to halt our slide toward the global chaos of autistic closure and violence,"

Žižek, in his most recent magnum opus *The Parallax View*, implies that mandated enjoyment and consumption (satisfying the lack of being and the lack of having) should not blur our realization of the intricate capitalist game of obfuscating class struggle as multiple struggles of ethnicities, cultures, and genders.[84]

CONCLUSION

The representation of male immigrants during the pre-referendum decade merely as narrative vehicles or as objects of displaced desires through identification, projection, or transference foregrounds the stalemate in the construction of gender identities outside their specific historical contexts. Ignoring the "social and political nature of male subjectivity" and privileging only "its habitual dependence on some form of intimacy,"[85] the "intimate other" has resulted in a series of ineffectual, sketchy characters (such as the seductive Latin American Pablo, the compassionate Bulgarian sailor, the Italian charmer Nino, the volatile "New" Russian Borkine, and the stateless, intellectually challenged Momo) stuck in the world of narcissistic desires of their filmmakers. And while the post-1995 referendum films have failed to offer any purely formal resolutions in the public or private sphere of the protracted "dialogue of the deaf" between locals and immigrants, they have creatively contained the latter within an enclosed space *outside* the Québécois nation—a space whose perfect metaphor is the stowaway container. Whether ineffective fathers, illegal immigrants, or frustrated young adults—and whether gay or straight—Roman, Walid, Sandu, Hamid, Manuel, Ahmed, David Cohen, Dédé, Atanas Katrapani, Angelo, and Nino (and Myriam and Hanna for that matter) are imagined as impaired outsiders to Québécois mainstream *de souche* society and identity. Some of them (Roman, Walid, Hamid, Nino) are crushed or "normalized" under the pressures of the law and the family tradition. Others (Ahmed, Manuel, David Cohen, Atanas Katrapani, Angelo) survive those pressures because of their arduously attained new identities as dreamers, poets, and sages, dwelling beyond the traditional social and political spheres of male subjectivity formation. And while Philippe's liquid identity seems most adaptable to a postmodern existence in the comfortable limbo between the local and the global, and away from the social and the political, it is nonetheless shattered by his need to deal with the Real beyond the territory charted by his sexual desires and material demands.

About two hundred years ago Karl Marx warned that a "spectre is haunting Europe, the spectre of Communism," and mobilized the world proletariat for an epochal, protracted, and largely successful class struggle. Now Bauman has followed suit with his warning about the "spectre of redundancy hovering over the liquid modern world," which is turning its "labours and creations" into cultural and human waste. Says Bauman:

[The forces of globalization] reshuffle people and play havoc with their social identities. They may transform us, from one day to another, into refugees or economic migrants...They may withdraw our certificates of identity or invalidate the identities certified... We hate those [displaced] people because we feel that what they are going through...may well prove to be, and soon, a dress rehearsal of our own fate.[86]

Abiding by the prophecies of Marx and Bauman, the world is on the brink of yet another protracted and epochal conflict between the privileged and the deprived, one in which antagonistic social, national(ist), and political discourses and identity practices engender exclusionary ethnic and gender formation. This conflict could become nastily external, with newcomers clinging ever so strongly to their solid gender identities and traditions (oftentimes strikingly intolerant). Or it could be assuaged by keeping "inner distance" from the universal injunctions of cravings and desires, planted there by the "game of shadows" of the globally polarizing intricacies of "virtual capitalism."[87] Or it could be transcended through the spiritual vistas of wisdom and of the arts.

NOTES

1 In his latest works, Zygmunt Bauman has replaced the terms "modernity" and "postmodernity" with "solid modernity" and "liquid modernity."
2 Zygmunt Bauman, *Wasted Lives: Modernity and Its Outcasts* (Oxford: Polity, 2004), 116.
3 Regine Robin, quoted in Bill Marshall, *Quebec National Cinema* (Montreal and Kingston: McGill–Queen's University Press, 2001), 267.
4 Julia Kristeva and Kelly Oliver, *The Portable Kristeva* (updated) (New York: Columbia University Press, 2002), 271.
5 Ibid., 271.
6 Daniel Salée, "Quebec Sovereignty and the Challenge of Linguistic and Ethnocultural Minorities: Identity, Difference, and the Politics of Ressentiment," *Quebec Studies* 24 (Fall 1997): 6–23 at 9.
7 September–October 2007. The debate was triggered by the Hérouxville town council controversial's "code of conduct," drafted in January 2007 to ensure measures against those practices of immigrants that were deemed unsuitable by the 1,500 residents of Hérouxville (a town completely devoid of immigrants). The "code of conduct" quickly garnered international attention, prompting heated province-wide hearings and challenging the provision of reasonable accommodation—a legal obligation to modify a law or a norm when it is contrary to fundamental rights stipulated in Canadian Charter of Rights and Freedoms. In fact, most of the Québécois presenters opted for no accommodation whatsoever.
8 This study is partly based on my postdoctoral research at York University (1999–2001), conducted under the guidance of Professor Peter Morris; and on a conference paper delivered at the Making It Like a Man! conference at the University of Regina, June 2004.
9 Société de développement des entreprises culturelles.
10 Conseil des arts et des lettres du Québec.

11 Pierre Falardeau's *15 février 1839 / 15th of February, 1839* (2001) venerates an iconic Quebec event: the execution by the Anglos of the patriots from the Lower Canada rebellion. Partly financed by Telefilm Canada.
12 Falardeau's *Octobre/October* (1994) is about Pierre Laporte's assassination by the FLQ (Front de Libération du Québec, a left-wing terrorist group, operating from the early 1960s through 1970 and precipitating the October Crisis of 1970) and is told from a separatist point of view. Produced by the NFB.
13 *Land of Hope* was released in 1996 but was conceived and shot before the October 1995 referendum.
14 Kristeva, *The Portable Kristeva,* 281.
15 Tania Modleski, *Feminism Without Women: Culture and Criticism in a "Postfeminist" Age* (New York: Routledge, 1991), 7.
16 Fredric Jameson, *The Political Unconscious Narrative as a Socially Symbolic Act* (Ithaca: Cornell University Press, 1981), 79.
17 Sherry Simon, "The Intimate Other: Representations of Cultural Diversity on Quebec Film and Video (1985–1995)," in *Textualizing the Immigrant Experience in Contemporary Quebec,* ed. Susan Ireland and Patrice J. Proulx (Westport: Praeger, 2004), 51–57.
18 Julia Kristeva in Madan Sarup, *An Introductory Guide to Post-Structuralism and Postmodernism,* 2nd ed. (Athens: University of Georgia Press, 1993), 122–26.
19 Ibid., 122–26.
20 Ibid., 122–26.
21 Ibid., 122–26.
22 Michel Brault's film rhymes with anglophone Giles Walker's *90 Days* (1985), an earlier, lighter version of a similar story in which the gender roles are reversed. Walker's romantic narrative, also geared to a heterosexual marriage, features Blue (Stefan Wodoslawsky), a soft-spoken intellectual and a loner, who challenges his arrogantly philandering friend Alex (Sam Grana) in their bid for the perfect relationship by choosing a mail-order bride from Asia. As it happens, he turns into a latter-day Pygmalion in his clumsy efforts to introduce his Asian wife-to-be (Christine Pak) into the North American way of life. The result is some hilarious moments of cultural incongruity. Whatever poignancy is left to the social message is blunted by rendering the ominous immigration machine harmless: the officer in charge of the deportation procedure in the event the marriage fails to materialize within 90 days (hence the title) is depicted as an overweight, pipe-smoking, sweet-natured fellow. Since *90 Days,* the female immigrant *other* has reappeared twice on Quebec screens, again in films by male Anglo directors: as a mysterious revolutionary (*So Far Away and Blue,* 2001, dir. Roy Cross) and as a steamy lover (*Café Ole,* 2000, dir. Richard Roy). Instead of bringing a refreshing change, however, the female gender seems to only enhance exploitative narrative stereotypes, established a decade or so earlier and discussed here.
23 Simon, "The Intimate Other," 57.
24 According to Adrian Carr, "the ego-ideal, Freud suggested, is established through three different forms of identification: 'First, identification ... in the original form of (an) emotional tie with an object; second, in a regressive way... (as) a substitute for a libidinal object-tie (*or narcissistic identification* [author's italics]), as it were by means of introjection of the object into the ego; and thirdly... (as) a new perception of a common quality shared with some other person who is not an object of the sexual instinct." Carr, "On Reading Emotions and Emotionality in Organizations," in *Radical Psychology* 1, no. 1 (Summer 1999): http://radicalpsychology.org/vol1-1/Carr.html#Note1, accessed April 25, 2011.
25 Simon, "The Intimate Other," 55.

26 Benoit Pilon's fiction short, *Regards voles / Stolen Glances* (1994, 34 min.) is yet another case of narcissistic identification, where a lonely *de souche* female protagonist fantasizes about an absent Romanian immigrant by entering his apartment and going through his things only to meet him just before the open ending.
27 Marshall, *Quebec National Cinema*, 278.
28 Jean Laplanche and J.B. Pontalis, *The Language of Psycho-Analysis* (New York: Norton, 1974), 210.
29 Christine Ramsay, "Leo Who? Questions of Identity and Culture in Jean-Claude Lauzon's *Léolo*," *Post Script* 15, no. 1 (Fall 1995): 23–37.
30 Kristeva, *The Portable Kristeva*, 281.
31 Young Pascale Bussières appears in her debut role as one of the girls, Chantal.
32 Kliment Denchev is arguably one of the few immigrants to have achieved brief but vigorous popularity amongst young TV audiences in the early 1980s with his Radio-Canada show *Klimbo*.
33 Kristeva, *The Portable Kristeva*, 282.
34 According to psychoanalysis, the main characteristic of transference is the "experience of feelings to a person which do not befit that person and which actually apply to another. Essentially, a person in the present is reacted to as though he or she were a person in the past... The person reacting with transference feelings is in the main unaware of the distortion" Ralph R. Greenson, *The Technique and Practice of Psychoanalysis* (New York: International Universities Press, 1967), 151–52.
35 However, it is also believed to form the basis of mature psychological processes such as empathy and intuition. Spillius identifies multiple motivations for projective identification, including controlling the object, attaining its attributes, purging a bad quality, and avoiding separation. Elizabeth Bott Spillius, *Melanie Klein Today: Developments in Theory and Practice* (London and New York: Routledge, 1988), 81–83.
36 Kristeva in Sarup, *An Introductory Guide*, 122–26.
37 Ibid., 122–26.
38 The film was released in March 1996 but was ready by October 1995.
39 One of the best examples of fetishizing immigrant male sexuality is Jacques Benoit's 1989 film *Comment faire l'amour avec un nègre sans se fatigue*, which, while reaching out for global commercial success with its generic *mise-en-scène* and supranational (some say stereotypical) treatment of (white) female and (black) male sexuality, leaves the familiar terrain of Quebec national cinema and comes closer to what Marshall defines as "world texts," which tend to "unravel the national altogether." Marshall, *Quebec National Cinema*, 283.
40 Laura Mulvey in Steve Neale, "Masculinity as Spectacle: Reflections on Men and Mainstream Cinema," in *Feminism and Film*, ed. E. Ann Kaplan (Oxford: Oxford University Press, 2000), 256.
41 Neale, "Masculinity as Spectacle," 257.
42 Kristeva, *The Portable Kristeva*, 279.
43 On referendum night on 30 October 1995, Jacques Parizeau, then Quebec premiere and leader of the sovereignist Parti Québécois, declared that the referendum had been lost because of "money and the ethnic vote," a remark that cost him his political career.
44 Salée, "Quebec Sovereignty," 12.
45 Roland Barthes in Marshall, *Quebec National Cinema*, 269.
46 Displacement is generally described as a neurotic defence mechanism, one that separates emotion from its real object and channelsg it to someone or something less menacing in order to avoid dealing directly with the real threat. In scapegoating, negative feelings are displaced onto powerless minorities.

47 Kristeva, *The Portable Kristeva*, 282.
48 Ibid., 282.
49 Marshall, *Quebec National Cinema*, 283.
50 Kristeva in Sarup, *An Introductory Guide*, 122–26.
51 Kristeva, *The Portable Kristeva*, 277.
52 Written by Gerald Wexler, the scriptwriter of *Margaret's Museum* (1995), the story about the rebellious twelve-year-old son of Portuguese immigrants has more literary than cinematic value in spite of some good acting and moments of bittersweet humour.
53 Members of the FLQ.
54 Marshall, *Quebec National Cinema*, 279.
55 Mathieu Kassovitz's *La Haine/Hate* (1995) is the most famous example of this trend.
56 Slavoj Žižek, *The Fright of Real Tears: Krzysztof Kieślowski between Theory and Post-Theory*. London: British Film Institute, 2001), 128.
57 Ibid., 127–28.
58 Jaques Lacan in Dylan Evans, *An Introductory Dictionary of Lacanian Psychoanalysis* (London and New York: Routledge, 1996), 48.
59 Slavoj Žižek, *Cogito and the Unconscious*, Vol. 2 (Durham: Duke University Press, 1998), 81.
60 Slavoj Žižek, *The Ticklish Subject: The Absent Centre of Political Ontology* (London: Verso, 1999), 367–68.
61 Usually involving self-ironic, self-conscious representations of the immigrant experience by immigrant script-writers and directors, mixing (therefrom the name *masala*, "mixed spices") genres and modes.
62 Or in Deepa Mehta's debut feature *Sam & Me* (1991).
63 Kristeva, *The Portable Kristeva*, 282.
64 Thomas Waugh, *The Romance of Transgression in Canada: Queering Sexualities, Nations, Cinemas* (Montreal and Kingston: McGill–Queen's University Press, 2006), 418.
65 Barbara Creed, *The Monstrous-Feminine: Film, Feminism, Psychoanalysis* (London and New York: Routledge, 1993), 25.
66 This lavishly shot period epic, set in Quebec at the end of the nineteenth century, represents a novelistic insight into the uneasy relations between a Sicilian immigrant community and the *de souche* Quebecois provincial society, seen through what Marshall calls a "post-Quiet Revolution optic." Marshall, *Quebec National Cinema*, 281. The tensions are brought to a head when the Sicilian immigrant Giuseppe (Tony Nardi) accidentally kills a local bully. Giuseppe's wife Ninetta (Enrica Maria Modugno) stays behind against the will of her imprisoned husband and his family, who want her to go back to Italy. The murder, the ensuing trial, and even the growing tensions between immigrants and locals set in motion the story of Ninetta and the Lamoureux family, who assist her bold efforts to save Giuseppe's life and to establish herself in Montreal after his death on the gallows. The director strikes a delicate balance between Italian immigrants and Québécois *de souche;* between an outside and an inside look at the events, allowing for what Mikhail Bakhtin would call dialogical interpretation of characters and situations and of their "infinite open-ended possibilities." In addition, the temporal detachment of *La Sarasine* from sensitive contemporary issues, compounded by its "Quebec style of 'quality'" (ibid., 281), help the director avoid stereotyped, monological representations of immigrants of the sort that beset Quebec cinema of the 1990s, discussed above.
67 Marshall, *Quebec National Cinema*, 282.

68 Waugh, *The Romance of Transgression in Canada*, 418.
69 Salée, "Quebec Sovereignty," 19.
70 Deliberate silence on a subject could also be read as hysterical reaction.
71 Late at night the police are summoned to a Quebec village, where an elderly lady has been shot to death and a teenage black boy (Iannicko N'Doua-Légaré) is found in coma, bruised and beaten. The audience is invited to reconstruct the truth, *Rashomon*-style, from the misleading cues of the witnesses, three men and two women. The film is a blunt picture of frustrated Québécois *de souche* masculinities, whose violent crisis is triggered by the silent (!!!) presence of the black boy, who happens to be in the wrong place at the wrong time. Yet again, as in the films from the pre-Oedipal phase, the black boy is only a catalyst for the cathartic outburst of these unemployed or underemployed characters. *The Negro*, however, is the only film so far to openly tackle the sensitive issue that immigrants are constantly seen in Quebec as a visible sign of cultural threat.
72 Žižek, *The Ticklish Subject*, 368.
73 Angelo Restivo, "Lacan According to Žižek," *Quarterly Review of Film and Video* 16, no. 2 (1997): 193–206 at 201.
74 Bauman, *Wasted Lives*, 117.
75 Slavoj Žižek, *The Parallax View* (Cambridge, MA: MIT Press, 2006), 297.
76 Kristeva, *The Portable Kristeva*, 281.
77 Ibid., 290.
78 The capital of Bulgaria.
79 Restivo, "Lacan According to Žižek," 198.
80 According to Kristeva, the "symbolic control of the various semiotic processes is, however, tenuous and liable to break down resulting in an upheaval in the norms of the smooth understandable text." Kristeva in Sarup, *An Introductory Guide*, 122–26.
81 Bauman, *Wasted Lives*, 126.
82 Ibid., 130.
83 Ibid., 127–28.
84 Žižek, *The Parallax View*, 297.
85 Julian Stringer, "'Your Tender Smiles Give Me Strength': Paradigms of Masculinity in John Woo's *A Better Tomorrow* and *The Killer*," *Screen* 38, no. 1 (1997): 25–41 at 38.
86 Bauman, *Wasted Lives*, 128.
87 Žižek, *The Parallax View*, 384.

III: THE MINORITY MALE

CHAPTER 7

The "Hood" Reconfigured: Black Masculinity in *Rude*

D.L. MCGREGOR AND SHEILA PETTY

The concept of masculinity has emerged as an important area of concern as theorists seek to broaden understandings of gender. As Stephen Whitehead explains, "the concept of the masculine subject is useful" because "it highlights the multiple discursivity that posits individuality on the subject, while also acknowledging the performative character of this constitution."[1] However, despite Whitehead's assertion that it is possible, even desirable, to conceive of masculinity as a fluid state in which "ideal representations of man/masculinity are not grounded and inevitable," there remains an insistence on masculine subjectivities that are structured as gendered first, a position that gives gender primacy over other social forces.[2] Most important, these constructs serve to erase or diminish other categories of experience by assuming that there is an imaginary social space that is not only masculine first, but also equally shaped by similar flows of Western history. Such constructs fail to deal with the reality of "minoritization," the process by which social "groups are denied access to power" through the systemic racism and social barriers created by a dominant that is determined to relegate them to "subordinate power relations."[3]

For black theorists who have, historically and socially, been in the position of challenging the integrity of white universalisms and Eurocentric histories that deny them equality, Whitehead's insistence on gender first poses a significant problem. If, as Whitehead would have it, the ontology of masculinity is premised "as a primary force, an unconscious activity that is independent of linguistic expression or interpretation," then how can a black man, denied full subjectivity by a system that privileges white imperatives, have equal access to these processes?[4] Frantz Fanon answers this inquiry cogently when he argues that "the black man has no ontological resistance in the eyes of the white man," because black subjectivity is fixed in "crushing objecthood" by "white eyes, the only real eyes."[5] From this perspective, achieving status as a gendered male subject whose experience is modified by race is an utopic impossibility because histories of slavery, colonialism, and exile have defined such individuals first by race and then by gender. In other words, the real-life experiences of such individuals confirm that they are black men as opposed to men who are black.

As constructs, black masculinities are highly contested and are negotiated within "the racial and cultural boundaries of a counter-hegemonic blackness which stands for the black nation, the black family, and the authentic black (male) self."[6] Bordered by depictions "in the popular imagination...as naturalized and commodified bodies in the case of athletes; as symbols of menace and threat in the case of black gang members; and as noble warriors in the case of Afrocentric nationalists," the black masculine subject straddles "competing and conflicting claims" all seeking to define the relations among race, masculinity, and society in a hostile environment.[7] In the African Canadian context, black male identities are faced with negotiating many competing imperatives: as Cecil Foster notes, though "we Blacks in Canada have our own history and experiences that make our expectations and levels of national and cultural consciousness," the polycultural makeup of the black population renders it entirely possible to ask the question, "Is there really such a thing as a black—or, as some call it, an African—community in Canada?"[8] Comprised as it is of "several distinct segments," including "Caribbean immigrants, African immigrants and those who have lived in North America for several generations," it is tempting to view the Black Canadian population as "so culturally different and dispersed that there is no real bond or common denominator" among such diverse black peoples.[9] The answer, suggests Foster, is deceptively simple: all of these multiple communities within a community are united by "the challenge of realizing that the mainstream does not differentiate among these groups"; in this way is created the commonality of experiencing life as black individuals in a Canadian context.[10] However, there are consequences to living in shifting flows of "black performativity" and multiple "black political identifications" where black male identities must be forged and practised in unstable circumstances.[11] The irony, as George Elliott Clarke succinctly states, is that "the constant challenges" to African Canadian identities "create fissures and disjunctures in the culture that make it what it is—as fraught with indefinition as Canada itself."[12] Placed in this perspective, it would seem that establishing black male identity in Canada is fraught with tensions and contradictions.

Black populations in Canada have met these challenges by developing powerful and constructive strategies for coping with the unique demands of living within Canadian borders. In speaking of black artists across disciplines, Rinaldo Walcott argues that their "imaginative works" fashion intricate "analyses" within "black diasporic invention and (re)invention" that stake out "the space of the in-between, vacillating between national borders and diasporic desires, ambitions and disappointments."[13] This is the ground staked out by filmmaker Clement Virgo in *Rude* (1995), the first feature film directed by an African Canadian filmmaker. *Rude* sparked a vigorous debate among film theorists interrogating the nature of black identity and masculinity in Canada. As Walcott notes, the film "opened up the space for thinking differently about Canada as a racialized space, and more specifically, a Black space."[14] Though the film is comprised of several narrative strands that are interwoven into a complex depiction of African Canadian identities, it is through the character of Luke that Virgo offers a normative depiction of black masculinity as a shifting territoriality, created at the interstices of global flows and practices of blackness encompassing Caribbean, African American, and Canadian cultures.[15] In particular, this chapter will explore how Virgo's creative engagement with the formal properties of the black action film genre in this narrative strand offers rich analytical possibilities for considering how African Canadian black masculinity dialogues with, and departs from, other constructs of black masculinity.

RUDE, THE FIRST CANADIAN BLACK ACTION FILM

Rude comprises three story strands about three young black individuals who face life-altering choices over the course of an Easter long weekend: Maxine, a window dresser, deals with the painful decision of aborting an unplanned pregnancy; Jordan, an aspiring boxer, is involved in a gay-bashing incident that forces him to confront his own homosexuality; Luke, once a high-profile drug dealer, returns home to his family after being incarcerated for his criminal activities. Virgo then unites these disparate lives through Rude, a pirate radio broadcaster whose commentary provides a social context through which to view the struggles of both individual characters and the community as a whole.

Of the three story strands, Luke's is significant because Virgo undertakes a deconstruction of what Walcott has termed the "two primary problems" delimiting discussions of African Canadian identities, namely, "the proximity to and influence on Canada of America" and "the dominance and impact of American cultural production on Canada."[16] As seems to be the case in virtually all aspects of Canadian life, America's presence on the border as "one of the most powerful capitalist and imperialist nations" in the world has influenced how Black Canadians view themselves and how they are viewed both within Canada and in the larger context of the global environment.[17] For example, in discussing a 1992 study for Multiculturalism and Citizenship Canada, Foster points out that "the mainstream Canadian culture sees no difference between the Blacks in Canada and those in the United States" despite the fact that black communities in the two countries have vastly different cultural perspectives.[18] This failure to recognize that "the black communities in the two countries—although claiming the same source of Africanness and even some of the same heroes and spiritual leaders—are strikingly different in their attitudes and history" accounts in large part for Canada's failures when "it tries to adopt solutions and models that might have worked in the United States."[19] To a degree, the very notion of black Canadianness operates under dual pressures: it is "an absented presence" operating under the threat of "erasure" as a result of both its invisibility in the official histories of Canada and an overwhelming, imperialist threat of a blackness as defined by American imperatives.[20] If, as Walcott argues, "the specific and localized concerns of black Canadians" are generally dismissed as "null and void," the quest becomes one of staking an affirmative space for a blackness in Canada that can differentiate itself from flows of African American blackness and also locate black identities within a shifting black diasporic and transnational context.[21]

In *Rude*, Virgo fashions Luke's story strand as a critique of the influence of American media stereotypes by framing the story within, and in opposition to, what has been described variously as the "black action film" or "gangsta rap" genre.[22] Tremendously influential in the early 1990s, these films "apply a clever concatenation of trendy rap music, rap singers turned actors, and volatile filmic action to the political and social issues that concern African Americans."[23] Including works such as "John Singleton's *Boyz n the Hood* (1991), Mario Van Peebles's *New Jack City* (1991), Ernest Dickerson's *Juice* (1992), Bill Duke's *Deep Cover* (1992), and Matty Rich's *Straight Out of Brooklyn* (1991)," these films "feature characters that oppose, flourish, or are assimilated into the political and social climate of poverty, crime, drugs, and violence" as articulated "within the spatial confines of the inner-city projects or the ghetto."[24] Generally "'male-focused,'" these films sought to explore the stressors facing young black males as they defined their masculinity within social forces intrinsically shaped by white racist oppression.[25] This was not an unproblematic goal: though the "rise of the black urban gangster" as a central figure in these narratives undoubtedly gave voice to "the source(s) of frustration and rage" experienced by young black males, it also served to "to construct or reconstruct the image of black masculinity into one of hyper-blackness based on fear and dread."[26] The desire "to turn dominant representations of black male bodies into a contested cultural field" may have arisen as a means of alleviating the inequities of "inner-city life" by increasing "awareness and political pressure for positive change"; but, under pressure exerted by "the capitalist politics of the Hollywood system," the end result is that the films present "stereotypical constructions of black characters"—constructions that divide young black males into either bad or good social subjects depending on their conformity to white precepts of social behaviour.[27] From this perspective, black action films might be perceived on one level as reinforcing certain racist stereotypes already at play in white society.

THE AFRICAN-CANADIAN 'HOOD: A COMPLEX SITE OF BLACK MASCULINE IDENTITIES

Instead of adopting the stereotypical binary oppositions so often forwarded in black action films, Virgo enters into a dialogue with the social impetuses that create them, thereby transforming what might be described as "Americanité" experience into a complex "imagining of an African-Canadian 'hood."[28] For example, Luke functions as neither a "good" black male nor as a "gangsta," but rather occupies a conflicted ground bridging the two extremes as the hub of the narrative strand. Ranging inwards to this centre are a variety of competing influences: Jessica, the mother of Luke's son, represents the apex of socially acceptable blackness as an idealistic policewoman; Yankee, Luke's white ex-employer, symbolizes destructive social forces as a drug lord determined to bring Luke back into the fold; John, Luke's young son, is filled with longing for the material things he sees all around him; Reese, Luke's younger brother, aspires to surpass Luke's legendary "success" as a drug dealer. Each of these characters will present Luke with a challenge that will ultimately change the way in which he views himself as a black male and as a subject of, or perhaps more accurately as an *agent within*, society.

As is the case with many black action films, the setting of *Rude* serves as "a process of rearticulation" of the city as "both a utopia—as a space promising freedom and economic mobility—and a dystopia—the ghetto's economic impoverishment and segregation."[29] Yet Virgo's depiction of Toronto's Regent Park projects without ever attaining the specificity of locale accorded to "South Central L.A., Watts, Bed-Stuy, Red Hook, and Harlem," all neighbourhoods depicted in black action films.[30] Instead, Virgo de-emphasizes specificity in favour of a more fluid concept of city and neighbourhood, one that reflects the diasporic space in which Black Canadian masculinities are articulated. This is established within the opening of the film, which begins with a slow-motion shot of a striking male lion as he turns and walks toward the camera. This image, which will be restated in each of *Rude*'s three storylines, connects the film's characters metaphorically to Africa, but also to Rastafarian symbolism, thus evoking Caribbean contexts. The lion thus reflects the flows of diasporic consciousness within which Luke's black masculinity will be transformed.

As the opening progresses, a series of long shots of Toronto set the urban backdrop against which Luke's narrative strand will unfold. Images of the city rising out of the distant lakeshore are accompanied by the voice-over narration of Rude's pirate radio broadcast as well as by several shots depicting details of an inner-city neighbourhood. Though Walcott argues that the neutrality of locale implied by this strategy suggests that "place is clearly not an issue," there is an alternative way to view Virgo's ideological intent.[31] Like the lion, the city is subject to currents of histories that circulate across and through it, making Toronto a specific locale but also linking it to the rise of other metropolises around the globe. When Rude states that her "signal stretches from the land of the Zulu Zulu nation to the land of the Mohawk nation," she is connecting the imperial power of Toronto to past and present histories of colonization, including those experienced by black diasporic peoples. In this way, Toronto becomes both a literal symbol of the Canadian dominant and a figurative imaginary where Black Canadians must, as Rude describes it, "steal Babylon's airwaves" in order to force a re-evaluation of "their immigration policy." Against this backdrop, it can be argued that Luke's redefinition of his black masculinity occurs in an imaginary geography that is simultaneously Canadian and global in scope.

Masculinity is also placed at the heart of *Rude*'s ideological concerns in the opening. Rude's narration, which graphically depicts sexual congress from a male perspective, becomes the frame within which each of the film's three story strands are introduced through a montage of images. For example, the first images of Luke show him burning a portrait of himself, representative of his pre-incarceration life. As the burning portrait is depicted in a close-up that reveals a contrast between Luke's younger self and the older one obliterating that image, Rude comments: "This one is for the boys. The D-O-G-S." Here he is signalling that an interrogation of black masculinities will drive each storyline. Furthermore, by introducing Luke in a context of artistic cultural production, Virgo is providing him with a roundness of character that resists an either/or categorization of his character. Luke's position as artist and convicted drug dealer suggests the presence of both constructive and destructive social traits and is representative of the conflicted ground he occupies as the narrative strand's central focus.

Another sequence in the opening makes this position clear. Depicted in a medium-long shot, Luke stands in front of a striking wall mural and contemplates the collage of images, which include depictions of slavery, of Christianity, and of urban decay. A young black man approaches him and tries to buy drugs. When Luke does not respond to his request, the young man states: "Aw, c'mon man. I know you. I know who you are." As the film develops, it is revealed that the mural is Luke's and that its location marks the "corner" where he used to sell his drugs. The juxtaposition of the mural as an evocation of diasporic context in a Canadian social space, and the corner as a place of transaction, serves to foreground the economic oppression of Eurocentric commerce and profit as a determining factor in Luke's conflict. In addition, the fact that it is a young black man who approaches Luke as a customer demonstrates one of the narrative strand's central ironies: Luke's economic advancement is shown to be based on the victimization of his own race. In this way, the mural's images are an expression of "spatiality and historicism" that "can be construed as entering into a dialectic which exposes discursive power structures."[32] Functioning as signs of "physical and psychological containment," the mural and the corner thus serve as a crossroads and as a reminder that Luke's current crisis is the result of global histories of repression interlocked with one another.[33]

The economic discourse that Virgo constructs in *Rude* demonstrates a commonality with similar concerns voiced in black action films. The link between black masculinity and an intense investment in material gain has been cited numerous times as one of the causal effects of racial inequality in African American societies. For example, as bell hooks argues persuasively, "by the late sixties and early seventies most black men had made the choice to identify their well-being, their manhood with making money by any means necessary," but were barred from advancing through education and other means because of poverty and the barriers created by systemically racist cultural milieux.[34] This prompted "a shift in class values" where making money became "the primary marker of individual success" rather than "how one acquire[d] money," allowing "hustlers in black communities to be seen as just as hardworking as their Wall Street counterparts."[35] Viewing "the market-driven capitalist society" as a new "plantation" where "the everyday work world becomes the location where that [racist] dominance can be enacted and reenacted again and again," some black males turned to the "vibrant yet deadly drug economy" as "an outlaw job arena where money—big money—can be made."[36] Thus, as a result of its inherent inequities, contemporary dominant society emerged "as a modern Babylon without rules, without any meaningful structure of law and order, as a world where 'gangsta culture,'" for some segments of black society, had become "the norm."[37] Hence, gangsta culture, and by extension the drug trade, often function in black action films as an almost romanticized space where the ultimate fall of the gangsta figure is of less consequence than the power of his rise.

Virgo offers considerable evidence that economic factors play a determining role in Luke's temptation to rejoin his old life. But Luke does not accept this proposition without contestation: his African Canadian masculinity may be strongly influenced by economic concerns, but it is also defined by and against other imperatives. To maximize this strategy, Virgo constructs a series of ideological interchanges between characters that explore drug culture as an expression of "autodestruction within the black community" as well positing other constructive social discourses that could offer succour from it.[38] The character of Reese offers a case in point. Reese is first introduced as a prototypical gangsta as he and his companion, Junior, shake down another drug dealer in a stairwell while the drug dealer's fourteen-year-old lover looks on. Depicted in a high angle close-up that reinforces his entrapment, the young drug dealer is brought to his knees by Junior, who holds a knife to his throat. Desperate to strike a deal, the dealer offers Reese the girl as a hostage until he can make good on the money he owes. Reese pulls the terrified girl to him and, portrayed in a low-angle two shot, he pulls out a gun and forces the girl to point it at the drug dealer. Against the backdrop of the dealer's off-screen pleas, Reese offers to look after the girl if only she will pull the trigger. Finally, the girl does so and the weapon strikes on an empty chamber, revealing that the gun is empty. On the surface, the psychological violence of Reese's actions situates him within the gangsta stereotype, but the fact that the gun is not loaded suggests that he falls somewhat short of achieving that status. This is not to suggest that the weapon is unloaded due to incompetence on Reese's part: it is clear that he is aware of the weapon's status and that he is using it for intimidation purposes. However, the fact that Reese does not resort directly to violence also argues for a kind of hollowness at the centre of the stereotype, as if Virgo is suggesting that Reese only possesses the *illusion* of power rather than power itself.

Virgo furthers this position by foregrounding "capitalism's complicitous links to the narcotics network" through the relationship between Yankee and Reese.[39] Yankee's status as a white drug lord to a degree departs from the general convention of black action film, in which white complicity with the economics of the drug trade is generally an implied subtext: by linking white power explicitly to the drug trade, Virgo is positing it as a "new" plantation where historical discourses of racism and slavery are made contemporaneous. This creates a category outside the so-called "dualism of the 'good' and 'bad' nigger," by providing a racist social backdrop against which the auto-destruction of black characters unfurls.[40] Furthermore, the choice of the name "Yankee" for this character ironically alludes to the dominance of American economic interests in Canada as well as evoking a colonizing relationship founded on manifest destiny. This is illustrated in the club scene where Yankee is first introduced. It opens with a series of medium and close-up shots of African artifacts and painted images of Africans. Virgo then juxtaposes these with a medium shot of Yankee positioned in the centre of the screen, discussing a financial transaction. The connection between purchased or owned objects and commerce, along with Yankee's position of absolute control, renders him as a metaphorical slave owner profiting from black labour. Later in the scene, Yankee's "ownership" of Reese is demonstrated as Reese informs him that he has told the drug dealer who owes money to pay it to him directly at the club. Yankee's response is depicted in a striking canted medium shot in which Reese is positioned in the foreground on left frame while Junior is positioned in the background near the centre of the frame: Yankee's location, on the right, is given visual dominance through lighting that not only highlights his whiteness but also serves to isolate him from his black employees. While Yankee lectures him like a child, Reese is portrayed in a tight high-angle close-up that accentuates his discomfort. The contrast between Reese's downcast eyes and nervous smile and Yankee's evident revelry in his own superiority makes it abundantly clear that any power Reese believes this affiliation affords him is subsumed by their master–slave relationship.

The relationship between Luke and Yankee has similar overtones. When Yankee hears that Luke has returned, he goes with Reese to Jessica's apartment to try and convince Luke to return to his employ. At this point in the narrative strand, Luke has been trying to re-establish his relationship with his young son. Alone in the apartment while Jessica is at work, Luke and John are depicted in a medium shot sitting at a table as Luke makes the child a sandwich. As the camera dollies in, John complains that Luke is putting on too much peanut butter, a comment that illustrates how Luke's incarceration has distanced him from knowing John's most basic tastes. Nevertheless, there remains an awkward affection between the two, evidenced by the tenderness on Luke's face at the end of the sequence as he gently touches John as he eats. This scene of domesticity is disturbed by the arrival of Reese, who walks into the apartment without knocking, trailed by Yankee. Virgo selects a medium-long shot of the dining room to depict this encounter, thus visually emphasizing the forces gathering against Luke. Luke is seated on frame left, with the table acting as a barrier emphasizing his separation from both Reese and Yankee, who take standing positions on frame right. John, seeing the fast food that Reese carries, moves frame right to join him and greets his uncle with an ease that is clearly absent from his relationship with his father. With Reese, John, and Yankee assuming visual prominence on right frame, Luke's isolation is complete.

After Reese takes John out of the room, Yankee and Luke are left alone to speak. In a tone that initially suggests deferral, Yankee expresses respect for Luke because he did not inform on other members of the operation when he was arrested. This is, however, an illusory act because the argument Yankee advances for Luke rejoining his organization is intended to directly undermine Luke's sense of masculinity. For example, when Luke refuses to discuss the matter because of John's presence, Yankee suggests that "this concerns his future too," implying that working for him is the only way for Luke to fulfill his duty to support his son. Later in the discussion, Yankee reiterates this position when he states: "You gotta make money to take care of the kid. You gonna make Reese keep doing it? That's what he's been doing since you were in the joint." Each of these comments is intended not only to accentuate Luke's helplessness in a system stacked against his economic advancement, but also to position Yankee and the narcotics trade as the only means for Luke to secure his son's future.

Interestingly, Virgo at no time suggests that Luke is an inadequate or disinterested father; rather, he uses his open concern for his son's future as a means to generate debate. The pressure to measure success by the ability to provide materially is demonstrated during a scene where John assists Luke as he adds to his mural. As Luke paints, he notices John's silence and asks him what is wrong. John replies that he does not want to return to school because "everyone in school has new everything. New baseball cap, new sneakers, new everything." The disdain that John expresses for the "no-name running shoes" purchased for him by Jessica indicates how status is defined by material possessions: without these items, John clearly feels alienated from his peers. Later, as they prepare to return home, Luke impulsively gets John an ice cream from a cart tended by an older boy. As John unwraps the treat, Luke reaches into his pocket and suddenly realizes that he does not have the money to pay for it. The older boy tells Luke to forget it, stating that "I get at least one [unpaying customer] a day." Virgo first portrays Luke's reaction to this dismissal in a close-up that accentuates his deep humiliation and allows the audience to contemplate the poignancy of Luke's inability to provide even such a simple luxury.

What differentiates Virgo's approach to this issue is that he offers a counter-narrative to the importance of material possessions as a marker of status through the influence of Jessica's character. As a police officer, Jessica may, on the surface, appear to embody what Guerrero has described bitingly as "upwardly mobile, black 'exceptions'" who prosper in white society by conforming to appropriate dominant social constraints.[41] Such "deracinated, 'safe' middle class characters" make up the reverse side of the good–bad black dichotomy as representations of how conformity to white society is necessary for even a modicum of economic advancement.[42] However, Jessica's character lives straddling two worlds, as evidenced by her acceptance of Reese, whose role in the narcotics trade would logically be known to her. By accepting some financial assistance from Reese during Luke's incarceration and by allowing him to play a continuing role in John's life, she is evidencing the tolerance toward hustling that hooks describes as the result of recognizing the "demoralizing effects of not receiving a living wage" in a corrupt work arena that demands black males endure "racialized humiliation."[43] In this way, Jessica is inscribed as both within and outside the good black stereotype.

The relationship between Luke and Jessica represents a major departure from the general construction of male–female relationships in black action films, which often relegate female characters to minor, often highly sexualized roles that are subordinate to those of males. Most important, interactions between Luke and Jessica are often depicted in two-shots that emphasize shared visual space. For example, during an intimate scene in their bedroom, the couple discusses the ramifications of Jessica's decision to become a police officer. At the culmination of this discussion, during which Luke evidences both a distrust of police authority and fear for her safety, Luke and Jessica are depicted in a medium two-shot. Though Luke sits on the edge of the bed and

Jessica is kneeling on the floor at his feet, the composition of the shot gives them equal importance in the frame. Thus, when Jessica ends the discussion by stating, "This is what I want to do," and Luke signals his acceptance of her decision by replying, "Okay," there is a strong sense of mutual respect and understanding between them.

A similar structure is used in a later scene where Luke discusses the implications of his economic situation and his inability to pay for Luke's ice cream. Once again in the bedroom, Luke and Jessica are portrayed in a loosely framed two-shot that dollies in as Luke sits on the bed drawing and Jessica sits on the edge facing him. The physical arrangement of the shot creates a shared social space that transcends their individual discussion and places it in the larger context of the struggles facing black culture. When Luke frames his humiliation in material terms by saying, "What am I to give my son when he is a man? I gotta give him more than just life," he is expressing his ability to provide for John's material well-being as a marker of his own masculine worth as well as his worth as a father. Jessica's response—"You gave him more than just life"—serves to suggest that more is at stake here than material needs. Though she reaches to touch him, Luke is unable to meet her gaze, and this sense of separation is enhanced by the intimate composition of the shot. Hence, despite their shared social space and investment in their culture, Luke and Jessica are estranged because of their differing visions of affirmative black masculinity.

Despite Jessica's assurance, Luke decides to return to Yankee's employ. However, he does not make this decision without conflict, as evidenced during a scene that takes place in Yankee's office as they discuss the details of Luke's return. In a canted medium shot, Luke's back is visible through a barred window, with a striking African shield suspended from the roof above him. Yankee faces him, and as he holds out his hand to Luke, says triumphantly, "Welcome back, my man." Yankee's use of the possessive in describing him indicates that he has "purchased" Luke and that Luke has surrendered his autonomy as a black male. However, this is not an easy surrender: both the composition of the shot and Luke's refusal to shake hands over the deal indicate entrapment in a system that he cannot seem to escape as long as he values his masculinity in terms of material wealth.

Once Luke has assumed this subordination, three events serve to alter the trajectory of his life. Standing against his mural, Luke resumes his old sales territory on the corner. Portrayed in a long shot that places him in context with the images of slavery and colonialism behind him, Luke radiates misery, a state that is heightened as the camera slowly zooms in. This shot is intercut with a close-up of the lion, eyes held in direct address, walking out of darkness and into the light as it approaches the camera. The juxtaposition of these images suggests that Luke is redefining himself in light of an intrinsic strength drawn from flows of black culture. This position is affirmed a little later in the sequence when, in a restatement of his first encounter at the wall, a young black man importunes him for drugs. At first Luke does not respond, but when the customer demands, "Are you a dealer, or aren't you a dealer?" Luke finally states simply, "No. I'm not." By making this assertion, Luke begins the process of recovering his power to determine his own future.

The second part of this redefinition of Luke's masculinity occurs during a confrontation he has with Reese in a stairwell. Reese, fired by Yankee, has been catapulted into a crisis of identity by the erosion of his self-image. When Luke comes upon him in the stairwell, Reese is doing drugs. As Luke approaches, he pulls the gun on him and they struggle for control. Reese pulls away and, aiming at Luke's head, discharges the empty weapon repeatedly. Then, tossing the gun to Luke, he calmly sits down and continues preparing his fix. In this sequence, Reese acts, in effect, as a mirror of what Luke may become if he remains in Yankee's employ. Furthermore, the empty weapon and his pointless action of discharging it at Luke, rather than at Yankee who is the true source of his devaluation, reflects Reese's impotence. By using this tactic, Virgo is suggesting that, far from being individualized, the seeds of self-hatred and auto-destruction exemplified by black-on-black violence occur in a racist social matrix that must be acknowledged. To make this point, Virgo depicts Luke in a loosely framed close-up as he stands, backed into a corner, looking down at Reese. Luke's words—"When are we going to grow up, Reese? When do we become men?"—suggest that in order to surmount the barriers of society, black males must become actively engaged in resisting auto-destruction and self-hatred by refusing the economic structures that condemn them to preying on one another.

Luke initiates this agency by quitting Yankee's employ, stating, "You're looking for a nigger. I am not a dealer." The choice of terminology serves as a critique of the gangsta image as it conflates this economic position with slavery. It also signals Luke's determination to separate himself from forces that seek to ensure the oppression of black males by taking responsibility for his own life and masculine identity. Though "the message of personal responsibility" may be viewed as an appeal to socially friendly "conservative values" that "appeal to a politically mixed black audience and to a crossover white audience," Virgo nevertheless seeks to demonstrate that the values associated with the exercise of black masculinity have a profound effect on the quality of life in black communities.[44] The ending of Luke's narrative strand bears this out when Jessica, who sees Luke on his corner, makes him leave the apartment. John, distraught by this turn of events, runs away to the street, where he is picked up by Yankee, who in turn forces a confrontation with Luke in front of the mural. The culmination of the conflict occurs when Yankee points a gun at John's head and Luke, desperate to protect his child, puts the empty weapon to Yankee's head. Yankee's response to this move is to declare: "I'm going to blow his fucking brains out and save him the trouble of being blown away when he's twenty." As Virgo cuts to a long shot composed of Luke on frame left, Yankee on frame right, and John positioned in the centre background between them, a chain of violence is created that flows from Luke to Yankee and finally to John. In effect, Virgo is signalling that the ultimate stakes of the narcotics trade are not the material wealth it provides but the cycle of violence it perpetuates on young black men. It is significant that the standoff is resolved when Jessica arrives on the scene and shoots Yankee: the final image of the narrative strand is a medium long shot that depicts Jessica, John, and Luke as a restored family unit. Though Virgo has been criticized for creating "a homogenized black subject" through the reification of heterosexual black masculinity as "'correct' black masculinity," a charge supported by this ending, it is worthy of note that Luke's redefinition of self is accomplished in part by the agency of a black woman whom he treats as an equal.[45] This suggests that however the politics of the action are read, black masculine paradigms must also reject what Derrick Bell describes as "the macho sexism of their white counterparts" in favour of "work[ing] toward a more natural and healthy equality between the sexes."[46]

CONCLUSION

In *Rude*'s critique of, and dialogue with, the stereotypes of the black action film genre, Virgo seeks to explore both points of contact and the significant differences between black diasporic minority experiences in Canada and those in the United States. The appropriation of the gangsta paradigm, which he transforms into a global framework, allows Virgo to depict Black Canadian masculinity from an interstitial perspective that best contextualizes black experience on the unstable ground of the Canadian nation.

NOTES

This chapter expands on ideas that originally appeared in *Contact Zones: Memory, Origin, and Discourses in Black Diasporic Cinema* by Sheila J. Petty (Detroit: Wayne State University Press, 2008). Reprinted by permission.

1. Stephen M. Whitehead, *Men and Masculinities: Key Themes and New Directions* (Cambridge: Polity, 2002), 208.
2. Ibid., 219.
3. George S. Dei, "Racism in Canadian Contexts: Exploring Public and Private Issues in the Education System," in *The African Diaspora in Canada: Negotiating Identity and Belonging*, ed. Wisdom J. Tettey and Korbla P. Puplampu (Calgary: University of Calgary Press, 2005), 94.
4. Whitehead, *Men and Masculinities*, 213.
5. Frantz Fanon, *Black Skin, White Masks,* trans. Charles Lam Markmann (New York: Grove Press, 1982), 110, 109, 116.
6. Herman Gray, "Black Masculinity and Visual Culture," *Callaloo* 18, no. 2 (1995): 401–5 at 404.

7 Ibid., 402.
8 Cecil Foster, *A Place Called Heaven: The Meaning of Being Black in Canada* (Toronto: HarperCollins, 1996), 18, 20.
9 Ibid., 21.
10 Ibid.
11 Rinaldo Walcott, *Black Like Who?* (Toronto: Insomniac Press, 1997), xii.
12 George Elliott Clarke, "Contesting a Model Blackness: A Meditation on African-Canadian African Americanism, or The Structure of African Canadianité," *Essays on Canadian Writing* 63 (Spring 1998): 1–55 at 17–18.
13 Walcott, *Black Like Who?*, xii.
14 Rinaldo Walcott, ed., *Rude: Contemporary Black Canadian Cultural Criticism* (Toronto: Insomniac Press, 2000), 7. Though John McCullough gives a nod to *Rude*'s grounding in "black film aesthetics," he argues that the film's "effects lies not in its verisimilitude but in its storytelling" (23). According to McCullough, this places the film "fully within the Canadian film canon" because "its narrative structure is visual, connotative, contemplative and finds its exemplary form" in a "mythic tale." John McCullough, "*Rude*; or the Elision of Class in Canadian Movies," *CineAction* 49 (1999): 19–25 at 23. This position is perhaps somewhat misleading because *Rude*'s mythic narrative and aesthetic structure owe as much or more to the narrative and aesthetic traditions of black diasporic cinema, a differentiation that places the film both within and outside the oeuvre of English Canadian cinema. Hence, though *Rude* certainly offers commentary on what it means to be black in Canada, and has a place in the Canadian film canon, its aesthetic conventions are predominantly drawn from outside this tradition.
15 The film's two other story strands present alternative discourses of masculinity in addition to Luke's. For example, Maxine's story focuses on her struggle to decide the fate of her unborn child after the breakup of her relationship with André, a mysterious man whose face is never seen on-screen and who comes to represent the absent black male. The final storyline concerns Jordan, a boxer who is struggling with his homosexual identity in the face of his own community's disparagement of such sexual orientation.
16 Walcott, *Black Like Who?* 20.
17 Ibid., 20.
18 Foster, *A Place Called Heaven*, 24.
19 Ibid., 25.
20 Walcott, *Black Like Who?* xiii.
21 Ibid., 26.
22 Kenneth Chan, "The Construction of Black Male Identity in Black Action Films of the Nineties," *Cinema Journal* 37, no. 2 (1998): 35–48 at 35.
23 Ibid., 35.
24 Ibid., 35, 36.
25 Ibid., 35.
26 Ibid., 36; Gray, "Black Masculinity," 403.
27 Gray, "Black Masculinity," 403; Chan, "The Construction of Black Male Identity," 36.
28 Christopher E. Gittings, *Canadian National Cinema: Ideology, Difference, and Representation* (London and New York: Routledge, 2002), 257. Gittings further argues that Virgo's choice was based on attracting production funding, a position that Virgo substantiated when he stated that funders would recognize the specific fundamentals of a 'hood film as "commercial elements." Ibid., 256.
29 Paula J. Massood, "Mapping the Hood: The Geneology of City Space in *Boyz N the Hood* and *Menace II Society*," *Cinema Journal* 35, no. 2 (1996): 85–95 at 88.

30 Ibid., 88.
31 Walcott, *Black Like Who?* 57.
32 Chan, "The Construction of Black Male Identity," 43.
33 Ibid., 44.
34 bell hooks, *We Real Cool: Black Men and Masculinity* (New York and London: Routledge, 2004), 17. hooks notes that "black males whose brute labor had helped build the foundation of advanced capitalism in this society had never been paid a living wage." As a result, "more than any group of men in this nation black males have realistically understood wage slavery" and are "far less likely" to accept the proposition "that employment will lead to self-esteem and self-respect." hooks, *We Real Cool*, 19, 21.
35 Ibid., 18, 19.
36 Ibid., 25, 24, 19.
37 Ibid., 25–26
38 Chan, "The Construction of Black Male Identity," 40.
39 Ibid., 39.
40 Ibid., 42.
41 Ed Guerrero, "The Black Man on Our Screens and the Empty Space in Representation," *Callaloo* 18, no. 2 (1995): 395–400 at 397.
42 Massood, "Mapping the Hood," 87.
43 hooks, *We Real Cool*, 24.
44 Chan, "The Construction of Black Male Identity," 43.
45 Walcott, *Black Like Who?* 60.
46 Derrick Bell, "The Sexual Diversion: The Black Man / Black Woman Debate in Context," in *Traps: African-American Men on Gender and Sexuality*, ed. Rudolph P. Byrd and Beverly Guy-Sheftall (Bloomington: Indiana University Press, 2001), 171.

CHAPTER 8

"Keepin' It Real"? Masculinity, Indigeneity, and Media Representations of Gangsta Rap in Regina

CHARITY MARSH

> *The police organize us. We're all Aboriginal and they all stick us in one place.*
> —ROBIN FAVEL, A.K.A. BURDEN

The city of Regina, Saskatchewan, is burdened with a highly contentious reputation as one of Canada's most violent and socially impoverished cities. This reputation is mapped onto the neighbourhoods known as "North Central" and the downtown "Core" through a discourse of both "true" accounts and sensationalized racist and gendered narratives offered up by a multitude of media sources. That discourse is then often reproduced by minoritized, marginalized, and disenfranchised young people, who adopt cultural signifiers, tropes, and practices associated with mythologized gang lifestyles as represented in mainstream hip-hop and gangsta rap cultures. For many Aboriginal youth in these neighbourhoods, participating in gangsta life represents a reclamation of (urban) territory, the creation of community or "family," a sense of belonging, safety from rival gangs, the accumulation of social status within the 'hood, and a means to cope with systemic issues linked to poverty and racism. But involvement in gang culture also means a life filled with violence and crime, higher potential for early death, and an internalized hierarchy of social status that mimics the patriarchal and racist structures of the colonialist society—structures that bind these neighbourhoods to their current social conditions.

Within hip-hop culture—and specifically in rap music—there is an emphasis on the relationship between place and meaning. This emphasis speaks to why and how rap music is created, as well as to why, in the global realm, the meanings associated with the genre are easily recognized and transferable.[1] Whether the city is a large metropolis like New York or a small city encoded with a rural sensibility like Regina, hip hop is an urban music culture with intimate ties to the city and especially to the racialized spaces of its inner city neighbourhoods.[2] In his work on hip-hop culture in America, media theorist Murray Forman (2004) argues that the city is audible in rap music: "Rap music takes the city and its multiple spaces as the foundation of its cultural production. In the music and lyrics, the city is an audible presence, explicitly cited and digitally sampled" (203). One outcome of these close connections is the transference of the sounds associated with one city or neighbourhood to another through the marketing and consumption of rap music and hip-hop culture. In his comparison of rap in two European cities, Andy Bennett (2004) argues that "hip hop is culturally mobile. Hip hop culture and its attendant notions of authenticity are constantly being 'remade' as hip hop is appropriated by different groups of young people in cities and regions around the world" (177). The globalization of rap music offers the potential for one cityscape to appropriate and adapt another, as well as possibilities for shared identifications among local residents.

In the case of Regina gangsta rapper Robin Favel (a.k.a. Burden), the typical American gangsta rapper archetype *and* his own experiences of living in Regina's notorious 'hood play a significant role in his practice as an artist and as an Aboriginal man living in North Central. Favel, who performs many of the stereotypes associated with gangsta rapper culture—fashion, vernacular, gesture, rituals—embodies the particular crisis that is North Central and, more generally, Regina. Following a standoff between Favel and the police in North Central on 17 August 2007, documentary filmmaker Cory Generoux told journalists that "Robin is the personification of [North Central]."[3] In Favel's rap music, Regina's 'hood, and one of its narratives—the rise in Aboriginal gang culture in Canada—can be heard alongside (and integrated within) the audible sounds of gangsta life as portrayed in American hip-hop culture (i.e., regional or turf rivalries, depictions of class struggle, run-ins with the law, the possession or coveting of "bling," attitudes of sexism, and "family" loyalty). For Favel, and for media sources that represent him and his 'hood, the genre of rap—more specifically, gangsta rap—provides a framework, an almost cookie-cutter approach to a complicated narrative that is both colonialist and minoritizing.

In this chapter I build on Forman's argument (2002, 2004)—that the city shapes rap music and is the foundation of its cultural production—as an approach to discussing how gangsta rap in Regina, specifically gangsta rapper Robin Favel (a.k.a. Burden), and Regina's 'hoods are represented in the media and in the community. Integral to this analysis is an understanding of how masculinity and indigeneity are signified and mapped onto these places, onto the bodies that inhabit them, and onto the cultural practices attributed to them by the media. An examination of Christine's Ramsay's work on APTN's series *Moccasin Flats* and its adaptation of the themes and styles of the American 'hood film genre will make even clearer the impact of American archetypes on the neighbourhood at hand. Worth noting here is Ramsay's compelling argument that *Moccasin Flats* gives "a distinct voice to the particularities of the urban experiences of Regina's aboriginal youth" (2010, 4). As a way to think about these particularities as alternative narratives that may be (or have been) employed by community members in order to deconstruct problematic stereotypes and misrepresentations, I draw on Paul Gilroy's critique of how the family trope is encoded in hip-hop culture as well as Taiaiake Alfred's concept of what it means to be a contemporary indigenous warrior. This research is also shaped by the following questions: How do stereotypical performances of gangsta rapper masculinity impact a community like North Central? Why are there no stories of women in relation to the gangsta figure other than the narratives of women as reproducers of culture (mothers) or as symbols of wealth (prostitutes/girlfriends/"bling")? How do media representations of hip-hop culture, and its *seemingly* natural associations with gang culture, reproduce and glorify rather than challenge conventional definitions of race and masculinity? What is the relationship between contemporary colonialism in Canada and the adaptation of gangsta rap culture by Aboriginal men, such as Robin Favel, who live in North Central? Using these questions as starting points for further discussion, my aim is to make sense of the continuing impacts of colonialism as manifested in Regina's gangsta rap culture, and of the ongoing violence inherent in the forging of a nation immersed in capitalism.

THE HIP-HOP GANGSTA: FIGURE OF FOLKLORE

Laying claim to the gangsta persona is a favorite theme in hip hop.[4]

In hip-hop folklore the gangsta figure represents the hero and the villain; more often than not, he is a tragic masculine figure.[5] As reproduced for mass consumption by the music, film, television, and news industries, the American hip-hop gangsta lifestyle offers a particular fantasy of hypermasculinity based on the accumulation of wealth, power, prestige, sex, and respect born of intimidation and fear. Because of its ties to power, wealth, and a discourse of authenticity, "laying claim to the gangsta persona is a favorite theme in hip hop" (Kelly 2004, 95). The hip-hop gangsta figure represents an alternative to the familiar narrative of colonized male bodies by repositioning a marked, racialized body as a site of privilege and power produced through capitalist gains. Power is assumed to come from "owning" the street, and the gangsta identity is generated by practices of naming and claiming that are ever present in hip-hop culture. To appear more gangsta and more ghetto lends credibility to one's identity as an authentic gangsta hip-hop artist.[6]

In spite of hip hop's idealistic origin myth—a commitment to politically conscious lyrics, reclamation of public spaces, and a significant connection to community through creative arts practices—hip-hop culture symbolizes a mythology of masculinity in which there persist archaic gendering principles based on patriarchal norms. These principles are reproduced through discourses of sexism and misogyny, as well as other strategies of exclusion and violence (e.g., colonialism).[7] "As sexism and misogyny are largely extensions of normative patriarchal privilege, their reproduction in the music of male hip-hop artists speaks more powerfully to the extent that these young men… are invested in that privilege" (Neal 2000, 247). And though Neal goes on to suggest that these artists are not solely responsible for reproducing that privilege, the argument needs to be made that these artists are responsible for their actions and behaviours as well as for the conventional narratives of oppression that they consistently adopt and reproduce. Those artists who attempt to challenge or disrupt such archetypes are pushed to the outside, where their voices, attitudes, and exceptionalism can easily be ignored or are less threatening to the status quo.

This investment in patriarchal privilege is perpetuated in media representations of the gangsta hip-hop lifestyle as well as among those who participate in gangsta hip-hop culture. The outcome is a masculinity that is meaningful only in relation to a subservient feminized other, a "bros before hoes" attitude, and to the trope of the hetero-normative family in which women are relegated to the role of reproduction. Within hip-hop culture, ideals of authenticity are perpetuated through conventions such as the family. In his criticism of how the family trope is adopted in hip-hop culture, Gilroy (2004) argues: "The family is the approved, natural site where ethnicity and racial culture are reproduced. In this authoritarian pastoral patriarchy, women are identified as the agents and means of this reproductive process" (89). This trope is also an important strategy in many Aboriginal cultures in Canada: women are viewed as reproducers of culture but are trapped in a patriarchal family system that continues to oppress and marginalize them.

For Gilroy the quest for authenticity in hip hop is riddled with highly problematic and essentialist associations: "Those definitions of authenticity are disproportionately defined by ideas about nurturance, about family, about fixed gender roles, and generational responsibilities. What is authentic is also frequently defined by ideas about sexuality and patterns of interaction between men and women that are taken to be expressive of essential, that is, racial, difference" (89).

The mapping of these essential differences in relation to the family trope is also relevant in contemporary Aboriginal culture so that "for many, idealization of nurturing/motherhood has been reified and has gained political currency within nationalist and cultural difference discourses" (LaRocque 2007, 55). For Aboriginal women generally, this too has resulted in their being relegated to role of reproducers of culture in a context of patriarchal and colonial oppression. Political theorist Joyce Green (2007) explains: "Contemporary Aboriginal women are subjected to patriarchal and colonial oppression within settler society and, in some contexts, in Aboriginal communities. Some Aboriginal cultures and communities are patriarchal, either in cultural origin or because of incorporation of colonizer patriarchy" (22).

The concept of authenticity has become deeply embedded in the discourses of nationalism and cultural difference, so much so that "this authenticity is inseparable from talk about the conduct and management of bitter gender-based conflicts, which is now recognized as essential to familial, racial, and communal health" (Gilroy 2004, 89). In other words, the argument presented around remaining healthy as a cultural community has become entrenched in highly problematic and essentialist notions of cultural authenticity, which actually perpetuate rather than disrupt power relations and the status quo.

In her work on indigenous feminisms, Green (2007) warns that

> rejecting the rhetoric and institutions of the colonizer by embracing the symbols of one's culture and traditions is a strategy for reclaiming the primacy of one's own context in the worlds, against the imposition of colonialism. But, in the absence of an analysis of the power relations embedded in tradition, it is not necessarily a libratory [sic] strategy. Each choice must be interrogated on its own merits, relative to the objective of a contemporary emancipatory formulation that will benefit Aboriginal men, women and children. (27)

Consequently, how authenticity is understood in relation to gangsta rap culture created in North Central, for example, is deeply embedded in contemporary systems of patriarchy and colonialism—systems that determine how masculinities and femininities are performed and read.[8] Moreover, because "hip-hop's grip on American [and arguably North American] youth allows for the circulation of sexist and misogynistic narratives in a decidedly uncritical fashion" (Neal 2004, 247), it is critical to analyze how these narratives are understood, re-enacted, and mediated, as well as how they are mapped onto other locales and nations where hip hop has traversed borders and been appropriated (and adapted).[9]

For young Aboriginal men participating in gang culture in Regina, however, the form of masculinity conventionally associated with hip hop, no matter how problematic, implies a "new" status that works against the signifiers associated with a lack of power or emasculation. It is a masculinity inextricably linked to capitalism. One only has to turn to the first issue of *Criminal Intelligence Service Saskatchewan* (Winter 2005), which states that "in Saskatchewan, the 'gangster' lifestyle is an attractive alternative for many aboriginal youth. The implications of extreme concentrations of poverty, violence, absent parenting and urban migration, combined with blocked opportunities and substance abuse have created an environment that is conducive for the recruitment of youth into gangs."[10]

The reasons why Aboriginal youth turn to gangs can be found in the notion that gang life offers an alternative lifestyle and, for young men, an alternative masculinity. It is reported that for some, participation in gang culture has actually enabled a reconnection with culture, traditions, language, and community, "a sense of belonging, recognition, and self-esteem as they are establishing their personal identity and networks."[11] Though this may seem counterintuitive, it also demonstrates how the effects of colonialism can play out. "The experiences of the Aboriginal youth or adults who join gangs are too commonly rooted in personal experiences of colonialism, poverty, and discrimination, all of which affect the relationship of the individual to the community and to others."[12] Thus, gang life and its offerings can represent an alternative.

To understand how institutionalized and seductive this form of gangster masculinity (and all it symbolizes) has become, one need only compare the privileges and rationales for becoming involved in gang culture with those privileges and rationales associated with other institutions representing a brotherhood. For example, the privileges that accompany membership in a men's club on Wall Street or in the police force—community, security, loyalty, belonging, social status, networking, and capital—are ironically similar to those of a "street" gang despite the perception of one as "good" and the other as "bad."[13] Yet the gangsta archetype, rather than deconstructing the racist narratives attached to the "black man" or "indigenous man," substantiates familiar stereotypes, and gangsta remains synonymous with all young black or indigenous men, recoding them as dangerous, as a group to be feared, confined, and heavily policed.[14]

In relation to these unsound terms, gangsta culture is read and represented as also being synonymous with rap and hip-hop culture. Thus Aboriginal youth, especially young Aboriginal men dressed in hip-hop fashion, living in Regina's North Central or the Core are often read through this racist and ageist lens, and this contributes to a climate of fear of "the Aboriginal man" as dangerous and untrustworthy. Through such a climate it becomes even more evident how masculinity is integral to colonialism, locale, and power.

The music of hip hop, though diverse in approach, content, and delivery, is often used by different media sources, including the news, film, and television industries, to portray a stereotypical gangsta lifestyle and a persistent view of rap as negative and bound to the streets. Society at large still refuses "to distinguish between enabling, productive rap messages and the social violence that exists in many inner-city communities and that is often reflected in rap songs" (Dyson 2004, 63). There is an overarching generalization that because these life experiences are being represented in rap, the music only glorifies or glamorizes a gangster lifestyle. And though this may be the case in some instances, there are also examples of critical engagement with and critiques of gangster culture that express concerns about the social crisis and attitudes of the culture and that provide various strategies for challenging these narratives.[15]

The music culture and lifestyles associated with hip hop are highly racialized and read as Other. Much as with gangsta rap's evolution in African American communities, the themes expressed by it in Western Canadian inner cities with high Aboriginal populations are "drawn from the conflicts and contradictions of [Aboriginal] urban life" (ibid., 63). This distinction between more progressive and socially conscious rap music—depicting life experiences from inner city and marginalized communities—and the rap music that expresses a highly romanticized capitalist narrative of the gangsta lifestyle is often controversial among hip-hop artists themselves. To be "keepin' it real" can represent one's status on the street, or it can mean that one identifies with the roots and routes of hip-hop culture and its politically and socially conscious ideals. Yet proving that one has or has had a legitimate place on the street or in the 'hood still plays a significant role in determining a rapper's status, for "the 'hood prevails as hip-hop's dominant spatial trope" (Forman 2004, 156).

THE 'HOOD: CANADA'S WORST NEIGHBOURHOOD[16]

The 'hood prevails as hip-hop's dominant spatial trope.[17]

In the past few years, the social, cultural, and economic conditions experienced by many people living in Regina's inner city neighbourhoods (North Central and the Core) have come under scrutiny in APTN's critically acclaimed television series *Moccasin Flats;* in the now infamous article from *Maclean's* 12 January 2007 issue titled "Canada's Worst Neighbourhood"; current scholarly criticism (Ramsay 2008); in media accounts of Regina gangsta rap artist Robin Favel's ongoing confrontations with police; and in Cory Generoux's film *Dogz Lyfe: Burdens of a Gangster Rapper* (2008).

Journalists' reports and other media representations of Regina's 'hoods, though at times fictional and incomplete, generally tell stories of racial segregation, culture loss, poverty, and other systemic impacts of colonialism, including patriarchal and hetero-normative sensibilities. These stories have become the impetus for a reactionary politics on the part of the municipal government and have upset community groups that have been attempting to demonstrate the vitality, creativity, and caring nature of these communities and of the city generally.[18] The national media attention has led to an injection of money into North Central and the Core in the form of new subsidized housing projects, support for social training programs for children and youth, an increase in community watches, a possible new high school building for Scott Collegiate (the only high school in North Central), funding support for community arts projects for youth, and the creation of artistic works, including hip-hop culture and its four primary elements (dj, rap, break, graffiti arts).[19]

The themes of space and place should be understood as "profoundly important" to the meaning found in hip-hop culture. The history of hip-hop culture is telling in that "virtually all of the early descriptions of hip-hop practices identify territory and the public sphere as significant factors, whether in the visible artistic expression and appropriation of public space via graffiti or B-boying, the sonic impact of a pounding bass line, or the discursive articulation of urban geography in rap lyrics" (Forman 2004, 155). For hip-hop artists, their home turf is often an integral part of the evolution of their art. "In practice, artists' lyrics and rhythms must achieve success on the home front first, where the flow, subject matter, style and image must resonate meaningfully among those who share common bonds to place, to the posse and to the 'hood" (208). In the case of Robin Favel, his flow, subject matter, style, and image represent the stereotypes of a gangsta rapper's life as well as the ongoing systemic impacts of colonialism in Regina.

To understand the urban landscape of Regina, one need only draw on the metaphor of the railway tracks—and who lives on which side of those tracks. With the CPR railway running through the middle of the city, residents have been divided into north and south along the signifiers of race and class. Ramsay explains how Regina's landscape evolved into its contemporary condition:

> In the 1960s, as people began immigrating from reserves to urban centres across Canada, Regina's downtown became a site of racial and class division between Aboriginals living mostly north of the CPR railway tracks that run along Dewdney Avenue, in an increasingly decaying North Central, and whites living "south of Dewdney" and in the burgeoning middle-class eastern and western suburbs, giving the lie to the colonizers' vision of Saskatchewan-style social justice and equality for all Canadians. (2010, 109)

The incredible wealth of parks and trees, the symbols of government, and the business districts of Regina are for the most part south of the tracks. North Central, a community initially read as working class, is now represented both within and outside the city as the 'hood or ghetto, which is code for home to Regina's poorest residents and most "dangerous" elements.[20]

The lie representing the colonizers' vision of social justice and equality that Ramsay refers to in the above passage is at the heart of the article "Canada's Worst Neighbourhood," written by Jonathan Gatehouse and published by *Maclean's* in 2007. Beginning with the question, "How did the province where Medicare was born end up with a city this frightening?" Gatehouse sets up the contradiction between Saskatchewan's reputation as a socially progressive province and the reality for those who live in its inner cities. The article continues with a report on the issues plaguing the neighbourhoods of North Central, the Core, and the entire city of Regina. Focusing specifically on poverty and gang-related behaviours, Gatehouse narrates his own experiences of being toured around North Central, creating vivid images of horrific circumstances connected to drug use, prostitution, poverty, and crime. Through Gatehouse's journalist lens, a national audience is introduced to one of many aspects of Regina's inner cities that are often left ignored by those living outside North Central.

For those on the outside, the 'hood is represented and viewed as a seedy urban underbelly, as a frightening place filled with crime and criminals. The 'hood is a place to be simultaneously observed and ignored, and the people who live there are objects to be stared at and understood only in relation to that place—under surveillance by the authorities but ignored by the rest of the city. One drives through the 'hood to look out at this "war zone" from behind the safety of a car window and a locked door, and only during daylight. It is a place of both fear and wonder, a place that seems both *un*real and *too* real. And the constructions of these readings—filled with hate and prejudice—are available to us within Canada's contemporary colonialist and racist nationalist framework, a framework that dehumanizes the Other, that constructs a false sense of security through obvious but invisible borders, and that permits ongoing unspeakable acts of psychic violence toward Aboriginal people.

The bordered areas of Regina's urban landscape can also be read in relation to similar circumstances in other cities across Canada and countries around the world where colonial rule persists in its effects, even though understood as over. Reflecting on South Africa's apartheid, J.M. Coetzee (2008) explains the significant impact that urban boundaries have on the economy and social status: "The institution of boundaries made upward mobility for blacks, and downward social mobility for whites, near to impossible, congealing class antagonism and race antagonism into a solid mass; while the machinery created to police those boundaries turned into the expensive, tentacular bureaucracy of the apartheid state" (106).

In making this connection to apartheid in South Africa through Coetzee's work, I am arguing that contemporary colonialism in Canada as enacted on a national level plays a primary role in what is happening in Regina and

North Central. Furthermore, I support Ramsay's argument that "the so-called 'Queen' City's deposing and descent into a metropolitan dystopia cannot simply be laid at the feet of its North Central citizens" (2010, 110). The existence of struggling neighbourhoods like North Central is entrenched in the historical and contemporary discourses of nation building and colonialism in Canada.

The lens through which Gatehouse represents North Central focuses on its "Third World" conditions—the poverty, violence, desolation, health crisis, drug trade, and gang culture, the rise in the number of Aboriginal youth who are forced to live in squalor, the lack of infrastructure and government support, the refusal of governments (municipal, provincial, federal) to provide for basic needs, and the continued denial by those living outside the 'hood that these conditions, and the people living in these conditions, exist. "Rather than Fiacco's 'it's all in the attitude "I love Regina"' campaign," Gatehouse suggests, "a real solution to Regina's crime woes will require a national effort to address the underlying social issues—poverty, unemployment and exclusion" (2007, 5). Indeed, when one looks beyond the borders of Regina, one finds that other inner city neighbourhoods and reserves are suffering horrific circumstances and that, also as in Regina, the issues are buried under statistics related to health (suicide, alcoholism, drug addiction, domestic violence) and crime (rise in gang culture and related activities). The result is a shift in blame as well as strategies for problem solving that are linked to the *symptoms* of crisis rather than to causes. The statistics presented in the 2005 *Criminal Intelligence Services Saskatchewan* report, as well as the Native Women's Association of Canada issue paper on Aboriginal Women and Gangs prepared for the National Aboriginal Women's Summit in 2007, directly link the rise in Aboriginal gang activity to the recruiting grounds found in correctional institutions. Gang life also offers incentives: "The gangs' allure—money, excitement, and a ready-made family—is hard for authorities to combat."[21] The effects of colonization are not limited to the past. Colonialism continues to affect contemporary lives and entire communities in multifaceted ways.

Gatehouse should be commended for reporting on the conditions of North Central and for helping publicly motivate people to take action to address these situations. However, as Ramsay suggests, "the portrait of a cheerless destiny [is not] the complete picture" (2010, 110) of North Central. As Ramsay conveys in her work on *Moccasin Flats* and its portrayal of the city: "Regina and North Central must be understood in the context of the racist legacies of a colonial nationalist modernity; the forces of postmodern globalization; the culture of urban poverty; the tensions between American media imperialism, Aboriginal cultural traditions, and masculine identity; and the dignity, resilience, and hope of the individuals and families who call these places home" (ibid.).

Though the *Maclean's* article painted a picture of North Central for the nation, there was little focus on any of the celebratory elements that exist there in spite of such horrific circumstances. North Central is home to vibrant, productive, and creative communities that want "to be involved in the solutions" (Brenda Mercer, in Gatehouse 2007, 5). For example, there are a number of community initiatives directed toward Aboriginal youth in North Central and the Core, such as the pedagogical methods found in project-based learning, which have been adopted at Scott Collegiate. This form of programming has succeeded in encouraging participation, attendance, and interest at the high school. In the fall of 2008, Scott Collegiate partnered with Sask In-Motion and the Interactive Media and Performance (IMP) Labs (Faculty of Fine Arts), along with the Faculty of Education at the University of Regina, to offer a program based on hip-hop culture and its creative elements. Hip-hop culture in this context shifts meaning away from the negative stereotypes associated with hip hop and presents alternative forms of masculinities and femininities. It also offers a collaborative and supportive mentoring environment, one that enables creative outlets for students to discuss and reflect on their lived experiences. Considering that most graduates of Scott Collegiate are women, the hip-hop program[22] has created another strategy for helping young Aboriginal men stay in school and finish a diploma. This is just one of the alternative programs that Gatehouse did not take up in his article.[23]

One week after Gatehouse's article was published, *Maclean's* published a second article, "For Regina, Anger Is No Substitute for Action," written by the editors in response to the reaction of Regina's mayor, Pat Fiacco, who referred to the article as a "shameful, sensationalistic, one-sided attack on his beloved city."[24] The editors pointed out that Gatehouse's sources had included civic leaders and community members, as well as statistics on crime, unemployment, and health. The editors went so far as to restate the original evidence that the city and the province were covering up the poor living conditions and high crime rate. They did so by calling into question arguments made by the Government of Saskatchewan's senior policy fellow, Fred Burch, who suggested that the indicators being used to calculate crime statistics in Saskatchewan were misleading and unfair. Though it is essential to analyze crime statistics and to call into question the methods used for analyzing statistical evidence—methods that are generally based on problematic and inconsistent categorical definitions, which leave little or no room for context—the process of scrutinizing the method of analysis often derails or limits the examination or actions needed to address the systemic problems underlying the crime statistics. In other words, the emphasis shifts away from the content, and the research becomes lost in the bureaucracies of method reform. The *Maclean's* editors criticized Fiacco for denying and massaging the facts, then concluded their article with wary praise for his organizing of the first City Hall summit with the leaders of southern Saskatchewan's First Nations. But they also offered this warning: "Engaging native leaders and facing up to these important issues will do far more to improve Regina's image—and the facts that drive the image—than creating a media bogeyman and demanding that everyone put on a happy face."[25]

In the 17 January 2008 edition of *Maclean's*, the editors published another article, titled "Regina, One Year Later." The follow-up was a brief report on what had happened in North Central in the year since the original article was printed:

> A new sense of optimism has taken hold. Neighbourhood organizations have benefited from a steady stream of new funding for youth employment and skills training programs, with the prospect of more, particularly from Ottawa. Local businesses have stepped up to rescue the image of their city with money and volunteer time. There has been greater interaction between city hall and the native community, and talk of a new urban reserve. Just last week the Regina Police Service announced the creation of a new police district in the inner core—explicit recognition of the challenges the area faces. And citizens from all over the city have gotten more engaged.[26]

From the editors' point of view, their coverage of Regina's "dirty little secret" generated a national embarrassment and "played a small role as a catalyst for change."[27] More generally, there is a sense throughout the article that even though the coverage did not represent North Central outside of its social ills, the impact mainly benefited the community.[28] And though there have indeed been some benefits such as new funding initiatives for youth training programs and newly directed resources to North Central, the sensational reporting—with taglines such as "Canada's Worst Neighbourhood"—and the article's emphasis *only* on violent crime, prostitution, gang violence, drugs, and poverty—perpetuated a mapping of these social issues and their detrimental effects onto Othered bodies, in this case primarily on Aboriginal bodies and Aboriginal communities. Instead of formal acceptance of responsibility by governmental and institutional bodies, this kind of reporting often generates a "moral panic" and further embeds places, spaces, and people in a racist and racialized framework. This racialized discourse, no matter how it is mediated, can only be read as a violent discourse—as a contemporary colonial violence committed against individuals and communities by a media industry that has everything to gain and very little to lose.

THE JOURNEY OF ROBIN FAVEL: "I'VE GOT EVERYTHING TO GAIN, NOTHING TO LOSE"[29]

> Space and place are important factors that influence identity formation as they relate to localized practices of the self.[30]

In the recently released documentary film *Dogz Lyfe: Burdens of a Gangster Rapper* (2008), Robin Favel self-identifies as a gangster and a rapper living in North Central, drawing heavily on the popular phrase "keepin' it real," which began circulating in American hip-hop culture in the 1990s. "I just keep it real, and that's the respect I get, you know? Just keep it real and don't try to front. People enjoy hearing the truth as jagged as it may sound, you know?"[31] For Favel, "Keepin' it real" refers to his life philosophy, the way he lives his life as a gangster, the way he creates his raps and tells stories: "I feed off the energy I get from my people around me...which are so called gang members or drug dealers. So we sit on the range and they tell me stories, we exchange stories and most of the stories they tell me I just put them in rhyme form."[32] For Favel, music has become an outlet for conveying stories of the street and his experiences of growing up and living as an Aboriginal man in North Central. These stories are not necessarily symbolic of all young men who live in the 'hood, in spite of the media's tendency to portray Favel as the face of Aboriginal youth living in the 'hood; however, some of the anger and rage felt by a generation of Aboriginal youth, who suffer the ongoing influences of colonial legacies, can be heard in his raps.[33]

Dogz Lyfe is the name of the group that Favel (a.k.a. Burden) raps under. When asked the reason for the name in an interview, Favel responded: "The Dog Soldier is the last line of defence for the tribe."[34] Initially a duo of Favel, from Piapot First Nations, and Cameron Nicholls/Dellagnese (a.k.a. Infamous) from Regina, Dogz Lyfe began working together in 2003. They performed at rap battles, open mic nights, at the Crow Hop Café, and in other venues around Saskatchewan and Manitoba. Performing for a number of organizations across the region—including the MacKenzie Art Gallery, Big Soul Productions, Renegade Productions, the Saskatchewan Writer's Guild (Moose Jaw), the Regina Folk Festival 2003, the Royal Saskatchewan Museum's 2004 Youth Forum Symposium on Sustainability, and the 2004 National Aboriginal Achievement Foundation—Dogz Lyfe began to make a name for themselves. In 2004, Infamous left the group. Burden went on to produce a second album, this one titled *Ransom* (featuring Favel's sister, Danielle Favel, a.k.a. Dee).

Favel raps from the place of the inner city. Much as in narratives of the 'hood film genre and in the television series *Moccasin Flats*, in Favel's music "the city centre and its economy are re-imagined from the perspective of the ghetto as a 'structuring absence' that excludes [the ghetto]" (Ramsay 2010, 114). The result is that the audience is reminded that the ghetto narrative exists only in relation to the rest of the city. In telling stories, whether his own or those of people around him, Favel offers a glimpse into the life of a gangster living in North Central, sometimes performing the stereotypical gangster persona—"We live the life of hustlaz, gangstaz / can the lord even save us / people make assumptions / fuck y'all haters / this one's for the g's and the playaz"[35]—but other times politicizing such stereotypes and challenging the state—"Canada's crossing their fingers / we don't rise and stand firm / rise together against the oppressor."[36]

In journalistic discourse (print, online, radio, and television alike), Favel is portrayed as a "loose canon," a young Aboriginal man who has been influenced by the likes of commercial gangster rapper 50Cent—"I listen to anybody who sings the real street, relates [to] the street and gets respect from the street while making it big... [In terms of a major label] 50 cent's G-Unit is where I want to be"[37]—and who eagerly relays to reporters stories about gang life and its influences on the streets of Regina: "'You really don't got to look far in this city,' he said. 'Everybody I grew up with is gang members [...] Gangs have hundreds of soldiers out there on the street initiating kids.'"[38] Obviously these sound bites are not always fully contextualized; thus, "truths" by both the subject of a story (Favel) and the conveyor of the story (media sources) can be exaggerated, sensationalized, or recontextualized to construct a story that presents a crisis, creates a climate of fear, and is worthy of news coverage.[39]

On Saturday, 18 August 2007, Favel and two other men found themselves in a standoff with the police,[40] who had responded to an anonymous call received at 6:19 a.m. about "a male entering the home with a firearm."[41] The difference from other Favel-related news was that in this instance Favel called Cory Generoux, a filmmaker who was documenting Favel's life for the new film *Dogz Lyfe: Burdens of a Gangsta Rapper* (2008). Generoux came to the scene with his video camera and recorded the standoff and subsequent arrests on film. Throughout the process, Generoux talked with Favel on his cellphone, finally convincing Favel to give himself up. Following the arrests, Generoux, responding to reporters about the connections between North Central and Favel, commented about how "the hip-hop musician is representative of the statistical numbers that are too often used in discussion of the neighbourhood."[42] It was at this point that Generoux made the statement I referred to earlier in the chapter: "[Favel] is the personification of that [North Central]."[43] In the media coverage, Favel's identity as a hip-hop (gangsta) rapper was constantly repeated, which reaffirmed the connections among violence, gang activity, and hip-hop culture. For Generoux, who had already created the short promotional video "The Journey of Robin Favel"—a teaser for the full-length film *Dogz Lyfe*—the footage became another layer to the Favel narrative.

At the beginning of the film, Infamous makes a connection between Favel's rap name, Burden, and Favel's life: "Burden is the burden of the city." The significance of the name "Burden" is not lost on Favel. This name, and the name Dogz Lyfe, which is tattooed on Favel's back, are explicit political statements concerning how he views his relationship to society.[44] In 2005, while talking to a CBC news reporter, Favel made it clear that he "sees the police

Arrested on camera

Regina Police Service was kept busy on Friday morning during a stand-off that resulted in the arrest of three people.

Subject of documentary in custody

By VERONICA RHODES
Leader-Post

Cory Generoux sat on the median and watched as Regina Police Service officers and SWAT members surrounded a North Central home with their weapons drawn, waiting for its occupants to surrender.

Speaking into his cellphone, Generoux tried to reassure one of the men inside the home, Daniel Favel.

"The best thing to do right now is to come out, come out relaxed," Generoux said while he glanced back at the officers standing ready outside the house.

Just minutes later, a black-shirt-wearing Favel and another man emerged from the home. An officer yelled for the men to put up their hands and walk slowly to their right.

Generoux picked up his videocamera to capture their arrest on film, which was followed shortly after by the surrender of a third man.

For the past 10 months, Generoux has been documenting the life of Favel, who has been called one of the province's most talented First Nations rap artists. But along with garnering praise for his music and acting skills, he has also accumulated a lengthy criminal record, which includes a recent two-year stint in prison for assaulting his former common-law wife.

According to police spokeswoman Elizabeth Popowich, officers arrived at the home in the 900 block of Athol Street after receiving an anonymous call at 6:19 a.m. of a male entering the home with a firearm.

See Arrest on Page A2

Documentary filmmaker Cory Generoux (middle) films Friday's incident.

Figure 29 "Arrested on Camera," *The Leader-Post*, 18 August 2007. Copyright 2007 The Leader-Post. Used with permission.

Figure 30 Poster for *Dogz Lyfe: Burdens of a Gangster Rapper*. Design by Cory Generoux (2008).

as the enemy and blames them and the correctional system for creating more gang members."[45] Describing both the jails and the 'hood, Favel remarked: "They organize us. We're all Aboriginal and they all stick us in one place."[46] In other words, though he is invested in gang culture and implicates himself as a gangsta, Favel is aware of and understands the role of the police as an arm of the state in creating the modern nation—a role that includes constructing North Central and Regina.

For Generoux, *Dogz Lyfe* (2008) represented an important journey for both Favel and himself. In the press release for the film, Generoux stated: "This was not an easy documentary to make but it was an important one... Our Elders tell us to never forget about those walking the broken circle, those who have strayed off the Red Road, incarcerated and living negatively." As the subject of this film, Favel "represents the very essence of why it is important not to forget, why it is important that the voice not get lost in the wind." And for Favel, his music has become an important symbol for his past *and* future life: "For most of his life, Robin Favel has lived a life of crime, has been a member of one of the most notorious gangs in Saskatchewan, The Native Syndicate, and has been in and out of jail numerous times." Yet in the documentary, Favel embraces his music as a possibility for something different, as a way to resist the narrative that already seems predetermined based on his previous actions.

There are also moments in the film where the audience bears witness to an important anxiety that Favel suffers, one relating to his grandmother and his young daughter. Favel's grandmother, accompanied by his young daughter, arrives to take Favel home after he is released from the penitentiary. Prior to that, Favel had worried out loud that his daughter would have forgotten him and not known him as a father. The presence of his grandmother and daughter at this moment speak to another crisis of colonialism and its intersections with patriarchal systems of power and privilege. Here, the film highlights the harmful impacts of Favel's lifestyle and his performed masculinity, as well as predetermined caretaking roles, the latter too often being performed by grandmothers, who go unrecognized yet are always called upon to pick up the pieces and heal the wounds even while relegated to the position of Other. Coming back to Gilroy's critique of how the family trope is adopted in hip hop, and to LaRocque's (2007) description of how Aboriginal women live—"as victims of colonization and patriarchy, yet as activist and agents in their lives; as oppressed, yet as fighters and survivors; and as among the most stereotyped, dehumanized and objectified of women, yet as the strong, gracious and determined women that they are" (53)—the impact of gangsta rapper masculinity is severe, and so is the impact of the media's representations of that masculinity, especially on a community like North Central. At the moment when Favel hugs his grandmother, and then again when he embraces his daughter, these images bring to the fore the crisis that accompanies this masculinity, which is embedded in the "capitalist desiring machine" (Deleuze and Guattari 1972), is integral to colonialism, and ultimately sustains the tragic figure.

A critique of colonialism must include a critique of masculinity. Yet from Frantz Fanon (1961) to Taiaiake Alfred (2005), many theorists of colonialism have neglected analyses of masculinity and male privilege, or substantial gender analyses. Where are the stories of the women being told—stories that move beyond the tropes of mother/bitch/ho'? Where are the stories of alternative masculinities, the masculinities that lie outside these hip-hop representations and the stereotypes offered up through the colonial lens? Why are they not represented in journalistic discourse?

CONCLUSION: "DECLARATION OF WAR"

In *Wasáse: Indigenous Pathways of Action and Freedom*, Taiaiake Alfred calls for a rethinking of what it means to be an indigenous warrior. Critiquing the conventional reified representations of indigenous warriors offered up in the media, Alfred (2005) argues that

> we cannot hold on to a concept of the warrior that is gendered in the way it once was...The Indigenous warrior...must be rethought and recast from the solely masculine view of the old traditional ways to a new concept of the warrior that is freed from colonial gender constructions and articulated instead with reference to what really counts in our struggles: the qualities and the actions of a person, man or woman, in battle. (84)

In other words, one cannot simply declare "I am warrior"; rather, one *becomes* a warrior through actions that are motivated by a "sense of responsibility to alleviate suffering and recreate the conditions of peace and happiness" (86). A warrior "takes action to change the conditions that cause suffering for the people in both the immediate (self-defence) and long-term (self-determinate) sense" (87). And most important, "the warrior does not focus on abstract or historical injustices and believes wholeheartedly that the ability to generate change is within the power of the people" (87).

In relation to gangsta rap in Regina, this concept of an indigenous warrior is lost. Favel's hip-hop masculinity, though repeatedly represented through a colonialist and racist lens in the media, only serves to perpetuate predictable narratives bound within a capitalist, patriarchal, and colonialist framework. These narratives offer little or no disruption of the status quo; hegemony is solidified. Yet Favel cannot be written off so easily, as is illustrated in the film *Dogz Lyfe: Burdens of a Gangsta Rapper*. There are moments in his music and in the telling of his stories where Favel leans just slightly away from the capitalist desiring machines toward the possibilities of something else, something different. Robin Favel is indicative of the crisis facing marginalized and minoritized Aboriginal youth living in North Central and, more generally, the crisis that is Regina. He raps about how the violence of colonialism (and the construction of the nation-state) is threatened by his own violence—the violence of the gangsta rapper—which is in turn confronted by the police and then challenged by the technocratic programs of the state. Yet Favel also romanticizes the hip-hop gangster life, the ghetto, and patriarchal privileges associated with money, power, and the oppression of women and one's community. His idea of "keepin' it real" continues to swing back and forth like a pendulum, always in question.

Robin Favel and his 'hood, North Central, continue to be represented by the media as something to be feared and as something dangerous. These representations, however, symbolize the uncertainties and anxieties embedded in Canada's contemporary colonial practices, and they speak to the ongoing violence inherent in how a nation is constructed. Returning to the quotation that began this chapter—"The police organize us. We're all Aboriginal and they all stick us in one place"—it is apparent that Favel, too, is engaged in a critical dialogue about colonialism and its current impacts. And though his voice is heard through the medium of gangsta rap, and he often falls into the dominant tropes associated with a problematic hip-hop masculinity, rap is an integral place for Favel to tell his stories. As has been demonstrated historically, rap music and hip-hop culture have the power to bind "locale, resistance, innovation, affirmation, and cultural identity within a complex web of spatialized meanings and practices" (Forman 2004, 155). These meanings and practices are diverse even in North Central, and therein lies the possibility for powerful resistance to and disruption of existing narratives.

NOTES

The Social Sciences and Humanities Research Council of Canada, the Canada Research Chairs program, the Canada Foundation for Innovation, the Saskatchewan Advancement for Education programs, and the Faculty of Fine Arts at the University of Regina have generously supported the research for this chapter. I want to express my gratitude to Dr. Christine Ramsay for her invitation to write a chapter for this collection and her encouragement to write on this subject. I also want to acknowledge the contributions of Cory Generoux, director of the documentary *Dogz Lyfe: Burdens of a Gangster Rapper* (2008), who took the time to meet with me in August 2007, and who shared some of his own stories, which have enriched and complicated my analysis. Finally, my thinking around contemporary colonialism in Saskatchewan has been significantly informed by Darci Anderson's research on ethical relations in Saskatchewan, and by my community-based research projects in Regina and numerous communities in northern Saskatchewan.

1 For a discussion on rap music as an important global culture, see Tony Mitchell, "Another Root: Hip-Hop Outside the U.S.A," in *Global Noise: Rap and Hip-Hop Outside the U.S.A.*, ed. Tony Mitchell (Middletown: Wesleyan University Press, 2001), 1–38; and Andy Bennett, "Hip-Hop am Main, Rappin' on the Tyne: Hip-Hop Culture as a Local Construct in Two European Cities," in *That's the Joint! The Hip-Hop Studies Reader*, ed. Murray Forman and Mark Anthony Neal (New York: Routledge, 2004), 177–200. For specific examples of how rap has been appropriated in western Canada, see Adam Krims, *Rap Music and the Poetics of Identity* (Cambridge: Cambridge University Press, 2001); and Charity Marsh, "'Bits and Pieces of Truth': Storytelling, Identity, and Hip Hop in Saskatchewan," forthcoming in *Perspectives on Contemporary Aboriginal Music in Canada*, ed. A. Hoefnagels and B. Diamond (Montreal and Kingston: McGill–Queen's University Press, 2011).
2 Murray Forman, *The 'Hood Comes First: Race, Space, and Place in Rap and Hip-Hop* (Middletown: Wesleyan University Press, 2002).
3 Veronica Rhodes, "Arrested on Camera," *The Leader-Post* (Regina), 18 August 2007. http://www.canada.com/reginaleaderpost/story.html?id=979625f0-06, accessed 1 April 2008.
4 Reagan Kelly, "Hip-Hop Chicano: A Separate but Parallel Story," in *That's the Joint! The Hip-Hop Studies Reader*, ed. Murray Forman and Marc Anthony Neal (Routledge: New York, 2004), 95.
5 One need only look to Tupac or Biggie Small for famous examples of the tragic masculine figure who is represented as both hero and villain.

6 One example I offer is rapper 50 Cent. 50 Cent's tales of living as a gangster, and his multiple scars from being shot, have given his hip-hop persona legitimacy. These narratives are used to promote his image and music as well as his film, *Before I Self Destruct* (2008).

7 Though there is an extensive repertoire of rap that challenges these attitudes, sexism and misogyny can easily be found in lyrics, images, and attitudes, and also in the persistence with which women are objectified as possessions and as signifiers of wealth. In spite of an increased presence of women in hip-hop culture—examples include Missy Elliott, Queen Latifah, Lady Sovereign, and MC Lyte—the privileges associated with patriarchy are firmly entrenched. Examples can be found in the lyrics of Dr. Dre and Snoop Dogg's "Nuthin' But a 'G' Thang," http://www.sing365.com/music/lyric.nsf/Nuthin-But-A-G-Thang-lyrics-Dr-Dre/941B60C911F835E348256887002507CD; Too $hort's "Ain't Nuthin' Like Pimpin'," http://www.lyricstime.com/too-short-ain-t-nuthin-like-pimpin-lyrics.html; and 50 Cent's "P.I.M.P.," http://www.absolutelyrics.com/lyrics/ view/50_cent/p.i.m.p, all three accessed 22 October 2008.

8 Indigenous studies scholar Emma LaRocque calls attention to the importance of context and the contradictory ways of reading how Aboriginal women live: "as victims of colonization and patriarchy, yet as activist and agents in their lives; as oppressed, yet as fighters and survivors; and as among the most stereotyped, dehumanized, and objectified of women, yet as the strong, gracious and determined women that they are." Emma LaRocque, "Métis and Feminist: Ethical Reflection on Feminism, Human Rights and Decolonization," in *Making Space for Indigenous Feminism*, ed. Joyce Green (Halifax: Fernwood, 2007), 53–71 at 53.

9 See Mitchell, "Another Root"; Bennett, "Hip-Hop am Main"; and Marsh, "Bits and Pieces of Truth."

10 *Criminal Intelligence Service Saskatchewan* 1, no. 1 (Winter 2005).

11 "Aboriginal Women and Gangs: An Issue Paper," prepared for the National Aboriginal Women's Summit, 20–22 June 2007, 1.

12 Ibid., 1.

13 These examples were part of a discussion that Darci Anderson and I had during and following a panel discussion held in Regina on 25 October 2008 in conjunction with the *Mispon Indigenous Film Festival*. Addressing the Chief of Police, one audience member repeated a comment that had been conveyed to him about how the police and correctional services in Canada could be viewed as the "biggest" gang. The Chief of Police responded with a statement suggesting that the psychological profile of police officers was quite different from those of a gang member. In an effort to contextualize the previous statement, Darci Anderson then asked why white men of the corporate world joined men's clubs. Listing off reasons such as community, brotherhood, networking, and status, Anderson suggested that young Aboriginal men in Canada joined gangs for much the same reasons that people joined the police force, and that businessmen joined men's clubs.

14 In Canada there have been a number of documented cases of racial profiling. One only has to scan the headlines in stories filed by the *Globe and Mail*'s Kirk Makin: "Police use racial profiling, appeal court concludes" (17 April 2003, A1); "Police engage in profiling, chief counsel tells court" (18 January 2003, A1). In Saskatchewan recently, there was an investigation into the death of Neil Stonechild, who, along with many other Aboriginal men and women at various times, had been dropped off outside the city limits by police during the freezing winter. This practice had even been given a name: "The Starlight Tour." Susanne Reber and Robert Renaud, "A Cold and Desperate Walk," *Maclean's*, 14 November 2005, 94–100.

15 For example, see Marsh, "'Bits and Pieces of Truth.'" Hear examples of alternative and challenging lyrics in Eekwol's song "Let's Move" from her and her brother Mils's 2007 album *The List;* and Oyé!'s performance of "Chan Chan" featuring rapper Def3 at http://interactivemediaandperformance.com.
16 This is the title of the article from the 15 January 2007 issue of *Maclean's* written by Jonathon Gatehouse.
17 Murray Forman, "Ain't No Love in the Heart of the City: Hip-Hop, Space, and Place," in *That's the Joint! The Hip-Hop Studies Reader*, ed. Murray Forman and Mark Anthony Neal (New York: Routledge, 2004), 156.
18 For video responses, go to "North Central Regina 'Through Our Eyes,'" http://ca.youtube.com/watch?v=9UmEv-I1Q-k&feature=related, and "Canada's Worst Neighborhood...Northcentral?" http://ca.youtube.com/watch?v=S2lQMZ_rc60, accessed 18 September 2008.
19 For an in-depth analysis of community-based arts programming around the hip-hop elements in Saskatchewan, refer to Marsh, http://www.charitymarsh.com/Dr._Charity_Marsh/Indigenous_Hip_Hop.htm).
20 The pairing of poverty and crime is not a new phenomenon, however problematic or unfounded. Doug Cuthand, "Less Poverty Means Less Crime," *The Leader Post* (Regina), 25 August 2008, A3.
21 Jonathon Gatehouse, "Canada's Worst Neighbourhood: How Did the Province Where Medicare Was Born End Up with a City This Frightening?" *Maclean's*, 15 January 2007.
22 Hip-hop culture has historically been gendered male for a variety of reasons. In its infancy, hip hop was about the reclamation of public space and the building of community on the streets. The public sphere has long been understood as a male privilege, whereas the private sphere (i.e., the home) has been interpreted as the place for girls and women. Throughout the evolution of hip-hop culture, the exclusion of women, or the relegation of women to the status of objects, has become entrenched. Thus, hip-hop, its cultural practices, and the technologies associated with these practices continue to be gendered—problematically so—in masculine terms. And though there are a number of women who participate in the culture and perform as rappers, DJs, B-Girls, and graffiti artists, the culture continues to reflect a patriarchal norm.
23 Understandably, this particular hip-hop program had not yet started. But this is not the first program dedicated to youth in this 'hood challenging the stereotypes and conditions through creative practices. http://www.macleans.ca/article.jsp?content=20070115_139375_139375
24 Gatehouse, "Canada's Worst Neighbourhood," http://www.macleans.ca/article.jsp?content=20070129_139986_139986.
25 Mayor Fiacco's and a local radio station's outrageous reaction to the initial article—throwing copies of *Maclean's* into a woodchopper—demonstrates an explicit denial of Gatehouse's report. Yet the report forced the mayor (and the city council) to take some action. Gatehouse, "Canada's Worst Neighbourhood."
26 The Editors, "Regina: One Year Later," *Maclean's*, 17 January 2008, http://www.macleans.ca/canada/opinions/article.jsp?content=20080117_95971_95971.
27 Ibid.
28 It is also significant that most if not all of these benefits are tied to the economy, which is narrow in its scope and imagination in terms of what is important to healthy and safe communities and neighbourhoods.
29 Robin Favel, in *Dogz Lyfe: Burdens of a Gangsta Rapper*, dir. Corey Generoux. Regina: Cooper Rock Pictures, 2008.
30 Forman, "Ain't No Love," 155.

31 Favel, *Dogz Lyfe*.
32 Ibid.
33 The impacts of contemporary colonialism on Aboriginal women in relation to the discourse on hip-hop culture are taken up later in this chapter.
34 Go to http://www.soundclick.com/bands/default.cfm?bandID=45117.
35 "Hustlaz," *Dogz Lyfe*, featuring Big Sav. Go to http://www.soundclick.com/bands/default.cfm?bandID=45117&content=music.
36 "Declaration of War," *Dogz Lyfe*. Go to http://www.soundclick.com/bands/default.cfm?bandID=45117&content=music.
37 Go to http://www.soundclick.com/bands/default.cfm?bandID=45117.
38 Favel, quoted by *CBC News*, 22 March 2005, in Daniel Johnson, "Robin Favel A.K.A. Burden," http://www.joybuzzard.com/danieljohnson/robinfavel.html, accessed 2 May 2011.
39 For a discussion of the relationship between music cultures and media-related moral panics, see Charity Marsh, "Understand Us Before You End Us: Regulation, Governmentality, and the Confessional Practices of Raving Bodies," *Popular Music* 25, no. 3 (2006): 415–30.
40 See Figure 1.
41 Veronica Rhodes, "Arrested on Camera," *The Leader-Post* (Regina) 18 August 2007, A1.
42 Ibid.
43 Generoux, in ibid.
44 Refer to Figure 2.
45 Johnson, "Robin Favel A.K.A. Burden."
46 Ibid.

CHAPTER 9

Fixing Stories "Is Sure a Lot of Work": Watching "the Men's Dance" in *Medicine River* and *Green Grass, Running Water*

PETER E. CUMMING

In the 2003 Massey Lectures, *The Truth about Stories: A Native Narrative*, Cherokee/Greek/American/Canadian author Thomas King claims that stories "control our lives"; that stories "told one way [can] cure, [but] told another way [can] injure"; that stories "try to set the world straight"; and that if we want a different ethic, we need to tell "a different story."[1] Indeed, a central conceit in King's 1993 novel *Green Grass, Running Water* (the single most frequently taught novel in university Canadian Literature courses in 2001)[2] is that of "fixing" the world through "fixing" stories—that is, through fixing our modes of narrative practice. In both his 1989 novel *Medicine River* and *Green Grass*, one way King "fixes" his stories is by steering his male protagonists away from Western traditions of individual male heroism toward Native valorization of community relations; in the process, he "re-visions" practices of minoritized Native male subjectivity in a way that parallels and corroborates feminist constructs of subjectivity-through-interrelation. As Sandra Harding argues, "there are suggestions in the literature of Native Americans...that what feminists call feminine versus masculine personalities, ontologies, ethics, epistemologies, and world views may be what...other liberation movements call Non-Western versus Western personalities and world views."[3] However, though King's Native views of community and the minoritized male may dismantle some of the tight connections between narrative structure and Western, hegemonic masculinities, this is not always sufficient to deconstruct normative masculinities and construct alternative ones; in fact, as I argue in this chapter, the more narratologically conservative novel *Medicine River* may unpack Western constructs of gender more fully than the aesthetically more radical novel *Green Grass, Running Water* by "re-visioning" rather than merely reversing traditional constructs of femininity and masculinity.[4]

An understandable preoccupation with issues of race, ethnicity, postcoloniality, and postmodernity in King's fiction—with the borderlands between "Indian" (King's preferred term for "Native American") and "white" worlds, and between oral storytelling and postmodern novel writing—risks eliding not unrelated and equally important issues of *gender* in King's work. As King suggests of his 1999 novel *Truth and Bright Water*, the novel is set "on either side of the border; one Indian, one white... *The other issue that I can play with is that border between men and women*."[5] Only by reading across what Teresa de Lauretis calls "several axes of difference"[6]—across race, ethnicity, narratological structure, *and* gender—can we recognize both the radical subversions and the potential limitations of King's fiction.

In *Medicine River*, rather than merely reversing power relations between women and men, King productively envisions new roles for each through the creation of strong, independent female characters like the aptly named Louise Heavyman; a feminized male trickster, Harlen Bigbear, who acts as "male mother" to his community; and Harlen's protégé, Will Horse Capture, a male protagonist who, rather than performing as the self-sufficient, isolated "walled city"[7] of the Hegelian subject, learns instead to define himself through his "relations": with his absent father and wandering brother; as a member of the basketball team; in his friendship with Louise; in his adoptive paternity of Louise's daughter South Wing—based not on insemination but on participant parenthood; and ultimately in his position in the community not as an outside photographer but as an inside member of a very extended family.

However, while King *seems* to re-vision gender even more overtly in his multi-levelled, comic tour de force *Green Grass, Running Water*, through gender-bending characters ranging from four ancient Indians of indeterminate sex and gender to the footloose professor Alberta Frank to "Moby-Jane, the Great Black [Lesbian] Whale,"[8] he may be merely reversing power relations between men and women—in what Gayatri Spivak calls "the founding of a hysterocentric to counter a phallic discourse"[9]—rather than exploring life-sustaining alternatives for women and men. In *Medicine River*, strong female characters are complemented by Will's and Harlen's *rejection* of destructive masculinities (the basketball team, with "Leroy's [station] wagon, the drum, a case of beer, a bunch of...cheap cigars, and a general idea of which way north is,"[10] not to mention violence, sexual braggadocio, spousal abuse, and criminal assaults) and *adoption* of typically "feminine" strengths (companionship, participant parenting, cooperation, community building, and nurturing). Conversely, in *Green Grass*, the strong female characters in the novel's realistic thread, having suffered from the abuse, stupidity, and indolence of men, incessantly emphasize the weakness of the decidedly unheroic male characters (hapless Lionel Red Dog, his "slick"/"sleazy"[11] rival, Charlie Looking Bear, and even his potentially heroic uncle, Eli Stands Alone). Even on the mythical level of the texts, whereas in *Medicine River*, the trickster Harlen works in constructive, cross-gendered ways (as King says, Harlen's job "is to make sure that the world is in good health. And in order to do that... [he has] to use... a more feminine approach to that world... a softer and tenderer method of arranging the whole community"),[12] in *Green Grass*, Coyote seems to work exclusively in destructive, typically "masculine" ways (impregnating the Virgin Mary and Alberta and dancing the dam away). Thus, while *Medicine River* actively contests Hegelian views of the male subject as isolated and dominating, *Green Grass* gets bogged down in Derrida's first "phase" of deconstruction—a simple reversal of the hierarchy of men over women— without exploring any possible "third term" for the doomed men in the text. While Will in *Medicine River* becomes more fully human through his feminization, Lionel in *Green Grass* almost always remains the butt of a First Nations Battle of the Sexes, inevitably doomed to personal failure in a world consisting exclusively of superior women and inferior men. While central male characters in *Medicine River* demonstrate growth as new and better men, those in *Green Grass* seem locked into pathetic, dead-end masculinities—reinforced not only by the past experiences but also by the self-fulfilling prophecies of the women in their community. While *Medicine River* seems profoundly optimistic about progressive masculinities, *Green Grass* seems deterministically pessimistic in its treatment of directionless men cast adrift by their loss of traditional masculinities. As Valerie Compton notes in her review of *Green Grass*, "What hope is there for the future of men and women who, in King's vision at least, always completely misunderstand each other?"[13]

SEARCHING FOR BALANCE

For King, Native cultures emphasize not "right and wrong" but "balance."[14] *Medicine River* ultimately strikes such a balance better than *Green Grass*: whereas women and men admirably tap into each others' strengths in *Medicine River* (as Constance Rooke suggests, "It's as if males are moving towards female strengths, and females towards male strengths"),[15] women's strength in *Green Grass* seems continuously predicated on—and also generative of— men's weakness. Thomas Matchie and Brett Larson suggest a link between King's fiction and Joseph Meeker's connection between comedy and balance: "In comedy we are a part of nature, and what is important in this mode is a return to balance."[16] However, the fictional universe of *Green Grass* remains lopsidedly out of balance when it comes to women and men: the novel's comedy, always at the expense of its male characters, depends not on a restoration of balance but on women always being superior to men. Replacing misogyny with misandry may be (at best) a necessary phase in the dismantling of patriarchy, though as Robert Scholes, responding to Derrida and Culler, notes, "the question that needs asking here is whether the phase of reversal ever accomplishes anything in social terms."[17]

In both novels, King's female characters are refreshingly strong, independent, and assertive individuals, repositories of traditional Indian culture, and spiritual and economic leaders of their communities. In *Green Grass*, on the mythic level of the text, First Woman revolts against the "grouchy GOD" of Genesis, packs her bags, and leaves the garden, the man Ahdamn in tow.[18] On the realistic level, Lionel's sister Latisha, despite having been abused by her white ex-husband, George Morningstar, both runs a successful tourist café and maintains cultural traditions of and positive relations with her community. And Alberta, professor of history and erstwhile lover of both Lionel and Charlie, is, in Lionel's understatement, "an independent woman."[19] As a child, Alberta asks her mother why women cannot, like her father, go to the mountains; her mother tells her there is "[no] reason why they can't."[20] As an adult, Alberta, like Louise in *Medicine River*, prefers to keep her men literally at a distance: "Alberta liked having two men in her life, especially when they were both over two hundred kilometers away...Apart from no men in her life, two was the safest number."[21]

In one of King's characteristic reversals, it is not Alberta or any women who are dependent on, or desirous of, marriage; as Alberta sees it: "Men wanted to be married. More than sex, Alberta was convinced, men wanted marriage."[22] By contrast, Alberta "just want[s] a child. I don't want a husband."[23] Carol Gilligan argues that since "masculinity is defined through separation while femininity is defined through attachment, male gender identity is threatened by intimacy while female gender identity is threatened by separation. Thus males tend to have difficulty with relationships, while females tend to have problems with individuation."[24] But in both novels, Will, Lionel, and even Charlie seem less threatened by (male–female) intimacy than Louise, Alberta, and Latisha; conversely, these women seem far less threatened by separation from men than the men do from women. The male characters desperately seek relationships with the female characters; the female characters seem to have little need or desire for the male characters. As Margaret Atwood notes of King's short story, "One Good Story, That One," "Adam is stupid, and Eve, who is generous, level-headed, peace-loving and nurturing, comes out the hero of the story."[25]

If King's women, admirably, have control of their lives in both traditional culture and the contemporary world, in *Green Grass*, King's men seem to have control in neither. If women are strong and independent, men, particularly in *Green Grass*, are weak and dependent. Granted, their very ineffectuality may make them less stereotypically patriarchal. Nonetheless, many of the men in *Green Grass* come off as sheer bumblers; indeed, much of the humour—as conventionally as in stand-up comedy routines—depends precisely on this. Typically, they are infantilized by King's female characters (as, of course, women in patriarchy have so often been infantilized by men): when Alberta dreams of having a baby in the hot bathtub with her, "just as she got it settled on a breast, she would discover that the baby had somehow turned into Lionel. Or Charlie";[26] and when Norma concludes that "[a] woman who gets married and has a child winds up with two babies."[27]

At their worst, *Green Grass*'s women essentialize men. Even in *Medicine River*, Will's mother and her friend Erleen dismiss men as "two raisins and a noodle, and a cupcake for brains" and also as an ugly "cucumber,"[28] but these re-visions of phallus as noodle and cucumber are not typical of that text as a whole. By contrast, in *Green Grass*, misandry—as regressive as it is comic—seems systemic. For Alberta, "Charlie and Lionel weren't much different from Bob [her chauvinistic first husband] and Amos [her abusive, alcoholic father]."[29] It is one thing that Latisha's husband, George Morningstar, a white wannabe Indian, is "bone-deep stupid."[30] However, it is quite another when, even at what should be their best moment, at the end of the novel, when Norma, Latisha, and Alberta prepare to rebuild Norma's mother's cabin after the dam has burst, both Charlie and Lionel—men—remain extremely dense, while all the women know exactly what to do:

"The porch post," [Norma] said....
"You want that thing?" said Charlie.
"Use it on the new cabin," said Norma....
"What new cabin?" said Lionel.[31]

The novel's pivotal scene at the traditional site of the Sun Dance seems to perpetuate, naturalize, or even valorize a rigid separation and hierarchization of the sexes in which women in the tepee (all women, Native or white) share dismissive views of men while sending the men (all men, Native or white) outside to paint their faces, cut wood, and participate in the "men's dance." Though Eli never becomes comfortable with the desire of Karen (his white, Toronto wife) to be part of the Sun Dance, the other women readily accept Karen there (more than they do Eli)—seemingly *because she is a woman*. Contrary to bell hooks's contention that women may "find 'common bonds' of affinity more easily with men of their socioeconomic and cultural group than they do with women across barriers of class or race,"[32] Karen's instant camaraderie and solidarity with the other women may even suggest that gender is a more primary—and substantial—determinant of interrelation than race or ethnicity: "by ... the third day in camp, just as the men began to dance, Karen found her voice, and Eli... was flushed from the lodge. 'Go on, Eli,' Norma told him...'Go outside and chop some wood...Us women got talking to do.'"[33] Similarly, Norma asks George (his maleness superseding his whiteness) to "go on out with the men... [T]here's always wood to be chopped."[34]

While there are occasional non-gendered activities at the Sun Dance, notably involving children, almost all adult activities are rigidly separated by gender. Both (white) George and (Indian) Eli like the "men's dancing" best.³⁵ George's outsider view of the "men's dance" *might* suggest progressive potential: "'Why are they skipping?' he asked. 'Why are they holding hands?' 'What do they do inside the double tepee all day?'"³⁶ But Eli's remembrance of the men's dancing aligns the ceremony disturbingly with traditional masculinities associated with death and domination: "[O]ne of the dancers would pick up a rifle and lead the other men to the edge of the camp, where the children waited... [T]he lead dancer would breach the fortress of children and fire the rifle, and all the children would fall down in a heap, laughing, full of fear and pleasure."³⁷

Moreover, this separation of the sexes cannot be blamed only on the elder women: the younger women Latisha and Alberta reinforce it as readily as Norma. Women, young and old, exploit the ample opportunity for jokes based on assumed sexual difference, female superiority, and male incompetence. When Lionel's lover, Alberta, and sister, Latisha, discuss Alberta's options for having a baby, Latisha concludes, "'With alternatives like Charlie and Lionel, [artificial insemination] makes perfect sense.'"³⁸ With gender again seeming to take precedence over race, Connie, a white police officer, concurs that a "[m]an's a nice thing to have around but so's a dishwasher."³⁹ Men, in fact, are almost completely dispensable to the women in *Green Grass*. After Alberta discovers the autoerotic possibilities of a hair dryer, rather than wait for Lionel to accompany her to the Sun Dance, she says, "Let him get his own hair dryer."⁴⁰ Jeanette, an older tourist, finds consolation in the fact that her husband will die before her and considers Latisha's "[throwing George] away" a "happy ending."⁴¹

Even when men show small signs of changing for the better, the female characters deny men the possibility of change. When Latisha and Alberta both express surprise that Lionel and Eli have come to the Sun Dance, Norma says, "'No point pouring water on a spark,'" only to have Latisha and Alberta dump buckets of water on Lionel's pathetically small spark of change:

> "Must be snowing in hell," said Latisha....
> ... "It's his birthday. Most men don't even start to get smart until after they turn forty."
> ... "Then what happens?"⁴²

Against the combined wisdom of women as a homogeneous group (despite Alberta being a professor, Latisha a self-made restaurateur, and Norma a traditional elder), even the most earnest of men has little chance to be more than a buffoon. Ultimately, through the eyes of Alberta and the novel's other female characters, all men share a very limited repertoire: "Lionel wasn't pushy and slick like Charlie. He was sincere and dull. And when she thought about it, Alberta wasn't sure that there was anything in between. Maybe all men were like that, Charlies and Lionels. Or worse. Maybe, in the end, they all turned into Amoses, standing in the dark, angry, their pants down around their ankles."[43]

The pervasive "*bone*-deep stupidity" of men in *Green Grass* may imply that this condition is biologically determined, inextricably linked with men's dubious possession of penises. It may also suggest either misandry (all men *are* bone-deep stupid) or a more subtle misogyny (women are only capable of seeing men as bone-deep stupid and therefore are incapable of allowing men to grow out of that stupidity). Asked why "the women in your fiction are so much more intelligent than the men," King offers a benign interpretation of this imbalance: "It is not so much that the women are smarter than the men... [M]en are simply more privileged and with that privilege comes a certain laziness... Lionel has had a pretty easy go of it and he hasn't made anything out of it."[44] Ironically, King, an author not usually given to limiting the scope of his vision to "how things are," defends these characterizations here with an argument of verisimilitude: that's just the way things are. To the contrary, as Stephen Tyler suggests, discourse is the "maker of the world, not its mirror... The world is what we say it is, and what we speak of is the world."[45]

IMPOSSIBILITIES OF "THE MEN'S DANCE"

Critics disagree about who the central character in the complex narrative structure of *Green Grass* is (or, more correctly, who the central characters are): for Alan Nustak, it is the four old Indians;[46] for Diane Turbide, the five contemporary Blackfoot Indians;[47] for Candace Fertile, the professor Alberta, caught between Charlie and Lionel;[48] and for Sandra Martin, Eli Stands Alone.[49] However, Malcolm Jones Jr. most accurately sums up *Green Grass* as being "chiefly the story of Lionel Red Dog....[b]ut...also the story of his Uncle Eli... Alberta, Lionel's girlfriend...Latisha, Lionel's sister...four aged Indian escapees from a mental institution...[and] the talking coyote."[50] Just as *Medicine River* is centrally about Will, but always about Will in relation to the rest of his community, so *Green Grass* is centrally about Lionel, but always about Lionel in relation to the other characters of his community. Both the mythological and the realistic characters in *Green Grass* all converge on Lionel and the "fixing" needed in his life. The gap between Lionel's aspirations to and fantasies about the role of the traditional, Western, male hero and his actual performance make him a comic hero. Yet as he tries to piece his life together on his fortieth birthday, Lionel demonstrates some small degree of heroism in his attempt to shed traditional masculinities and—like Will in *Medicine River*—in his discovery of his need for help from and relationships with others. Unlike Will, though, Lionel is ultimately not able to inhabit the skin of a fully grown human—because the women in his life will not allow it.

From the age of six, Lionel has wanted to be precisely a traditional male Western hero: "John Wayne. Not the actor, but the character. Not the man, but the hero."[51] But facing his fortieth birthday, Lionel finds his life "had become embarrassing."[52] In Lionel's misguided attempts to turn his life completely around on his fortieth birthday, King humorously deflates the heroic, redemptive transformations of the traditional Western male hero. The man who would be John Wayne now resolves that "[t]omorrow, he would begin to floss"[53] and fantasizes about Alberta eagerly dropping her career to have his babies.[54] The male hero of Western literature surely needs such deflation. As Atwood asks: "[L]ike Walter Mitty, does each man contain within him both an ordinary, limited and trivial self and a heroic concept, and if so, which should we be writing about?"[55] Indeed, both Will in *Medicine River* and Lionel in *Green Grass* are more interesting as the "limited" and "trivial" selves Atwood describes. However, to make Lionel central to his community and the novel *Green Grass*, yet to offer him practically no scope for substantial growth as a character, may lead to both a narrative and a political dead end.

Though Jace Weaver's assessment of Lionel as "the rather lazy protagonist of *Green Grass*"[56] and Diane Turbide's as "a mild-mannered underachiever"[57] may be overly harsh, Lionel is hardly much of a self-starter: his name, "Lionel Red Dog," is more mock-heroic than heroic. (As is, of course, that of Will Horse Capture in *Medicine River*.) Constantly vacillating about going back to university, Lionel is told by his father: "If you're going to go... you probably better get going.... Maybe they got an age limit at that university ... When your grandfather was thirty-two... he was dead."[58] Yet out of all the needy people in the world, it is Lionel whom the four old Indians choose as in need of fixing. Weaver, and following him, Sharon Malinowski[59] seriously misread the novel when they argue that the four old Indians "are determined to avert an environmental disaster about to take place in Canada. During their picaresque adventure they become involved with some offbeat modern Natives,"[60] for the old Indians intentionally set out to "fix" the "balance" *in Lionel's life* rather than to oppose the dam project.[61] When the Indians first meet Lionel, his "standing in a puddle of water"[62] suggests both that he is in need of "fixing" and that he is capable of "rebirth." With advice from Norma, prodding from the four old Indians, and mentorship from his Uncle Eli, Lionel reluctantly ends up at the Sun Dance, where he performs his most conventionally heroic act, helping to stop George from taking pictures of the Sun Dance. In this atypical scene, Eli Stands Alone no longer stands alone; his nephew, Lionel Red Dog, acts true to his name; and, in one of the most sustained sections of narrative in the novel, there is a rare moment of interdependence and solidarity between men and women.[63] Just for a moment, Lionel is a hero, connected with and equal to the rest of his community.

More important, though, in terms of rejecting "old" and adopting "new" masculinities, Lionel shows himself strongest at two points toward the end of the novel. Significantly, though, at both points, his gestures toward connection, intimacy, and caring are rebuffed by the women in his life. When Lionel finds out that Alberta is pregnant, far from demonstrating undue anxiety about the paternity of the child, he expresses concern for Alberta and tries to negotiate a relationship of equals with her: Lionel "watched Alberta leaning over and debated how he should try to comfort her. Wondered if he should hold her or talk to her. Tell her a joke. Or just stay out of the way."[64] Surrounded by women who do not need him, women who, like Norma, want to live his life for him, women who, like Alberta, want to live their lives without him, is it any wonder that Lionel, who reaches out for connection and is rejected, ends up deciding that the best he can do for others is to "just stay out of the way"? Similarly, at the end of the novel, when Alberta, Latisha, and Norma begin building a cabin to replace the one Norma's mother built and that Eli lived in until the dam broke, the community of women cajoles Lionel into staying and helping—on *their* terms. However, when Lionel decides that "maybe when the cabin is finished ... I'll live in it for a while. You know, like Eli," even though he has been constantly likened to Eli and mentored by Eli throughout the novel, Norma closes down this possibility, at least for the moment: "'Not your turn...It's my turn. Your turn will come soon enough.'"[65] But will Lionel's turn come?

Given these unequal power dynamics, Dee Horne's celebratory reading of changes among men and women in *Green Grass* seems far too generous: "King...re-presents an alternative discourse...that is neither patriarchal nor capitalistic ... a world in which men and women are equal...and tricksters attempt to unbend what is bent."[66] In *Green Grass*, men and women are *not* equal: women are superior to men, and men, having abandoned traditional masculinities, have few other opportunities for productive lives. Tricksters in *Green Grass* may *attempt* to unbend what is bent, but as the novel repeatedly emphasizes, some tricksters cause as much damage as healing, creating new imbalances while attempting to rectify old ones: "'We fixed up part of the world,'" says Hawkeye, but Ishmael adds, "'Unfortunately,...part of it got messed up too.'"[67] "'Is it time to apologize?' says a characteristically unrepentant Coyote... 'Is it time to be helpful?'"[68]

King says that "[s]omeplace in [Native culture], there's a strength. And someplace in there, people are managing, not just surviving, but actually prospering. And I want to see these people in my fiction."[69] Though in *Medicine River*, some of King's male characters seem to be managing, perhaps even prospering, in *Green Grass*, King's male characters may be doomed to just (barely) surviving. Following Judith Butler's conception of "gender trouble," Linda Lamont-Stewart contends that the "gender trouble" produced by androgynous characters in *Green Grass* "may not bring about the collapse of the power structures within which they perform their gender crossings, but it does succeed in exposing the binary logic upon which authoritarian power structures are founded."[70] To the contrary, *Green Grass*'s rigid definition of, separation of, and hierarchization of the sexes in the realistic characters, combined with a masculine Coyote and narrator who get the first and last words of the novel, all suggest "gender trouble" of another sort. It may well be that, both traditionally and more recently, women tend to lead Native communities while men typically drag their heels. However, the fictional universe in *Green Grass*—a world in which all men are dependent on women while all women are only encumbered by the nuisance of men, a world in which men are either sleazy, abusive, or spineless while women are consistently strong and successful in both traditional and contemporary worlds—seems to go far beyond empowering women and a female-centred society: for here, women's power seems predicated completely on men's weakness.

In both *Medicine River* and *Green Grass*, leather jackets symbolize hegemonic masculinities that clearly need to be shed. Refreshingly, in *Medicine River*, Harlen and Will productively come to recognize that a leather jacket that prompts a violent fight between men "is a poor substitute for friends and family":[71] consequently, Will develops his identity not through the isolation and violence of normative masculinities but by his nurturing of Louise's baby South Wing—he shakes her rattle, sings her a parenting song, and buys a top for her, the top his own father never bought for him. To the contrary, in *Green Grass*, Lionel, for a time, wears the fringed buckskin jacket—variously belonging to John Wayne[72] and Nasty Bumppo.[73] Ominously, the chorus of mythical "Indians" comment on the leather jacket: "'It's pretty old' [said the Lone Ranger]. 'But these things never wear out,' said Ishmael. 'Yes,' said Hawkeye. 'You can wear them forever.'"[74] To his credit, Lionel, who has wanted all his life to be John Wayne's character,[75] eventually finds the jacket uncomfortable, "as if the jacket was suffocating him."[76] But though Alberta knows that Lionel "could use a new jacket"[77] and though Lionel sheds this jacket of old masculinities, reeking of a "stale, sweet smell, like old aftershave or rotting fruit,"[78] unlike Will in *Medicine River*, Lionel in *Green Grass* can find no adequate jacket to don once he throws off this mantle of patriarchy—and the gold blazer of Bill Bursum's television store. Thus, unfortunately for Lionel, the other male characters in *Green Grass*, and readers seeking a representation of progressive masculinities in the novel, as a result of the inability of male, female, and androgynous characters and of Coyote, the narrator, and the novelist to find new clothes for new men, Alberta's pessimistic conclusion about men seems dangerously like the conclusion of the novel itself: that "[m]aybe, in the end, [all men ended up like her father Amos] ... standing in the dark, angry, their pants down around their ankles."[79]

CONCLUSION

For Denise Low, "King delivers an optimistic message [in *Green Grass*]: that opposites can reconcile, that bad movies can be amended, and that creation is not stuck in the atrocities of the past."[80] Granted, many stories *are* "fixed" in both *Medicine River* and *Green Grass*. But fixing stories, as the four old Indians discover, "is sure a lot of work":[81]

> "[Y]ou have to get it right," said Hawkeye.
> "And," said Robinson Crusoe, "you can't tell it all by yourself" ...
> "Everybody makes mistakes," said the Lone Ranger.
> "Best not to make them with stories."[82]

Unfortunately, in terms of gender, the stories in *Green Grass* may ultimately remain stuck as "fixed" (meaning rigid and unchanging) stories rather than being liberated as "fixed" (meaning new and better) stories. The climactic earthquake and the breaking of the dam toward the end of *Green Grass* brings an "ominous sound of things giving way, of things falling apart";[83] though "things fall apart" invokes Chinua Achebe's famous novel of cultural dissolution, the Sun Dance and cabin-rebuilding scenes in *Green Grass* may instead wistfully suggest that a return to traditional values, complete with men being men and women being women and both being separate, is the only possible alternative to the present state of men being only and always bumbling lost souls and women being only and always effective community leaders. In either case, though at least some of King's Indians recognize that even a phrase as "nice" as "[a]s long as the grass is green and the waters run" is a metaphor, "and no one signed a contract for eternity,"[84] the one construction that seems eternal in *Green Grass* is the construction of women and men as separate and unequal beings. If, then, as Thomas King persuasively suggests in his Massey lectures, stories control our lives, then this matters. And if, as he maintains, we need to tell a different story in order to set the world straight by seeking "a different ethic," then when it comes to constructions of new and better practices of masculinity, *Medicine River* presents us with just such a story while *Green Grass, Running Water*—for all its aesthetic pyrotechnics—falls short of doing so.

NOTES

1 Thomas King, *The Truth about Stories: A Native Narrative* (Toronto: Anansi, 2003), 9, 92, 60, 164.
2 "Which Have *You* Read?" *University Affairs* 43, no. 1 (2002): 8.
3 Sandra Harding, "The Instability of the Analytical Categories of Feminist Theory," *Signs* 11, no. 4 (1986): 645–64 at 659.
4 For my celebration of King's revisioning of masculinities in *Medicine River*, see "Coyote Meets Hegel: 'Male Mothers' and Absent Fathers in *Medicine River*," in

"Some 'Male' from Canada 'Post': Heterosexual Masculinities in Contemporary Canadian Writing," Ph.D. diss., University of Western Ontario, 2002, 182–236; here, I focus more concertedly on my perhaps more contentious disappointment in the limitations of King's representation of masculinities in *Green Grass, Running Water*.
5 Thomas King, "Interview with Thomas King," by Jeffrey Canton, *Paragraph* 16, no. 1 (1994): 2–6 at 4. Emphasis added.
6 Teresa de Lauretis, "Eccentric Subjects: Feminist Theory and Historical Consciousness," *Feminist Studies* 16, no. 1 (1990): 115–50 at 137.
7 Kathy E. Ferguson, *The Man Question: Visions of Subjectivity in Feminist Theory* (Berkeley: University of California Press, 1993), 44.
8 Thomas King, *Green Grass, Running Water* (Toronto: HarperCollins, 1993), 164.
9 Gayatri Spivak, "Displacement and the Discourse of Woman," in *Displacement: Derrida and After*, ed. Mark Krupnick (Bloomington: Indiana University Press, 1983), 184.
10 Thomas King, *Medicine River* [1989] (Toronto: Penguin, 1991), 104.
11 King, *Green Grass*, 99.
12 Thomas King, "Interview with Tom King," by Constance Rooke, *World Literature Written in English* 30, no. 2 (1990): 66–67.
13 Valerie Compton, review of *Green Grass, Running Water*, by Thomas King, *Quill and Quire* 59, no. 3 (1993): 46.
14 Thomas King, "Introduction," in *All My Relations: An Anthology of Contemporary Canadian Native Fiction*, ed. Thomas King (Toronto: McClelland and Stewart, 1990), ix–xvi.
15 King, Rooke interview, 67.
16 Thomas Matchie and Brett Larson, "Coyote Fixes the World: The Power of Myth in Thomas King's *Green Grass, Running Water*," *North Dakota Quarterly* 63, no. 2 (1996): 164–65.
17 Robert Scholes, "Reading Like a Man," in *Men in Feminism*, ed. Alice Jardine and Paul Smith (New York: Routledge, 1989), 211.
18 King, *Green Grass*, 57.
19 Ibid., 142.
20 Ibid., 214.
21 Ibid., 36–37.
22 Ibid., 37.
23 Ibid., 148.
24 Carol Gilligan, "Woman's Place in Man's Life Cycle," in *The Second Wave: A Reader in Feminist Theory*, ed. Linda Nicholson (New York and London: Routledge, 1997), 198–215 at 201.
25 Margaret Atwood, "A Double-Bladed Knife: Subversive Laughter in Two Stories by Thomas King," *Canadian Literature* 124–25 (1990): 243–50 at 249.
26 King, *Green Grass*, 213.
27 Ibid., 116.
28 King, *Medicine River*, 62.
29 King, *Green Grass*, 74.
30 Ibid., 159.
31 Ibid., 352.
32 bell hooks, quoted in Lynne Segal, *Is the Future Female? Troubled Thoughts on Contemporary Feminism* (London: Virago, 1987), 61.
33 King, *Green Grass*, 171.
34 Ibid., 281–82.
35 Ibid., 283, 116.

36 Ibid., 283.
37 Ibid., 116.
38 Ibid., 295.
39 Ibid., 255.
40 Ibid., 296.
41 Ibid., 113.
42 Ibid., 308.
43 Ibid., 149–50.
44 King, Canton interview, 4.
45 Stephen Tyler, quoted in Gerald Vizenor, "A Postmodern Introduction," in *Narrative Chance: Postmodern Discourse on Native American Indian Literatures*, ed. Gerald Vizenor (Albuquerque: University of New Mexico Press, 1989), 4.
46 Alan Nustak, "Sudden Acclaim Is a Surprise for Aboriginal Writer," *The Gazette* (Montreal), 11 April 1993, section F.
47 Diane Turbide, "A Literary Trickster: Thomas King Conjures Up Comic Worlds," *Maclean's* 106, no. 18, 3 May 1993, 43, 45.
48 Candace Fertile, "Novel Works on Many Levels," review of *Green Grass, Running Water*, by Thomas King, *Calgary Herald*, 6 February 1993, section A.
49 Sandra Martin, "This Land Is Whose Land?" *Quill and Quire* 60, no. 5 (1994): 24.
50 Malcolm Jones, Jr., "Life Off the Reservation: A Cherokee Writer as Darkly Funny as Twain," *Newsweek*, 12 April 1993, 60.
51 King, *Green Grass*, 202.
52 Ibid., 201.
53 Ibid., 202.
54 Ibid., 344–45.
55 Margaret Atwood, "Writing the Male Character," in *Second Words: Selected Critical Prose* (Toronto: Anansi, 1982), 412–30 at 426.
56 Dee Horne, "To Know the Difference: Mimicry, Satire, and Thomas King's *Green Grass, Running Water*," *Essays on Canadian Writing* 56 (Fall 1995): 255–73 at 270–71.
57 Turbide, "A Literary Trickster," 43.
58 King, *Green Grass*, 68.
59 Sharon Malinowski, ed., *Notable Native Americans* (New York: Gale Research, 1995), 235.
60 Jave Weaver, "Thomas King," *Publishers Weekly*, 8 March 1993, 56–57 at 56.
61 King, *Green Grass*, 105, 106, 141.
62 Ibid., 90.
63 Ibid., 322.
64 Ibid., 344–45.
65 Ibid., 354.
66 Horne, "To Know the Difference," 270–71.
67 King, *Green Grass*, 357.
68 Ibid., 191.
69 King, quoted in Malinowski, *Notable Native Americans*, 235.
70 Linda Lamont-Stewart, "Androgyny as Resistance to Authoritarianism in Two Postmodern Canadian Novels," *Mosaic* 30, no. 3 (1997): 115–130 at 128.
71 King, *Medicine River*, 255.
72 King, *Green Grass*, 161.
73 Ibid., 327.
74 Ibid., 252.
75 Ibid., 202.
76 Ibid., 318.

77 Ibid., 149.
78 Ibid., 318.
79 Ibid., 150.
80 Denise Low, review of *Green Grass, Running Water*, by Thomas King, *American Indian Quarterly* 18, no. 1 (1994): 104–6.
81 King, *Green Grass*, 266.
82 Ibid., 10.
83 Ibid., 346.
84 Ibid., 224.

CHAPTER 10

Masculinity in a Minority Setting: The Emblematic Body in Simone Chaput's *Le coulonneux*

NICOLE CÔTÉ

I would like to examine here an issue at the confluence of minority masculinities in Canada: minority studies and globalization. François Paré[1] examines the paradoxical identity configuration that is specific to minorities in a globalized world and that transforms the individual's relationship to identity and origin. He argues that minorities oscillate between an acute and painful consciousness of their marginal status, and oblivion. In our postmodern world, oblivion seems to be one of the strategies by which minority cultures adapt. Indeed, Pare argues that oblivion might not necessarily be a negative strategy, as it allows individuals to move beyond their paralyzing status toward a reinvention of identity, which is then projected into the future. By refusing to dwell on the vulnerability of their first culture, by developing a sense of belonging to the main culture — even though it might mean endless negotiations — minorities construct a necessarily hybrid identity. Franco-Canadians follow this trend.

Nonetheless, this oblivion strategy takes a toll on identities. Minorities, according to Paré, as a result of oblivion, that survival strategy, suffer both from the *atopical* — the loss of a sense of belonging to a specific territory — linked to "wandering, migration and disorder";[2] and from the *amorphous*, linked to "the negative, death and the privation of being."[3] For instance, traces of this oblivion strategy — that is, symptoms of minoritization — can be found in the texts produced by this culture. In other words, Franco-Canadian literature buries its minoritization characteristics deeper into its textual fabric. Minorities thus, in their cultural texts, display both an "ontological lack" — a constant feeling of being invisible or in the process of vanishing — and "practices of dislocation at work in all minority cultures."[4]

Subjectivity being traditionally founded on the relation to an excluded or subordinate *other* who suffers the above symptoms, I would like to investigate how symptoms of minoritization affect the display of masculinity of *Le coulonneux*'s main protagonist and narrator.[5] I am thinking here first and foremost of Gabriel Tardiff's minoritization as a Franco-Canadian and North American, but my analysis will also consider the fact that he is a white hetero male, his identity thus showing a mixture of minority and majority traits. I will compare his status to that of his female equivalent in years and ethnic belonging, Amandine. If we consider, as Butler contends, that "sexual and racial differences are not discrete axes of power"[6] and that gender is a way of "doing," of styling the body, a "sculpting of the original body into a cultural form,"[7] what does this Franco-Canadian novel tell us about the minoritization of the hegemonic gender? What does it tell us about Gabriel's relation to his body—his self-styling—and to other sexed bodies?

In accordance with Paré's findings about oblivion as an alternative strategy of survival for minorities, *Le coulonneux* often buries the minority status of its characters and their environment. This burying is manifested in the obliterating strategies of the male and female characters, of which the strangest might be a desire for invisibility. The protagonist Gabriel, of Franco-Manitoban heritage, suffers symptoms of minoritization typical of Franco-Canadians. Yet being male and white, he holds a certain majority status. How does this particular configuration of power shape his hetero masculinity in relation to the female protagonists?

STRATEGIES OF OBLIVION: THE ATOPICAL AND THE AMORPHOUS

The protagonist of *Le Coulonneux* is emblematic of the exiguity symptom that Paré discussed in his *Littératures de l'exiguïté*, for in him are condensed the "*atopical*, that which has no place assigned,"[8] according to Paré's typology, and the amorphous, linked to negation and to ontological lack.[9] According to Paré, the "atopical" is at the same time a condition of cultural exiguity and a symptom of the oblivion present in the works produced in minority conditions. In *Le coulonneux*, among the two types of distanciation from the self that I mentioned earlier, the most obvious, the "atopical," translates into the relentless pursuit of some elusive desire by taking the road, which brings about a constant disorientation—a sort of permanence amidst the transitory—an itinerancy. In *La distance habitée*, Paré defines itinerancy thus: "a group of practices of dislocation, the dislocation at work in all the minority cultures: *shifting*, diglossia, assimilation, displacement, compromise and delegation of identity."[10]

I would argue that Gabriel's desire for obliteration is on one side manifested in his burning desire to take the road, a desire that, because it is adirectional, would point to the *atopical*. Bizarrely, the territories traversed during his journey are strictly described geophysically, as if they were without geopolitical reality, as if, metonymically related to Gabriel's body, they could only fall into oblivion (or is it because this is Canada, a huge country that Americans and Europeans alike manage to forget in their statistics, a measure of our self-effacement?). Another aspect of the *atopical* in this novel is the fact that the Franco-Canadian culture and language that Gabriel belongs to is—characteristically—mentioned only toward the end, when he is searching for his roots. Gabriel's desire for obliteration also points to the *amorphous*, linked to "the negative, death and the privation of being," an "ontological lack" that I would argue is again a somatic translation of his minority status, Gabriel's "ontological lack" translating into a very particular, ambiguous but ever-changing relation to flesh.

BODY DYNAMICS: DISAPPEARING ON THE ROAD

Le coulonneux seems to be under the sway of a centrifugal force that destabilizes space and, with it, any idea of a firmly rooted culture. I would argue that what is hidden in hegemonic cultures—the fight for a unified collective identity, the various strands of identities left uncollected—becomes obvious in a minority setting. Paré contends that "in minority societies...the ground on which identity lies seems to give way."[11] Paré's remark is here metaphorical, but it is precisely what one can say of Gabriel's wanderings, experienced as an absence of space, inasmuch as the space being covered is only really inhabited at the moment when the narrative stops. Paré explains that "in the negotiation and often the desertion of his or her primary identity, the minority subject is being traversed by this emblematic distance which divides him-her and constitutes his-her only language."[12]

Gabriel Tardiff, 17, drives away from his unfinished studies in his old Chevrolet, which will be his home base during his North American journey. Gabriel leaves without a precise destination in mind, yet he follows an itinerary that traverses the main cultures of North America. At the symbolic term of seven years, Gabriel is ready not only to confront the lacks brought by his culture, from a hegemonic standpoint, but also to find its benefits, his roots. Thus even though his trip appears first as *itinerancy*, it will in the end be revealed as *itinerary*. In other words, his experience of vagrancy will become vectorial, thanks to the hegemonic masculine culture he was raised in, which traditionally allows for transformation through a quest.

However, this will not be the case for Gabriel's female counterpart, Amandine Collard. Gabriel's unconscious strategies of oblivion seem to find a tragic echo in Amandine, Gabriel's neighbour in St-Boniface, barely older than he is, and just as obsessed by the elsewhere, as she will find herself unable to give a meaning to her travelling. A sculptural beauty, she indifferently offers her body to whoever is ready to drive her around. Nonetheless, the drives remain only drives in that their destination is of no import. Amandine is on the road—she drives for the sake of driving, rather than to discover the world. Metaphorically, she is going nowhere: her story turns round and round. Gabriel finds her seven years later still obsessed with running away, her male school friends having been replaced by long-distance truck drivers. Her agency is now clearly problematic in that she chooses neither her destination nor the man who drives her when she runs away, leaving it to fate. The only choice she makes is to leave, knowing that she will always be back. Abandoned by her parents, living with a grandfather forced by necessity into her adolescent life, but with whom she entertains no affective relationship, Amandine seeks compulsive flights from her daily reality, flights that perpetually propel her toward the shifting centre of her trauma. The minoritization of her French people in Western Canada—Amandine being the daughter of Belgian immigrants—as well as her orphan status contribute to her vulnerability as a female. The trips even seem to worsen Amandine's mental alienation, since they disorient her and never translate into the exploration of a cultural territory, as they do for Gabriel. In the end, even though Amandine seems to be the feminine counterpart to Gabriel in her burning desire to leave, her itinerary, rather than being linear and vectorial, will be circular. Travelling, for the women of the same generation as the male protagonist, seems to be devoid of scope, as trips are geographically restrained. Abel, Hirch, and Langland maintain that the development of the protagonist in the traditional *bildungsroman* in the feminine, instead of following the linear progression common to the male protagonist, builds up in a circular fashion, while allowing brief epiphanic moments in an otherwise repetitive life.[13] Even though decompartmentalization seems a strategy used by all travelling characters to avoid the suffocation consequential to their minority status, access to a true voyage—that is, one that allows for discovery and renewal—is granted only to the young male that is Gabriel.

Furthermore, the narration, which focalizes on Gabriel (but which is not Gabriel's), apparently unaware of its ideological stakes, compares the journeys of Gabriel and Amandine using a marked gender divide: "Both shared the same desire of escape, the same temptation to severe all bonds. But they did not know yet that, when the moment of leaving would come, one would leave to lose herself, the other, to find himself."[14] The narrator is correct in that Gabriel's deterritorialization experiences are transcended whereas Amandine's lead to further alienation. My hypothesis is that, women suffering a double marginalization in the context of exiguity, female authors are more likely to choose a male protagonist, to counterbalance a double (cultural and gender-biased) and thus an unbearable marginality. Amandine is a secondary character with a very second-hand chance of surviving; thus we can say that the novel, unaware of its stakes, is realistic.

BODILY EQUATIONS: DWINDLING INTO NOTHINGNESS

I have attempted to show how the protagonist materializes the economy of his disappearance by movement—that is, by covering a territory in a linear manner—in opposition to his feminine foil, who covers territory in a circular fashion. By absenting himself from a territory whose very existence is problematic, Gabriel avoids recognizing the perceived insufficiency of his culture, a forgetting necessary to his survival. This oblivion, nonetheless, will morph into awareness when he encounters other cultures.

To this strategy of obliteration, Gabriel has added one that materializes in a disgust toward flesh, its expansion on the human frame, a somatic translation of his minority status. During Gabriel's trip, his disgust will morph into a self-denied—which he interprets as forbidden—access to women characterized by their physical fullness. That what precisely disgusted Gabriel before his seven-year trip (west, and then southward on the American continent)—overflowing flesh—should be the object of an obsessive nostalgia points toward a fascination for the flesh that is—by proxy—an embodiment of one's idealized presence, and thus status, in the world. Gabriel endorses a traditional hetero-male position by projecting onto women's bodies his own symbolic status within the sphere of symbolic exchanges—a status, as we shall see, that changes somewhat at the term of his quest.

Butler posits that "if the body is synechdochal for the social system per se or a site in which open systems converge, then any kind of unregulated permeability constitutes a site of pollution and endangerment."[15] A revelatory passage about Gabriel links metonymically the bodies to family, family to society, and Gabriel's hatred of society to the compulsive urge to be on the road: "He could not stand crowds—it was a proliferation of the Tardiff[16] family—avoided mass, fairs, public places. Could only feel himself breathing... [in] a vagrant existence, on the roads of the world, far from the worn traces of human existence."[17]

The self—it is truer in the case of a minority—is always already other than him/her-self, a stranger to itself. But in the case of Gabriel, the other, rejected self, is invested as an abject other. In the following passage, Butler, interpreting Kristeva's concept of the abject, contends that every human being establishes the contours of his/her corporeal self by first expelling what s/he does not consider as belonging to his/her-self, which allows us to understand the necessity for Gabriel to clearly delineate the contours of his self as a member of a minority constantly in danger of being engulfed by the hegemonic culture: "The abject designates that which has been expelled from the body, discharged as excrement, literally rendered 'other.' This appears as an expulsion of alien elements, but the alien is effectively established through this expulsion. The construction of the 'not me' as the abject establishes the boundaries of the body which are also the first contours of the subject."[18]

Gabriel reacts by ejecting not the hegemonic culture, but the weaker terms of his minority culture, the women and his family, vulnerable parts of his identity.

Gabriel is at the beginning most disgusted by bodies that fill up space, and this phenomenon starts with his family, as we have just seen: "The bodies of others repulsed him. Their smell, their hairiness, their flabby roundness. Their noise as well...their animal presence, their silly self-importance. He himself practised silence, obliteration. Wanted to resorb to his bare bones, to shed the excess flesh. Already, he felt superfluous, felt that his build, not so imposing, claimed more space than deserved."[19]

Any excess of flesh, be it his or not, torments Gabriel. Perhaps, belonging to the majority gender, Gabriel wants to project a spartan ideal of hypermasculinity on every body. His is a hypermasculinity that strangely espouses the desire of the minoritized to take the least space possible and that translates into the desire for a hard, dry, cold body, reduced to the essential, rid of its excess flesh, softness, warmth, even of secretions, all qualities associated with the feminine: "Gabriel, lying as a cadaver between the limp bodies of his brothers, was listening to their overflowing life: the pulse in their veins, the gurgle in their guts. Touching their skin damp with perspiration, he coiled back upon himself to avoid their fat calves and their flabby thighs brushing against his cold foot."[20]

Gabriel's bodily practice could also correspond to Foucault's practices of austerity, which the latter ties "to the production of a certain kind of masculine subject," according to Butler.

We saw that Gabriel's distantiation from his brothers stems from his perception of their excess of flesh, which brings them closer to the feminine. But why this hatred of the feminine? One could link the feminine, the traditionally minoritized gender, to the "malaise" of the minoritized. We have seen that one of the main survival strategies for the minoritized is oblivion, denial. Given that, to be defined as a human being, one must be sexed—that is, gendered, as Judith Butler reminds us—it is very tempting for a member of a minority to clearly exhibit his masculinity to counter his vulnerability. Nonetheless, Gabriel's hypermasculinity paradoxically incorporates, by its purified shape, the desire for evanescence that the minoritized harbour. According to Butler's reading of Foucault,[21] these "practices of austerity do not attest to a single and abiding prohibition, but work in the service of crafting a certain kind of self."[22] But as I hope to have shown here, in the case of a hetero male belonging to a minority group, one of the strategies for associating with the hegemonic group would consist in coming as close as possible to a male regulatory ideal to compensate for one's already vulnerable status as a member of an ethnolinguistic minority. If this were not clear, the goal here is—when one belongs to an ethnolinguistic minority—*not* to be associated with another minoritized group—here the feminine, identified by most cultures with the body, and especially with excess flesh. Women are the minoritized "other," "defined by a masculine perspective that seeks to safeguard its own disembodied status through identifying women generally with the bodily sphere,"[23] says Butler, summarizing de Beauvoir's intuition.

Thus the desire of the adolescent Gabriel, before he takes the road, will coalesce on the sculptural Amandine, because "her flesh hugged perfectly the shape of her bones,"[24] evoking not the organic, but rather marble or porcelain. Amandine would reveal herself to be, under Gabriel's hands, "dry, flexible, incorruptible."[25] She would act as a shield against the immanence of the flesh, associated again with femininity. Had Gabriel dared approach her, he would have learned "to disregard men and their carnal exhalations; with her he would have learned the secret of impermeability."[26]

By a strange reversal, Amandine's body—venerated by Gabriel as that of a statue with its perfect lines, devoid of the excesses that appear to Gabriel's eyes as the worst of obscenities—attracts all excesses from men. Amandine's body, the very idea of a receptacle, empty *khôra*, inert and indifferent to emotions, becomes a site of debauchery. Amandine, with her scapegoat body—foreshadowing her mental alienation—is minoritization brought to its ultimate consequence. Back from his seven-year trip, Gabriel will find her "fine and transparent as an everlasting flower."[27] A long minoritization process will have brought her to the desertion of her body, a desertion that cannot take place without the alteration of her mind. I would argue that Amandine's character is the locus where traditional ideology resists, where the minoritized feminine is condemned, marked by the abject; her status thus contrasts with that of Gabriel, the minoritized masculine, who remains "pure" despite similar sexual encounters on the road. Indeed, according to Amandine's sister, the chaste Camille, Gabriel is "pure, chaste and infatuated with the sky… destined to life," whereas poor Amandine is "destined to the darkness of nights, of bars, of closed rooms where she will attempt to quench in the arms of morons the last remains of her light."[28] Despite her "easy girl" appearance as a teenager, Amandine is just as disgusted as Gabriel by the body and bodily functions: "Their mouths on her had inspired her a disgust both visceral and metaphysical: all these stories of mingled breaths, of effluvia from bodies falling prey to death, had turned her stomach."[29] As if Amandine had always been aware, in her self-loathing, constant purifying of her body either by fasting or by submitting to the burning rays of the sun, that the body, and especially the female body, became the locus of the dislocating forces imposed on exiguity cultures. Butler argues, following de Beauvoir, that men dispose of their own bodies, projecting their bodily existence onto women, the body being "a symbol of human decay and transience."[30]

When, on his return, Gabriel announces that he has bought Amandine's family house in order to write by the river that he loves, Amandine objects—"I don't like the smell of this river…It smells hair and rot. Meat, rotten meat"[31]—

thus projecting her own body onto the river's odour. Amandine's disgust is a symptom of an emotional disaffection that will allow her to let men touch her without feeling agitation—whether pleasant or unpleasant—but that will lead her to the threshold of madness. Her point of view is that of an outsider to her body, of an internalized (Anglo?) male gaze. Amandine, who refuses to inhabit her body—thus objectifying it—will by the same token allow her casual encounters to objectify her. One of the reasons why living outside her body is so disastrous to Amandine is that living a decorporalized, intellectual life is not sanctioned for a female. Few women end up doing it, and when they do, it is often at their own expense.

In sum, Gabriel and Amandine both practise types of absence to the world that are itinerancy and an asceticism of the body that abjects, and thus ejects, the feminine. Paradoxically, these types of absence to the immediate reality will grant the male protagonist an availability that will allow him to better absorb other cultures, perhaps because a decorporalized masculinity is sanctioned in North America's hegemonic Anglo culture. This openness to other cultures will, in turn, make possible a salutary return to his own culture. As Jacques Brault said, the encounter with the other is necessary to the recognition of one's own culture.

Turning our attention to the young women with whom Gabriel had affairs during his voyage, we see that Gabriel is partial to women who live, like him, on the threshold of death. The first lover he meets, Patti, is so thin as to appear translucent, her body already surrendering to death. While he caresses ghostly Patti, Gabriel cannot but let his mind wander to the thought of Gloria, a Black American waitress with a full silhouette who kept an ironic distance from him in the restaurant where he washed dishes. The second woman he meets when he works in the Rockies is Sarah, whom he rescues from a certain death by immersion. When Gabriel reanimates her, she asks him through her tears why he hasn't abandoned her to her drowning. A painter, she confides that she had come to the mountains in order to be obliterated by the white of snow. Gabriel meets during this early part of his voyage women who reflect his fear of embodiment (Patti) and his desire for obliteration (Sarah), two sides of the same coin. Full, fleshy women exhibiting a flourishing femininity are American, black or white inaccessible beauties. Their very inaccessibility seems born of the hegemonic American culture to which they belong. Gabriel's "ontological lack" would then be signified by his forbidden access to women whose physical fullness is a marker of a hegemonic and thus successful culture. That what precisely disgusted him before his trip—the excess flesh—would, during that same trip, be the object of an obsessive nostalgia with non-francos, non-Canadians—points to a desire to join the hegemonic culture. Gabriel's affairs with emaciated women point to an alternative desire to espouse or be engulfed by his minority condition. One could link this paradoxical phenomenon to Paré's notion of the flickering ("clignotement"), where the minority subject alternates between an exacerbated conscience of oneself in the world and an evanescent one, a desire to disappear into oblivion.

Only the third woman with whom Gabriel will have an affair at the very end of his travels, Maliyel the Mexican, will help him synthesize his life thus far. By her very difference, Maliyel points to his ethnic roots. Recognizing the specificity of his quest, calling him "mi pequeño escritor"—Maliyel uses interpellation, a performative, producing the very effect she describes, thus allowing Gabriel to finally make a narrative (a vector) of his thus far desultory wanderings. Moreover, by recognizing Gabriel's newfound love for Camille, Maliyel will generously deliver Gabriel to the world a second time, this time the lost world of his origins as now reinterpreted by his narrative. As a good feminine Other, she will give meaning and form to his wanderings: he will become a writer and use as raw material the events lived and acquaintances made during his long trip. The fact that Maliyel does not belong to either of the traditional two white North American linguistic groups seems to situate her, in Gabriel's eye, as an impartial outsider. Her disinterested role, that of a Greimassian adjuvant, comes very close to that of the benevolent black male helping the white all-American hero get where he needs to be, as portrayed in Hollywood action films of recent decades.

Two words about the elusive Camille, Amandine's younger virginal sister, whose childish face begins to reappear to Gabriel seven years after having left their town, while he is with Maliyel in Mexico. When Gabriel comes back to his native St-Boniface, his quest to write is intermingled with the need to retrieve her. His absolute certainty of finding Camille and keeping her for himself seems particularly self-centred, especially since he knows nothing of her whereabouts and is unaware that she herself has embarked on a journey from a near reclusive student in a convent to the shack of a Métis single mother, where she learns self-reliance. Even though there is no certitude that Camille will be back to Gabriel, the narrative seems to leave no doubt about it, because of the love they feel for each other.

Though Camille is presented as a conservative feminine presence, Gabriel essentializing her by associating her with nature (as a child she preferred to stay in the woods rather than play with dolls), Camille is also presented as the antidote to the self-hatred of the minoritized: because of her love of everything organic, she is not repulsed by bodies and living processes: "Nothing repulsed me. Everything, in my mouth, had the taste of blood, of salt and of the sun. I embraced proliferation, perfume and putrefaction."[32] The French vernacular particular to this region—snubbed by the European French mother of Camille and Amandine—is associated by Camille with the expansion of flesh on the frame, probably because the Western Franco-Canadian matrons are described as tall and large. Camille embraces this baroque excess of life and thus becomes the symbol of the inscription of the non-normative in the geolinguistic landscape. The fact that Gabriel chooses her as his ultimate bride/lover, at the very end of his journey, indicates that he has overcome his fear of the flesh and, by the same token, that he has accepted to "register" his origins in the landscape of his life. Camille is also associated with the local because her travels, contrary to Gabriel's, have remained regional, Camille delving deeper and deeper into the history of the region by sharing first the life of Catholic nuns in a convent, then that of a Métis mother in the woods. The fact that Camille is a very young virgin is to be read, I imagine, as Gabriel's—a prerogative of the masculine—intact chances of starting a new life as a writer with his young bride. But of course one can wonder why the very qualities that he is supposed to have earned must be reflected precisely in his young virginal lover. I would argue that however absent Camille is during Gabriel's transformative quest, she is a projection of Gabriel's ideal self, of suddenly mythic dimensions, since she represents both Gabriel's newly disalienated self and "nature." She is thus both a progressive and a conservative character. Marianne Hirsch says of the novel as a genre that it can harbour such dichotomy in its polyvocality—which Bakhtin voiced before her:

> The novel is the optimal genre is which to study the interplay between hegemonic and dissenting voices. In recent years, narratologists have analyzed the novel's polyvocality, revealing the novel's conflicting discourses that make possible, within the structures of the novel, the interrogation of dominant cultural codes and assumptions. Thus the novel is at once, as Rachel Blau du Plessis finds, "the place where ideology is coiled" and the place where it can be called into question.[33]

CONCLUSION

I would like to summarize here by suggesting that if the minoritized can be defined by their hesitation between a hyperconsciousness of their minority and a desire for erasure, this ambivalence, as shown in the Franco-Manitoban novel *Le coulonneux*, is experienced quite differently according to one's gender. Thus, while Gabriel is afflicted by all the symptoms of minoritization at the beginning of his voyage, and while he never tries to define his quest, it can still be considered a success, as he comes back to his roots and to love. We have seen that Gabriel's itinerancy morphs into an itinerary at the very end of his voyage. Similarly, his various love affairs, from the point of view of his final destination, seem to have existed only to prepare his inevitable reunion with Camille, Amandine's virginal sister.

Gabriel has had to travel to the confines of his continent to recognize desires that he had hidden with his origin. He thus shows real possibilities of transcendence, especially since on his return to his native region, he will devote himself to writing while waiting for Camille. The voyage from then on will be metaphorical for Gabriel: writing is a self-discovery voyage, one that promises the structuring of the self's narrative: it allows for a quasi-transcendence. Gabriel's belonging to a hegemonic gender and to a white community seems to compensate for his belonging to a linguistic minority. As if it were not difficult enough to be from a minority culture, a second minoritization, that of gender, traces the fine line between quasi-transcendence and immanence.

NOTES

1 François Paré, *La distance habitée* (Ottawa: le Nordir, 2003). Paré is a winner of Governor General's and Trillium Awards in Canada. Other specialists of Franco-Canadian identity as expressed in literature, such as Lucie Hotte (Canada Research Chair at University of Ottawa), have noticed a recent trend in all minority groups that points to a need to reach beyond ethnicity, to abandon identity motivations. Hotte's studies deal with the same phenomenon as Paré, *conscience* and *oblivion*, but from socio-historical angle. How do groups that are traditionally characterized by their in-between identities, by their unrecognized status, deal with the uprooting brought about by globalization?
2 *Littératures de l'exiguïté* (Ottawa: Le Nordir, 1992), 22.
3 Ibid., 22.
4 Paré, *La distance habitée*, 27; my translation.
5 Simone Chaput, *Le coulonneux* (Saint-Boniface: Les éditions du blé, 1998).
6 Sara Salih, in Sara Salih with Judith Butler, eds., *The Judith Butler Reader* (Oxford: Blackwell, 2004), 3.
7 Ibid., 21.
8 *Littératures de l'exiguïté*, 22; my translation.
9 Ibid., 22; my translation.
10 Ibid., 27; my translation.
11 Paré, *La distance habitée*, 10; my translation.
12 Ibid., 12; my translation.
13 Elizabeth Abel, Marianne Hirsch, and Elizabeth Langland, eds., *The Voyage in Fictions of Female Development* (Hanover: University Press of New England), 12.
14 Chaput, *Le coulonneux*, 112; my translation.
15 Salih, *The Judith Butler Reader*, 107.
16 *Le coulonneux*, 22; my translation.
17 Freud argues that the ego is first and foremost a bodily ego.
18 Salih, *The Judith Butler Reader*, 107.
19 *Le coulonneux*, 20; my translation.
20 Ibid., 21; my translation.
21 Salih, *The Judith Butler Reader*, 309.
22 Ibid., 309.
23 Ibid., 28. Butler adds: "By defining women as 'Other,' men are able, through the shortcut of definition, to dispose of their bodies, to make themselves other than their bodies—a symbol of human decay and transience, of limitation generally—and to make their bodies other than themselves. From this belief that the body is other, it is not a far leap to the conclusion that others are their bodies, while the masculine 'I' is a noncorporeal soul."
24 *Le coulonneux*, 192; my translation.

25 Ibid., 192; my translation. The narration, focalized here by Gabriel, says: 'Nothing in her which would be viscous or slimy; the sun had purified her'; my translation. Note the disgust with which femininity is associated. It needs to be masculinized (the sun is associated with the masculine in our cultures) to be desirable. Quite another paper could be written taking as a thesis the derivative nature of heterosexuality, as Butler argues.
26 *Le coulonneux*, 195; my translation.
27 Ibid., 195; my translation.
28 Ibid., 111; my translation.
29 Ibid., 194; my translation.
30 Salih, *The Judith Butler Reader*, 28.
31 *Le coulonneux*, 210; my translation.
32 Ibid., 93; my translation.
33 Abel et al., *The Voyage in Fictions of Female Development*, 9.

IV: CAPITALIZED, CORPORATIZED, COMPROMISED MEN

CHAPTER II

The Politics of Marginalization at the Centre: Canadian Masculinities and Global Capitalism in Douglas Coupland's *Generation X*

KIT DOBSON

In his 2009 novel, *Generation A*, Douglas Coupland sets out to revise the ideas and tropes from his debut novel, *Generation X*, published eighteen years earlier, in 1991. In *Generation A*, bees have all but disappeared from the world because of the development of the drug Solon, which is toxic to bees and causes humans to experience time in the perpetual present, thereby alleviating anxiety about the future—and also causes catastrophic environmental and social collapse. When five disparate people are stung by bees, they become the subjects of intense scrutiny and end up sequestered on Haida Gwaii, where Serge, the shadowy and ultimately nefarious scientist, asks them to tell stories to one another, because the experience of storytelling and narrative is what produced the initial desire in him to inhabit a perpetual present and create Solon. Throughout the novel, the characters experience an overwhelming desire to make their own lives "string together to form a story—something that makes sense of events [they] know have no meaning."[1] As Coupland's five protagonists—from Canada, the United States, New Zealand, France, and Sri Lanka—tell stories and create narratives for their own lives, readers witness a shift over the past eighteen years: whereas the characters of *Generation X* appear to blame the older generation for a lack of narrative coherence in their own lives (and go on to make stories for themselves in order to rectify this lack), the characters in *Generation A* have no such expectations and simply deal with the perpetual presentism around them (prior to beginning to render their lives as narratives via storytelling).

It seems highly appropriate to include a discussion of gender politics in the work of Douglas Coupland, especially *Generation X*, in a volume focusing on masculinities in Canadian arts and culture. Since publishing his first novel in 1991,[2] Coupland has begun more consciously to position himself as a representative white Canadian male, making it his particular practice in his two *Souvenir of Canada* books to speak as a sensitive, artistic guy's guy about the things that supposedly make Canada Canadian,[3] all the while continuing to produce novels that document the quirks of North American—and, increasingly, global—society. As his career continues, he has worked in sculpture and visual art, theatre, cinema, television, and the written word, and has become a household name. His own public persona—as a sort of ironic Everyman—has now led to the insertion of a version of himself into his 2006 novel, *JPod*, which begins with one character claiming to feel "like a refugee from a Douglas Coupland novel," and another rejoining, "*that* asshole."[4] Coupland inserts himself into *JPod* as an obnoxious character, much like Martin Amis in *Money*, preferring simply to steal other people's life stories rather than make up his own. Andrew Tate, in the first academic monograph written on Coupland, suggests that *JPod*'s use of Coupland marks a "willingness to critique his own reputation and to mock the legacy of his fiction,"[5] but the novel suggests more than that. That Coupland's persona has now been recognized to the point that he can insert himself into his own novels in such an act of self-mockery suggests a very conscious act of creating his self. Returning to his breakout debut novel is therefore a means of going back to the genesis of this creation; doing so provides a means of examining how heterosexual-identified white male bodies therein were conceptualized in the early phases of his work (this, even though Coupland himself is gay—a theme that rarely surfaces in his work), while providing a means of reading the broader problematic of how to theorize dominant masculinities in the context of the discourses of globalism that proliferated throughout the 1990s and into the new millennium.

Generation X is an episodic novel for hipsters of the early 1990s, one whose narrative wanders through the lives of friends and their families on the western edge of the United States prior to the millennium as they attempt to find themselves within a postmodern world of apparent disconnections and ruptures. The novel focuses on three characters: Dagmar Bellingshausen, a reformed Torontonian advertising executive with dual Canadian–American citizenship; Claire Baxter, self-exiled from a large and wealthy California family; and the narrator, Andrew Palmer, who is disenchanted with his middle-class family in Oregon. Andrew, as the narrator, delivers much of the novel's content and emerges as the main protagonist. These characters have all experienced a loss—whether perceived or real—of economic security under the new global order they see emerging, and their response is to absent themselves from these global flows as much as possible. The novel tracks the adventures of the three characters through Palm Springs, which is deliberately positioned as a marginal space in the Californian landscape, as they work their menial jobs, with Claire suffering through a relationship with the overbearing hypercapitalist Tobias. Much of the novel takes place in the neighbouring bungalows in which the characters live, around their shared pool, or along the quiet streets of the dying California suburbs, as they detail their minor exploits and petty acts of vandalism. Between these daily events, the three characters share their perspectives on the current state of the world and tell stories to one another. These stories are sometimes about their own pasts and are sometimes short fictions set on "Texlahoma," a mythical asteroid on which the year is permanently 1974. This year has been chosen because it is said to have been the last year in which real wages increased in the United States.[6] The story concludes with the three characters retreating deeper into what they see as marginal space, as they move over the border and into Mexico. It expresses an overall sense of playfulness as well as hopelessness, with the three protagonists voicing their displeasure with the world as the baby boomer generation has left it.

The somewhat loose sense of dissidence that Andrew, Dagmar, and Claire express is tied to the immediate context of the narrative. That same dissidence has had a shifting history in English Canadian writing, one that suggests some of the theoretical questions the novel raises. Margaret Atwood's 1972 "thematic guide to Canadian literature," *Survival*, gives the following model for conceptualizing dissidence:

> The tendency in English Canada has been to connect one's social protest not with the Canadian predicament specifically but with some other group or movement: the workers in the thirties, persecuted minority groups such as the Japanese uprooted during the war. English Canadians have identified themselves with Ban the Bombers, Communists, the F.L.Q., and so forth, but not often with each other—after all, the point of identifying with those other groups was at least partly to distinguish oneself from all the grey WASP Canadians you were afraid you might turn into.[7]

Atwood identifies here what she already sees as a substantial trend in English Canadian writing in 1972. Importantly, though, the risks that are posed when one appropriates the voice of another go by unnoted. It is key to observe that such appropriations may misrepresent those who are being spoken for or enact a violence upon them. Moreover, if one accepts Alan Sinfield's definition of dissidence as a "refusal of an aspect of the dominant,"[8] then dissenting by actively identifying against one's own subject position, when it is one of dominance, amounts to identifying against oneself in the process of appropriating a position of marginality. Atwood's "grey WASP Canadians" are, in her formulation, both the dissenters and the dominant, a problematic that requires more space for consideration than she gives.

In the nearly forty years that have elapsed since *Survival* had its massive impact on Canadian literary studies, however, attempts to connect social protest with particular groups seem to have shifted, with marginalized social groups beginning to articulate for themselves the violences done against them,[9] and with subjects coming from positions of cultural privilege and dominance beginning throughout the 1990s to articulate grounds for dissidence on economic terms as a response to the rise of popular ideas about globalization. Problems remain, however, with how the language of marginalization has been used in these latter discourses, as well as in how the processes of global capitalism are affecting different groups unevenly, greatly impacting the Third World, but receiving the most attention when they have impacted privileged Western subjects negatively. That is, dissidence need no longer be simplistically connected to "persecuted minority groups" or to those who occupy clear positions of marginality, because those who experience Atwood's rather narrowly conceived "Canadian predicament" have their own grounds for disagreement with the system, particularly economic ones. But even as dissidence is articulated by "grey WASP" subjects in positions of power and dominance such as those of Coupland's protagonists, problems concerning the appropriation of marginalized voices return in the rhetoric used by the dominant. The question this chapter asks, in order to discuss how discourses of marginalization have been used in the West as grounds for articulating dissidence in the context of 1990s and 2000s globalization, is as follows: What happens to "mainstream" Canadian men in the light of global capitalism? I want to suggest that one important response to globalization, as it impacts the "mainstream" Canadian male, has been to belatedly adopt the language of identity politics in order to describe the situation. This usage is one way in which the supposedly unmarked nature of such bodies has become visible; at the same time, it has created a number of theoretical problems. The theory goes something like this: economic globalization has been perceived as effecting a sort of levelling for this identity group in that it has enabled straight, white men to claim a position of marginalization as a result of the economic shifts of global capitalism, whose narratives no longer ensure that these men will retain their positions of privilege and security. This claim to marginalization has risked functioning as a silencing of other voices, thus re-enacting the pattern analyzed by Atwood, except that now the "grey WASP" centre is articulating dissenting views as its own. The articulation of dissent through tropes of marginalization, however, still risks eclipsing well-founded protests against the system coming from a variety of other subject positions. My purpose here is not, however, to criticize the position of the privileged dissident simplistically. Rather, I discuss how this state of affairs has arisen and suggest that this shift is both alarming—given the continued privilege of the normative male subject in contemporary Canada— and, in some senses, a welcome relief from the political complacency for which this group was critiqued throughout the 1990s, particularly along generational lines.[10] At the very least, appropriating the discourses of marginalization to oneself is, I believe, a step up from appropriating the marginalized voices of others, particularly when reasons for using such discourse can be analyzed and therefore considered for their political utility.

This chapter has two main sections: in the first, I sketch a portion of the theoretical context through which globalization was theorized in the 1990s and into the 2000s; in the second, I hone in on what I take to be an exemplary text in order to support my theoretical framework. That text, of course, is Douglas Coupland's *Generation X*, which had a major sociological impact in defining a generation of North Americans. It is a novel that also nicely illustrates my thesis, for it makes direct use of the language of marginalization to which I have been referring. My intent, however, is not to scapegoat *Generation X* or its author in criticizing how mainstream men do politics; while I see similar moves taking place in Coupland's other texts, his writing continues to evolve, and *Generation A*, his most current book at the time of this essay, demonstrates a more pluralistic world view. Moreover, the trials and tribulations of global capitalism lead normative male subjects to appropriate discourses of marginalization in many places. This chapter reads *Generation X* as a way of approaching these politics, and as a starting point for further consideration of how such politics might be conducted in the future.

DISCOURSES OF MARGINALIZATION AND LATE CAPITALISM

My first step, then, is to provide a theoretical framework for reading globalization as a process that undermines the security and privilege—both economic and psychological—of the mainstream Canadian male. In 1991, the same year in which *Generation X* was published, Fredric Jameson made it a virtual truism that postmodernism can be somehow equated with "the cultural logic of late capitalism."[11] From the current perspective, postmodernism is fast becoming a movement whose moment is receding into the past. It is something that Linda Hutcheon, a prominent and formerly enthusiastic theorist of the movement, now declares to be "over,"[12] and it can therefore be examined in terms of its history and how it sheds light on texts produced in the last fifty years or so. In this period, postmodern and post-structural social and literary analysis has repeatedly suggested that the world is defined by structures that, while constituted as permanent, natural, or self-evident, can be demonstrated to be socially determined. The result is that transcendental assumptions or ideas of permanence have been radically disrupted, giving way to a space of play or open-endedness.

This same state of affairs holds for analyses of capitalism, and Jacques Derrida's work of dismantling the assumptions of Western metaphysics has been successfully extended to this realm.[13] The connections between capitalism and postmodernism have been well-noted: contemporary economic structures have been thought of as "disorganized capitalism,"[14] in which the financial structures supposedly organizing the world are shown to be chaotic and arbitrary. The structures of production have also been thought of as processes of "flexible accumulation,"[15] in which capital is defined, increasingly, by its mobility and by its need to remain flexible in terms of its investment patterns in order to maximize profitability. This model has allowed for an analysis of economic globalization in which capital is defined particularly by its flexibility and by its impermanent, decentred nature, as those who control it seek to make it mobile or flexible, especially, David Harvey suggests, "with respect to labour processes, labour markets, products, and patterns of consumption."[16] Notably absent from this list are those who control the means of production, but capitalism itself, as an experienced condition, has become decentred, even though critics have demonstrated that it maintains an insistently patriarchal logic[17] and that production itself has become concentrated via corporate ideologies at the same time as its effects have been dispersed on a global scale.[18] The economic processes of globalization have thus been characterized in analyses by a decentring of geographies—which Arjun Appadurai, in a seminal work of the late 1990s, discusses under the rubric of deterritorialization,[19] following the post-structural theorization of Gilles Deleuze and Félix Guattari[20]—as issues of place become subsumed to the demands of capital in the global economy. The resulting "new global cultural economy" is one that, for Appadurai, "cannot be understood in terms of existing centre–periphery models."[21] Appadurai suggests instead that "something like a human version of...chaos theory" is needed in order to adequately account for the movements of this decentred world.[22] Global capitalism has thus been seen to create conditions in which knowable, reliable social structures are undermined and rendered chaotic.

In such an analysis, the formerly secure centres of the Western world are displaced, destabilized by shifts in the economic environment. Given the ultimate loyalty of capitalism only to itself, territorial linkages come to be disconnected, as corporations move their workforces overseas in order to maximize profit and exploit Third World labour and are rewarded for doing so by receiving increased returns. The human costs of such flows are not directly considered in the economic model, as people in the West are marginalized through job loss, while those in the Third World become a new, super-exploited proletariat. Given the mobility of their employers—many of whom will happily relocate their production facilities should they face labour unrest—this proletariat has not yet been able to constitute itself as a coherent body or act effectively against its oppressors, because these oppressors are located in other parts of the world. And in the West, in Canada, the disenfranchised and laid-off workers—sometimes hired back as independent contractors or on short-term contracts for work that cannot be sent offshore, with lower benefits or less security—have lost what little stable footing they might have had. The West/non-West distinction thereby becomes less clear, as workers in all parts of the globe experience destabilizing effects.

This framework has been discussed at length in and around Michael Hardt and Antonio Negri's controversial books *Empire* (2000) and its sequels *Multitude* (2004) and *Commonwealth* (2009),[23] which have featured prominently in debates about globalization.[24] *Empire*, in particular, has had a large impact on how globalization has been thought and theorized, largely because of its authors' ambitious attempt to provide a coherent picture of the contemporary moment.[25] One of *Empire*'s key postulates is that the contemporary world under global capitalism is not defined simply through imperialism—particularly American imperialism[26]—but by Empire, which is a condition in which ever-increasing portions of the globe are brought under the sway of capitalism as an imperial force unto itself that does not rely on national or state structures. For Hardt and Negri, the contemporary world is subordinated by an imperial structure that is not simply part of a nation-state extending its sovereignty, as with the Western imperialisms of the nineteenth century. Rather, it is part of a process through which nation-states are themselves undermined, as their legislative jurisdictions are broken down in order to pave the way for the further incursions of capital. In their analysis, capital has become the world's mobile agent. Individual citizens can be physically restricted from crossing borders when such movements hinder capitalism, while those borders are increasingly fragmented for the flows of money. The critical point of this analysis here is the decentring of Empire itself as a broader project that transcends individual nation-states. This Empire, if it is in the process of consolidating its power and sovereignty, as Hardt and Negri contend, creates the conditions for destabilizing privileged Western subjects from their positions of power. That such citizens might still construct themselves as Western and as endowed with cultural privilege and power, however, demonstrates that Hardt and Negri's theories remain, of course, theoretical. Spaces in which such subjects might view themselves as disenfranchised or decentred, alternatively, suggest ways in which Empire is becoming global. Empire is, at present, an at best incomplete process through which we are living. Reading the gap between earlier discourses of Western privilege and more recent ones of uncertainty or trepidation—one can easily analyze the doctrines from the period of the George W. Bush regime as representing fears about losing the West's position of hegemony—reveals how social changes have operated by extrapolating local spaces onto global capitalism, thereby profoundly unsettling normative subjects and creating different questions for political actors seeking change from positions of supposed dominance.

GENERATION X AND THE TROPES OF THE MARGINS

The impacts of these theorized processes on mainstream Canadian men are, I hope, beginning to suggest themselves. The racially and sexually privileged Canadian male can be seen, in this model, as suddenly losing any absolute claim to cultural primacy. The decentring of global forces as a result of global capitalism enables him to see himself as marginalized in economic terms, as production migrates offshore—for example, with companies like Roots and Levi's shutting down their Canadian production facilities, as both have done in the past decade. Those who are most affected by these processes may not, indeed, be the privileged, white, male segments of the population, but these moves perform a philosophically levelling function, as geographical spaces dominated by otherwise privileged white, male bodies fall under the sway of global capitalism, and as these dominant bodies are thereby able to include themselves among the marginalized by virtue of contemporary economics. It is important to see this shift as a specifically gendered one in this light, for it provides privileged men with a material basis for post-structural and post-modern narratives of decentring. In this case, the decentring is seen not as a cause for celebration, but rather as one that creates uncertainty and a loss of privilege. The oppressed remain oppressed under global capitalism, but the oppressive classes of white males have also been enabled to see themselves as oppressed. This is a shift that needs to be recognized and discussed.

This process is well documented in Vancouverite Douglas Coupland's *Generation X,* as discourses of economics and marginalization enter directly into the novel and feature prominently in the discussions of Andrew, Dagmar, and Claire. Andrew recounts his feelings of distress to Dagmar and Claire about having had a conversation with an older Japanese businessman who emphasized "the necessity of wealth being transportable" when he was working in Japan.[27] These words introduce considerations of a world of flexible accumulation to the novel, in which the culturally dominant characters are decentred. Coming after the baby boomer generation, Andrew and the other characters complain that their parents had more than they do and that they are marginalized by contemporary society. Their solution is to drop out of the rat race; thus, they move to Palm Springs in order to avoid urban centres and to engage in "occupational slumming," which a note printed in the margin of the text defines as "taking a job well beneath one's skill or education level as a means of retreat from adult responsibilities and / or avoiding possible failure in one's true occupation."[28] This series of decisions is positioned as one means of being dishonestly "promised heaven" in their lifetimes as children and later finding themselves having to make do with the earth instead.[29] Daniel Grassian states that "Andy, Dag, and Claire gradually come to believe that they have been 'colonized' by popular culture and attempt to remove themselves from that enforced, fragmented mentality by extracting themselves from American culture itself,"[30] moving to increasingly marginalized spaces as they discover that the popular psychology with which they had been reared was deceptive. Their dissidence is characterized by non-participation in the economic and political processes around them as they attempt to step outside of history. The narrator Andrew acknowledges this state of affairs in noting that he and his comrades "live small lives on the periphery" and that they "are marginalized and there's a great deal in which [they] choose not to participate."[31] The purpose of this dissidence, Andrew states, is "to find a personal truth."[32] This truth, it seems, is individual, transcendental, and ahistorical.

This ahistorical search has led to readings of the novel as "a meditation on the end of history."[33] This history ends for generation X, it seems, with the end of the Cold War. G.P. Lainsbury maintains that "the end of the cold war is an anticlimactic end of history for the characters of *Generation X*, because they had always taken for granted that the end of history and the end of the human species would be synchronous events. Now they have to try to reconcile themselves to living in an era where they will die alone and their deaths will signify nothing."[34]

With the failure of the world to end in the nuclear conflagration that would bring the Cold War to a close, the subjects of the novel find themselves displaced, their beliefs disrupted. Dagmar is particularly obsessed with the atomic bomb: he visits test sites in the American desert, discusses having "Bomb anxiety,"[35] and makes up stories about dying when the bomb lands, dying in a manner that is both serene and grotesque. His realization that the dropping of the bomb might not end the entire world, but merely a small portion of it, leaves him shaken, as his truths are uprooted. The lost truths of the world in which Dagmar, Andrew, and Claire live are those that have been disrupted by globalization, in which history ends instead with the conclusion of the Cold War and the apparent triumph of global capitalism. The characters grapple with their desires for the simple "truths" of ontological plenitude and social significance in this new space. Instead, they find global capitalism imposing its levelling effects, theoretically undermining the differentiation between global subjects and the hierarchies around which their early childhood narratives were constructed, especially the binaries of West/non-West and democracy/communism.

This position is troubling on at least two grounds. The first is the difficulty of abstracting oneself from history, as Andrew and his fellow exiles attempt to do. This debate became a theoretical one that developed during the early 1990s, concurrent with the publication of *Generation X*. Francis Fukuyama then argued that the end of the Cold War and the seeming victory of the United States signalled the end of history itself, as democratic liberalism and global capitalism displayed themselves as the highest forms of human organization.³⁶ History itself, he argued, reversing Marx's communist teleology, culminated in a static model of global capitalist society that was yet to evenly distribute itself to all people. For the characters of *Generation X*, however, the so-called victory of capitalism over communism is not so much a triumph as a failure. The emphasis on the stagnation of real wages in the United States, far pre-dating the fall of the Berlin Wall and the Soviet Union, suggests that, should history end with globalization, a world of freedom and prosperity will not arise in its place. The idea that history has somehow managed to end, moreover, is clearly suspect.³⁷ Rather, as Jacques Derrida suggested in his uncharacteristically direct demolition of Fukuyama's premise, the end of the Cold War might instead signal merely the end of a "*certain* concept of history" rather than of history itself.³⁸ The history that is ending, Derrida posited, is the history of metaphysical certainties and teleological development in which capitalism can be seen as an expression of the pinnacle of human achievement. That is, the end of the Cold War may signal an end of a dialectical, more modern or Hegelian than post-structural conceptualization of history, with all its narratives of human progression, which is exactly the type of history that Fukuyama sought to enshrine. The potential for reformulating the terrain and expectations of history would then be opened up, as the theorization of history would now be allowed to move from simple diachronic analyses of cause and effect to a more dispersed form in which events would instead unfold according to a genealogical model rather than relying on narratives of origins and endpoints. For the characters of *Generation X*, history as the story of capitalism versus communism may have ended, and the promise of less linear narratives may arise in its stead, leading to a further disruption of hierarchical narratives that privilege Western "development" over non-Western "backwardness."

This development, however, does not appear to have positive effects on the characters of the novel, despite its antiracist potential. The second ground on which Andrew, Dagmar, and Claire's malaise is troubling arises out of the first, in which the arrival of the end of history is envisaged in Fukuyama's writing as a passive process, one that simply happens with the triumph of global capitalism. In this process, the powers and privileges of the world are to be evenly spread over the globe—they are, in other words, to be decentred as privileges are expanded. But there is a substantial difference between the passive process of history ending and the active operations of capitalism, a difference that Fukuyama does not substantially address. This slippage also occurs in *Generation X*, in the passage cited above, as the characters position themselves in society. When Andrew states that he and his comrades "are marginalized" in the passive voice, he is articulating an anxiety about the passive dispersal of Western privilege. However, he proceeds in the same sentence to state that there is also "a great deal in which" he and his friends "choose not to participate." It seems that, if the characters in the novel are the first subjects to experience the metaphysical displacements of global capitalism, then the prior experiences of marginalized people living in diaspora, exile, or poverty must somehow be discounted. Tate puts it as follows:

> Coupland's characters are fugitives from the story of middle-class aspiration, hoping to forge a new identity. The idea that this activity somehow negates class identity is, however, rather more problematic. A skeptical approach might suggest that Andy, Claire and Dag are tourists, visiting a world without pension schemes, healthcare benefits and stock options as a retreat from the less palatable elements of consumerist society but who always have the opportunity to return to this more secure financial world.[39]

Andrew's calling himself and those around him marginalized, while possibly an apt characterization of their situation within the United States, becomes an insensitive claim when placed in a global context, Tate suggests. Nevertheless, the subjects of *Generation X* privilege their own marginality as a position from which to criticize those who are more fully implicated in capitalism, especially Claire's boyfriend Tobias, whom Andrew calls "smug and bland" and whom he sees as embodying "all of the people of [his] generation who used all that was good in themselves just to make money."[40] Lainsbury suggests that an "inability to draw distinctions, the lack of a sense of the hierarchical" is typical of generation X,[41] and Andrew's claim to marginality may reflect one such lack of recognition of the different material situations of those impacted by global capitalism, despite the theoretical levelling that has occurred among those of his generation.

Criticisms of generation X as a sociological group suggest that Andrew's failure to recognize his own privilege can be read more broadly in North American society of the period. Helene Shugart noted then that while the generation X mentality is supposedly "multicultural," this "claim seems to be an empty one," as it is happy with its own platitudes and erasure of otherness.[42] Other criticisms of the generation X mentality as ignoring the marginalized have been more pointed: J. Giles has suggested that the mentality "doesn't resonate much beyond the white middle class,"[43] while Lynnea King has accused the art of generation X of completely lacking "diversity and representation."[44] These are points that may well hold true of *Generation X* itself, as the subjects of the text can be seen as reflecting a sometimes glaring ignorance of the experiences of the oppressed in order to claim their own position of marginality (again, it is important to separate the text from Coupland here, whose texts have become increasingly varied in their representations). After Andrew goes home to Oregon to visit his family for the Christmas holidays, he states that "when you're middle class, you have to live with the fact that history will ignore you. You have to live with the fact that history can never champion your causes and that history will never feel sorry for you. It is the price paid for day-to-day comfort and silence. And because of this price, all happinesses are sterile; all sadnesses go unpitied."[45]

The narrator here constructs fulfillment and plenitude as lack, implicitly desiring recognition for his marginalization while ignoring the hardships faced by those whose causes are championed by history, those who are more materially marginalized. That capitalism is an alienating and marginalizing structure is not what I seek to contest here, and Andrew may have a basis for his argument. What is risky, rather, is that he suggests at this point not only that he and his friends are marginalized by the structures of late capitalism, but also that they are in some ways marginalized by the marginalized themselves, or at least by those whose marginalization is recognized as such, and who thereby prevent his own claim to marginality from being heard.

Andrew's contention that the subjects of *Generation X* are marginalized must be both questioned and put into context. While the expressions of malcontent with capitalism voiced in the text have certainly been echoed from other quarters, the specific complaints of its subjects ring somewhat hollow. The narrator states that he and his companions make conscious decisions to "put themselves on the margins of society."[46] This deliberate profession of marginalization—and the active pursuit of such positioning—does not render their concerns invalid, but it does render their justifications for making them suspect. Within the specifically Western setting that the text invokes, their irritations seem to register as valid critiques of the system. However, when situated in the transnational context of the contemporary modes of capitalist alienation against which the subjects of *Generation X* agitate, complaints about economic disparity come off as insensitive remarks in the face of global populations affected by industrial collapse or by the processes of global domination and exploitation. Reading the text in this broader context makes it seem possible that the disenfranchisement the characters express elides and thereby elicits the suggestion that their marginalization arises in part from having been displaced from positions of dominance—be it economic or ontological—precisely *because* they do not accompany their expressions of malaise with specific analyses of the dynamics of global capitalism from which they feel alienated. To psychologize their reactions, one can read sublimated expressions of fears that what would once have been their employment is migrating offshore and is now being monopolized by the marginalized in other locations. The simple solution is to give up on the prospect of finding fulfilling employment entirely. Andrew and Dagmar treat their jobs at Larry's Bar as necessary but disposable inconveniences, as Claire does her job at the Chanel counter at a department store. As far as they are concerned, the hope of finding satisfying employment is long gone. If the characters of *Generation X* dissent against the structures of society, therefore, they also risk oppressing those who are hierarchically subordinated to the West, in a perhaps unconscious expression of a desire to retain the position of hegemony against which they ostensibly dissent, from which they express a sense of alienation, and for which they express nostalgia in their endless storytelling about 1974.

CONCLUSION: MARGINALIZATION, DISSENT, AND THE CONTEMPORARY MAINSTREAM MALE

My goal here is not to vilify *Generation X*. I think that the text points toward an important trend in 1990s conceptualizations about how straight, white, male subjects have coped with interpreting the world under globalization by using its tropes—the ideas of economic deterritorialization and displacement—as means of participating in the language of marginalization. This is a gendered discourse in *Generation X* despite Claire's participation in the trio of lost hipsters. Andrew suggests that acts of self-marginalization such as his and Dagmar's are "harder for women...than men,"[47] and though he does not explain exactly why this is, it is not difficult to surmise that women are already marginalized within patriarchal culture, which hinders their freedom to adopt and reject various marginalized stances. Claire's marginalized position is thus already assured prior to the levelling discourses of global capitalism. Coming from a position of supposed cultural dominance and normativity, however, Andrew and Dagmar do not have obvious points for resistance aside from the economic realm. Engaging in discussions of marginalization from this perspective, though, risks occluding the challenges faced by global subjects who come from positions clearly marked as other and who face intersecting oppressions. *Generation X* is a brilliant illustration of this occlusion, given the characters' relative lack of demonstrated awareness of marginalization beyond the privileged world in which they live. The lingering question has to be about how troubling these constructs may or may not be. Coupland's writing in *Generation X* recognizes a problematic issue for formulating alternative masculinities from what is constantly reified in cultural discourse as a position of dominant normativity. Dissent against the structures of late capitalism, when coming from a position of privilege, needs to be a carefully nuanced and articulated process, and *Generation X* indicates some of the pitfalls involved.

This problematic is well demonstrated in the conclusion of *Generation X*. At the end of the episodic narrative, Dagmar and Claire ditch their jobs and move from California to Mexico in order to start a small hotel for generation X hipsters in San Felipe. Andrew, after hesitating about leaving his world behind, follows them across the border and into the unknown. Grassian rightly identifies this move as "another attempt to flee postmodern American culture,"[48] one that replicates the logic of the trio's original move to suburban California. On the trip there, Andrew sees the people trapped on the borders of Empire—the vendors who work on the crossing without traversing it—while he crosses over it easily, given his privileged position. Hardt and Negri's Empire is in a sense embodied in Andrew, who, as a form of Canadian/American mobile capital—driving his car and bringing his possessions and relative wealth with him—is able to traverse the world of capitalist imperialism, while borders remain staunchly erected for the impoverished. Robert McGill argues that Coupland's novel *Girlfriend in a Coma* requires its characters to "find utopia within their state"—California—because there is no further westward expansion toward which its characters can look.[49] In *Generation X,* Coupland's characters, after seeking a suburban utopia in California, decide to move south in order to find a utopic space. Despite their fixation on eschatology, history has not yet ended with the triumph of global capitalism: barriers persist, and capitalism still has many corners of the globe left to permeate. Andrew and his friends are thus moving over to what he describes as the "lunar, granular, parched, and desperate" side of the border,[50] consciously deciding to adopt this position of metaphorical lack and isolation from capitalist abundance.

The hotel that the three plan to start, however, may be another iteration of Empire itself, as these Canadian and American citizens move further away from the centres of privilege in California in order to colonize a piece of what might be considered marginal soil. But does this colonization take place in the name of entrepreneurial capitalism? Or, alternatively, might their movement away from security and privilege offer a genuine means of articulating and situating mainstream dissent against contemporary capitalism? These answers will likely vary based on readership of the text. The political questions remain, however, concerning the extent to which dissidence is possible for the mainstream Canadian male, whether such dissidence can be situated on such marginal soil, and to what extent the site of economic disparity is valid for such subjects to situate their projects of articulating social alternatives.

NOTES

1. Douglas Coupland, *Generation A* (Toronto: Vintage Canada, 2009), 2.
2. Douglas Coupland, *Generation X* (New York: St. Martin's, 1991).
3. Douglas Coupland, *Souvenir of Canada* (Vancouver: Douglas and McIntyre, 2002) and *Souvenir of Canada 2* (Vancouver: Douglas and McIntyre, 2004).
4. Douglas Coupland, *JPod* (Toronto: Vintage Canada, 2006), 15.
5. Andrew Tate, *Douglas Coupland* (Manchester: Manchester University Press, 2007), 164.
6. Coupland, *Generation X*, 40.
7. Margaret Atwood, *Survival: A Thematic Guide to Canadian Literature* (Toronto: Anansi, 1972), 242.
8. Alan Sinfield, *Faultlines: Cultural Materialism and the Politics of Dissident Reading* (Oxford: Clarendon, 1992), 49.

9 Roy Miki does just this in discussing the cited passage from *Survival* in *Broken Entries: Race, Subjectivity, Writing* (Toronto: Mercury, 1998), 102.
10 For a thoughtful, sociologically grounded version of these arguments, see the studies in Stephen Craig and Stephen Bennett, eds., *After the Boom: The Politics of Generation X* (Lanham: Rowman and Littlefield, 1997). A somewhat weaker thesis is discussed in Bernard Rosen's *Masks and Mirrors: Generation X and the Chameleon Personality* (Westport: Praeger, 2001), which suggests that all citizens of Generation X have flexible politics, which they use cynically in order to adapt to their world.
11 In 1991, Jameson expanded his earlier essay of the same name into the book-length study *Postmodernism, or, The Cultural Logic of Late Capitalism* (Durham: Duke University Press, 1991).
12 Linda Hutcheon, *The Politics of Postmodernism*, 2nd ed. (London: Routledge, 2002), 166.
13 For Derrida's own contribution to discussions of capitalism, see especially his *Specters of Marx: The State of the Debt, the Work of Mourning, and the New International,* trans. P. Kamuf (New York: Routledge, 1994).
14 Claus Offe, *Disorganized Capitalism: Contemporary Transformations of Work and Politics* (Cambridge, MA: MIT Press, 1985).
15 David Harvey, *The Condition of Postmodernity* (Cambridge: Blackwell, 1989), 141ff.
16 Ibid., 147.
17 See, for example, Carla Freeman, "Is Local:Global as Feminine:Masculine? Rethinking the Gender of Globalization," *Signs: Journal of Women in Culture and Society* 26, no. 4 (2001): 1007–37; and Saskia Sassen, "Women's Burden: Counter-Geographies of Globalization and the Feminization of Survival," *Journal of International Affairs* 53, no. 2 (2000): 503–24.
18 Arif Dirlik, "The Postcolonial Aura: Third World Criticism in the Age of Global Capitalism," in *Dangerous Liaisons: Gender, Nation, and Postcolonial Perspectives,* ed. A. McClintock et al. (Minneapolis: University of Minnesota Press, 1997), 517.
19 Arjun Appadurai, *Modernity at Large: Cultural Dimensions of Globalization* (Minneapolis: University of Minnesota Press, 1996), 37–39.
20 Throughout Gilles Deleuze and Félix Guattari, *A Thousand Plateaus: Capitalism and Schizophrenia,* trans. Brian Massumi (Minneapolis: University of Minnesota Press, 1987). Neil Smith has recently noted that analyses of the global that celebrate or focus on processes of deterritorialization often neglect that, for Deleuze and Guattari, every deterritorialization is accompanied by a subsequent reterritorialization. Neil Smith, *The Endgame of Globalization* (New York: Routledge, 2005), 51.
21 Appadurai, *Modernity at Large,* 32.
22 Ibid., 46.
23 Michael Hardt and Antonio Negri, *Empire* (Cambridge, MA: Harvard University Press, 2000); *Multitude: War and Democracy in the Age of Empire* (New York: Penguin, 2004); and *Commonwealth* (Cambridge, MA: Harvard University Press, 2009).
24 See especially Paul Passavant and Jodi Dean, eds., *Empire's New Clothes: Reading Hardt and Negri* (New York: Routledge, 2004); Gopal Balakrishnan, ed., *Debating Empire* (London: Verso, 2003); and Atilio A. Boron, *Empire and Imperialism: A Critical Reading of Michael Hardt and Antonio Negri* (London: Zed, 2005) for responses to Hardt and Negri's work.
25 This ambition and reach has led to many critical and at times unfavourable reviews. See Timothy Brennan, "The Empire's New Clothes," *Critical Inquiry* 29, no. 2 (2003): 337–67, for a sometimes harsh version thereof.

26 Hardt and Negri, *Empire*, xiii–xiv.
27 Coupland, *Generation X*, 57.
28 Ibid., 113.
29 Ibid., 7.
30 Daniel Grassian, *Hybrid Fictions: American Literature and Generation X* (Jefferson: McFarland, 2003), 89.
31 Coupland, *Generation X*, 11.
32 Ibid., 88.
33 G.P. Lainsbury, "*Generation X* and the End of History," *Essays on Canadian Writing* 58 (1996): 232.
34 Ibid., 233–34.
35 Coupland, *Generation X*, 70.
36 Francis Fukuyama, *The End of History and the Last Man* (New York: HarperCollins, 1992).
37 This point has been critiqued and rejected by many writers. Edward Said, for instance, stated in a lecture shortly after Fukuyama's book was published that "we are nowhere near the end of history" ("Culture and Imperialism," York University, Toronto, 10 February 1993). His book *Culture and Imperialism* refines this point, stating that Fukuyama's premise is "a radical falsification of culture" as it attempts "to strip it of its affiliations with its setting," that is, its connection to time and hence its context (New York: Vintage, 1993), 259. Edited volumes variously critiquing Fukuyama's postulate have appeared as well: see Christopher Bertram and Andrew Chitty, eds., *Has History Ended? Fukuyama, Marx, Modernity* (Aldershot: Avebury, 1994); and Timothy Burns, ed., *After History? Francis Fukuyama and his Critics* (Lanham: Rowman and Littlefield, 1994).
38 Derrida, *Specters of Marx*, 15.
39 Tate, *Douglas Coupland*, 6.
40 Coupland, *Generation X*, 81.
41 Lainsbury, "*Generation X* and the End of History," 236.
42 Helene Shugart, "Isn't It Ironic? The Intersection of Third-Wave Feminism and Generation X," *Women's Studies in Communication* 24, no. 2 (2001): 162.
43 J. Giles, "Generalizations X," *Newsweek*, 6 June 1994, 63.
44 Lynnea King, "Generation X: Searching for an Identity?" *Post Script* 19, no. 2 (2000): 8–18.
45 Coupland, *Generation X*, 147.
46 Ibid., 88.
47 Ibid., *Generation X*, 88.
48 Grassian, *Hybrid Fictions*, 94.
49 Robert McGill, "The Sublime Simulacrum: Vancouver in Douglas Coupland's Geography of the Apocalypse," *Essays on Canadian Writing* 70 (2000): 258.
50 Coupland, *Generation X*, 172.

CHAPTER 12

Dangerous Homosexualities and Disturbing Masculinities: The Disabling Rhetoric of Difference in Barbara Gowdy's *Mister Sandman*

SALLY HAYWARD

In "Compulsory Able-Bodiedness and Queer/Disabled Existence," Robert McRuer engages with Adrienne Rich's feminist critique of compulsory heterosexuality and her theory that "lesbian existence" is central to the construction of heterosexual relations.[1] In positing that "the system of compulsory able-bodiedness that produces disability is thoroughly interwoven with the system of compulsory heterosexuality that produces queerness," McRuer is able to take Rich's analysis of compulsory heterosexuality beyond its connection to "lesbian existence" to include an analysis of ability and disability.[2] While Rich argues that compulsory heterosexuality utilizes an alternative lesbian existence to "[buttress] the ideological notion that dominant identities are...the natural order of things," McRuer argues that compulsory able-bodiedness utilizes disability for the same reasons. In McRuer's words, "compulsory heterosexuality" and "compulsory able-bodiedness" are imbricated systems: "compulsory heterosexuality is contingent on compulsory able-bodiedness and vice versa."[3] These intertwined systems depend on "disciplines of normality" for the (re)production of "dutiful (or docile) able-bodied" and heterosexual subjects and for the deployment of queerness and disability as marginal subject positions.[4] However, while the (re)production of able-bodied, heterosexual subjects constitutes the common ground of all identities, "queer/disabled existence...can never quite be contained."[5] It remains to inform heterosexual able-bodied identities not only of their "naturalized" and "normalized" dominance, but also to inform these dominant identities of their "mutual impossibility" and "mutual incomprehensibility."[6]

It is this "mutual impossibility" and "mutual incomprehensibility" that Barbara Gowdy thematically explores in her novel *Mister Sandman,* as she tells the story of Doris and Gordon Canary, who struggle to deal with the illegitimate birth of their daughter's child, Joan, and Joan's ensuing diagnosis of autism. While on one level, this novel appears to be a close study of a conservatively "normal," 1950s-style heterosexual family, on another level, *Mister Sandman* exposes how the forced, disciplinary compliance with sexual, gender, and ability norms creates an environment that is both dysfunctional—oppressive and repressive—and destructive.

In the novel, the conflated and interwoven discourses of heterosexuality, homosexuality, and disability work not to affirm normative identities but to trouble them, interrupting and exposing as dysfunctional the cultural truism that assumes as "natural" the dominance of the heterosexual, able-bodied male individual and "his" family.[7] In troubling these "normative" conceptions, Gowdy calls attention to the disabling and "queer" aspects of "normal" heterosexual, able-bodied existence, an existence that is dangerous precisely to the extent that it demands individual repression and oppression. Gowdy goes further, however, when in an attempt to affirm difference, she makes disability central to the novel's portrayal of both heterosexuality and homosexuality. Paradoxically, while this representation might be seen as an attempt by Gowdy to make disability "*foundational to both cultural definition and to literary narratives that challenge normalizing prescriptive ideals*,"[8] it is, while appearing central, ultimately conceived as peripheral: disability is an extreme example of the radically different other who must always be figured as unequal and relegated to the margins of the norm. In other words, disability is deployed and utilized as a sign of liminality: a sign of the limits of sexual possibilities and social and "corporeal unruliness," especially when it comes to hierarchizing and delineating "acceptable" practices of masculinity, and an indication of the need to contain unruly masculinities within the normative and "natural" prescriptions of the heterosexual family.

In this chapter, I argue that though *Mister Sandman* conflates homosexuality and disability in potentially constructive ways, exposing the impossibility and incomprehensibility of a normative, heterosexual existence, this representation is compromised by Gowdy's tendency to metaphorically appropriate disability rather than explore it as a valid and equal subject position. While a normatively established male identity is enlarged to include a tentative and limited acceptance of male homosexuality and its practice within the heterosexual family, disability—and disabled identity in particular—undergoes a representational and rhetorical erasure, functioning only to the extent that it is able to serve as "a barometer by which to assess [the] shifting values and norms" of the dominant, able-bodied, and predominantly heterosexual culture.[9]

THE SECRET SHAME OF QUEER SEXUALITIES

In that this novel challenges the norm, it seems that one of its main aims is to challenge comfortable depictions of the Canadian late 1950s and 1960s normal individual and family. In doing this, Gowdy produces a counter-narrative, a re-vision that shows an era and the institution of the family in crisis.[10] In this novel, no one is "normal": Doris Canary, the mother, is a practised liar and a bisexual who has a string of lesbian affairs; Marcy, her daughter, is heterosexual and "uprightly" promiscuous, reading the Bible and compulsively seeking satisfaction through numerous sexual encounters; Sonja, another daughter, is overweight and inert and finds sensual if not sexual pleasure in working industriously as a bobby pin counter in the home; Gordon Canary, the father, a book publisher and editor, is a gay man who is torn between his allegiance to his "normal" heterosexual family and his own biological and "abnormal" sexual desires. Joan, Sonja's asexual and "brain damaged" daughter, is central to the novel. She is the "reincarnation baby" who mutely receives and records the family's darkest secrets. Under the burden of these forbidden desires and secrets, the family is, as Gowdy suggests, falling apart. It cannot sustain relationships outside the monogamous, heterosexual, and able-bodied model, and it remains "stalled in a maze of false dichotomies"—healthy versus unhealthy marriages, well-behaved versus misbehaving children, straight versus gay sexualities, beautiful able-bodies versus deviant disabled bodies—that prevent individual family members from "determin[ing] the meaning and place of sexuality in their lives."[11]

At the same time, however, that the family members cannot sustain these deviant relationships or know where they stand in relation to these false, socially constructed dichotomies, they are defined by them. The behaviour of everyone in the family is to some extent determined by the lies, the pretence, and the secret shame that accompany their inability to live their lives in "straight lines."[12] While Doris recognizes that her desire for Gordon and her lesbian "yearning for women [runs] on two separate tracks," she also knows that "loving women [is] dangerous" because it is outside the bounds of what "normal" women do; it is something to be kept secret, reserved for times when "the coast was clear—your husband at work, your oldest girl at a pin-clippers seminar, your middle one at school, and your littlest one in the closet."[13] Similarly, while Marcy believes it is "natural" to have many "Beloved" boyfriends, she is compelled to pretend to conform to the monogamous heterosexual norm by keeping one acceptable "school or public boyfriend (a boyfriend she brought home to meet her parents)" for show.[14] In secret, however, Marcy keeps many "back door boyfriends"—both dangerous and sick outcasts—that she can, with her sexual favours, heal and cleanse.[15]

Notably, when Marcy decides to give up her secret other life for a decent, "sharper, calmer, narrower," and monogamous life, she changes her name to

Marcia.[16] This strategy is an indication that her secret life has become untenable. She must, "in order to live in an unliveable situation," conform in body and in name to what is socially expected of her.[17] Once Marcia has embraced her new name, shed her false eyelashes,[18] and confessed to her boyfriend that she wears a padded bra, a "manufactured cleavage," she is free to decide to "maybe even get married eventually."[19] In more radical terms, Sonja's marriage possibilities rest on her ability to shed her inhibitions and manufacture a liking for Henry Bowden's "wormy" kisses,[20] while Doris and Gordon's happiness rests, at least to some extent, on Doris's ability to coax the homosexual Gordon to orgasm by arousing his penis's "helpless pluck" with her lips.[21]

Ultimately, however, despite their desire for normality, the propensity these women share for diverse and dangerous sexualities cannot be repressed. While Doris dreams and daydreams about kissing women,[22] Marcy develops a "split personality. One for day, one for night," in order to satisfy her desire for a variety of men,[23] and Sonja craves, not men, but the "buoyancy, the lightness, the bubble feeling" she experiences when she "mechanically" counts and clips her bobby pins onto cards.[24] In a culture that is "ventilated by [the] uprightness" of privileged "normal" heterosexual relationships, their "queer" sexualities are seen as abnormal.[25]

This conflation and internalization of queer sexualities with abnormality is not restricted to women. Gordon's intense desire to envision himself as a heterosexual male, an "ordinary father,"[26] structures his view of his own masculinity as it exists within and for the heterosexual family: for Gordon everything good and "normal" can be associated with this family-oriented "normal" heterosexual masculinity, and everything bad or "abnormal" can be associated with homosexuality. According to Gordon, "real" men, men who have "manly sex," are heroes, Tarzan figures, whose sexuality is rewarded and legitimated,[27] while homosexuals are, like Gordon, "sick...ungrown, unmanly."[28]

This view of himself is confirmed in the scholarly books that he reads first as an eighteen-year-old and then as a mature man searching for "information" and for "a kind of punishing reassurance that it was true": he *was* "afflicted." In these books, "Mental Disorders" and "Sexual Deviance" are synonymous terms that confirm for Gordon that his desire for other men is "unnatural," uncontrollable, and somewhat monstrous. Unable to find a remedy for his "affliction," Gordon believes that "the only decent thing" he can do is "keep [his] affliction under wraps, live with it...Hide it."[29] Unfortunately, his attempt to "bury it alive"[30] comes back to haunt him, emerging in an explosive list of expletives through which he defines himself, "bellowing 'D' words—'Degenerate! Deprived! Deviate! Dystopia!'"[31]

Gowdy would seem to be implying here that repression returns full force in the unconscious use of language to determine Gordon's identity as not only deviant but also sick, ill, and dis-abled. Gordon, aware of the ubiquity of language and its ability to fix meaning in definitive classifications, points out that the men who write books like *Curing the Male Homosexual* and *Demonology and Homosexuality* are speaking from neutral subject positions that leave unknown their identities and the identities of the "other" about which they speak. However, their presence is everywhere, confirming for Gordon in "printed...perfect block letters" that he is not a "real" man.[32] While wondering who these "oddly featureless" men were—"were they homosexuals?"—Gordon realizes that he has only the dry, scholastic, densely footnoted, but also shocking, operatic...bland passages" to provide for him "a kind of punishing reassurance that it [is] true," he is homosexual. He appears to realize at this point that it is these oppressive "clinical descriptions," these words written by unknown men, that officially define, label, and diagnose those who stray from the "norm."[33]

As Gordon observes, in these narratives the "official diagnosis," which is designed to take the "mystery" out of the description, becomes at best a matter of opinion and at worst a blatant or confused misrepresentation.[34] Once, when Gordon looks up "brain damage" in one of his books, he is surprised to find the definitions and descriptions "vague and overblown, wacky even." In one example, the "damaged brain" is metaphorically described as a "red balloon bursting in a bucketful of noodles"; in another example, it is compared to a "berserk telephone exchange run by demented operators."[35] Later, when Gordon falls asleep, his dreams continue in this illogical, metaphorical, and somewhat ominous vein, as homosexual images—"snake clusters"—are conflated with images of the extermination of those deemed unacceptable: the "mental defectives," the promiscuous, and the homosexuals. All of these individuals are conflated in his dreams, envisioned in relation to "the braided limbs of gas chamber corpses."[36]

This metaphorical and metonymical conflation of homosexuality with mental and moral disability, which positions both homosexuality and disability as contiguously undesirable subject positions, is presented as a somewhat frightening "problem." The image of the disordered body and mind, conflated as it is with disordered sexuality and embroiled in the mangle of "gas chamber corpses," serves to remind the reader of early-twentieth-century eugenics discourses that claimed disability and death to be the ultimate and severest consequences of homosexual impulses.[37]

According to Michel Foucault, this discursive and practical eugenic ordering of society revitalized "the type of political power that was exercised through the devices of sexuality" and, I would argue, disability.[38] Inasmuch as homosexuality and disability are seen as "contrary to nature,"[39] the disabled or homosexual individual becomes an "everyday monster...a monster that has become commonplace" in the eyes of the community in which he or she lives.[40] This individual embodies "a principle of intelligibility in spite of [his or her] limit position as both the impossible and the forbidden."[41]

It is possible to know the monstrous, not only because he or she lacks the " sufficient mental self-possession to resist by himself certain deficiencies," but also because, seen through "the reality of lack," these "imbeciles and degenerates"[42] must always be corrected and contained within "the play of relations of conflict and support that exist between the family" and other norm-educing institutions.[43]

Gordon points to this form of insidious containment when, conflating homosexuality and disability, he points to the biological and social ramifications of the unacceptable practice of homosexuality. Blaming his daughter's "slowness" on his homosexuality, he asks himself,

> What is mayhem?...Now, today, he wonders if it isn't him. He doesn't mean her *knowing* that she has a strange father, what he's suddenly wondering is, if a queer father, by unconsciously failing to emit certain normal masculine impulses, plays havoc with his daughter's temperamental development. Her *intellectual* development! Jesus, what if she's slow because he's queer?[44]

The association of queerness here with what he sees as his daughter's biologically inherited brain damage is, for Gordon, an indication of his failed masculinity. His guilty feelings concerning what he perceives to be his "abnormal" creation—his daughter, Sonja—are what enable him to correct himself, as he tries hard to be what they want him to be: "an ordinary father."[45]

There is a sense of irony here. It is not biology that creates Sonja's intellectual disability, but rather not knowing that she has a "queer" father. There are, Gowdy implies, far-reaching psychological consequences to living this secret sexual life. Sonja's cognitive slowness here is an unfortunate by-product of a sexuality that cannot speak its name. Disability is the ultimate punishment for failing to live and experience one's sexuality honestly and openly. This failure on Gordon's part to recognize disability as a valid subject position is consistent with Gowdy's claim, in an interview with the *Bookreporter* in June 2000, that she has "no desire to write from the point of view of characters who are cruel or stupid or brain-damaged. Such people are usually incapable of the kind of reflection that gives a novel its moral core."[46]

THE MONSTROUS AND LIBERATING POSSIBILITIES OF DISABILITY

It may come as no surprise, then, that Joan, who is inscribed into the centre of Gowdy's text, is, though brain-damaged, not intellectually slow. Joan's disability is attributed to a "head-first fall onto the floor" at birth. However, though this caused "a bruise to the left of her soft spot, a mauve quarter-sized circle," which in turn caused her autism, Joan, the reader discovers, is no ordinary autistic.[47] Being autistic, Joan has problems with social interaction, and her communication skills are, if not lacking, different in the extreme; yet as an autistic savant, Joan is gifted. She has extraordinary skills that surface in her ability to play music skilfully by ear and in her ability to memorize information. Doris qualifies Gordon's recognition that in Joan's brain "certain functions appear to have suffered some degree of injury" by pointing out that brain damage is something that happens in a certain part of the brain, but "you can be a genius in one part of your brain and still be brain-damaged in another part."[48] It is this idea of genius, rather than disability, that appears to intrigue Gowdy.

The autistic "brain-damaged" "midget"[49] savant is no "retard,"[50] as some people might initially suspect when first introduced to the silent child; she is "a genius" who "learned fast"[51] and who, by the end of one month, can write any letter read to her and "[add] and [subtract] double-digit numbers in her head."[52] Similar to Gordon, Joan is acutely aware of the power of words to define, stigmatize, and violate those who are different. Joan, who refuses to speak, knows that when words are printed or spoken they are drained of their colour, reduced or transformed so that the "whole story, or even the true [story]" is not told.[53] Words, it would seem, have the ability to evoke the power of God, but as Marcy notes, "more than that, they are weapons."[54]

Interestingly, it is not Joan but the other members of her family who believe that Joan "suffer[s] from words." While Sonja believes that words are dangerous and that Joan's inability to speak is some kind of karmic retribution for abusing language in a previous life—"as a gossip maybe. As a tattletale"[55]—Gordon believes that words perform a violence. Rather than reflecting and preserving the "climate of the mind," they dislodge, dry, and shrink the original meaning. For Sonja, Joan's silence is a punishment; for Gordon, Joan's muteness is "highly evolved." His need to assign meaning to Joan's disability means that he alternates between believing that Joan is "deliberately foreswearing words out of an instinctive sense that it [takes] only one to flatten you," and believing that "she'll come around" and speak eventually.[56] When he discovers Joan's tapes in the basement, he is ecstatic that he has discovered Joan's "first written communication." This "breakthrough," however, has more to do with Gordon's own desire to make Joan "normal" that it has to do with Joan's own reality, which is more focused on listening and recording than it is on speaking.[57]

Despite Joan's persistent silence, or perhaps because of it, when the family needs solace, they instinctively turn to Joan. Joan, who lives in the closet because she cannot bear the daylight, is used as a "sounding board" by all of the family: there was a "regular pilgrimage throughout the day—Doris always racing in, Sonja dropping by...[and] Marcy joining her before and after school."[58] Every day after work, Gordon lies on the floor of her closet and "pour[s] his heart out" to her. In there, he feels he can say anything, tell her anything, in part because he does not think she understands, and in part because "never in her face has he witnessed reproach or shock. Never, not under any circumstances."[59] In confessing to the silent and non-judgmental child, in "extracting from the depths of [himself]...a truth," in telling her "what [he] is and what [he] does," Gordon finds a false sense of freedom.[60] He feels, as he states, "aghast, but refreshed as well," free for one brief moment from his own particular brand of oppression.[61]

Ironically, though appearing as if she understands nothing, Joan sees, hears, and remembers *everything*. She is the one who "knows" the family's darkest secrets. She knows about the many boys that Marcia has slept with, she knows that Doris "love[s] to have sex with bare naked women," and she knows about Gordon's love for other men.[62] She has heard him speak the "dead giveaway words—'lover,' for example, or, worse: 'queer,' even 'Al Yothers.'"[63] Within this textual configuration, Joan is both "the metaphorical signifier" of the traditional heterosexual family's "social and individual collapse" and the "reincarnating spirit" that allows the Canarys to acknowledge to themselves and to one another their "true" identities.[64]

In this way, Joan can be seen to exist at the centre of the novel. In one respect, she comes to stand for the margin that has come to the centre: a dysfunctional but "uniquely" different individual, a "case of special interest"; but in another respect, her role in the novel is functional. She is "a crutch" on which the narrative depends for its "representational power, disruptive potentiality, and analytical insight."[65] In the process, Joan becomes a function of the plot, a literary device that grounds the family in their "adverse truths," making them "recognizable" to themselves and to one another as she forces them to confront the truths about one another that "[demand] only to surface."[66] In this scenario, Joan's own identity is annihilated. Because the family thinks she does not understand, she becomes a blank slate, an asexual, and a metaphorical "family dog" onto which they can project their worst fears and desires.[67] Ultimately, she exists for her family and for the reader only to the extent that she enables them to affirm their own "normal" humanity to themselves.

DANGEROUS MASCULINITIES

Clinging to this sense of shared and acceptable humanity, Gordon, more than anyone else, repeatedly attempts to repress his homosexual desires. When Gordon first meets Al Yothers, the man who comes to fix Gordon's office radiator, he fights his attraction by staring at "a proof reader named Tom Hooks, a surly kid with insolent little hips and fluttering blue eyes...to reassure himself that his desire isn't fatally pinned to one man but is spread out, restored to its old, harmless sprawl."[68] Additionally, Gordon uses his desire for Al Yothers as a "catalyst to return him at last to [the] sanctified threshold" of his wife's "capsized body."[69]

Kept within this secretive and restorative context, Gordon's homosexuality is somewhat acceptable. The "heterosexual romance" can, it seems, withstand a certain amount of deviance and difference as long as this difference is framed by the "white lies" that are themselves representative of the "heterosexually defined" "way things are."[70] In this context, it is clear that compliant, assimilable homosexual masculinities are more acceptable than those which are figured as completely antithetical to the institutionalized heterosexual family. Creating a hierarchy here, Gowdy outlines for her readers exactly which kinds of homosexual masculinities are acceptable or unacceptable in this heterosexual universe.

In the novel, Al Yothers—Sonja and Gordon's boyfriend and Joan's father—represents an "unacceptable" homosexuality. Al sits on the border; he is neither clearly heterosexual nor definitively homosexual. However, this alone does not define his exclusion (after all, Doris admits that she is bisexual and is clearly accepted as part of the family). His exclusion, rather, is dependent on the fact that he uses his sexuality subversively, refusing to subscribe to any ethical and/or normative mores, rules, and standards in his relationships with Sonja and Gordon.

Al, who represents the symbolic "Mister Sandman" of nursery rhymes, steals Gordon's civilized dreams and his heterosexual vision of a "normal" family away from him. Playing with the Freudian *"unheimlich,"* the unfamiliar or the uncanny, Gowdy reiterates this idea of the dream through the repeated invocation of the song, "Mister Sandman."[71] The dream, which in the song "Mister Sandman" represents a desire for an elusive mystery man, and an elusive "peaches and cream" sexuality, speaks to Gordon's desire to delete any (heterosexual) decency and to romantically imagine himself and Al as a couple together: "Is *he* the dream?" Gordon wonders as he listens to the song.[72] In invoking this song, Gowdy is playing with Freud's notion that the uncanny is "that class of the terrifying which leads back to something long known to us, once very familiar" and now strange.[73] In other words, Gowdy makes the strange become familiar, the secret known, as the song, and the fantasy—made real in the man, Al Yothers—returns time and time again to remind Gordon of his dread and fascination for his hidden or repressed homosexuality.

In Freud's terms, the Sand-Man of nursery rhymes, Hoffman's story, *Nactstucken,* and Offenbach's opera, *Tales of Hoffman,* is at once an inanimate idea that reminds us of that to which we must return, and "a wicked man" who comes to naughty children at night when they won't go to sleep and tears out their eyes. According to Freud, the "morbid anxiety connected with the eyes and with going blind is often enough a substitute for the dread of castration."[74] In that Al Yothers, as a symbolic Freudian "Sandman," robs Gordon of his vision, he represents the castrating father figure who threatens to destroy Gordon's "normal" sense of himself as a man. By extension, Al's reappearance in a network of dangerous signs mirrors Gordon's own queer sexuality that, precisely because it has always "been here" below the surface, represents a threat to the individual physical and mental health of his "normal" family. In other words, Gordon's and Al's deviance is dangerous precisely because it creates an incomprehensible reality for the heterosexual family.

Unable to read the signs of this queer sexuality, the family itself becomes an anxiety-ridden location, a place that inspires and manifests inferred or imagined, rather than known, terror. Afraid of a sexuality that she cannot see or know, Marcy "[dates] fuzzy male shapes with erections she [grabs] on to like...white cane[s],"[75] while Sonja, confusing men with objects, rejects men in preference for her pin clipping and the "bubble feeling" she gets from this activity.[76] Doris, the mother, who turns to lesbianism at least in part because of Gordon's neglect, naively "[wraps] her fingers around Gordon's penis,...to have something to hold on to in the world."[77]

Al Yothers, however, holds on to nothing but empty, shallow facts that he gleans from encyclopaedias. Though Al boasts to Gordon that he has "read [the encyclopaedia] right through twice" and is on "his third go-round, up to the D's," his claim that all he is interested in is "[t]he facts" and "[t]he truth" seems superficial. Moreover, his frequent urging of Gordon to test him on his knowledge and memorization skills—"Gimme some C's. I've got the C's down cold"—is ridiculous considering that he is often "idiotically wrong." Gordon's statement that "the truth is only a version" becomes ironic in Al's presence when the truth is seen, more significantly, as "aversion."[78]

One version the reader gets of Al's aversive behaviour is when Al first meets Gordon. They go to a "new Chinese restaurant," and Al, characteristically rude, loudly makes fun of Gordon and his role as a "civilized" "family" or "famry man," and of the "'Chinks,' their eating habits (slurping, shovelling it in), the food they themselves eat (Labrador retrievers and stray cats), their feelings (none)." Because Al is seemingly unaware that his behaviour is not only politically incorrect but also obnoxious, it is possible to assume here, as Gordon does, that Al, metaphorically, is "drawing a blank."[79]

The assumption that Al is some kind of an "idiot," however, must be revised when it becomes apparent that much of his behaviour is conscious and deliberate. His pointed humiliation of Gordon, for example, takes on an ominous tone when, having heard of Gordon's painful boyhood experience, he laughs uncontrollably and calls Gordon a "jerk...a *friggin' jerk!*"[80] Comparing Al to Joan here, it might be possible to argue that if Joan is disabled by her autism, by her inability to communicate and socially interact with others, and by her lack of emotion, Al, in a similar way, is compromised and disabled by his inability to relate to the feelings of others and by his lack of morals. However, this insensitive lack of morality becomes paradoxical when, after finishing the affair with Gordon, Al functions as a moral judge, insightfully and consciously exposing Gordon's moral weakness: according to Al,

Gordon is "the pornographer of lost causes...A taker...You go around acting like you're a giver but you're a taker."[81]

Al, it would seem, identifying himself to his lovers as "Yours," exists in a similar way to Joan, to reveal to people their deepest dreams and fears. He is "theirs" in that he "cures" them of their shame, forcing them to confront who they are by, ironically, reading not the fictions but the "facts, the truth," of what lies below the surface. He defines, in other words, not only what is written on the page but also what is written in between the words or palimpsested word upon word—as in the repeated and modified phrase, "Al was here"—on the skin, in the mirror, on the material of everyday existence. In some respects, then, "screwing Al is the breakthrough cure" for Gordon.[82] In rescuing Gordon's "capsized body," Al not only forces Gordon to come to terms with who he is but also acts as the "catalyst" that "returns him at last to this [homosocial] sanctified threshold."[83]

In other respects, however, Al is a threat because he exposes the heterosexual "fiction" to be little more than a comforting myth. It is a myth that keeps everyone safe and normal precisely to the extent that it demands they keep their "fantasy-land" lives a secret and precisely to the extent they are able to "act" or "appear" normal. In revealing this fiction, Al exposes the heterosexual family as a constructed and privileged artifact. His refusal, within this construct, to provide *any* "straight answers" or identifications means that, unlike the members of the Canary family, he cannot be "yanked into straight lines."[84] He has to "[blow] this turkey-trot town" because he has no place, within this text and within this "fictionalized" culture, to go.

Al, then, has the worst kind of disability. He is the "'eccentric' or 'mildly insane'"[85] "orange-haired giant"[86] who disturbs the social and moral order precisely because he refuses to conform to its normative ethical and moral standards. Consequently, Al's existence, much more so than his daughter Joan's, represents a "mutual impossibility and mutual incomprehensibility."[87] He must, to create even the suggestion of a possible happy ending, be expurgated from the lives of the family and from the pages of the text. His double-edged heterosexual/homosexual masculinity is doubly dangerous in that it demands repetition. It will, as he makes clear to Sonja, go on "to infinity." Perhaps not surprisingly, then, his parting shot to Gordon, "watch your back,"[88] combined with his comment to Sonja, "no matter which way you look, darlin', there we are," suggests his, or an-other's, hauntingly familiar and somewhat dangerous return.[89] Like the Sandman who returns to steal the children's dreams and vision, Al exists in this text to remind the reader that the defective, the depraved, and the deviant exceed the text's and the culture's ability to define or imagine the norm.

Perhaps not surprisingly, then, when Al calls "time's up" on his relationship with Gordon, he disappears physically from the text.[90] He exists only as a reminder of a dangerous masculinity that must not be able to (re)surface in physical form. The appearance and reappearance of the constantly mutating mark that he leaves on Gordon's back, "Al was here," is a reminder of both the need to erase the physical memory of the dangerously deviant, and the impossibility of this erasure.[91] Gordon, however, who is to some extent able to keep his homosexuality hidden, is allowed to return to the comfortable arms of his homosexual Presbyterian minister—a man who preached that "God forgives everything"—and his heterosexual family.[92]

RESTORING NORMALITY; NEGATING DISABILITY

Ironically, it is Joan, the asexual, autistic savant/dwarf, who holds on to nothing remotely "normal," who facilitates Gordon's return to the "normal" heterosexual family, when she exposes the "truth" of Gordon's repressed desires to his family. Embedded in her musical composition, which the family listens to when Joan is sick in hospital, are the words spoken by the family when taken unaware. Taking "a word from here, a word from there"[93] and splicing them together, Joan forces her family to confront not only their secret sexual identities but also the lie, the "agreed upon common ground" against which homosexuals and the disabled are compared and judged. When, for example, the tape reveals that Gordon "[has] orgasms with queer men," he and the rest of the family are forced to consider that this is not simply "shock value" but a sincere attempt to reveal the "tremendous lies" that heterosexual normativity demands.[94]

In doing this, Gowdy subverts uncannily what is considered "normal," making the normal, the abnormal, and the familiar, strange. Gordon Canary, as the "normal" male head of the household and the symbolic centre of the heterosexual family, is revealed to be the "abnormal" yet hauntingly familiar centre that must be thoroughly examined, and reinscribed, as Joan is, into the family. While Marcia leaves, still trying to figure out how "to feel how she feels,"[95] Sonja is reinscribed into the family as a "crazy lady," a "monkey [caught] in the middle" of her family's dysfunctionality.[96] Doris, too, becomes acceptable because she admits that she still has sexual feelings for her husband—"I must be what they call a bisexual"[97]—and because she tells Gordon that she might not have taken the "plunge" if Gordon had been able to give her a "normal sex life."[98] However, if Gordon is to be allowed to remain in the family, he must fulfill his role as the "normal" male head of the household and take "absolute responsibility" for his wife and children. He can be gay, it seems, as long as he does not make any "bones rattle," as long as he continues to pretend, "to lie through his teeth," about his sexual orientation, and as long as he continues to take a "curiously resigned comfort" in the illusion.[99]

At the end of the novel, Gowdy reiterates this need for secrecy and pretence when, having revealed that the "abnormal" is a "normal" or "recognizable" construct, she creates an ironic sense of liberation. This happens when the family, having heard the truth, are able to metaphorically "[burn] the evidence," put the past behind them, and "come out" and play.[100] In this night-time scenario, the family plays ball: "they form a circle and keep tossing, industriously, carefully. Without a word."[101] Gordon, here, freed from Al's influence and freshly inspired by his new lover, the minister, is one of the players. Yet his liberation, and the sexual liberation of the typically heterosexual Canadian family, is far from complete. They, and Gordon in particular, are still constrained by the tossing, the need to be industrious, the need to be careful and, above all, silent. Gordon has come out in the open, revealing his "queer" truth to Doris, his wife; yet his homosexuality, similar to Joan's disability, is still closeted by the night as well as by his admission that, if asked about his sexual orientation, he will undoubtedly continue to pretend and so compromise the truth about the ways he practises his masculinity.

At this point in the novel, it is easy to forget Joan, who has, it would seem, served her purpose in this fictionalized account. Having revealed to the family members their secret, hidden truths, and having almost paid the price for it with her life, she is allowed to return home. Carried over the threshold by her freshly committed father, she, like the rest of the family members, returns to her regular routine. Bridging the boundaries and limits of normality, she plays the piano—both the "funeral march" and "honky-tonk piano"—and shuts herself in her closet to read "old *Life* magazines";[102] at night, she comes out with the rest of the family to play ball. It is significant, however, that Joan's echoing of the "screen door banging" is now only "so-so," and that, instead of only tossing the ball to her father, she now "throws the ball" to the new players.[103] Metaphorically, handing responsibility to the able-bodied members of the family, Joan's importance to the narrative decreases. She has served her purpose, destabilizing cultural meanings and exposing the limits of sexual liberation, and now her presence, which has always been somewhat defined by her absence, is of only marginal significance.

In one respect, Gowdy's conflation of dangerous homosexualities with deviant disabilities indicates that a tolerant-minded, modern sensibility might well be open to reincorporating certain homosexual subjectivities—and perhaps, like Joan, certain gifted people with disabilities—into the "normal" family; in another respect, this conflation points to the fear, fantasy, or desire to eliminate people who threaten the "normal" social order. Subjectivities that stray too far from the norm, this novel implies, are a threat that must either be eliminated from the dominant narrative, as Al is, or contained within the "normal" or "natural" heterosexual, and able-bodied framework, to which the family is central. It would seem that within this heterosexual, normative, and familial frame of reference, people with disabilities are useful to the extent to which they serve as a reminder of the acceptable limits of deviance or to the extent to which they serve as models of "overcoming" deviance in the most extreme of circumstances. Joan reveals the shifting values and norms of the modern heterosexual family, exposing the dysfunctional consequences of an insistence on heterosexuality, while also pointing to the limits of a cultural and rhetorical acceptance of sexual and able-bodied difference. Within this limited able-bodied narrative, Joan, as a representative disabled person, is destined, paradoxically, to remain both a hypothetical model that readers can identify with, and a representative or metaphorical figure that is, in either respect, denied any real existence.

NOTES

1. Adrienne Rich, "Compulsory Heterosexuality and Lesbian Existence," in *Blood, Bread, and Poetry* (New York: Norton, 1986), 23–74, 88.
2. Robert McRuer, Robert. "Compulsory Able-Bodiedness and Queer/Disabled Existence," in *Disability Studies: Enabling the Humanities* (New York: Modern Language Association of America, 2002), 89.
3. Ibid., 89. McRuer's larger project here is to argue for the inception of a new academic area: Queer/Disability studies. Queer/Disability studies would resist the norm, offering a new perspective that would challenge a heterosexual, able-bodied culture and its elusive "ideals" by refusing to limit "the kinds of bodies and abilities that are acceptable or that would bring about change" (97).
4. Ibid., 92. The "disciplines of normality" is a term originally used by Susan Wendell in *The Rejected Body: Feminist Philosophical Reflections on Disability* (New York: Routledge, 1996).
5. McRuer, 97.
6. Ibid., 93.
7. David Mitchell and Sharon Snyder, *Narrative Prosthesis: Disability and the Dependencies of Discourse* (Ann Arbor: University of Michigan Press, 2000), 16.
8. Ibid., 51.
9. Ibid., 51.
10. Brett Josef Grubisic, "Review of *Mister Sandman*," *The Reader* (Winter 1995), http://www.collectionscanada.gc.ca/eppp-archive/100/202/300/newreader/newreader.b03/Readers/Archive/1995Winter/gowdy.html http://collection.nlcbnc.ca/100/202/300/newreader/newreader.b03/Readers/Archive/1995.
11. Rich, "Compulsory Heterosexuality," 67.
12. Barbara Gowdy, *Mister Sandman* (Toronto: Harper Perennial Canada, 1995), 260.
13. Ibid., 63–64.
14. Ibid., 195.
15. Ibid., 107.
16. Ibid., 188.
17. R.D. Laing, *The Politics of Experience and the Bird of Paradise* (Harmondsworth: Penguin, 1967), 95.
18. Gowdy, *Mister Sandman*, 192.
19. Ibid., 188.
20. Ibid., 143.
21. Ibid., 164.
22. Ibid., 165.
23. Ibid., 224.
24. Ibid., 58–59.

25 Ibid., 225. The implication that Sonja finds a mechanical and disconnected sexual pleasure in her relationship with "things" hints at the way modern relationships are increasingly determined by their connection to a consumer culture, where everything has a measurable value, and to lifeless objects in general.
26 Gowdy, *Mister Sandman*, 119.
27 Ibid., 82–83.
28 Ibid., 70.
29 Ibid., 70–71.
30 Ibid., 85.
31 Ibid., 121.
32 Ibid. 70–71.
33 Ibid., 70–71.
34 Ibid., 70–71.
35 Ibid., 72.
36 Ibid., 72.
37 Ibid., 72.
38 Michel Foucault, *A History of Sexuality: Volume One* (New York: Vintage, 1990). 149. In *A History of Sexuality: Volume One* (New York: Vintage, 1990), Michel Foucault argues that "beginning in the second half of the nineteenth century, the thematics of blood was sometimes called on to lend its entire historical weight toward revitalizing the type of political power that was exercised through the devices of sexuality." This "eugenic ordering of society" (149), which leads unavoidably to genocide, is, for Foucault, the "dream of modern powers" (137). If originally, "one had the right to kill those who represented a kind of biological danger to others," then one might say that in modern times "the ancient right to *take* life or *let* live was replaced by a power to *foster* life or *disallow* it to the point of death" (138).
39 Ibid., 38. In conflating dangerous homosexual masculinities with deviant disabilities, Gowdy points to the fear, fantasy, or perhaps even wish fulfillment made real in the Nazis' eugenics plans of the 1930s and in Canada's sterilization programs—both of which were attempts to eliminate people who threatened the "normal" social order.
40 Michel Foucault, *Abnormal* (New York: Picador, 1999), 57.
41 Ibid., 57.
42 Ibid., 300.
43 Ibid., 57.
44 Gowdy, *Mister Sandman*, 118.
45 Ibid., 119.
46 Bookreporter.com, http://www.bookreporter.com/authors/au-gowdy-barbara.asp.
47 Gowdy, *Mister Sandman*, 22.
48 Ibid., 119.
49 Ibid., 56.
50 Ibid., 219.
51 Ibid., 67.
52 Ibid., 67.
53 Ibid., 95.
54 Ibid., 102
55 Ibid., 69.
56 Ibid., 69.
57 Ibid., 242
58 Ibid., 56–57.

59 Ibid., 117.
60 Foucault, *A History of Sexuality*, 59–60.
61 Gowdy, *Mister Sandman*, 57.
62 Ibid., 250.
63 Ibid., 117.
64 Mitchell and Snyder, *Narrative Prosthesis*, 47.
65 Ibid., 49.
66 Foucault, *A History of Sexuality*, 60.
67 Gowdy, *Mister Sandman*, 57.
68 Ibid., 30–31.
69 Ibid., 30.
70 Rich, "Compulsory Heterosexuality," 72.
71 Sigmund Freud, "The Uncanny," in *On Creativity and the Unconscious* (New York: Harper, 1958), 122–61 at 122.
72 Gowdy, *Mister Sandman*, 185.
73 Freud, "The Uncanny," 123–24.
74 Ibid., 137.
75 Gowdy, *Mister Sandman*, 188.
76 Ibid., 138.
77 Ibid., 163.
78 Ibid., 35–36.
79 Ibid., 35–36.
80 Ibid., 84.
81 Ibid., 92.
82 Ibid., 90.
83 Ibid., 30.
84 Ibid., 260.
85 Ibid., 181.
86 Ibid., 1.
87 McRuer, "Compulsory Able-Bodiedness," 93.
88 Gowdy, *Mister Sandman*, 93.
89 Ibid., 52.
90 Ibid., 90.
91 Ibid., 94.
92 Ibid., 127.
93 Ibid., 251.
94 Ibid., 252–55.
95 Ibid., 263.
96 Ibid., 265.
97 Ibid., 261.
98 Ibid., 260.
99 Ibid., 255.
100 Ibid., 264.
101 Ibid., 266.
102 Ibid., 265.
103 Ibid., 266.

V: ABJECT MASCULINITIES

CHAPTER 13

What Do Heterosexual Men Want? Or, "The (Wandering) Queer Eye on the (Straight) Guy"

THOMAS WAUGH

> *I've always been curious about heterosexuality, the fact that heterosexuals exist seems to me improbable. But you just have to throw a rock and you're likely to hit one. They're everywhere. I've tried asking them about their roots, the genesis of their heterosexuality, but they're unable to understand the question. It seems that they think of heterosexuality, a term incidentally they rarely have any reason to use, as the degree zero of sexual identity, so normal it is completely without qualities or attributes. Recently though I found this magazine, it's from 1977, it's called* The Rendezvous, the Midwest Voice of Swinging, *and I think it sheds some light on the phenomenon of sexuality. I've been using it as a guidebook to the spectrum of heterosexual behaviour. Like many strange and foreign things it is simultaneously alluring and repulsive—mostly though it's repulsive. I'm fairly appalled that the continuation of the species seems predicated on certain types of heterosexual behaviour. But I look forward to a more biotechnologically advanced future, when this will no longer necessarily be the case.*
> —STEVE REINKE, *UNDERSTANDING HETEROSEXUALITY* (1994)

INTRODUCTION

In the winter of 2004 I spent seven weeks in India, unfortunately during the never-ending cricket tournament between that country and their nuclear rival Pakistan. With roughly two billion eyes glued to the urgent television spectacle of strained and sweaty men hurling, batting, and desperately chasing a hard round object, it was hard to get service in a restaurant, or even have a conversation with a male person. I came back to Canada just in time to experience 60 million eyes here glued to the spectacle of strained and sweaty men swiping and desperately skating after another hard round object, a puck this time, and furthermore doing what they don't in cricket—blocking and hitting each other with sticks and fists, and plotting to kill each other. Meanwhile, the big-screen box office smashes of the season were *Lord of the Rings: The Return of the King* (Peter Jackson, 2003), *Passion of the Christ* (Mel Gibson, 2004), and *Troy* (Wolfgang Petersen, 2004), spectacles about strained, sweaty, and bloody men fighting and flogging each other over round objects. (Admittedly only one of these epics revolves around a ring, but there is a crown of thorns in one of the others, and an apple of discord offstage in the other.) It's not completely clear from all of these films what stakes the sweaty bloody men are really fighting over—whether property, land, women, status, the redemption of transgression, or the shame of defiled bodies and murdered "cousins." Not that it really matters—they're just doing these things because they're men. Meanwhile the small screen had been full of the spectacle of real wars rather than fictional ones, men fighting, killing, and torturing each other. The domestic news was highlighting an election, yet again, full of men arguing with each other about tax cuts, health care, and women's reproductive rights (as well as scandals, now forgotten, about men sending each other to jail for sexual abuse of girls in British Columbia or avoiding sending each other to jail for sexual abuse of boys in New Brunswick). We saw a flurry of full-page election ads from the Defence of the Family foundation, mostly of one white dad holding one white boy child and cheerfully accompanied by one white mom. All in all, that year that saw the triumph of same-sex marriage turned out to be a very big year for heterosexuality, for heterosexual men in particular.

As a queer outsider to this phenomenon, I'm so mystified by all these competing spectacles that, like Toronto video artist Steve Reinke before me, I initially wanted to investigate heterosexuality, heterosexual men in particular, and share with you the question of what heterosexual men really want. I don't really believe that heterosexual men really want the eyebrow waxing and other consumerist makeovers that *Queer Eye for the Straight Guy* wanted us to believe that season, so a reflection is in order. Since I am a film scholar and the hook for this essay was an arts conference, exhibition, and festival, I would like to do so through the realm of representation. Reinke's 90-second commentary for his 1994 tape is spoken over a close-up scan of illustrated come-on classifieds inside the sleazy, yellowed found document he mentions, a 1970s swingers' magazine. The artist clearly shares my perplexity at the contradictions of heterosexuality in general and heterosexual men in particular. Reinke has the not uncommon tendency to define a group by stigmatizing representations of its least upright members, and *Swingers News* offers the gamut of unattractively photographed over-forty individuals engaged in so-called "outer limit" sexualities from sex-for-money on down.[1] Like Reinke, I too have found, this time in the realm of cinematic representation rather than archival newsprint, that "heterosexual" is a concept never deployed by any of these folks involved in the phenomenon itself. Reinke is apparently right that heterosexuality is invisible, "without qualities or attributes," "the degree zero of sexual identity."

Stalled at the outset by this invisibility and panicking about the implications of a degree zero object for this presentation, I did a Google on "What do heterosexual men want?" and got exactly one hit—myself. Broadening my search, I tried "What do men want?" and got 3,000 Google results, a more statistically significant collection to be sure, but these were mostly discourses from *Cosmo*-type women's magazine copy about what women wanted men to want, heterosexual by default, usually focused on relationships and sex, and the tag "from women" was usually added on to the question. In contrast, "What do women want?" got 18,400 results, providing answers like sex aids, Brad Pitt, financial independence, and Erica Jong's 1998 book title *What Do Women Want?*—itself an appropriation of the hackneyed old male question that originated in one of the perennial male crises of the postwar period (it even cropped up in a National Film Board film description, *The Masculine Mystique* [1984], but we'll come back to that). In short, women are clearly both subject and object of most of the questioning about either gender and its desires. I decided to narrow my search, as Google wisely suggests. "What do gay men want?" got seven results; "What do lesbians want?" got fifteen results, most connected to the recent *Charley's Angels* films (2000, 2003); "What do heterosexual women want?" got exactly zero hits, with Google's suggestion that I check my spelling. In sum, no one in the cybersphere or anywhere else is asking questions that connect sexual orientation to real-world gendered and sexual subjects, least of all heterosexuals, be they men or women, and this must be very discouraging for all concerned. My frontline colleagues in queer politics, culture, and academia have been complaining for thirty-five years about the invisibility of LGBTQ people and issues, but in fact it's heterosexuality that doesn't leave a trace. A helpful comparison is with Richard Dyer's analysis of whiteness: "the 'invisibility of whiteness as a racial position in white (which is to say dominant) discourse is of a piece with its ubiquity...At the level of racial representation...whites are not of a certain race, they're just the human race."[2] And likewise for heterosexual men.

Reinke and queer outsider artists are not the only ones making eyes at the straight guy and the whole invisible phenomenon in which he is enmeshed. Queer academics and theoreticians have achieved some of their most important insights with regard to heterosexuality rather than queerness itself. According to Jonathan Katz in a book called *The Invention of Heterosexuality*, the eponymous invention as a discursive formulation happened around the turn of the century, a couple of decades after homosexuality as a concept came into play.³ On another wavelength, according to Judith Butler,

> the "reality" of heterosexual identities is performatively constituted through an imitation that sets itself up as the origin and the ground of all imitations. In other words, heterosexuality is always in the process of imitating and approximating its own phantasmatic idealization of itself—and *failing*. Precisely because it is bound to fail, and yet endeavors to succeed, the project of heterosexual identity is propelled into an endless repetition of itself. Indeed, in its efforts to naturalize itself as the original, heterosexuality must be understood as a compulsive and compulsory repetition that can only produce the *effect* of its own originality; in other words, compulsory heterosexual identities, those...phantasms of "man" and "woman," are theatrically produced effects that posture as grounds, origins, the normative measure of the real.⁴

I'm not sure what Butler would do with the sad banality of Reinke's found magazine, but certainly these midwestern Swingers do seem the ultimate instance of compulsive and compulsory repetition of some kind. Stiffly posing for the camera, they are imitating for the most part the centrefold formulas of the decade that themselves are seemingly phantasmatic idealizations of some absent or elusive original.

In another register, another Toronto video artist with a queer eye, Stev'nn Hall, like Reinke a mad genius for found image editing and appropriation, chimes in on this problem. His 1999 tape *Bondage Television* seems inadvertently to be backing up Butler's insight into the repetitiveness and imitativeness of heterosexual male performance. This satiric compilation diabolically strings together snippets of Hollywood male action films from the 1980s and 1990s, glimpses one after another of Gibson, Stallone, Willis, Schwarzenegger, and their ilk, strung up in climactic moments of villainous torture, just on the brink of their respective movies' final cataclysm of hetero-patriarchal vengeance and affirmation. Perhaps a personal SM scrapbook of an obsessive compiler, *Bondage Television* is also an uncanny insight into the indulgent male heterosexual fantasy of hyperbolic submission and impotence that justifies ultimate power. Hall's intuition is that these moments are more essential to these films' appeal than their final perfunctory moments of ambiguous triumph, and one would be justified in concluding, based on this evidence and Gibson's and Stallone's impeccable heterosexual credentials, that what heterosexual men really want is to sweat, strain, and struggle, to indulge in shame, suffering, pain, abjection, and humiliation, and to flaunt their bombastic pectorals and vulnerable effulgent armpits at audiences of millions in an excess of vulnerability, exhibitionism, and surrender. Theatrically pro-

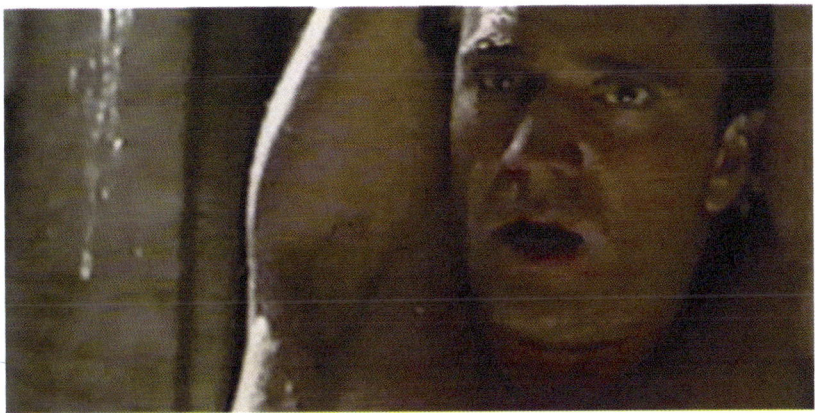

Figure 31 *Bondage Television* (Stev'nn Hall, 1996). The male heterosexual's ultimate fantasy of hyperbolic submission and impotence. VHS frame grab. Courtesy Stev'nn Hall.

duced effects indeed! Hall's snippets are formulaic narrative tropes of course, but I think they speak eloquently about male masochism and the entropy that inextricably binds submission and mastery together in gender performance. The tape speaks also, incidentally, about the failures of Canadian masculinity in living up to dominant American models, at least insofar as Hall's wry branch-plant recycling operation can be seen to stand in for the project of Canadian popular culture as a whole. Gibson's *Passion of the Christ*, bursting forth at the height of the test of American hetero-patricharchal domination somewhat to the east of Jerusalem and endless replaying Stallone and Gibson torture scenes but in Aramaic, simply echoes Hall's insights in its *alluring and repulsive* manner. However, rather than pursuing this analysis of abjection in the male action genre and its fundaments of male masochism (I am indebted to such authors as David Savran and Margaret Robinson for having already laid excellent groundwork in this respect),[5] I would like to take a slightly different route in this chapter and briefly consider a more self-reflexive field of discourse, cinematic as well as scholarly, on abject masculinity somewhat closer to home.

THE MASCULINITY INDUSTRY

> I don't consider fighting indecent.
> I've seen greater indecency in the violence of silence, the silence
>   that engenders sadness, the sadness that engenders anger.
> Do we have the right to our own anger?
> What do we do with it?

> I know my anger well, I use it often.
> Everything I've done, I've done with a lot of anger, but is there a clearly defined line between healthy anger and destructive anger?
> Love hate love hate
> Can we live with one and get rid of the other?
> —Dan Bigras, *Le ring intérieur / The Ring Within* (2002)

Queer video and macho potboilers are of course not the only reflections on hetero-masculinity. Over the past twenty-five years there have emerged from within the belly of the beast itself, (1) a substantive interdisciplinary scholarly corpus called men's studies, a subdiscipline set up as a outgrowth and answer to the older, bigger, and wiser women's studies; (2) a political movement whose rhetoric is primarily backlash or socially conservative resentment, whose membership seems to include a disproportionate number of divorced men burdened with alimony payments and/or who have lost custody, and whose theoretical component includes dubiously grounded denunciations of misandry in the educational setting and the society at large,[6] and whose parallel socio-cultural vector is usually associated with Robert Bly and *Iron John* and his white middle-class whiners who first turned up in the 1980s; and finally (3) a robust cinematic current embracing both pop and parallel sectors, which I shall come back to.

I have always distanced myself from this masculinity industry within academia, partly because I am naturally a little suspicious of its political agenda and find its customary exclusion of queer perspectives very symptomatic of deeper complicity and phobic avoidance. Bryce Traister has wryly and incisively critiqued this field, which he calls "Academic Viagra":

> To some degree, cultural "masculinity studies" has become a code term for "heterosexual masculinity studies"...One of the effects of this recent interest in heteromasculinity...has been a restoration of the representations of men—produced by men and analyzed for the most part by men—to the center of academic cultural criticism...Heteromasculinity studies is the academic answer to the regressive politics of "menz ideology" now proliferating in mainstream periodicals, radio and television.[7]

The discipline has had the effect, in Traister's view, of reviving and justifying the erectile tissue of old-style canonical cultural studies, which were always, after all, about masculinity anyway.

Aside from ideology, I also find the insights of masculinity studies slightly droopy in comparison to the robustness of women's studies and queer studies over the same time period. Some of the queer entries into the field with regard to cinema have been firm indeed: I am thinking of Richard Dyer, Steve Cohan, and Robert Lang, among others.[8] Female masculinists have participated broadly in the discipline, but sometimes don't have a much better record than their hetero-masculine colleagues in terms of queer inclusivity. Take Susan Bordo in her 1999 book *The Male Body: A New Look at Men in Public and in Private:* consider how oblivious she is to the already existing seminal work on the male body within the framework of gay/queer studies, such as Dyer's brilliant analysis of the male pinup, which predates her book by fourteen years (Bordo 1999; Dyer [1985]1993). Why should she have had to reinvent it? Or take Judith Gardiner's 2002 anthology *Masculinity Studies and Feminist Theory,* which offers fourteen authors plus herself and a self-congratulatory introduction by hetero-masculinity studies pioneer Michael Kimmel but not a single gay male voice (Gardiner 2002). The silencing and marginalization of queer voices and insights within masculinity studies has at the same time begun to be alleviated, and many other anthologies that have surfaced in recent years have one or two queer chapters, sometimes tokenistic and sometimes integral elements of the overall thrust, but never approaching the tilting point to be sure. At least film scholar Peter Lehman's twenty contributors in his exemplary *Masculinity: Bodies, Movies, Culture* includes one lesbian and five gay male scholars.[9]

Nevertheless, my personal distancing from the academic masculinity field is probably one I can no longer afford. The polite tolerance of queer studies within academe, as long as it remains safely marginalized in non-funded interdisciplinary programs as at my own university, is in some ways not much better than the silencing of yore. Queer studies in the university would clearly benefit from more allies, and protein supplements from a masculinity studies network, re-energized and no longer mired in hetero-masculinism, would not do any harm.

The *cinematic* vector of the masculinity industry is of more immediate concern to me in this meandering set of queer specular speculations on the straight guy. The pop culture wing extends from *Falling Down* (Joel Schumacher, 1993) and *Fight Club* (David Fincher, 1999) to their Canadian analogues *Men with Brooms* (Paul Gross, 2002), the Cronenberg oeuvre, and a score of commercial features in Quebec, of which the garage league hockey epic *Les Boys* I, II, and III (Louis Saia, 1997, 1998, 2001) may be the most interesting, as I have discussed elsewhere.[10] Of more concern here and now is the parallel sector of documentaries and art films that have been especially dynamic within Canadian cinemas since the early 1980s. Not surprisingly, festival movies such as *I Love a Man in Uniform* (David Wellington, 1993) and *Un zoo la nuit* (Jean-Claude Lauzon, 1987), and experimental films such as those of Bruce Elder, have received excellent attention from film scholars such as Christine Ramsay and Lee Parpart.[11] So it is the countertradition of non-fiction and docu-fiction on hetero-masculinity, continuous and dynamic for more than fifty years, especially in Quebec but also in English Canada, that solicits my lingering attention here. Many of these latter films are from the NFB, and either focus directly on the problematic of gender, or do so obliquely through such rubrics as mental illness, parenthood, or juvenile delinquency, from *Being Different* (Julia Murphy / Gudrun Parker, 1957) across the decades to *Who Is Albert Woo?* (Hunt Hoe, 2000) and *Life with Dad* (Ray Harper, 2002). My assessment of the liveliness of this current is not shared by NFB English-language cataloguers, who have many subject categories pertaining to women and girls but not a single one pertaining to the invisible category of men and boys (a search even for the keyword "masculinity" turns up only a single title, and heterosexuality draws a complete blank, with the suggestion from the NFB website to check the spelling). Nevertheless, the category does exist, and when I say continuous, I mean that this large corpus in both English and French has emerged over the generations in spurts and cycles inflected as ever by the *zeitgeist*, absorbing the day's iconography, whether the youth revolt of the 1960s or the diversity politics of the 1990s.

One perverse English cycle from the NFB in the 1980s cannot be seen in any other way except as backlash to Studio D, that uppity embodiment of women's agency and subjectivity in film. I'm thinking of such titles as *The Masculine Mystique* (John N. Smith and Giles Walker, 1984), which the Studio D insiders used to snickeringly call "the masculine mistake" but which the studio brass apparently liked so much they gave a huge budget the following year to the same artistic perpetrators to make the even more execrable *90 Days* (1985). This latter "light" comedy explores the traffic in mail-order Third World brides without any critical edge whatsoever and had the temerity to represent Canada abroad in some of the countries implicated in that same traffic during the dark days of the then recently elected Tory regime— Free Trade indeed! The best film in this cycle, in my opinion, is from a slightly later phase, *Fathers and Sons* (1992), a fine autobiographical essay by heterosexual West Coast writer Colin Browne about his relationship with his military father, packed with insights by both gay and straight men—who usually have in common, after all, their socialization within the heterosexual family. The backlash cycle on the French side at the Board also includes some honest and risk-taking work such as heterosexual Yves Dion's beautiful docudrama *L'homme renversé* (1986). (The French side is aided rather than hindered by the cataloguers this time: a search for the category "*condition masculine*" on the French side of the website comes up with a very fruitful list of 27 titles produced over 40 years. The English studio definitely needs to roll some cataloguer heads: one of a more recent cycle on masculinity, the self-reflective and ironic *Project Grizzly* [1996], is classified solely under "Animals Mammals in the Wild; Animals Research, Evolution and Animal Behaviour." But I digress ...)

With this latter film that uses forest mammal stalking as a pretext for understanding human testosterone in the working-class hinterland, belonging to the genre I call "boys in the bush," we have been drawn back into the sports formula. After all, sports is the most frequent prism through which hetero-masculinity has been examined by poets of hetero-masculinity at the NFB and in many other places. This pattern extends way back as far as *Le Sport et les hommes / Of Sport and Men* (Hubert Aquin, 1959), which has become quasi-canonical because of the participation of Roland Barthes and Aquin in the film. But *Of Sport and Men* is not really about men at all, since in those pre-feminist dark ages of the 1950s, *hommes/men* was used generically, which makes the film all the more symptomatic when seen retroactively since it's exclusively about males. Women are 99-percent absent, represented only by one or two sexist shots where a skirt of a spectator is flared by the wind à la *Seven Year Itch* as racing cars roar past. One might expect other kinds of turbulence in this compilation project about grand prix racing, hockey, bicycle racing, soccer, and bullfighting co-written by a discreet gay man, Barthes, and produced by a discreet gay man, Guy Glover. But the film was directed by a writer, Aquin, whose work is characterized by the compensatory mechanism of homosexual panic (according to Peter Dickinson),[12] so none of the complex dynamics of ambiguity and contradiction that inevitably crop up in hetero-masculine sport mythologies show up in this film, except as complete denial and oblivion. Not only women are missing, but also all appearance of complexity is expunged from this diverse collection of archival footage. (Not to mention even suggestively homoerotic nuances: it does not help that the first three sports are notoriously anti-erotic because of their dependence on a mechanical apparatus and/or protective exo-skeletons that anticipate *Project Grizzly*—in contrast to the sensuous corporeal celebration and epidermal display of the latter two sports, soccer and bullfighting.) Aside from the possible exception of recurring thigh massage tropes and a congratulatory male–male kiss in the Tour de France segment, the montage of this film that is about men and sport produces a discourse that is consistently and repressively about neither "men" nor the full range of maleness at all.

But I don't want to dally on *Of Sport and Men*, rather simply point out that it is an ancestor if not the *ur*-film of the steady stream of self-reflexive hetero-masculinist sports films in the French studios at the NFB. The scope of these films ranges from hunting to hockey and volleyball, but their most symptomatic exercise is devoted to combat sports, on which documentaries surface predictably every five years or so. Two other founding documentaries in this tradition are quite familiar: Gilles Groulx's *Golden Gloves* and *La lutte/Wrestling*, both from 1961. The latter is a collective film that included at least one queer eye for the straight guy, Claude Jutra's, but compared with the sardonicism of *La lutte*, *Golden Gloves*, Groulx's tender, passionate homage to boxers, is much more prophetic of a generic tradition of tragic working-class male-focused populism that is alive and well to this day. Incarnated regularly by boxing in films by artists like Pierre Falardeau and the working-class sensibility he cultivates, *Rocky* à la Québécoise, more sentimental and more complicit, cruder and bloodier than Groulx's, this tradition reached its most recent version in 2002 with singer-filmmaker Dan Bigras's feature-length *Le ring intérieur / The Ring Within*. *Ring* treats "ultimate combat" and confirms the enduring chord that sports narratives strike among both the heterosexual male producing community and the corresponding audience. Though Bigras's film makes certain strides in terms of reflecting Quebec's increasing cultural diversity (most of the fighters are of Haitian descent), and in pushing point-of-view documentary aesthetics toward increased subjectivity and versatility (and budgets), it is ultimately an uncritical hodgepodge mystifying violence and anger through confused codes of race and class. The film is basically the white director's first-person sparring match first with the camera and then with his fighter subject, Charles Ali Nestor, a champion of one of the emerging fusion combat sports. The film lurches wildly among its various levels, part homosocial love story between filmmaker and subject, part social analysis of Nestor's biographical trajectory as juvenile delinquent redeemed through sport, part journalistic presentation of the growing ultimate combat circuit, and part aestheticization—nay *eroticization*—of the male body, movement, and conflict. Bigras's brooding first person voice-over, addressing Nestor, sums it up as cited above, and repulsed/allured me as much as any work in this decades-long trajectory of reactionary masculinist *ressentiment*.

But, contrary to the expectations I may have aroused, I am not going to take off cleverly to develop the image of the ring within as the hetero-masculine anus, something Brian Pronger and Mark Simpson have done extremely well without me.[13] I am not going to excoriate the themes of abjection and masochism in sports narratives, however fruitful this would be as a topic. Instead Nestor's talk of his childhood now redeemed by combat sport, his mention of his former activity as a bully now abjured, has triggered a veering off in another direction, has made me decide I can no longer talk about heterosexual men and their wants, nor about the cinematic masculinity industry per se, without focusing first on boys. But I don't want to talk about the boy bully as redeemed and redemptive male Other, which is what Bigras's film is all about, but about this Other's victim who is so invisible in Bigras's film. Boys are of course everywhere in the movies, as books as divergent as James Kincaid's *Erotic Innocence* and Murray Pomerance's anthology *Where the Boys Are* make clear.[14] But *dissident* boys' sexuality and identities, their place as gendered victim, remains a great unmentionable in cultural analysis (even in a progressive film like *Billy Elliott* (Stephen Daldry, 2000), which despite its breakthrough in tackling dance rather than soccer, delicately avoids the question of the hero's own sexuality, though at least the filmmakers resisted the temptation to construct a reassuring heterosexual socialization for the character and included a queer gender-dissident supporting player). On this tack, which may be at the core of what heterosexual men really want, I continue to be inspired by Eve Sedgwick and her suggestive comments about the "very dynamic relation" between shame and identity, about "the terrifying powerlessness of gender dissonant or otherwise stigmatized childhood,"[15] as a "a permanent, structuring fact of identity."[16]

THE ABUSE INDUSTRY

> *Graham James*: So what's the charge? Hunh? What's the charge? We were lovers? Personal history for 800. What is the expression that best defines the relationship between Graham James and Sheldon Kennedy? The battered wife syndrome? No. The Stockholm syndrome? No. The answer is in fact that we were hot for each other. We all make our own choices, Sheldon. Did you tell them about the good times? Don't forget to tell the cops about the good times [...]
> *Sheldon*: Turn that on. It's OK. I want you to tape that. I want people to know that I'm the guy. Guys don't like talking about his stuff. I want to talk about it. I want to talk about it for all the guys that can't. My name's Sheldon Kennedy, and Graham James, he stole something from me. My innocence and my love of the game. Kids always think that everything is their fault, you know. And I guess I had to learn to forgive myself. If it weren't for my wife Jana... What are we gonna do about these kids, eh? Because kids, they can't always protect themselves, you know. So that's what we have to do. That it's OK to say "Hey Mom ...," I just don't want any kids to have to feel the way I did. [Cut to pre-game locker room].
> The Sheldon Kennedy Story (1999)

Nestor mentions hockey in *Ring* as the setting for his explosion of violence and punishment and as his own formative experience of shame as immigrant/racial/criminalized other. This is handy, for hockey will allow us to make this radical switch in focus from men to boys. Every single film ever made in Canada about hockey—and there are many—anchors the motif of boyhood, the prevailing mythology of hockey as core of male socialization in Canada. But there is a very interesting small corpus within the safe, sentimental, and nostalgic framework of hockey culture that injects another motif, that of child abuse, whether parental violence as in Atom Egoyan's *Gross Misconduct* (1993) or sexual abuse in combination with parental violence, as in *The Sheldon Kennedy Story* (Norma Bailey, 1999). The connection between hockey and abuse is tenuous and ambiguous but also very tenacious—and no doubt it is just a matter of time before the Maple Leaf Gardens abuse scandal reaches the screen. Think of *The Boys of St. Vincent* (John N. Smith, 1998), that epochal epic of the Mount Cashel orphanage abuse scandal, co-scripted by two *Masculine Mystique* survivors Smith and Sam Grana together with Newfoundlander Des Walsh. The end of Part I celebrates the apprehension of the monster abuser in the lower depths of the orphanage, and does so by bringing all the boys out into the winter sunshine for a game of shinny, officiated by none other than the brother who has just caught his demon colleague red-handed, a whistle-blower in two senses. It is as if hockey immediately takes over its redemptive function within the world of traumatized masculinity in formation, just as combat does for Bigras, Nestor, and masculinity.

We'll shortly come back to Sheldon Kennedy, the Boston Bruin from Elkhorn, Manitoba, who came out publicly in 1997 as a sexual abuse victim at the hands of his coach Graham James, who had pleaded guilty to assaulting Kennedy sexually over five years (between the ages 14 and 18) when Kennedy was under his charge in the junior leagues in Swift Current[17] (the guilty plea prevented the facts of the case from being fully aired). But first let me acknowledge that we have just found ourselves in another cultural industry and broad generic territory, not the hetero-masculinity industry or the hockey hall of blame, but one that overlaps to a certain extent with it, and one that has been no less dynamic over the past twenty-five years, at the NFB and elsewhere—the abuse industry. Just when you thought that masculinity films within the NFB or outside it would be a solid thesis topic, here's another one crying out even more to be explored, another hitherto unrecognized genre family with an apparently steady socio-economic base, the abuse film. A preliminary taxonomical survey of the genre in its Canadian manifestation immediately finds a complex and gradated landscape, of which the true-life-story TV-movie male-victim melodramas like *Misconduct, St. Vincent,* and *Sheldon* are only the tip of a large, compartmentalized iceberg. Predictably alongside and somewhat earlier are the parallel group of female-victim melodramas, most from the 1980s, such as *Rien qu'un jeu* (1983), *Loyalties* (1986), and *Where the Spirit Lives* (Bruce Pittman, 1989), as well as a number of shorts including Lorna Boschman's *Family Secrets* (circulated as part of *Five Feminist Minutes*, 1990). There are several more commercial B-movie melodramas where the plot hinges on accusations of abuse that may or may not be true, mostly set in the United States, including an early tax shelter quickie *Improper Channels* (Eric Till, 1981), and one of the later tax shelter sequels *Prom Night IV: Deliver Us from Evil* (Clay Borris, 1992) that milks in its own way the then recent but in fact perennial abuse scandals in the Catholic church.

Without a doubt the documentary sector, mostly situated at the NFB, is more prolific and perhaps more significant. Here again the category search

Figure 32 *Touch* (Jeremy Podeswa, 2001). One of a sprinkling of gay-male-authored vital works told from the point of view of the queer boy object of intergenerational sexual exchange. Production still © Carol Racicot. Reproduced with permission.

is telling: twenty-seven titles respond to the "sexual abuse" category, and the "incest and sexual abuse" category brings up an overlapping list of almost forty titles (depending on how you count). Forty titles in less than 25 years is more than a minor industry: it constitutes a rather persistent cultural groundswell, the "coming out" of a hitherto unmentionable issue. In fact the films embody a full-blown social panic about an issue that, along with pornography and rape, in the late 1970s constituted a triangle of sexual political problems that the women's movement formulated as a major platform. It is interesting that this is the one the NFB responded to most heartily, from Studio D, from the regional studios, and also from outsourcing. The list includes well-known epochal works such as Beverly Shaffer's wrenching exorcism *To a Safer Place* (1987); Bonnie Dickie's *Sandra's Garden* (1990), a pastoral allegory of healing and lesbian community; and Maurice Bulbulian's epic of a scarred native community grappling painfully with its legacy from the residential school culturecide *The Nitinaht Chronicles* (1997), which echoes the already substantive current of works dealing with the First Nations situation. The pyramidal base of everyday works deals largely with female victims, though the experience of male victims is also well represented. Suspiciously, a disproportionate number of these works are not available for purchase online or at the Cine-Robotheque. I admit that my suspicions about such NFB anomalies usually end up running into bureaucratic ineptitude rather than ideological conspiracies. Nevertheless let me wonder about one larger suspicious aspect of this whole industry, namely, that the surge in abuse thematics not only matches the proliferating societal interest in the topic but also parallels the awakening of NFB interest in another social/sexual/political issue—queer communities, families, and identities. Will wonders never cease, an approximately equal number of queer-related documentaries suddenly appeared at the same time as the abuse industry, as if each surge authorized the other. I will come back to this curious convergence of abuse and the NFB's late great gay awakening a little bit later.

Rounding out the abuse industry landscape are a couple of other pockets of vital works, most notably a sprinkling of gay male–authored films from the last five years, told from the point of view of the queer boy object of intergenerational sexual exchange: first-person non-fiction by Atif Siddiqi and Kevin Kelly, and fiction by Jeremy Podeswa.[18] And to this group must be added, because there's no place else to put it, Claude Jutra's first film, *Le dément du lac Jean-Jeunes* (1948), a stunning child abuse melodrama, juvenilia in more than one sense. We shall see in a moment why this group of films, so eclectic that it can't be called a genre, is so important.

But first I promised we'd come back to Sheldon Kennedy. The final movements of Norma Bailey's made-in-Alberta CTV movie melodrama (woman-scripted as well as -directed, by the way) are encapsulated by the two devastating confessional speeches cited at the start of this section, the first offered privately by the finally incriminated abuser to his "victim," and the second publicly by the same abusee, now performatively transfigured by the public avowal of his shame in the penultimate scene of the film. The abuse story is told in present time from the point of view of the adult hockey player whose lingering trauma has created a crisis in his marriage, career, and psychic health. The spectator is shifted back into flashback episodes in the player's life: the post-pubescent boy's first victimization, the eighteen-year-old's final submission before he escapes up into the major leagues, rescued by the Calgary Flames! In the 1990s, the social-issue TV melodrama, the traditional game preserve of liberal pieties in the Just Society, became a privileged vehicle for considering what increasingly was cast as the national trauma of child sexual abuse, and was often anchored, as this film and *St. Vincent* are, in actual lives and events. *Sheldon* seemed on some level like a cheesy, defanged CTV version of *The Boys of St. Vincent*. Nothing is more sacred in Canadian culture than hockey, except perhaps heterosexuality itself, and when the two of them come under threat, safe sentiments and tears will flow. Kennedy had become something of a media sensation not only because of his poignant primetime revelation but also because of his subsequent rocky ride through substance abuse, career implosion, and media hijinks around a child protection foundation he had set up. Another critical success, *Sheldon* garnered both rave reviews from the usually somnolent Canadian network of TV reviewers and Gemini awards for the two male leads, martyr and demon.

The *St. Vincent* and *Sheldon* films offer similar elements of a mythology of sexual abuse that is intrinsic to both the fictional discourses of melodrama and the non-fiction discourses of media "reporting" and socio-cultural sex panics:

(1) *The demonization of the abuser.* So intense was Henry Czerny's portrayal of the abuser friar in *St. Vincent* (as he races down the orphanage stairs to corner cowering Kevin in the dank basement, his black cassock flaps like vampire wings) that at least one American reviewer compared the character to Ralph Fiennes's Nazi in *Schindler's List* (Steven Spielberg, 1993) and Anthony Hopkins's Hannibal Lecter in *Silence of the Lambs* (Jonathan Demme, 1991).[19] As for James, the coach is played as a snarling gargoyle who pops into the frame like Mephistopheles at every turn and who frightens the protagonist both as teenager and as adult, not to mention the adult Sheldon's pretty and pregnant "top model" wife.

(2) *The heterosexualization of the abused.* Queer kids get abused but the mythmakers and gatekeepers never choose those stories for transmission. In fact, excessive energy is devoted in both narratives to the overstated construction of the heterosexuality of the victims. "If it weren't for my wife Jana ..." has several possible connotations ... Written explicitly into his script is Kennedy's obsessive need to declare his heterosexuality, both during the abuse and years later as the accuser, to the abuser himself, to his wife, to the

media. Both *Sheldon* and *St. Vincent* offer climactic dénouements of hyperbolic heterosexual redemption, complete with tearfully smiling cutaways to female spouses supportive in the moment of crisis. Both production teams would no doubt go all the way to deny in their political correctness that sexual abuse has anything to do with sexual orientation, but when it comes to the dramatic crunch, what else is there but "compulsory heterosexual identities," the degree zero phenomenon that suddenly becomes shouted from the rooftops? In *St. Vincent* Part Two, one of the witnesses who accuses the Brothers is exposed under cross-examination for his record of petty drug and male prostitution offences, as well as—the clincher—for having himself as an older teenager perpetrated the cycle of abuse on younger boys in the orphanage. This character is given the trapdoor treatment by the scriptwriters (suicide or drug overdose?), but would have made a much more interesting protagonist than straighter-than-an-arrow Billy Budd—named Kevin here—as Bulbulian found out in his treatment of abuse victims turned abusers in the controversial *Nitinaht*.

(3) *The rendering of coercion as physical violence*. It is a matter of debate what proportion of sexual abuse is based solely on emotional and psychological manipulation, but the films make it clear that brute force is the modus operandi in these cases. The fourteen-year-old Sheldon is raped at gunpoint by his coach, and the physical abuse delivered by Brother Lavin in *St. Vincent*, by belt or by literally throwing Kevin across the room, is graphically depicted. This absolves the filmmaker of the need to sketch in the nuances of the emotional power an abuser has over his "victim," and just as significantly responds to real-life survivors like Kennedy who obsessively need to justify how a strong eighteen-year-old soon-to-be-professional jock could not or would not physically resist his middle-aged and out-of-shape assailant. Graham James is clearly getting warm when he mentions battered wives and Stockholm, and one wonders why the film drops the puck and skates away.

(4) *The use of flashback to invoke the therapeutic theory of recovered traumatic memory*. The recovered memory theories and therapeutic practices introduced in the 1980s—thereafter seriously challenged, and not only by resentful abusers—were a goldmine for scriptwriters. In both films, scenes of physical intimacy between adult heterosexual survivors and their female spouses are punctuated with flashbacks of the original assault. These are not literal recovered memories, of course (since the victims remember all too well), but they feed into a cultural trope of individual traumatic memory that is its own validation and corroboration. Bailey's editor is deft in linking two caresses of Sheldon's comely chest, the first by his erstwhile coach and the second by his wife, and the visual logic, topped off by the scene in which Sheldon lacerates that same comely chest in his self-blame, overwhelms any other logic.

(5) *The appropriation of "coming out."* The climaxes of both films (taking the two-part *St. Vincent* as a single work) are constructed around the

"coming out" of the abuse survivor, the courageous public declaration/accusation that performatively mobilizes the truth of past submission and present transformation in the moral resolution of the drama, the first before the microphones of the news media (cited above), the second in the forum of the courtroom. Although I have already decried the hysterical heterosexuality of those moments, I cannot escape their power in terms of my personal response. Their effect astonishes me, both the CBC sobriety and the CTV moral smugness and aesthetic cheese, and the tears well even as I fast-forward soundlessly past them to a cue. But I don't know whether it is because the sacramental ritual of queer identity has been appropriated and reapplied to the subculture of abuse survivors, whether some personal psychic dynamic occasions my tears, or whether there is a more fundamental cultural dynamic of modern narrative in play in which the confessional ritual motivates and propels the narrative of both political empowerment and melodramatic absolution (as British queer sociologist Ken Plummer has argued in *Telling Sexual Stories*).[20]

(6) *The evacuation of institutional and historical context*. Within a mainstream culture in which the Catholic Church is perhaps as sacrosanct as hockey (and heterosexuality), is it any wonder that neither *St. Vincent* nor *Sheldon* is able to penetrate the institutional and cultural dynamics of systemic abuse within the two micro-societies? Both directors give evidence of having been hampered from such penetration, but Smith comes closest I think in his devastating critique of the vestmented church hierarchy in its mode of damage control and smug denial. Bailey and her distinguished scriptwriter Suzette Couture dot many i's, to their credit, especially in fleshing out the script's hypothesis of direct continuity between parental physical abuse and hockey's systemic cultures of violence and *in loco parentis* sexual abuse. However, both directors ultimately yield to the overwhelming melodramatic impulse to individualize the phenomenon within the personae of a villain-to-end-all-villains and his saintly prey.

Aside from this commonality, *St. Vincent* is by far the superior film, even given the constraints of the TV social-issue melodrama, based on important distinctions between the two films. Take the matter of the nitty-gritty of sexual exchange, which abuse narratives in fact usually avoid or confuse out of discretion or ideological or psychic avoidance. Both films surprise with their relative frankness, especially when compared with the American TV-movie standard, for example, in the eroticization of the victims. It is not surprising that Kennedy should be set up as beefcake material, especially in the light of the marketing of actor Jonathan Scarfe (a heartthrob *ER* veteran), but it is significant that this is strictly through the eyes of his wife, never through James's eyes. Smith goes much further, and Jeannette Sloniowski has elaborated in detail on something that amazed me upon first viewing *St. Vincent* when it first came out in 1992 for its extreme brazenness, namely the sexualization of the prepubescent victims.[21] The sensual aestheticization of the boys' nude bodies in several shower scenes, in the swimming pool, and even in a nude lineup at the urinals (there is no frontal nudity), is an essential element in the construction of Lavin's subjectivity into the film. Similarly, Smith and his scriptwriters are surprisingly graphic about the exact genital behaviours in play, showing in bold and prolonged close-up Lavin's frantic kissing and caressing of the face and abdomen of the boy and showing, though not so boldly of course, the acts of anal penetration and fellatio that are remembered at the trial in Part Two. Bailey is much less clear, and the spectator is left wondering specifically what behaviours are in play, if any, beyond the depicted caress of hand on chest. This is crucial, for in the latter case, the constructed eroticization avoids responsibility, fails to account for the complexity of coercive sexual contact among males, fails to explore the sexual agency of victims and victimizer alike.

In short, *St. Vincent* is a film that is genuinely disturbing whereas *Sheldon* ultimately compromises with the most superficial of assurances. No doubt this profound difference is due to the fact that the abuser is the central subjectivity within Smith's film, whereas it is that of the "victim" that overwhelms and suffocates Bailey's. I agree with Sloniowski in her astute explanation of the mechanics of this refusal of identificatory comfort and what she calls "simple-minded" "assurances" for the spectator, and in her praise for the film's distinctive path away from the American model (noted also by most flabbergasted American critics).[22]

Since Kennedy had script approval, it is not surprising that "his" film is

1. Not the place to look for nuanced explorations of issues of intergenerational consent and coercion, including the semantic, political, and criminological nuances between pedophilia and ephebophilia.[23] Remember the difference between the 10-year-old and the 14-year-old victim in the two films. Kennedy himself referred to the crime as pedophilia even though he had been a teenager just past the legal age of consent at the time of the first sexual contact.
2. Not the place to look for the contradictions of male sexual response and juvenile and adolescent sexual agency. What might 300 teenage ejaculations over five years mean in terms of the overall framework of abuse?[24]
3. Not the place to look for the erotic complexity of homosocial mentorship, as explored most interestingly by Jane Gallop in a slightly different context.[25]
4. Not the place to look for scrutiny upon the cult of violent masculinity and homophobia within hockey and other sports cultures—a cult that valorizes the silence and stigmatization of both queer and victim.

Figure 33 *The Sheldon Kennedy Story* (Norma Bailey, CTV, 1999). "Abuser" coach James (left) confronts hockey star "victim" Kennedy, whose heterosexuality is affirmed by his pregnant wife, shown in soft focus between coach and player. DVD frame grab. Courtesy Sarrazin Couture Entertainment.

"Guys don't like talking about his stuff," Sheldon announces in my epigraph above, but in fact for all its laudable frankness, the film doesn't like talking about any of this stuff very much either. The *Sheldon* scriptwriter may well attempt to rush in but continually fears to tread: for example, the fag baiting of the protagonist by opposing players on the rink is no sooner depicted than it is defused by the script's encouragement of spectators to cheer Sheldon on when he pounds the fag baiter into a pulp. It likewise takes a risk in cannily but implausibly putting self-reflexive discourses into James's mouth when he confronts his former protegé, in the memorable scene transcribed above, but insights are soon dissolved into a desperate man's deluded self-rationalization: this is his last dialogue in the film.

Ultimately all nuance is lost in Bailey's conclusion, which is predicated on all of the means eschewed by Smith: the "comfortable assurances," the "morally reassuring notes," the sense of "triumph and revenge," and, in short, "closure"—again to use Sloniowski's phrases. Yet even Smith failed to push his work far enough to differentiate it from deeper and equally complicit and panicked mythologizations around child abuse, masculinity, and sexual diversity that abound in the hegemonic culture. By the mid-1980s and 1990s, the cool hip Canadian media fraternity no longer allowed itself the most flagrant of onscreen queer bashing, but along came the perennial bogeyperson the child molester to fill in the function of exorcising the terror of sexual diversity and "outer limit" desire. Along came the abuser as if in unconscious response to queer artists' exploration of the role of coming of age and mentorship in the transmission of queer cultures and their images of the emergent alternative families that would occupy centre stage in the courts and the media in the 2000s. Ultimately, for better or worse, whether at the NFB or on CBC or CTV, whether mediated through liberal hand wringing or tabloid demonization, whether left open by art cinema docudrama ambiguities or tightly sewn up by the resolutions of popular melodrama, Brother Lavin and Graham James are indeed the two queer Hannibal Lecters of Canadian cinema of the 1990s.

MAN ENOUGH

> *Ti-Guy*: Put five bucks on the table and I'll do it. You guys don't have the balls. None of you is man enough to do it. Not you, not you, none of you. [Clearing table to make room for the boys to strap down the neighbour's cat]
>
> *Narrator*: Tonight Ti-Guy Godin will be late for home. His mom will check his fingers, she's worried her son might be smoking on the sly. No Madam Godin. Your son fucks anything that moves. His dick is eaten by bugs. He swallows any pill he can just to forget you. That bath you force him to take before church on Sunday, just serves him to prostitute himself with his hockey coach. But don't worry he doesn't smoke—it makes him choke. [The cat is violated.] Sex I discovered between ignorance and horror. Deep down we all knew money was just a pretext and that he'd do it anyway. The betting just defanged the fear. The poor cat didn't defend itself ... [26]
>
> *Léolo* (Jean-Claude Lauzon, 1992)

I said that the group of queer-authored first-person fictions and non-fictions was crucial, however small it is. The abuse industry has understood that we shall never attain a full understanding of abuse as citizens and as film spectators if we do not listen to the voices and experiences of victims and survivors. But I would like to emphasize that *all* "victims" and survivors must be heard, including those who come to the fore relatively unscathed, as in the three queer first-person works I mentioned earlier. Abused or abuser or neither, the obfuscation of the queer child is one of the most distressing silences in contemporary representation, as Sedgwick has pointed out.[27] I underscore this distress by excerpting above a scene from the late heterosexual director Jean-Claude Lauzon's *Léolo*, which has almost never been discussed by critics and then inattentively and only in passing.[28] Well, there is one critic who has discussed it, Monte Solberg, MP from Medicine Hat, then pillar of the Conservative shadow cabinet and Calgary Flames fan, that well-known film expert so telepathically discerning that he doesn't even need to look at the films he's reviewing. Solberg denounced the prize-winning film on the floor of the Commons after a 1995 late-night CBC broadcast as "that kind of garbage" "shown across the country"..."A scene in which a child engages in an act of bestiality." The scene of course is much more and much less than Monte's description. In the film, we have been following the first-person account of the boy Léolo, who is observing the horrible ritual of abjection from the background, in the context of his socialization in an economically deprived Montreal neighbourhood, discovering sex "between ignorance and horror," and his seemingly relentless slide along with his family into catatonia. The scene, combining as it does the hard-edged poetic voice-over, the panicked mewing of the cat, and the deft chiaroscuro *mise-en-scène* of the circle of pubescent boys enacting their cruel ritual, is another of the repulsive but alluring kind.[29]

Léolo is a pretty sad kid himself, trying to murder his grandfather and ending up institutionalized like his whole working-class family. But one thing can be said for him as he obsessively jerks off watching the pretty older Italian neighbour girl Bianca and pays her for hand jobs—his initiation is cute, idealized, and solidly hetero-normative. No doubt pervert boy Ti-Guy with the infected dick helps deflect the anxiety away from Léolo's own rather perverted initiation. As Toles comments, Léolo "at some deep, knowing level, embraces the deed that an outcast surrogate [Ti-Guy] performs on his behalf."[30] On some literal level of Lauzon's mind, Ti-Guy is probably an abuse victim, and that may be true, though he is probably not a victim of his hockey coach as much as of his bully buddies who manipulate him into this grotesque shaming. But his more important function seems to be to crystallize the filmmaker's own ignorance and horror—about the anus (the film is bursting with images of coercive shitting), and about same-sex incest (Léolo spies on his grandfather in the bath, and sleeps in the same bed, in warm embrace, with his mature but slow and fearful muscle-bound brother Fernand). To me, Ti-Guy, the driven outcast who fucks his hockey coach and anything that moves, and performs this claim to fame for his admiring pals, is by far the most interesting character in this indulgent mess of a film, the queer boy par excellence who is right in claiming that he is more of a man than all his cowardly tormentors. I regret that Lauzon died before being able to make a film called *Ti-Guy* with all the intensity, excess, risk (and tenderness) of his other work.

But in gravitating inexorably to this charismatic queer outlaw child, for whom money is just a pretext, I almost forgot the point-of-view structure of the scene, the straight eye for the queer guy, and may seem to have veered off the topic of the wants of hetero-masculinity for the nth time. But I have not: the narration is read by Léolo's adult mentor after the aspiring child writer's ultimate incapacitation, and is very interesting. How does the

Figure 34 *Léolo* (Jean-Claude Lauzon, 1992): cartoonist Rick Trembles's take on "queer outlaw child" Ti-Guy's "horrible ritual of abjection." Courtesy and © the artist.

"heterosexual" boy Léolo know that Ti-Guy uses money as a pretext only and will fuck anything that moves? What is the meaning of the very meaningful eye contact that Ti-Guy shares with three of his witnesses and with Léolo himself before the act of abjection? I didn't have a conscious theoretical justification for my peripatetic but inexorable slide from the invisibility of heterosexual masculinity through the hetero-masculinity industry through hockey and sports-narrative mythologies on to the abuse industry and its melodramas of remembered traumas to end up with the unique, unwatchable, and unforgettable scene, repulsive and alluring, of this tormented queer kid defying his tormentors, satisfying their heterosexual wants and performatively embracing his humiliation and marginalization—and belonging.

It is not enough to leave you with a glib generalization about the abject shame that is at the heart of masculinity, the shame of male socialization into the world of power, and the desire to perennially re-enact that shame, but that is all I can do. If I conclude that abuse narratives in general, and that particular scene from *Léolo* that was so invisible to film critics but was denounced in Parliament, constitute both an important crystallization of the traumas as well as the powers and desires of heteromasculinity *and* a displacement of the responsibility for those powers and desires, am I beginning to understand this eclectic but commanding and terrifying corpus I have shared with you in this chapter? Coming from a place both outside of and belonging to hetero-masculinity, is it enough for me to point to the commonality and the continuities between so-called queer masculinity and so-called straight masculinity, to point to its border zones, like the ignorance and horror—but also pride and community—shared by hetero-masculine initiate Léolo and queer boy child Ti-Guy, who alone has the balls to do "it"? For this wandering queer eye on the straight guy to finally settle on the complicities and knowledges shared in that dark basement room by all the strung-out boys-becoming-men who know they are not "man enough," their repulsion as well as their allure, their shame as well as their desire, is a conclusion but not an ending.

NOTES

This essay is derived from the keynote address at the June 2004 Making It Like a Man! conference and exhibition in Regina, which was integrated with five video and film works and excerpts. While this published version undertakes to find the typographic equivalent of this audiovisual format, at the same time I have attempted to preserve the personal if not the oral character of the original presentation, as well as its reflection of its context: the particularly fraught political climate of the spring of 2004, which was full of war in the Middle East, along with a mixture of electoral campaign stress (which led to the election of Paul Martin's short-lived Liberal minority government) and Stanley Cup neurosis in both Canada and the United States.

1 I can't think about sex without evoking queer feminist anthropologist Gayle Rubin's "Thinking Sex" (in *The Lesbian and Gay Studies Reader,* ed. Henry Abelove, Michèle Aina Barale, and David M. Halperin [New York and London: Routledge, 1993], 3–44) and its basic concept of "outer limit" sexual practices and identities at the periphery of the hierarchy of the "sexual value system" of our society—everything that is "bad," that is not "heterosexual, marital, monogamous, reproductive, and non-commercial."
2 Richard Dyer, *White* (London and New York: Routledge, 1997), 3.
3 Jonathan Katz, *The Invention of Heterosexuality* (New York: Dutton, 1995).
4 Judith Butler, "Imitation and Gender Insubordination," in Henry Abelove, Michele Aina Barale, and David M. Halperin, eds. *The Lesbian and Gay Studies Reader* (New York and London: Routledge, 1993), 313.
5 David Savran, *Taking It Like a Man: White Masculinity, Masochism, and Contemporary American Culture* (Princeton: Princeton University Press, 1998); Margaret Robinson, "Making and Breaking Manhood: Masochistic Masculinity in *The Passion of the Christ* and *Fight Club*," *Socialist Studies Bulletin* 75 (Winter 2005): 25–28.
6 Such as Katherine Young and Paul Nathanson, *Spreading Misandry: The Teaching of Contempt for Men in Popular Culture* (Montreal and Kingston: McGill–Queen's University Press, 2001).
7 Bryce Traister, "Academic Viagra: The Rise of American Masculinity Studies," *American Quarterly* 52, no. 2 (2000): 274–304 at 275.
8 Richard Dyer, "Male Sexuality in the Media," in *The Matter of Images: Essays on Representations* (London and New York: Routledge, 1993), 111–22; Steve Cohan, *Masked Men: Masculinity and the Movies in the Fifties* (Bloomington: Indiana University Press, 1997); Robert Lang, *Masculine Interests: Homoerotics in Hollywood Films* (New York: Columbia University Press, 2002).

9   Peter Lehman, ed., *Masculinity: Bodies, Movies, Culture* (New York and London: Routledge, 2001).
10 Thomas Waugh, "Boys and the Beast," Chapter 7 in *The Romance of Transgression in Canada: Queering Sexualities, Nations, Cinemas* (Montreal: McGill-Queen's University Press, 2006).
11 Lee Parpart, "The Nation and the Nude: Colonial Masculinity and the Spectacle of the Body in Recent Canadian Cinema(s)," in *Masculinity: Bodies, Movies, Cultures*, ed. Peter Lehman (New York and London: Routledge, 2001), 167–92; Christine Ramsay, "Social Surfaces and Psychic Depths in David Wellington's *I Love a Man in Uniform*," *Canadian Journal of Film Studies* 4, no. 1 (Spring 1995): 3–26.
12 Peter Dickinson, *Here Is Queer: Nationalisms, Sexualities, and the Literatures of Canada* (Toronto: University of Toronto Press, 1999), 101–30.
13 Brian Pronger, *The Arena of Masculinity: Sports, Homosexuality, and the Meaning of Sex* (New York: St. Martin's, 1990); Mark Simpson, *Male Impersonators: Men Performing Masculinity* (New York and London: Routledge, 1994).
14 James Kincaid, *Erotic Innocence: The Culture of Child-Molesting* (Durham: Duke University Press, 1998); Murray Pomerance and Frances Gateward, eds., *Where the Boys Are: Cinemas of Masculinity and Youth* (Detroit: Wayne State University Press, 2005).
15 Eve Kosofsky Sedgwick, "Queer Performativity: Henry James's *Art of the Novel*," *GLQ: A Journal of Lesbian and Gay Studies* 1, no. 1 (1993): 1–16 at 4.
16 Ibid., 13.
17 For a fascinating insider queer memoir of and perspective on hockey culture in Swift Current and the impact of the abuse scandal on that culture and community, see Debra Shogun, "Queering 'Pervert City,'" *Torquere: Journal of the Canadian Lesbian and Gay Studies Association* 4–5 (2002–2003): 110–24.
18 Atif Siddiqi, *Solo* (NFB, 2003, 54 min.); Kevin Kelly, *A Super Natural Premiere* (1967, 6 min.); Jeremy Podeswa, *Touch* (2001, 29).
19 Peter Stack, "Painful Look at Pedophilia: *Boys* Based on True Story of Abuse in Orphanage," *San Francisco Chronicle*, 3 February 1995, C3.
20 Ken Plummer, *Telling Sexual Stories: Power, Change and Social Worlds* (London and New York: Routledge, 1995).
21 Jeannette Sloniowski, "Violations: *The Boys of St. Vincent*," *Canadian Journal of Communications* 21, no. 3 (1996): 1–10.
22 Ibid.
23 A very interesting book that recounts Canadian appeals court reflections on this nuance is Stan Persky and John Dixon, *On Kiddie Porn: Sexual Representation, Free Speech, and the Robin Sharpe Case* (Vancouver: New Star, 2001).
24 The total embargo on discussion around juvenile and adolescent sexual agency, sexual consent, and intergenerational sexuality, upheld for three decades as Steven Angelides has described ("Feminism, Child Sexual Abuse, and the Erasure of Child Sexuality," *GLQ: A Journal of Lesbian and Gay Studies* 10, no. 2 [2004], 141–77), has recently begun to be tentatively lifted in the new millennium, as demonstrated by the publication of Persky and Dixon's *On Kiddie Porn* (unfortunately almost unnoticed) and Judith Levine's more controversial *Harmful to Minors: The Perils of Protecting Children from Sex* (Minneapolis: University of Minnesota Press, 2002). See also Rachel Thomson, "'An Adult Thing'?: Young People's Perspectives on the Heterosexual Age of Consent," *Sexualities* 7, no. 2 (May 2004): 133–149; Jon Davies, "Imagining Intergenerationality: Representation and Rhetoric in the Pedophile Movie," *GLQ: A Journal of Lesbian and Gay Studies* 13, nos. 2–3 (2006), 369–85; and Thomas Waugh and Jason Garrison,

Montreal Main (Vancouver: Arsenal Pulp Press, 2010); as well as a small glut of recent feature films, from *L.I.E.* (Michael Cuesta, 2001) to *La Mala educación* (Pedro Almodóvar, 2004) and the exceptional Canadian *Whole New Thing* (Amnon Buchbinder, 2005). One book that would echo my question about the specificity of gendered physiology in relation to abuse, as well as my premise of the fundamental import of gender in any discussion about abuse, is Richard B. Gartner, *Betrayed as Boys: Psychodynamic Treatment of Sexually Abused Men* (New York: Guilford, 1999), though I experience a layperson's skepticism about many of its findings and implications.

25 Jane Gallop, *Feminist Accused of Sexual Harassment* (Durham: Duke University Press, 1997).

26 I have substituted the character's original French name for the "translation" of "Buddy" that he assumes thanks to the subtitles of the English version.

27 Eve Kosofsky Sedgwick, "How to Bring Your Kids Up Gay: The War on Effeminate Boys," *Tendencies* (Durham: Duke University Press, 1993), 154–66.

28 One of the few relatively substantive discussions of the scene is in George Toles, "Drowning for Love: Jean-Claude Lauzon's *Léolo*," in *Canada's Best Features: Critical Essays on 15 Canadian Films,* ed. Eugene P. Walz (Amsterdam: Rodopi, 2002), 291–92. However, I differ with Toles's reference to Ti-Guy as "unformed and insensible."

29 House of Commons, Debates, 10 October 1995.

30 Toles, "Drowning for Love," 291.

CHAPTER 14

Boy to the Power of Three: Toronto's Drag Kings

BOBBY NOBLE

Let me make a confession at the outset: I love drag kings. I am what you might call an academic fan of drag kings. I saw my first drag king show on June 29, 1995, when the Greater Toronto Drag King Society staged a "Drag King Invasion I," at a Toronto drag bar called El Convento Rico to an audience of about 600 screaming fans. It was quite a ride that night quite beyond just about anything else I had seen before. The performers were equal parts campy, sexy, outrageous, raucous, and utterly tenacious. The crowd was whipped into a kind of queer frenzy, and in a bar designed for drag queen performances, lesbian public cultures were permanently transformed.

This chapter will explore those transformations through three different waves of drag kinging in one major urban centre: Toronto. I borrow the wave metaphor from feminism and find it useful to characterize three different historical moments in the evolution of drag king cultures in Toronto. These are not easily characterized as generations; age ranges may not differ dramatically between groups and some kings travel comfortably between each wave, mentoring young generations of upcoming kings. But what is significant about these waves is the social, historical, and epistemological context that each maps. The first wave—the Greater Toronto Drag King Society—is easily situated *in* but not *of* lesbian performance contexts, such as those mapped by lesbian performance theorists, Jill Dolan, Kate Davy, and Sue-Ellen Case. Even as these drag king performances challenge the work of the lesbian theorists, historically this first wave overlaps with changes each notes

---

Reprinted by permission from *Sons of the Movement: FtMs Risking Incoherence on a Post-Queer Cultural Landscape*. Toronto: Women's Press, 2006, 53–75.

in the development of a body of literature on lesbian performances, such as those of the WOW Café and the performances of Lois Weaver and Peggy Shaw of Split Britches. Drag kings do not fit easily into the work of Dolan, Davy, and Case, but are significant in the sense that they begin to mark the rupturing of lesbian discourse, theory, and identity by what I call the butch-femme renaissance. This first wave of kings in Toronto begins to expand the circles around "lesbian" to map an imbrication with the then emerging queer theory and nation.

The second wave—The Fabulous Toronto Drag Kings—emerge, as waves do, at the end of the first wave. With the emergence of this troupe, drag kings are dis-identified with lesbian cultures even though they perform in lesbian contexts. What begins to emerge instead is an entirely different set of relationships marked by affiliations with both gay masculinity and trans masculinities. Where the first wave engaged in mimicry of masculinity, the second wave begins to complicate that mimicry through an increasing identification with masculinity and dis-identification with exclusively lesbian subject positions. I trace those identifications, dis-identifications, and the ways that a second wave begins to foreground a consciousness of race, especially of whiteness, into performances. Finally, I explore the work of one king in particular, Deb Pearce, and hir alter ego, Man Murray.

Finally, after the dissolution of the Fabulous Toronto Drag Kings, which overlaps with the emergence of a third wave that includes a variety of groups, including Big Daddy Kings and United Kingdom, and then with a fast fourth wave, Bois Will Be Boys and KingSize Kings—what I will develop as "bois to the power of three"—discernible gender identifications and affiliations are all but rendered incoherent. What exist instead are both self-referential (performances that signal the representational practices of the first wave and earlier lesbian cultures) and a plethora of gender identities off known gender maps. These are productively incoherent genders in No Man's Land. Moreover, what makes each wave newish, in addition to the existence of a new group of performers, is also physical performance space as discursive as well as geographical location, particularly bars in a large urban centre like Toronto, where different neighbourhoods with varying demographics lend each wave an entirely different character through its fan base.

One of the things that links these waves together, even through some pretty significant differences, is their proximity to discourses of masculinity and a dependence on this larger problematic for their condition of possibility. While not every performer identifies with masculinity, even the dis-identifications mark a persistent relation to larger, cultural scripts of gender. As Butler told us in 1990:

> The "I" who would oppose its construction is always in some sense drawing from that construction to articulate its opposition; further,

the "I" draws what is called its agency in part through being implicated in the very relations of power that it seeks to oppose. To be implicated in the relations of power, indeed, enabled by the relations of power that "I" opposes is not, as a consequence, to be reducible to their existing forms.[1]

She reminds us that thinking in excess of social construction renders any subject, and masculinity in particular, incommensurate with self-knowledge or unable to know that which makes it it/self. Self-consciousness, in other words, is not in and of itself the remedy as consciousness is conditioned by language and is a product of language at the same time. Curiously, then, it's often what the subject cannot know just yet that conditions what it can know. Two points here: First, these configurations of our sense of self are always ambivalent, that is, configured around what we think we know even as we are aware that there is more to a self than what ego knows about itself. Second, more remains leftover, then, undefined and these are the things which animate the self we do think we know. Drag kings draw out this ambivalence and stage it for both pleasure and parody. The work I want to do with drag kings is located at the meeting point of these ambivalent contradictions and paradoxes, a space I am hailing as yet another No Man's Land. If we cannot deny or disavow masculinity, as Homi Bhabha suggests we cannot, then we can, within the larger ideological and discursive economies of essentialism, racism, and heteronormativity, disturb or trouble its manifest destiny, deny, at the very least, its invisibility. By drawing attention to masculinity as a free-floating signifier, we rearticulate it, again to quote Bhabha, as prosthesis, "prefixing" the rules of gender and sexuality.

AT THE BUTCH-FEMME LESBIAN BAR: DRAG KING INVASIONS

First, I want to situate my reading of the "Drag King Invasion I" as lesbian cultural production at the crossing of "performativity and the loose cluster of theatrical practices, relations and traditions known as performance," and more precisely for my purposes here, "lesbian theatre."[2] The tension between performativity and performance fuels the erotic intensity of the drag king show. In other words, the tension or ambiguity between the so-called "reality" of the performance—its parody of the "hyper-masculine star" at his most contradictory and illusory, "stardom" as a technology of desire, and performativity or the identificatory processes themselves—marked the show that night as an important and pleasurable event.

Second, my reading of the show foregrounds the axiomatic, discursive, and historical slippage between the terms "camp" and "drag." On one axis of my rather oppositional taxonomy rests earlier lesbian feminist "performance" theorists Kate Davy, Jill Dolan, and Sue-Ellen Case, focusing on the woman-run performance spaces Split Britches and the WOW ("Women's One World") Café. To conflate the arguments of these three theorists would be a mistake; however, they not only share similar questions, they anticipate issues foregrounded in theories of performativity, and provide a lens through which I want to read the drag king show. Those are: the problematization of the field of representation itself; an interrogation of reading practices *vis-à-vis* performer-audience dynamics, and, finally, the outing of butch-femme subjectivities as constitutive of a "lesbian aesthetic." As Kathleen Martindale[3] suggested, much of this early work held high hopes for articulating a radical and political aesthetic. "While the utopian appeal of such anti-realist hopes for aesthetic activism is compelling...even the critics most responsible for producing these determinist readings concerning the new lesbian spectatorial communities came to acknowledge that they hadn't paid enough attention to the contradictions within discourses and within spectators."[4] Nonetheless I agree with Martindale's assertion that the demands on lesbian avant-garde writing/performance art for political accountability can be traced back to early feminist theory and practice, so I will set the stage by revisiting that work. I will return to those "contradictions both within discourses and within spectators" a bit later. Kate Davy attempts to discern an essential difference between what she identifies as gay Camp and a lesbian performance aesthetic. In her "Fe/Male Impersonation," Davy disparages what she identifies as the misogyny inherent in Camp, arguing that it not only says "something about women" to the men it is intended for, but it effaces women in the process. Moreover, Davy suggests gay Camp doesn't translate on the "lesbian" stage as Camp is driven by "a fierce masculine-feminine hetero-gendering," which cannot work for a lesbian aesthetic. Finally, Davy begins the outing of butch-femme subjectivities as a solution to the problems posed by male impersonation. Defined in opposition to female-to-male cross-dressing, butch-femme doesn't "hide the lesbian beneath" and as such "dismantles the construction of woman...challenges male sexuality...[and] challenges the heterosexual contract."[5] In other words, butch-femme as the motor of lesbian performance is "lethal."[6]

Jill Dolan is also concerned with the field of representation itself and the reading of lesbian theatre—that is, with the relations between the performer and the reader/spectator. In "'Lesbian' Subjectivity in Realism: Dragging at the Margins of Structure and Ideology," Dolan[7] eschews realism as a strategy of representation, arguing that realism offers "unhappy positionalities for lesbians...the ideological inflections of which are crucial to mark." One of the inflections that Dolan marks is not only the denial of butch-femme generally, but the feminization of the butch herself.

> By the mid-1970s, the sexual lesbian who engaged in butch behavior as a subcultural resistance to the dominant culture's gender and

sexual ideology was silenced by feminism, her transgressive sexual desire "femininized" through the woman-identification that neatly elided active sexuality as a precondition for lesbianism.[8]

In "The Discourse of Feminisms: The Spectator and Representation," Dolan goes on to theorize the position of the individual spectator and spectorial communities in the making of a specifically "lesbian" desire in representation. While Dolan posits a rather unitary and White spectator undifferentiated by class, gender, and race, she attempts to rethink the argument by film theorists Mulvey, de Lauretis, and Doan, which suggests that the series of "looks" built into the structure of film position the male spectator as subject and woman as the passive object of the male subject's active desire. Dolan too deploys butch-femme in a rhetorical move that anticipates Butler's notion of "citationality," arguing that butch-femme "quotes" gender to appropriate the male gaze for the purpose of "looking" and "reading" queerly both in the theatre and in the performance of the everyday as well:

> The drag role requires the performer to quote the accepted conventions of gender behavior. A woman playing a man...is quoting gender ideology, holding it up for critique...When the assumed gender role does not coincide with the performer's biological sex, the fictions of gender are highlighted.[9]

Finally, Sue-Ellen Case herself fully outs the butch-femme couple as the definitive subject positions in not just lesbian theatre, but in feminist theory as well. Paradoxically nodding in two directions at once, both through feminism and against feminism, Case's "Toward a Butch-Femme Aesthetic" attempts to resolve a theoretical impasse in thinking to date (circa 1988) about the lesbian subject. Case is in conversation with Teresa de Lauretis, who argued in "The Technology of Gender" that the female subject is already trapped within the concept of "sexual difference," either a biologically overdetermined "female subject" or evacuated significatory effect. De Lauretis interrogates the limitations of both positions and offers another perspective—again, from the "space-off"—that concept term borrowed from film theory, which identifies the space not visible in the representational frame but inferable from what that frame makes visible. This space is where we find the terms of a new perspective that will allow the "subject of feminism" to move between "the (represented) discursive space of the positions made available by hegemonic discourses and the...elsewhere of those discourses," at once both inside and outside of ideology.[10] In a very clever rhetorical move, it is within the "elsewhere" of de Lauretis's own "subject of feminism" that Case finds her dynamic duo, the butch-femme couple.

> The butch-femme subject could inhabit that discursive position [where] the female body, the male gaze, and the structures of realism function as only sex toys...In recuperating the space of seduction, the butch-femme couple can, through their own agency, move through a field of symbols, like tiptoeing through the two lips (as Irigaray would have us believe), playfully inhabiting the camp space of irony and wit, free from biological determinism, elitist essentialism, and the heterosexist cleavage of sexual difference. Surely, here is a couple the feminist subject might perceive as useful to join.[11]

As Bob Wallace[12] notes, the other axis—"performativity"—as signified in the last decade by "queer theory" generally and Judith Butler in particular, answers that of performance and its attendant identity politics by suggesting that all identity categories are performatives or acts of signifying systems that gain efficacy through stylized repetition. Gender is no longer an immutable and natural "fact" waiting for articulation in discourse, but is a fictional and discursive effect of signifying systems. Moreover, Butler's work problematizes the distinction between "sex" and "gender" as it was read in feminist theory. If the two are no longer suggestive of a biology vs. culture split as feminism argued, then logically, to quote Butler,[13] "man and masculine might just as easily signify a female body as a male one, and feminine a male body as easily as a female one." Thus, while *Gender Trouble* suggests that gendered performances such as butch-femme are not pathological imitations of heterosexuality, but rather are a kind of fictional imitation for which there is no original, Butler's next work, *Bodies That Matter*, through its interrogation of "sex," suggests that it too is fantasy, the effect of the reiterative regulatory sexual regimes.[14] Thus,

> if gender is the social construction of sex, and if there is no access to this "sex" except by means of its construction, then it appears not only that sex is absorbed by gender, but that "sex" becomes something like a fiction, perhaps a fantasy, retroactively installed at a prelinguistic site to which there is no direct access.[15]

While much of the work by the former lesbian performance theorists is very much grounded in its own historical moment—lesbian-feminism with its attendant essentialisms—this body of work attempts to map a kind of "performative," which Butler polished in her later and highly influential works. I suggest that the interrogation of "performance," as very tentatively mapped by Davy, Dolan, and Case, can be reconstituted as the three lenses through which to read the work of this early wave of drag kings: first, butch-femme in its 1990s manifestation as parody of a recognizably lesbian signifying system and heterosexual gender roles; second, the function of an audience or authorizing witness for such performances/performatives; and third, lesbian drag in its proximity to larger technologies of heterosexuality.

An impossibility structures this citation of the performative event at the Toronto bar that night, indeed in any live performance. Peggy Phelan notes that nostalgia, or "the wound of wishing to return," structures any attempt to report, record, or repeat that performative:

> Even at the seemingly simple level of the linguistic sign it is impossible for writers to convey the complete context in which a[n]...act occurs. To report it back, to record and repeat it, is at once to transform it and to fuel the desire for its mimetic return...Much of the writing [about performatives] is a record of a living relation between the writer and the artists she sees. This seeing is, necessarily, a distortion, a dream, a hallucination; writing rights it back toward reason by creating enabling fictions...The effort to "cite" the performance that interests us even as it disappears is much like the effort to find the word to say what we mean. It cannot be done.[16]

That night I remembered a range of mostly White masculinities staged in performance: Andy Gibb; John Denver and Placido Domingo; The Village People; Billy the Kid or other Nashville or Hollywood cowboys; Freddie Mercury; Guns N' Roses' Axl Rose and guitar player Slash; and Anne Murray herself. What underwrites these performances of masculine "stardom" as well as the conventional live music show is how each "star" signifies beyond just a "genre" of music. Each constructs gendered subject positions, types of physicality, identities, fashions, in other words, *star texts*, intertextual constructs produced across a range of often contradictory media and cultural practices.[17] In other words, each of these signifiers signals entirely different identitarian as well as musical discourses: disco (Gibb and The Village People); country ("Trouble"); folk (Denver); rock (Freddie and Axl); and whatever descriptor we might use to characterize the star text loosely organized around "Anne Murray."

What intrigued me about these performances was the obviously contradictory and at times hysterical visualization of the tensions of masculinity as a heteronormative discourse. Contrary to Davy's assertion[18] that male impersonation does not "say anything about men" other than their erasure of women, I suggest that male impersonation speaks volumes about masculinity. But I do think Davy is right that we need to learn to read lesbian drag differently, and I offer the following very tentative speculations about that reading paradigm. The drag kings' performance suggested to me that lesbian drag, as opposed to Camp, might depend not so much upon excess or an excessive send-off of heterosexual masculinity, but upon equivalency instead. To put this into other terms, if we define mimicry as "the parodic hyperbolization of a gender identity," and masquerade as "the nonironic or unconscious assumption of that identity," then it seems this dyke drag show did not spin around mimicry's distance from masquerade but rather upon its approximation to it instead. The drag kings' mimetic act takes masquerade, or the unconscious assumption of identity, as its object.[19] In other words, in targeting masculinity as a supposedly "natural" identity, the show simultaneously signaled both process and product, unveiling performance technologies, with "technology" both as a discourse naturalizing identity categories as well as the illusion-producing apparatus of the theatre/stage itself, and the performative or the fictive identities produced. While gay Camp foregrounds the performativity and excess of traditional femininity through its over-the-top parody, masculinity remains unmarked and underspoken. The drag kings foreground that cloaked status, and parody masculinity's own unspoken artifice, even though, as Butler[20] rather paradoxically suggests, "[a woman performing masculinity] is perform[ing] a little less, given that femininity is often cast as the spectacular gender." Moreover, it seems that Davy was both right and wrong—right in that male impersonation puts a different spin on its object than gay Camp, but wrong in that lesbian performance, at least in this particular manifestation in this moment, is as implicated in a "masculine-feminine heterogendering" as gay Camp.

Moreover, part of what this male impersonation speaks about masculinity is its contradictions and inevitable and thus repetitive failures. As Butler[21] suggests, "to the extent that gender is an assignment, it is an assignment which is never quite carried out according to expectation," where the addressee never quite inhabits the ideal s/he is compelled to approximate. In their parody of heteronormative masculinity as "failure," the drag kings flesh out Butler's assertion. For instance, the drag kings seem quite fond of hijacking musical acts that rely on either duets (Donny and Marie Osmond, John Denver and Placido Domingo) or groups (The Village People). The duet as a music convention is a form just asking for "trouble." And troubled it was. One of the most raucous points of the show that night occurred during the Domingo/Denver duet when, at the big climactic end of the song, John and Placido could no long hold back, and commenced kissing onstage. Similarly, as Axl Rose and his guitar player Slash finish flailing around on stage, Slash falls to his knees and gives Axl a rather enthusiastic blow job. While seeming to be great fun for most folks in the audience, including the gay male waiters and bar staff working that night, these particular performances foregrounded and parodied masculinity's hysterical fear of "feminization" *vis-à-vis* sexual desire between men.

Furthermore, the drag kings' impersonation of masculinity and parody of sexual desire between men relies on but also shifts away from what Case identified as the butch-femme couple and toward what I have identified earlier as a continuum of female masculinity. Evoking those axiomatic epistemological tensions outlined by Sedgwick in *Epistemology of the Closet*, that same-sex desire is understood either as an expression of the essence of one gender (gender-separatism) or as cross-gendering (gender transitivity), what overdetermines the male impersonation at the heart of the drag kings' show is a shift from the separatist to transitive trope, complete with its shifts in alliances and cross-identification. To quote Sedgwick,[22] "under a gender-separatist [trope], lesbians have looked for identifications and alliances among women in general [while under]...a [trope] of gender [transitivity]...lesbians have analogously looked to identify with gay men, or, though this latter identification has not been strong since second-wave feminism, with straight men." Clearly, the drag kings' performance could be grouped under gender transitivity and the proliferation of butch-femme subjectivities as anticipated by Case. (We will see later in the second and third waves that it is precisely this dynamic that these latter waves tease out; that is, there is a decided move away from lesbian affiliations toward ones with masculinity instead.) But fuelled by its referent "butch-femme of the 1950s," or Case's butch-femme couple, butch-femme of the 1990s will, as I will argue a bit later, in many ways far surpasses its own history, demonstrated by the proliferation of female masculinity in all its complexities: FtM trans-sexuality, butch-bottoms, soft butches, butchy-femmes, stone butch, fag butch, etc. Subsequently, the masculinities performed on the stage signify in very contradictory but remarkably rich ways, simultaneously as "butch," and in excess of "butch," an approximation of heterosexual masculinity, and an outing, queering, and poaching of that masculinity as well.

Elspeth Probyn[23] reminds us, in her essay "Lesbians in Space," to think about the question of human geography or, more precisely, the fact that bodies exist in relation to other bodies within socio-spatial sites as well. And the space of the performance that night was a queer bar, not a theatre. If I were to limit my definition of "stage" to what it was that we all supposedly looked at, then it would be difficult to go much further than discussing the kings on stage. But I want to suggest that we read the "stage" as the front door of the bar instead. The drag kings' performances do not take place in isolation; the audience, especially but not exclusively its femme audience, is as much a part of the performance as those in the spotlight. In fact, I would suggest that audience, or femme desire, is the central condition of the performance.[24] The audience, or at least the many panties that land on the stage, are props in the performance as much as the performers are in the show staged by the audience. But this contingent authorizing and contingent community is not made up of Dolan's undifferentiated, unitary subject. Nor is it Mulvey's passive female subject, the object of a masculine gaze. Rather, this was an audience made up of as many desiring and identifying boys and girls, actively reading against the grain of hegemonic gender and desire, desiring and authorizing not just the complex performances "on stage," but reading and read by the many other performances "off-stage" as well. Thus, what is staged and negotiated is not "lesbian identity" as ontology, but the beginnings of a very queer and eventually post-queer desire as it's constructed through the multiple identificatory and dis-identificatory positions opened up through and across the performances in that bar as a queer space. Identifications within and across the show as performative event constitute its seductiveness, not ontologies.[25]

If Butler is correct, as Lynda Hart suggests, that the power of lesbian subjectivity may be not in appearance but in disappearance, in "letting that which cannot fully appear...persist in its disruptive promise," then the drag king show that night was doubly potent.[26,27] The remarkable irony of the event was that, unlike the performances of Split Britches and WOW Café, this show did not have one single "Lesbian" on stage, short of Anne Murray, of course. Needless to say, there were lesbians performing both in, to, and around the bar. Indeed, "lesbian" was the defining condition of the show. But I suggest that this was a very different performance of "lesbians in space" than the realist, "positive-images" school of lesbian representational politics. That apparitional creature, the Lesbian, lurked continually in de Lauretis's "space-off" just outside of view, and no matter how hard one worked to catch a glimpse of her, she remained productively absent. The drag kings engage gender as "an inevitable fabrication," working gender against both identity and heteronormativity, staging, not "representing," lesbian desire.

I have been suggesting that a reading of the Toronto drag king show through the enhanced lens offered by performance theorists Davy, Dolan, and Case, as well as Butler's complex and rigorous theories of performativity, can layer the drag kings' queer performances of masculinity. What seems to be at stake in both bodies of work is, as Butler[28] notes, an "increasing politicization of theatricality." What Davy, Dolan, and Case remind us is that such an increasing politicization has an important set of both performance and epistemological histories.

LONG LIVE THE QUEER KINGS: THE FABULOUS TORONTO DRAG KINGS

Where the "Drag King Invasion I" suggested that heterosexual masculinity doesn't quite hold together, the Fabulous Toronto Drag Kings demonstrate that White masculinity doesn't always cohere together either. The Fabulous kings, later known as The Toronto Drag Kings, held court in Toronto for the last half of the 1990s. Produced by Clare Smyth ("Flare"), also a drag king performer, both the Fabulous and Toronto Drag Kings became a standard feature in the Toronto queer, lesbian, and performance scenes for over seven years. This wave, made up of a fairly consistent group of performers—Flare, Zach, Stu, Deb Pearce ("Dirk Diggler" and "Man Murray"), Jesse James

Bondage, Christopher Noelle, Chris, Moner, and Mitch[29]—introduced Toronto to some of the most innovative and long-lasting king performances around. This was also the first group to represent Toronto in the International Drag King Extravaganza, in Columbus, Ohio, October 1999, and many of these same kings—Dirk, Christopher Noelle, and Flare—have developed a kind of notoriety that has bumped them to a national level. For instance, Flare and Christopher Noelle appeared on *Queer as Folk*; Jesse James Bondage, Flare, and Dirk all appeared on the *Maury Povich Show*; and Christopher Noelle appeared in the Toronto Unity 2000 show with rock star Cyndi Lauper.

What this next wave of drag kings articulate in their performances is as vast and unique as the kings themselves. Themes include ironic spins on famous duets or groups; interesting or hyper-masculine characters from popular culture; famous musicians or artists; some, like the performances of Jesse James Bondage, perform songs that have had meaning at various points in time (especially popular are songs from a king's high school years). Other kings, like Mitch, imitate famous artists known for their genre-specific style or dance moves. As I discuss below in more detail, some kings emulated their favourite bands while others again, like Man Murray, impersonate famous Canadian icons rumoured to have queer histories (Anne Murray). While this group presented literally hundreds of performance scenarios, there are a few consistent tropes that I want to draw out here.

First, a stock favourite of a number of these kings are the places where masculinity, especially White masculinity, speaks volumes about itself in very ironic ways. That is, of course, through race and the operations of White supremacy. As I have suggested in *Sons of the Movement,* if one of the key elements of whiteness is that it disavows itself as a racialized identity, standing instead as the human race, as universal mankind, then a consciousness of race and the processes of racialization start becoming one of standard features of the second wave of kings. Two of the White kings in this troupe target precisely that paradoxical hyper-visibility and yet invisibility of whiteness: Zach does an impressive angry young White boy in his salute to Rage against the Machine. What makes this particularly effective is that Zach wears an "Anti-racism Action" t-shirt that shows a young White boy jumping up and down on top of a swastika. The effect is to mark whiteness from inside and articulate it against the invisibility of White supremacy. Moner too stages whiteness as a subjectivity simultaneously hyper-visible and invisible. Moner performs a song called "Pretty Fly (for a White Guy)." The lyrics of this song document the ways that White masculinity imagines itself in relation to men of colour, who are read as "hip" and "cool." "Our subject," so the lyrics tell us, "is not cool but fakes it." He dresses up, overcompensates to fit the part and to disguise the emptiness of whiteness: he listens to the "right" music (Vanilla Ice), cruises in a cool car (a Pinto), and tries "too hard" to imitate his fantasy of Black masculinity. The song inverts a White racist gaze back at itself, and shows whiteness to be both vacuous and hyperbolic. Moner's version of this song forces attention onto the artificiality of the White subject in the song and denaturalizes and makes that artifice even more ironic. As Moner said to me in conversation, "It's important to work the White boy persona—that's what I am." Whiteness is marked and articulated—that is, made to work by revealing itself. If you think about the verb to articulate, it means to divide into words, to pronounce or utter. But it also means to connect or mark with joints—that is, to be connected with sections. Thus, to articulate is to express fluently and to manipulate a site where component parts join (as in a knee or hip), to bring segmented parts together to enable functionality. These kings dissemble White masculinity, break it into parts, and then reassemble those parts to make them work differently, to render them dysfunctional. If White supremacy works best when it's hyper-visible and invisible, it cannot work in quite the same way when it is denaturalized, rearticulated, and, most importantly, de-cloaked.

In the same way that whiteness manifests itself and speaks through normative masculinity, gender is also spoken loudly through a queering of heteronormative male sexuality. A number of the kings stage the sexual failures at the heart of straight masculinity. For instance, during a number where Kelly, Flare, and Zach dress down to look like stereotypical ill-kempt, working-class men with huge beer bellies and perform "I Am Too Sexy," the men at one point drop their pants to show their butts to the audience. Two of the three are wearing men's underwear, which is what you might expect. But Flare's character is wearing girl's panties and subsequently gets chased off the stage for it. Chris and Stu do a similar routine, only their characters are hyper-masculine soccer players; one player (Stu) has a crush on the other (Chris) who at first refuses him, but then who returns his advances and finally carries him off the stage. The song is the "Cup of Life" by Mr. Contradiction himself, Ricky Martin. Ricky represents an entirely curious figure of masculinity. He's racially marked, but sings in English; s/he's hypersexualized as a man of colour, but that oversexualization is always already overdetermined as simultaneously in excess of heteronormative masculinity. What's parodied in these numbers is the sometimes very thin line between gay and heterosexual masculinity, where queer and ironic reading practices articulate the contradictions that masculinity often disavows and yet is unable to contain. The first wave of drag kings in Toronto similarly played with these tensions. Not to be outdone by the "original" Village People and their own parody of gay masculinity, the Fabulous Toronto Drag Kings' Village People parodies a parody in a performance that simultaneously signifies masculinity, hyper-masculinity, failed heteronormative masculinity, and White notions of queer diversity all at the same time. This wave of drag kings staged queer community when Flare, dressed in a sailor suit, performed Kermit the Frog's

"Rainbow Song" while the rest of the kings joined him on stage with rainbow flags in a group finale.

Moreover, the drag kings' mimicry of masculinity and parody of sexual desire between men relies on but also shifts away from what we might identify as butch-femme sexual identities toward a continuum of female masculinity, and then off the map completely to what I will call "something a wee bit different." What better ground to map that difference onto but the female masculinity as an open secret coded onto Canadian singer Anne Murray. Deb Pearce's Man Murray has been a stock and, clearly a beloved, feature of almost every drag king wave to date. What makes Man so pleasurable is how Deb's performance codes not just irony but layers of irony onto each other. Layering refers to the way that drag kings will map a king persona onto their own gender identities, allowing that identity to show through cracks in the mapping.[30] Deb draws our attention to Anne Murray's own layering of identity. Murray has long been rumoured to have a lesbian past; this rumour is virtually unverifiable. But what is far more interesting about this rumour is the degree to which it is fed by a disavowed spectre of masculinity around Murray's gender identity, including her deep baritone voice. Despite the signifiers of femininity that accrue around Murray—makeup including the requisite blue eye shadow, earrings, long gowns, feminine pantsuits, women's low-heeled shoes, and so forth—her performance of White femininity always seems to fail given it is layered onto a body that reads more masculine than feminine. That is, one could argue that Murray herself, as text, reads as a very toned-down male-to-female drag queen.

It is precisely these already existing ironic layerings around Murray that Man Murray foregrounds. In performance, Man wears a rainbow flag dress which replaces the evening gown, but many of the other markers seem consistent with the codes around Anne Murray: the short, masculine hairstyle, square jaw, broad face and smile, strong hand tightly gripping the microphone in a fist; pantsuits with slip-on shoes, step dancing where she moves awkwardly from side to side, etc. What makes this performance so effective— that is, what makes the irony so resonant—are the similar facial features that Anne Murray and Deb Pearce share. This is the face of White butch masculinity and was unequivocally the voice of female masculinity as well. How else might we characterize that deep baritone voice? Only for Anne Murray, femininity is layered—albeit unsuccessfully—onto female masculinity. But Man, of course, is not just layered, he's also queerly camped up. Man is packing a phallus not unlike the microphone Murray grips so tightly; Man draws out the awkwardness of body movements, dancing centred at the knees as they step from side to side, giving equally awkward facial expressions (the wink, complete with blue eye shadow and head nod, for instance); and inhabiting Murray's body through favourite songs, such as "Snow Bird."

Clearly, such ironic and simultaneous reiterations of failed heteronormative femininity, disavowed female masculinity, and queered gay masculinity return us to Sedgwick's axiomatic epistemological contradictions and to a post-queer No Man's Land. What overdetermines the male impersonation at the heart of the drag kings' show, such as Man Murray, is a shift from the separatist to transitive trope, complete with its shifts in alliances and cross-identifications.[31] In many ways, I think this latter turn toward masculinity has finally been taken. Christopher Noelle, for instance, plays on the different expectations between looking like a girl and identifying as a boy in his number "Sharp Dressed Man." Noelle comes out in a tight, black, slinky dress with hair down and proceeds to transform himself into a John Travolta–looking man (from *Grease*) in front of a mirror on stage to the song "Sharp-Dressed Man." The transformation from femininity into masculinity in some ways defies the premise I began with—that is, that femininity is about hyperbole, masculinity about understatement. Noelle puts on the man using as many accessories and props as he takes off. And Chris too (formerly Ricky Martin in the "Cup of Life"), who returns to do "Livin' La Vida Loca" Ricky Martin, also references this turn when he tells me "I am the straight man of the lesbians...It's hard for me to do the gay stuff onstage." Moner and Jesse also do a song, "Mr. Roboto" by Styx, which rearticulates these identifications with straight men. The narrator of the song is a self-made man, who allegorizes the natural and ultimately defamiliarizes the liberal humanist "man": "I have a secret I have been hiding under my skin...I am not what you think / Forget what you know / I am the modern man who hides behind a man so no one else can see my true identity."

Curiously, these rearticulations and performative deconstructions of masculinity are very telling of these affiliations with masculinity and dis-identifications with lesbian practices and identifiers. For instance, I asked nine of the kings one day if they identified or found themselves at all in the word "lesbian." All nine of them said no, including the one self-identified femme; they offered me a bevy of other words, but not one of them said "lesbian," suggesting that the history of lesbian politics has been both incredibly successful and a failure all at the same time. Barbara Johnson anticipated this kind of paradox when she wrote on the failure of success:

> If the political impulse of [lesbianism and/ or queer theory and/or performativity] is to retain its vital, subversive edge, we must become ignorant of it again and again. It is only by forgetting what we know how to do, by setting aside the thoughts that have most changed us, that those thoughts and that knowledge can go on doing what a surprise encounter with otherness should do, that is, lay bare some hint of an ignorance one never knew one had.[32]

In other words, if irony is less about controlled self-consciousness and about its failure instead, then these scenes of irony need to be read for what they reveal about ourselves and our identifications. To phrase this differently, what drag kings do is stage the things that whiteness and masculinity do not want to know and cannot know about themselves, to use irony to make these subjects strange and make their ambivalences work against what they think they do know. As a mode of critical politics, the scene of irony has to be inherently noisy and dialogic in the Bakhtinian sense—that is, that it is engaged in many conversations all at the same time. As a discursive mode of the unsaid and the unseen, irony is the ideal form in which to stage ambivalences, ambiguities, and contradictions. Meaning is made and confused, reduced and complex all at the same time. Drag king performances are both inherently dialogic, in conversation with both conservative and oppositional politics of gender, with lesbian feminism, queer theory, homophobia, feminism, with race and racism, with trans-gendered politics, etc., but also with the contradictions that fracture each. Irony troubles correspondences; it removes certainty that we mean what we say or, conversely, that reality is somehow reducible to some appearances. It also betrays the continuous and inevitable failure of the visual as an epistemological mode.

In addition to my arguments that: (1) drag kinging allows for the ironic rearticulations of whiteness and masculinity, especially of those things they cannot know about itself, and (2) that the culture of drag kings produces—indeed, necessitates—new affiliations across gender and sexual orientations, my own interest as of late has been in those performances of more abjected masculinities: the guys who perform, for lack of a better term (and I use this term affectionately) "pond scum." I remember listening to a friend talk once about a king character she was creating and developing. In her non-drag king life, she's one of the best-looking, most charming gentleman butches around: "He" she said, referring to her drag persona, "is nothing but pure pond scum... He's gross to women. He's entirely flirtatious in a way that is completely disgusting. He's constantly grabbing himself and making those offensive noises to women. He's a pig!" How might we begin to make sense of these somewhat paradoxical articulations of a kind of masculinity that, 15 years ago, we might have tried to intimidate into disappearing? What are the pleasures of watching, say, "Jay," who did a similarly stunning non-musical performance in which he impersonated an incredibly homophobic man who picks up what he thinks is a woman in a fag bar, has sex with her, then, upon discovering she was a drag queen, beats her up. Jay held his audience spellbound while he performed this scene. The larger question at stake in a performance like Jay's is similar to one articulated earlier by Hall. Hall[33] rereads Bakhtin to ask the question: "Why is it that the thing we deem socially peripheral... be[comes] symbolically central?" Why did Jay's character, a homophobic man, hold us spellbound that night in a dyke bar? Part of my answer lies in reformulating the question to ask what cultural work the category of drag kings does. My tentative answer is that when drag kinging emerged, it worked toward articulating an unspoken tension inherent in identity politics that continually asks what we are. Our political task must be not finding out what we are, but understanding the relations between what we say we are and what we deny we are. I am not implying that female or trans masculinities are actually Mr. Pond Scum at their core. But I do want to suggest that the power of the drag kings lies in their exposure of the impurity of categorization itself, especially those categories that have historically understood themselves to be bound, distinct, somehow discrete, and separate (like, for instance, our history of lesbian separatism and, for some of us, the history of White supremacy). These lines that are crossed are there to differentiate, say, lesbian from straight man, Black from White, but that line already allows "in" that which it is suppose to "ward off." It binds identities in the very same gesture through which it supposedly differentiates itself. By way of a conclusion, I suggest that the drag kings remind us, with Bakhtin,[34] that: "When one finds a word, one finds it already inhabited...There is no access to one's own personal ultimate word...Every thought, feeling, experience must be refracted through the medium of someone else's discourse, someone else's style, someone else's manner...Almost no word is without its intense sideward glance at someone else's." If this is true of words, then, of course, it must be true of our identity categories at the same time.

KINGS TO THE POWER OF THREE: BOIS WILL BE BOYS

With this third, and likely by now even fourth or fifth, wave of kings the proliferations of gendered subject positions move beyond "something a wee bit different" into something unrecognizable on our gender maps. Curiously, though, one of the stock features of continuing waves of kings is the presence of the boy. This boi—as either a lesbian boi, gay boi, or FtM boi—is an exceedingly popular trope performing either solo or with other boys (and hence the title of one of these new troupes, Bois Will Be Boys). Why is it that the boy bands—or, if not actual boy bands, then acts or performers that foreground *boyishness*—are such popular fodder for drag kings? Here in Toronto in the early 2000s several new boy acts appeared on the drag king scene, including the utterly compelling trans trio/*ménage-à-trois* New Cocks on the Block. But the boy has featured as a stock choice in drag king numbers—at least here in Toronto—for as long as drag kings have been performing. The New Cocks on the Block are a case in point: their 2003 appearance at the bar formerly known as Pope Joan (since closed) signaled a new turn in the Toronto drag king scene where several incarnations of the boy converged. The event at a lesbian bar was a convergence of those who, across a spectrum of subjects, might identify with the term "boi": butch bois, lesbian bois, trans bois, the trannyfag-boi, gay bois, and, judging by the demographics of the huge audience, the bio-boy (admittedly, in some instances, dragged out by their girlfriends for a night on the town, or so several of my straight female students later confessed).

If we agree that this boy is theatricalized and, by implication, denaturalized, soft, always stylized, and anti-heteronormative in his orientation to the imperatives of masculinity, then could we also agree, perhaps, that whether he appears on stage in a lesbian bar or in a fag bathhouse, or in a (bio-)boy band, this subject is always trans-gendered? Early twentieth-century depictions of the Brando and Dean types resisted such exteriorizations of masculinity evident in the "new" boys of culture: Leonardo di Caprio or the more numerous boy bands. These teen idols and objects of teenage girl fandom and consumption are sexualized through a feminizing gaze that is seductively threatened by the very thing boys supposedly lack: phallic power.

But one of the crucial triangulations that I am also seeing in this new wave is the way in which the figure of the boy/boi functions as a hybrid, antiessentialist hinge point between three different kinds of resisting masculinities: lesbian boi, trans-sexual boi, and drag king bois. This figure remakes manhood and gives us new vocabularies that are not just antiessentializing but simultaneously a-essentialist; that is, they draw our attention to the ways that we remake gender every day as fiction through our reading practices and our desires. But even as we attempt to remake gender as a fiction, these fictions are still heavily and sometimes violently regulated with heteronormative cultures. One of the results of that regulation is, of course, a particular relationship to cultural and political, and hence public trauma. Ann Cvetkovich's new book, *An Archive of Feeling: Trauma, Sexuality, and Lesbian Public Cultures*, argues a curious relation between trauma, sexuality, and public cultural production by suggesting that both power and trauma are productive rather than repressive. Unhappy with increasingly commodified self-help approaches to trauma, as well as with theories of trauma that overly individualize and decontextualize trauma from its socio-political frameworks, Cvetkovich provides a theoretical framework within which to theorize the role of trauma in the production of what she calls queer countercultural publics. I do not want to get lost in theories of trauma at this juncture, nor am I suggesting at all that drag kings are working out private traumas on the stage. This has always been an accusation levelled against queers, transfolks, gays, lesbians, bisexuals, etc.—that is, that somehow these queer and resisting subjects are a traumatic response to and interruption of heterosexual identity. That is not at all what I am arguing here, nor is it what Cvetkovich is suggesting either, but I do think it is necessary to draw our attention to a couple of axioms of queer theory and activism about trauma as they inform the performance cultures of female and trans masculinities. First, it is still traumatizing, both individually and culturally, to live under any of these signs of difference. Whether it be "queer" or "lesbian" (two signs that I will not posit here as mutually exclusive) or "gay" or "transed," and despite the many social and political gains made, it is still a traumatizing everyday experience to be different, although, of course, the everyday experience that I detail here is always mitigated by power vis-à-vis race, class, ability, ethnicity, nationality, and so forth. Moreover, both trauma and queer cultures have been marked by an unspeakability or unrepresentability in public cultures; both have had to aggressively insert themselves into the public domain, but each has also had to struggle to preserve histories and spaces.[35] Each has been marked by a permanent tension between "official" and "unofficial" narratives or knowledges; each has found/created languages in a kind of ironic or unconscious rearticulation of public/heteronormative languages. Finally, as Cvetkovich[36] herself notes, the memories of each have been embedded not just in narratives but also in material artifacts, which can range from photographs to objects whose meanings might seem arbitrary but for the fact that they are invested with a particular kind of value.

Quite apart from specificities of individual traumas (bashings, sexual abuse, loss, and so on), Cvetkovich posits what a number of other queer theorists, including Sedgwick and Butler, have and that is that social and political traumas give rise to counter-cultural public spaces. But Cvetkovich[37] takes this one step further and it is this argument that interests me in terms of drag king cultures: she particularizes these relationships to argue that if trauma presents an epistemological challenge, standing at the crossroads of the complex relation between knowing and not knowing, then it can be a particularly potent discourse with which to "sort through the everyday relation between categories rather than resolve them." Cvetkovich[38] puts it this way: "I am interested instead in the way trauma digs itself in at the level of the everyday, and in the incommensurability of large-scale events and the ongoing material details of experience...I hope to seize authority over trauma discourses from medical and scientific discourse in order to place it back in the hands of those who make culture, as well as to forge new models for how affective life can serve as the foundation for public but countercultural archive as well." One of the things that continues to be brilliantly reiterated in the performance of the New Cocks on the Block/KingSize Kings are the traumas of living in these incoherent bodies around which I centre a postqueer politic. I want to end this chapter on drag kings with their work because in the few performances I have seen, they struck a chord with me in how they staged a resistance to their traumas on the site of gendered bodies. As I noted much earlier in this chapter, the return to previously viewed performance art is structured by what Peggy Phelan identifies as a kind of nostalgia, or the wound of wishing to return.[39] These performances are ones I return to because in many ways, they overlap with many of my own experiences with an identity in transit. For me, as a trans person, two sets of surgeries occurred during my last few years in Toronto: breast-reduction surgery and chest reconstruction surgery. The butch body and the FtM body are each marked by different relationships to trauma: the first, at least in my experience, carried a profound ambivalence to breasts, while the second alleviated the first, but was not itself without traumas. The first performance I saw by New Cocks on the Blocks staged these bodies in trauma and in sometimes ambivalent transit. Two of the then original three performers of New Cocks came on stage with their chests wrapped in what was supposed to be the surgical tape used after breast reconstruction. Under that see-through material, drawn in red on their breasts, were bright red lines, again mirroring the incisions made to reduce breast size. At this point, not that long after my own surgery, I am not even sure I noted the song they performed, but I certainly made note of the trajectory of the performance. In the beginning of the performance they treated their chests as sites of wounding, but when the number came to a close, they had dramatically removed the see-through bandage and the red incisions, and celebrated their breasts. The message of the number was a clear refusal of the traumatizing interventions of breast reduction and removal. These are three very queer, young, non-operative trans-gendered youth with very unconventional bodies who, as part of a new trans wave, clearly seize authority over traumatized incoherent bodies from medical and scientific discourse in order to place those bodies back in the hands of those who make culture with them instead. They are not only bodies of incoherence, they are also, quite literally, bodies on the line, embodying new possibilities for matter-ing.

NOTES

1 Judith Butler, *Gender Trouble: Feminism and the Subversion of Identity* (New York and London: Routledge, Chapman & Hall, 1990), 123.
2 Andrew Parker and Eve Kosofsky Sedgwick, eds., *Performativity and Performance* (New York: Routledge, 1995), 1.
3 Kathleen Martindale, *The Making of an Un/popular Culture: From Lesbian Feminism to Lesbian Postmodernism* (New York: SUNY Press, 1996), 32.
4 Ibid., 30.
5 Kate Davy, "Fe/Male Impersonation: The Discourse of Camp," in *The Politics and Poetics of Camp*, ed. Moe Meyer (London: Routledge, 1994), 130–48 at 145.
6 Ibid., 145.
7 Jill Dolan, "'Lesbian' Subjectivity in Realism: Dragging at the Margins of Structure and Ideology," in *Performing Feminisms: Feminist Critical Theory and Theatre*, ed. Sue-Ellen Case (Baltimore: Johns Hopkins University Press, 1990), 40–53 at 42.
8 Ibid., 49.
9 Jill Dolan, "The Discourse of Feminisms: The Spectator and Representation," in *The Feminist Spectator as Critic*, ed. Jill Dolan (Ann Arbor: UMI Research Press, 1988), 1–18 at 116.
10 Teresa de Lauretis, "Technology of Gender," in *Technologies of Gender: Essays on Theory, Film, and Fiction* (Bloomington: Indiana University Press, 1997), 1–30 at 26.

11 Sue-Ellen Case, "Toward a Butch-Femme Aesthetic," in *The Lesbian and Gay Studies Reader,* ed. Henry Abelove, Michèle Aina Barale, and David M. Halperin (New York: Routledge, 1993), 294–306 at 305.
12 Robert Wallace, "Performance Anxiety: 'Identity,' 'Community,' and Tim Miller's My Queer Body," *Modern Drama* 39 (1996): 97–116 at 98.
13 Butler, *Gender Trouble,* 6.
14 Butler, *Bodies That Matter: On the Discursive Limits of "Sex"* (New York and London: Routledge, 1993), 15.
15 Ibid., 5.
16 Peggy Phelan, "Reciting the Citation of Others; or, a Second Introduction," in *Acting Out: Feminist Performances,* ed. Lynda Hart and Peggy Phelan (Ann Arbor: University of Michigan Press, 1993), 13–31 at 19–22.
17 As quoted in Christine Gledhill, ed., *Stardom: Industry of Desire* (New York: Routledge, 1991), xiv.
18 Davy, "Fe/Male Impersonation," n.p.
19 Diana Fuss, *Masculinity Studies and Feminist Theory: New Directions* (New York: Columbia University Press, 1995), 146.
20 Butler, *Gender Trouble,* 235.
21 Butler, *Bodies That Matte,* 231.
22 Eve Kosofsky Sedgwick, *Epistemology of the Closet* (Berkeley: University of California Press, 1990), 89.
23 Elspeth Probyn, "Lesbians in Space: Gender, Sex, and the Structure of Missing," *Gender, Place, and Culture* 2, no. 1 (1995): 77–84.
24 Robert Wallace, "Performance Anxiety," 102.
25 Lynda Hart, "Identity and Seduction: Lesbians in the Mainstream," in *Acting Out: Feminist Performances,* ed. Lynda Hart and Peggy Phelan (Ann Arbor: University of Michigan Press, 1993), 119–37.
26 Judith Butler, "Imitation and Gender Insubordination," in *Inside/Out: Lesbian Theories, Gay Theories.* ed. Diana Fuss (New York: Routledge, 1991), 1–31 at 29.
27 Hart, "Identity and Seduction," 134.
28 Butler. *Bodies That Matter,* 233.
29 Names are a curious thing with drag kings. Many have at least two, their birth names and at least one character name. Given that drag kings are part of a queer community, not all drag kings are comfortable using their full legal names. For clarity, I will identify kings primarily through their character names, although I will often use full names if I have received permission to do that. Some names mark a character or persona performed by a king while others might mark a trans identity taken on by the king and then, by extension, performed on stage. Character names, of course, are far more interesting given the way in which irony is built into them. Some names are spins on popular characters from Hollywood movies (for instance, Dirk Diggler is from the movie *Boogie Nights*; Man Murray references the Canadian singer Anne Murray), while others are ironic spins either on a birth name or character trait or popular identity. Names are an important feature of the performance long before a single king steps onto a stage. Moreover, many kings do identify as trans, but many do not, identifying themselves as butch, queer, gay, or, in some cases, femme or feminine.
30 Judith Halberstam, *Female Masculinity* (Durham: Duke University Press, 1998), 260.
31 Sedgwick, *Epistemology of the Closet,* 89.
32 Barbara Johnson, *A World of Difference* (Baltimore: Johns Hopkins University Press, 1987), 16.

33 Stuart Hall, "For Allon White: Metaphors of Transformation," in *Stuart Hall: Critical Dialogues in Cultural Studies*, ed. David Morley and Kuan-Hsing Chen (London and New York: Routledge, 1996), 143.
34 Mikhail Bakhtin, "Discourse in the Novel," in *The Dialogic Imagination*, Mikhail Bakhtin (Austin: University of Texas Press, 1981), 91.
35 Ann Cvetkovich, *An Archive of Feelings: Trauma, Sexuality, and Lesbian Public Cultures* (Durham: Duke University Press, 2003), 8.
36 Ibid., 7–8.
37 Ibid., 18.
38 Ibid., 20.
39 Peggy Phelan, *Unmarked: The Politics of Performance* (New York: Routledge, 1993).

CHAPTER 15

Life Without Death? Space, Affect, and Masculine Identity in the Work of Frank Cole

CHRISTINE RAMSAY

In *The Pearly Gates of Cyberspace: A History of Space from Dante to the Internet,* Margaret Wertheim concludes that "in the final analysis, our conception of ourselves is indelibly linked to our conception of space...Conceptions of space and conceptions of self mirror one another. In a very real sense, we are the products of our spatial schemes."[1] In thinking about the work of Canadian documentarist Frank Cole, Wertheim's concept of identity and spatial schemes intrigues me, especially as it can be related to questions of masculinity, emotion, and intersubjectivity in Cole's fourth and final film, *Life Without Death* (2000), which won the International Critics' Prize at the Thessaloniki Images of the 21st Century International Documentary Film Festival and the Certificate of Merit–Golden Gate Awards at the San Francisco International Film Festival, both in 2000. In addition to this recognition, a documentary about Cole's film and his life, *The Man Who Crossed the Sahara* (Korbett Matthews, 2008), premiered at Toronto's Hot Docs! Festival in 2008, where it was described by Gisele Gordon as "a gripping cinematic tale of artistic passion taken to the limits of human endurance."[2] Indeed, Cole's obsessive passion is legendary among Canadian experimental and avant-garde filmmakers, such as Mike Hoolboom, Philip Hoffman, and John Greyson, who share with Matthews a reverence for this fascinating artist who called himself "a child of the desert"[3] and who literally died for his art.

In 2009, Hoolboom, with film critic Tom McSorley, edited a book on Cole titled *Life Without Death: The Cinema of Frank Cole*. The book, accompanied by a DVD of Matthews's film, comprises a series of collected dialogues on Cole and his work by friends, filmmakers who knew him, and others who only knew *of* him—variously admirers as well as harsh critics of

Figure 35 Frank Cole, in a still from *Life Without Death* (2000). Courtesy of the Cole Family and the Canadian Film Institute.

his small but strangely luminous oeuvre. Where Matthews's film and some of the dialogues are interested in investigating Cole's individual psychological motivations, the questions motivating my contribution to *Making It Like a Man* and its theme of Canadian masculinities in practice involve how Cole's particular gendered spatial and emotional schemes are revealed in his aesthetic attitude, and how certain tropes familiar to representations of masculine identity in Canadian cinema might be at play in *Life Without Death*, that astonishing and enigmatic documentary self-portrait, the film many consider his masterpiece. As Hoolboom and McSorley suggest, *Life Without Death* all but begs us to read it through the optics of masculinity—masculinity at war with itself—what I and others see as a characteristic style of *Canadian cinematic masculinity:* "There is, in this compelling work, a lean musculature sculpted by the profound tensions between infinity and closure, between definite and indefinite, between reduction and irreducibility: in life and in cinema. This is an artist, in so many senses, at war, and the war is fought on the daunting, elusive fronts of memory, epistemology, the body, and time itself."[4]

MASCULINITY, AFFECT, AND DEATH

This chapter is informed by my interest in a striking cross-generic trend toward images of masculinity and death in works of Canadian cinema, which I situate in the context of a broader postmodern terrain of affective identities. Lawrence Grossberg argues that in the last decade or two, affect has become a dominant mode of communication in American culture, expressing a new attitude of "empowering nihilism"[5] as some men struggle to reassert their power in worlds that increasingly challenge male privilege. Christopher Sharrett concurs that apocalyptic images of violence and death are decidedly gendered forms of "mythic speech"[6] that make asocial masculinities intelligible in the new millennium as our belief in fictions of white male atomistic wholeness, rationality, and stability have been decidedly called into question. Affective masculine identities are indeed ubiquitous—identities that Christopher Faulkner describes as marked on the body—identities that show and test the limits of men's alienation, fear, hysteria, and rage with "the force of a charge" or a visceral "shock."[7] However, where nihilism, violence, and death are typically visited with a cartoon-style vengeance on *others* in Hollywood films, in Canadian and Québécois films their affective force tends to be expressed more contemplatively and reflexively, with ultimate challenge—and risk—to the *male self*, not others. I see this in the feature fiction films of our most prominent and accomplished *auteurs*, from David Cronenberg and Jean-Claude Lauzon through Atom Egoyan, Guy Maddin, Bruce McDonald, and Don McKellar, among others, and such is also the case in Cole's documentary self-portrait *Life Without Death*. Here the attitude of "empowering nihilism" is revealed *as fantasy* as the protagonist—and the filmmaker himself—is forced to negotiate the symbolic horizon of his own mortality and to face the difficult fact that, as Russian philosopher Mikhail Bakhtin puts it, we all owe God a death.[8]

According to Cole's longtime friend and occasional collaborator Richard Taylor, the filmmaker had a lifelong obsession with death, the symbolic negation of which is key to understanding his work. "He admired the painter Alex Colville," says Taylor, "and latched onto his fierce quote: 'Art is one of the principal means by which a human being tries to compensate for, or complement, the restlessness of death and temporality.'"[9] His first film after graduating from Ottawa's Algonquin College, *A Documentary* (1979), was an unblinking chronicle of his grandmother's death from cancer, which, while it shocked some audiences, was nonetheless very well received by critics at the Venice Film Festival. Her death left Cole's grandfather in such a state of despair, Taylor writes, "that Frank decided in his art and his life to challenge the archetypal experience of death itself,"[10] so much so that it became increasingly hard to tell where his art stopped and his life began. Melanie Scott concurs: "Those with whom he shared his life—and there weren't many—are unanimous in their agreement that Cole *was* his work... 'His art was his blueprint for life. His film was the way he communicated with the world.'"[11]

Haunted by the passing of his beloved grandfather soon after his grandmother, Scott says, Cole became "consumed with the belief that death is a temporary cancer that can be treated" and so "built up his body and soul with, respectively, exercise, vitamins, a strict diet and solitude."[12] However, his narcissistic obsession with "beating death" by surviving a self-documented gruelling 11-month, 7,000-kilometre solo trek by camel of the North African desert from Nouakchott, Mauritania, in the west to the Red Sea coast at Souakin, Sudan, in the east—by striving to make himself "a person the Sahara could not kill...a person whose outcome was life, not death"[13] —while it succeeded in producing the remarkable film *Life Without Death*, and in getting his name in the *Guinness Book of World Records*, inevitably led, as life will, to his own mortality, not immortal empowerment. For in April 2000, ten years after the first trek (which took place from 29 November 1989 to 3 November 1990), and just days after the Ottawa premiere of the film that documented it (which, characteristically, the reclusive filmmaker did not attend), Cole set out for the Sahara again, pursuing in his mind not a "death wish," but what he called "death's death."[14] This time he aimed to up the ante by taking a much more remote route and by making it a return trip.[15] While his parents and friends pleaded with him to reconsider, given that he had already proved himself more than capable of the desert's challenge, and given the increasing political unrest and banditry in the area,[16] he could not be deterred. His second trip ended in mid-October 2000 in death, as Karin Roman writes: "Four or five days after Frank left Timbuktu, a nomad found his body, bound and bludgeoned, in a shrub about 70 kilometres southeast of the city. Authorities believe he fell victim to banditry. Everything had been stolen: His camels, traveller's cheques, film, film equipment, even his boots."[17] Dental records and DNA testing identified his remains, which were sent, as his will stipulated, to a cryogenics institute near Detroit. While he was hoping that, after his death, the technology would eventually be developed that could bring him back to life, in the end his mourning family and friends were left to deal with the cold fact that the man's nihilistic and narcissistic bent ultimately led, not to the power of life without death, but to the vulnerability of all flesh.

Acclaimed documentary filmmaker Peter Wintonick, who knew Cole through their mutual producing partner Francis Miquet, understands him as a truly gifted documentarist, compelled to the practice of this harsh work "by his own inner obsessions. Frank lived life on the edge of life, and in the end, what he did was only really the most extreme example of what all documentarians do. Documenting life and death."[18] According to Wintonick, Cole saw himself and his art as mediating the ultimate human paradox: our terror of dying; and our tacit acceptance of mortality in order to go on living: "'I think that because we don't face death,'" he quotes Cole as saying, "'we can't face life itself. People should live very intensely—to have as much of life as possible.'"[19]

Ultimately, the unbearable experience of his grandfather's passing compelled Cole to want to face death himself. "I loved my grandfather," he says in voice-over in the opening minutes of *Life Without Death*. "I'd have faced death for him if it meant he could live." The entire film, while dedicated in the prologue to Cole's parents, is in fact structured around the traumatic memory of this absent loved one. It opens with black-and-white images of Frank with his grandfather on the latter's deathbed, then cuts to a high-angle shot of Frank sitting bare-chested on a chair and crying, naked and inconsolable in his grief. "It was my grandfather's death that made me decide to cross the Sahara desert by camel," Cole says in voice-over as the film's first images of the desert appear, superimposed on a map of the Sahara. We soon find out that Cole has brought his grandfather's ashes with him on this macabre journey to confront death by experiencing the absolute limits of life, and the film will flashback several times from the abject hardships of the trek—the extremes of heat and cold; the violent sandstorms; the dying camels and bleached animal carcasses haunting his path; the blistered and peeling skin; the unbearable loneliness; and the ever-present panic of getting lost and dying of thirst, of exposure, or at the hands of bandits—to the abject images of the dying old man. Significantly, these images of the grandfather return near the end of the film to effectively bookend it. And while the final frames take us back to the desert and a sequence of shots of dead animal carcasses, before Frank appears in close-up and, in the only moment of the film in which he speaks directly to the camera in synch-sound, cryptically declares what sounds like "Oh, live!" or "A life!"[20] as the frame freezes, still, this static shot would not be the film's final word: a postscript was added by Miquet at Cole's request in early June 2000, including footage Cole shipped home from the beginning of the second trek that April, which showed Cole "setting off again into the glowing light of a pristine Saharan landscape."[21] Moreover, he made Miquet promise that if he died in the course of the second crossing, his death would not be mentioned in the film that documented the first one. Miquet understood this to mean that if Frank could not be "eternal in flesh," then he wanted to be "immortal on film."[22]

THE MALE BODY AND EMPOWERING NIHILISM

Thus, the few people who knew the director closely are all adamant that he was not suicidal, not simply an unstable man with a death wish, as many perplexed audiences have assumed after seeing the film. After all, as John Steinbachs reports, he had been preparing for the trip since 1985, building his body, learning Arabic and first aid, and doing a dry-run 400-kilometre journey in 1988 in which he learned to ride a camel and spot water wells.[23] Rather, as Miquet says, he was "possessed with the idea of being immortal"[24] — which attitude, I would argue, can best be understood in the context of the mythic speech of the masculine impulse toward "empowering nihilism" elaborated above: in this case, the symbolic negation of dying by courting near-death in the desert and surviving, with the trauma indeed marked on his body with the force of a visceral shock.

Observers scrutinize Cole's masculinity and its portrayal of the marked body in different ways. For filmmaker Yann Beauvais in "A Sending Without Any Recipient," in the obsessive yet oddly blank and distanced close-up sequences on Frank's body wounds littered throughout the film (bleeding sores, blisters, burnt skin), there is "an incredible exhibitionism" that Beauvais ultimately finds manipulative, indicative of the "wilful blindness" motivating the director's voyage that is "overbearing" in its narcissism and neo-colonialist attitude toward others. He elaborates:

> The desert is only a test. What is significant are the extreme survival conditions that it affords to a sick-at-heart westerner. We experience this irritation again when the filmmaker brings up the civil and tribal wars that took place in some of the lands that were crossed, to the borders of Chad and Darfur. For the filmmaker, these wars are an obstacle. The overbearing quest sees only what deflects it, whatever delays its plan to cross the entire length of the Sahara. The life and death of others (as long as it is not the grandfather) is only collateral damage. The perseverance of the project plunges us into a web of contradictory sentiments. It is fascinating, but it is also unacceptable. We are almost in a double bind. But this double bind shows how the contemporary forms of colonialism — or should we say neo-colonialism? — show themselves today.
>
> The project, the crossing, is stronger than everything. Anything that interferes with its completion, or even postpones it, is brushed aside, is evil. Everything has to make way for the project, even the filmmaker's body.[25]

In contrast, in "I Come Here for the Rites of Your Unworlding," media artist Mike Cartmell understands Cole's body language in terms of a more self-aware and self-reflexive but nonetheless neurotic masculine fetishism (the sadomasochism of excessive bodybuilding and weight and diet control; the drive to masterful solitude; celibacy and the repression and/or displacement of feelings, emotion, and affect) expressed (and this is the *art* of it) in the very style of the film itself: "The 'Preparation' section is fetishistic in style, with the high-con black and white, the heavily and obviously foleyed sound effects, the minimalist staging, and it contains multiple and thoroughly eroticized fetish items: the dagger, the belt and buckle, the naked chest."[26] Not to mention the ultimate fetish object of the grandfather's ashes, which Cole ceremoniously drags with him across his desert warpath to beat death:

> Fetishistic belief is structured in the form of repudiation: *I know very well that* this is merely an ordinary bottle containing cinders, *but just the same*, it is for me the very substance of my lost loved one. And since it is the very one, the very other, my very master whose obscene living enjoyment compels my journey...it must accompany me, guide me, protect me, preserve me as I seek to overcome my foe in holocaustic utter burn. Consumption, consummation. Devoutly to be wished.
>
> At the same time, as it is the master it is my foe, it is what I needs must overcome, burn utterly. In being alive I am only dead; I am nothing, I am going nowhere, better I should be dead than him. In being dead he is unbelievably alive...He is everything, he will take me across millions of metres of desert, he overcomes and in overcoming must be overcome, I must become him. I must be the one who says, "I am become death, destroyer of worlds."[27]

What is *Life Without Death*, then, if not the eternal return to the masculine triumph of the will?

In any case, for me, what seems to be Cole's incomprehensible pursuit of "death's death" takes on profound meaning if considered from both of the above perspectives—as the empowered and empowering work of a unique Canadian artist attempting to live at the threshold of existence and speak the idiosyncratic language of his soul's desire, on the one hand; and as a question of the limits of personal and social identity for an atomistic and agonistic if not narcissistic and nihilistic masculine subjectivity, on the other hand.

"Like many gifted artists," Miquet writes, "Frank harboured a truth too painful to reveal. The film and I can only offer a superficial glimpse into his soul."[28] For Tom McSorley, who as director of the Canadian Film Institute mounted a retrospective of Cole's work in 2004, the minimalist, tableau style of *Life Without Death* made him think of Frank as "a landscape painter" of the desert.[29] It is a metaphor that might well have pleased Cole, given his admiration for Alex Colville. Ambiguously accepting and at the same time refusing the stereotypical imperialist Western images of the place as a manly

Figure 36 Frank with camel, in a still from *Life Without Death* (2000). Courtesy of the Cole Family and the Canadian Film Institute.

site for exploration and exploitation, or as a romanticized tourist destination with its breathtaking sand dunes and sunsets, Cole portrays the Sahara in a distinctly "anti-travelogue,"[30] unaffected, and minimalist aesthetic, with utmost respect for its meaning in Arabic: "brown and empty."[31] As filmmaker Mike Hoolboom puts it, "this confrontation with nothing is the place Frank Cole wrestles his pictures out of."[32] In such a space—the space to which his fear of death had "summoned" him "like a calling"[33] and in which he felt "most alive"[34] —in subjecting and abjecting his body to the elements, the man found what McSorley calls "a metaphor for his interior self,"[35] or, as Miquet puts it, an "extension of his own mind."[36]

GENDERED SPACES OF IMMORTALITY

The Sahara, unquestionably, was a metaphor for what Wertheim would call Frank Cole's "soul space"—the stark answer to his quest to find a place, or room, for his sense of his "self." In tracing the history and meaning of space in the West, Wertheim finds the heart of the story in "the age-old tension in Western culture between body and mind." "With respect to space," she says, "this tension has been played out in our shifting concepts of what we perceive as *physical space* and *spiritual space*—that is, our perceptions of a space in which our bodies are embedded, and a space in which our 'psyches' or 'souls' are embedded."[37] Whereas in medieval times, there was still a common belief in a space for both body *and* soul (the physical and spiritual were pictured as mirroring each other, with humans Janus-like on the borderline, facing a finite cosmos—the physical world—yet also turned toward the stars and God in the heavens beyond—the spiritual world), with modernity and its mechanistic philosophy, physical space is now said to extend infinitely in all directions, leaving no place for the soul. Hence the current postmodern scientific world view in which humans are increasingly seen as, and experience themselves as, atomistic machines whose bodies can be perfected and their lives technologically enhanced and extended (evident in the cryogenics craze that Cole himself ascribed to and in the cultural obsession with fitness and cosmetic surgery whereby we hope to free ourselves from the sins and "embarrassments of embodiment").[38] Moreover, it is a view in which the earth is reduced from an interconnected lifeworld enabling the survival of all plants and animals to a "lump of rock revolving in a vast Euclidian void,"[39] and the self is reduced to just a body, embedded in physical space alone—a supposedly infinite but ironically claustrophobic space that the isolated individualized body cannot transcend because it has no *other space* in which to place the soul.

Thus, Wertheim explains, modern Western culture creates pathologies of the self by failing to give space to this immaterial, spiritual aspect of the self—pathologies such as the obsessive desire to perfect and control the body on the one hand, and the obsessive desire to escape the body on the other hand—and she sees it as a gender-based phenomenon that is visible in postmodern cyberculture as well. The appeal of cyber-disembodiment to teenage boys in particular is well documented as they "surf the net"—the "muscular metaphor" that allows them to use technology to escape their awkward bodies and "metamorphosing flesh" and

> flee to a place where they regain power and control... "Surfing the Net" does not conjure up images of disembodied ethereality, but a vision of physical power—both for the human user and for the space itself. Where the cybernaut is endowed with the prowess of a surfer, the space is likened to the ocean. Real-life ineptitude is replaced by an image of physical grace. It is no coincidence that hackers and surfers alike are predominantly young men—as also are the major Christian angels: Michael, Gabriel, and Raphael.[40]

The interesting fact that Frank Cole was an avid and accomplished ocean surfer and high diver aside, what strikes me is the way in which the Sahara can be seen as the answer to the director's idiosyncratic and increasingly pathological quest for a space to put his soul: a space less "sexed up," hyperbolic, and hyper-real than the postmodern technology of cyberspace, certainly; but a space of escape through modern cinematic technology into a state of "empowering nihilism" nonetheless, where he could symbolically attempt to beat death and get control over his vulnerable flesh by filming himself surviving a living hell. As Beauvais writes: "The desert is a fascinating space...as well as a space that transforms our worldly existence...For the western man, the desert is a mirage that engulfs him in delectation. It is a pristine space to conquer, or to take complete control of. It is the ultimate frontier."[41] In Cole's own words: "For now I am only going to explain that I did it to prove something. I could prove it symbolically, not scientifically, because I am an artist, not a doctor. But I believe that symbolic proof might inspire others to discover scientific proof. Nothing is impossible."[42]

This narcissistic and ascetic fantasy of infinite consciousness and space without limits where nothing is impossible and in which one could live in disembodied solitude forever, like an angel, haunted Cole, as his friends attest. "He wanted immortality, not celebrity," says Taylor. "He wasn't willing to accept the inevitability of death."[43] As Miquet observed, if he couldn't be eternal in flesh, then he wanted to be immortal on film, and while he describes his friend as a genuinely warm, humble, and generous person who "was preoccupied with not wanting to appear heroic in the film," Miquet notes a decided contradiction in his motivation: "Frank was front and centre throughout most of the film which was inherently narcissistic. This he not only acknowledged but condoned. He derived a great deal of pleasure from seeing himself on-screen."[44] This is more than evident in the early weightlifting scene, which captures clearly Cole's self-conscious and self-satisfied smirk as he pumps iron in preparation for his gruelling sojourn. Thus, for Miquet, after the initial shock of hearing about Frank's murder, he was "overcome by emptiness. There was little meaning or redemption in this death—only tragedy. Something had gone terribly awry. Such a fate should not fall upon someone so possessed with the idea of being immortal."[45]

Yet from a Bakhtinian perspective on identity as intersubjectivity[46]—as an eternal dialogue based in the fundamental phenomenological principle of *I and the other in co-consciousness*—Cole is exactly the kind of man such tragedy might befall, someone whose acute solipsism made him unable to see and accept not only the inevitability of, but also the *value* in limits of, the self in its relation to others; and of life itself in relation to death. If something had indeed gone terribly awry in Frank Cole's self or soul, Bakhtin would understand it as a pathological imbalance in the relative moments of embodied consciousness that link human subjects inexorably together in the intersubjective dance of (co)-existence, which moments he calls I-for-myself, I-for-the-other, and the-other-for-me. I-for-myself is ongoing consciousness—how my self looks and feels to my own consciousness—and it is experienced from within as heterogeneous, cold, unbounded, unfinished, infinitely open and ongoing in its unique and once-occurent place in Being. From my position on the boundary of the world I see, I cannot see all of myself, cannot place myself as a whole object in the world, am unable to consciously experience either my own birth or my own death, and so perceive myself as both fragmented and limitless. Hence the uncanny feeling we get—as Frank Cole surely did—when we try to think of life before we were born or after we die. I-for-the-other is how my self appears to those outside it—as a limited, bounded, embodied whole object in space and time. Conversely, the-other-for-me is how outsiders appear to myself—as limited, bounded, embodied whole objects in space and time. Given this situation, what we are all called upon and ultimately have the choice to do for one another as an interdependent existential field of co-beings in co-consciousness is to give one another the value and warmth of embodiedness, which, as I-for-myself ongoing consciousnesses, we do not innately possess. Looking at another human being from within my unique horizon, or compass of vision, or place that I and *only* I occupy in existence, my perspective has a meaningful, contextualizing value relative to the other, which Bakhtin characterizes in terms of "excess."

In seeing an other, I *see in excess* of her, filling in the things that, from her unique compass of vision—from within her once-occurent, ongoing, unfinalized "I"—she cannot see (i.e., her face and its expression, the world behind her back, her context as an object-for-me in a whole series of relationships with others, etc.). Thus, I embody the other, consummate her, give warmth and form to her through my thoughts, words, gestures, and attitudes toward her. In short, I *author* the other: I am the mediating screen that produces the other as an *embodied consciousness* in space, time, and value. The mother–child bond is exemplary of this dynamic, as Bakhtin observes. In contemplating one another with our excess of seeing, subjects exist *dialogically*, as unique and individual yet at the same time interdependent centres of perception *outside* one another. For Bakhtin, there is not one *monologic* "I" or abstract consciousness. I am not the only consciousness in a world of others as objects, but an agential co-being in co-consciousness in a social multiplicity of "I's" who *need* one another to mutually author one another. Without such consummative, form-giving activity, such pathologies as doubling, madness, and suicide—not to mention the irrational obsession with limitlessness in the form of immortality—can come to haunt us.

Accordingly, I suggest that Frank Cole's spatial and emotional schemes are caught in an essentially narcissistic and cold I-for-myself attitude—in a masculine adolescent fantasy of infinite ongoing being that seems to leave no place, or space, for the soul to live and die where, ironically, his film itself attests it must: in the warmth of dialogue with other people. As Taylor suggests,

> in his heart, I'm sure Frank realized that the desert was not the best place to endure solitude...Perhaps he wanted to take that one last trip before coming back to begin a new life with people .... A friend

of mine I had introduced to Frank more than 10 years ago, landscape painter Joan Sutherland, received one of Frank's last letters on Oct. 11, a week before he was murdered: "Joanie—even in Timbuktu, you are not forgotten. I took six months and 3,000 km riding to get across the first country, Mauritania. Five countries still to go. Sahara feels endless. I long for life to be so endless too."[47]

So, how are we to understand *Life Without Death*? To make it psychologically and socially intelligible? For Taylor, it is the telling document of the life of a dear friend whose "confusion about heroism finally caught up with him."[48] For Tom McSorley and Geoff Pevere, they concur that there is something quintessentially Canadian at work here. "In his confrontations with vast, hostile and empty landscapes," McSorley writes, Cole was "typically Canadian":

> He was some other Terry Fox on some other marathon. Crossing and recrossing a continent of sand, he wrote a life's story in a book of sand, adhering to a tenacious, disciplined monotony. Stride after stride, he wrested form out of the hot, sandy temporal trudge. Walking was his war, and was always fought in no-man's land, alone under black-hole darkness or searing incandescence.[49]

Pevere's comparison is to our national cinematic tradition of troubled masculinity generally, and to the "sheer impulse to get as far from human concern as is geographically possible":

> As far back as *Nobody Waved Goodbye*, *Le Chat dans le sac* and *Winter Kept Us Warm*, and as recently as many of the films made by David Cronenberg, Atom Egoyan and Guy Maddin, one sees men walking away. Often it's an exodus from responsibility: family, love, commitment, sexual intimacy. Sex is an especially fraught arena in movies like Egoyan's *Exotica*, Cronenberg's *Dead Ringers* and Maddin's *Cowards Bend the Knee*, a blend of obsession and fear that invariably results in forms of almost rapturously high perversion.
> There is no sex in Frank's movies, but there is sexual tension. Galore. Indeed, it"s the kind of wire-humming sexual tension that can only come from such a strenuous denial of its release. And denial of the body—its desires, its functions, its very organic destiny—is a fact of Frank's movies. But one can't escape one's organic destiny, any more than one can transcend death, or hope to cross the Sahara desert alone more than once and expect to come out alive. Frank's films take such pathological flight from human contact, they are decidedly out-of-body experiences.[50]

For me, the film is the daunting work of a highly sensitive, serious, and gifted, if not neurotic and narcissistic, Canadian artist, as well as the haunting gendered self-portrait of a man in mortal crisis. Cole's was a subjectivity—a consciousness—that tried to abandon the limits of the body and take up *all space*—to live forever, infinitely. Hence the attraction of the ocean and later the desert—infinite open waves of water and sand—as the stark emotional and spatial schemes he sought out in which to place his soul.

DEATH AND THE SPACE OF THE OTHER

As Grossberg, Sharrett, and Faulkner suggest, such images of mortal crisis as a film like *Life Without Death* proffers function as gendered mythic speech—as affective allegories of the limits of social and personal identity for contemporary masculinities. One such limit involves the body. Another involves the spaces of dialogic intersubjectivity, self and other. A third involves the fear of death: the end of the self—an idea impossible to contemplate and singularly anxiety producing from the perspective of a narcissistic subjectivity yearning helplessly and hopelessly for absolute I-for-myself consciousness, life without death. For Bakhtin, my birth and my death—my beginning and ending—can never be part of my own consciousness because I cannot experience within myself the fact of my non-existence. Death experiences us, over and over, all souls; we do not and cannot directly experience it. I like the way Mike Cartmell puts it as well: death's "register" is "outside experience."[51] Inevitably, we all owe God a death. But my death is not mine to know or behold. For Bakhtin, death, like subjectivity, is a liminal phenomenon. It belongs to the category of the other: to the other pole of consciousness: to others as my form-giving witnesses after I die; and so ultimately to the *social* realm that works of art necessarily inscribe, even when they are as seemingly atomistic and solipsistic as Frank Cole's masterpiece.

As *Life Without Death* and his friend Francis Miquet attest, Frank Cole, the Canadian who crossed the Sahara, indeed "lived life on the edge of life":[52] at the cold extreme of I-for-myself consciousness, looking, he seems to have thought, in facing down his own death and making it like a man on the brown and empty horizon of abject nothingness, for an immortal place to put his soul. However, it seems to me that to really face death is to see that it irrevocably belongs not to the self, to the purview of my own consciousness, but to the life of the other—to those who might, depending on the quality of *being toward others* that I have manifested in living, mourn me and miss me and speak of me after I'm gone. Yet, and how ironically, isn't this exactly what Cole's film is about and accomplishes as he uses his artistic practice, and his very life, to pay homage to the death, and life, of the *other*—the beloved grandfather and his sacred vial of ashes whose passing has left, as every passing will, and as Cole's itself has done, what Bakhtin calls a hole in existence for those left behind?

NOTES

1 Margaret Wertheim, *The Pearly Gates of Cyberspace: A History of Space from Dante to the Internet* (New York: Norton, 1999), 308.
2 Gisele Gordon, http://hotdocs.bside.com, accessed 19 September 2008.
3 Ibid.
4 Mike Hoolboom and Tom McSorley, "All Franked Out," in *Life Without Death: The Cinema of Frank Cole,* ed. Mike Hoolboom and Tom McSorley (Ottawa: Canadian Film Institute, 2009), 4–7 at 6.
5 Lawrence Grossberg. "Postmodernity and Affect: All Dressed Up with No Place to Go," in *Dancing in Spite of Myself: Essays on Popular Culture* (Durham: Duke University Press, 1997), 45–65 at 45.
6 Christopher Sharrett, "Introduction," in *Mythologies of Violence in Postmodern Media,* ed. Christopher Sharrett (Detroit: Wayne State University Press, 1999), 9–20 at 10.
7 Christopher Faulkner, "Affective Identities," *Canadian Journal of Film Studies* 3, no. 2 (Fall 1994): 3–23 at 17.
8 Mikhail Bakhtin, *Art and Answerability: Early Philosophical Essays by M.M. Bakhtin,* ed. Michael Hoquist and Vadim Liapunov, trans. Vadim Liapunov (Austin: University of Texas Press, 1990), 54.
9 Richard Taylor, "Death of a Filmmaker," *Ottawa Citizen,* 28 January 2001, C4.
10 Ibid., C4.
11 Melanie Scott, "Life Without Frank," *Take One: Film and Television in Canada* 11, no. 37 (May–June 2002): 18–21 at 21.
12 Ibid., 20.
13 Ibid., 21.
14 Frank Cole, "Sahara Journal," in *Life Without Death: The Cinema of Frank Cole,* ed. Mike Hoolboom and Tom McSorley (Ottawa: Canadian Film Institute, 2009), 136–49 at 140, 147. In fact, as Mike Hoolboom reports in "In the Theatre," Cole's first film, *A Life,* was to have been called "*Death's Death,*" but he decided to rename it at the last moment. See Hoolboom, "In the Theatre," in *Life Without Death,* ed. Hoolboom and McSorley, 92–94 at 94.
15 Coway Daly, "Filmmaker's Duel with the Sahara," *Globe and Mail,* 11 January 2001, n.p.
16 Karin Roman. "Life and Death in the Desert," *Ottawa Citizen,* 15 February 2001, A4.
17 Ibid., A4.
18 Peter Wintonick with Francis Miquet, "Frank Cole (1954–2000): Life Within Death," *Point of View* 44 (Fall 2001): 20–23.
19 Ibid., 22.
20 The phrase has puzzled many viewers, including several contributors to *Life Without Death.* In his piece in the volume, entitled "The Placebo Singers of Howard Stone," John Greyson sheds some light on the subject. The phrase is a reference to Cole's first film, *A Life,* in which the director himself played the central character, Howard Stone, who uttered the word "*alif*" at strategic moments throughout the film. "*Alif,*" Greyson explains, is "the word for 'one,' ' the first letter of the Arabic alphabet," which Stone "tattooed onto his wrist in the middle

of *A Life*. He said it aloud and it sounded like 'a life.'" In Greyson"s analysis this tattoo was "a placebo, a blue sash standing in for a red wound, the cut of a blade"—a simple sign of solitude, a symbolic suicidal gesture of a man at war with himself, or both? See John Greyson, "The Placebo Singers of Howard Stone," in *Life Without Death*, ed. Hoolboom and McSorley, 95–103 at 97.

21 Francis Miquet (with Peter Wintonick), "Frank Cole (1954–2000): Life Within Death," *Point of View* 44 (Fall 2001): 20–23. 23.
22 Ibid., 23.
23 John Steinbachs, "A Long, Slow Trek to Justice: More Than Two Years after an Ottawa Filmmaker's Murder in the Desert, Mali Officials Claim They Have 2 Suspects in Custody," *Ottawa Sun*, 23 February 2003, 4.
24 Miquet, "Life Without Death," 23.
25 Yann Beauvais, "A Sending Without Any Recipient," In *Life Without Death*, ed. Hoolboom and McSorley, 152–54.
26 Mike Cartmell, "I Come Here for the Rites of Your Unworlding," in *Life Without Death*, ed. Hoolboom and McSorley, 162–76 at 169.
27 Ibid., 169.
28 Miquet, "Life Without Death," 23.
29 Scott, "Life Without Frank," 20.
30 Catherine Tunnacliffe, "True-Life Tales of the Unexpected: Hot Docs," http://www.Eyeweekly.com. accessed 28 June 2005.
31 Wintonick, "Frank Cole (1954–2000)," 21.
32 Mike Hoolboom, "Frank Cole Is Dead," http://www.cfi-icf/cole_mh.html, accessed 30 January 2005.
33 Steinbachs, "A Long, Slow Trek to Justice," 4.
34 Scott, "Life Without Frank," 20.
35 Ibid., 21.
36 Douglas Quan, "Filmmaker 'Thrived on Adversity': DNA Tests Confirm Body Discovered Bound and Bludgeoned in Sahara Desert Was That of Ottawa's Frank Cole," *Ottawa Citizen*, 11 February 2001, A1.
37 Wertheim, *The Pearly Gates*, 30–31.
38 Ibid., 21.
39 Ibid., 38.
40 Ibid., 26.
41 Beauvais, "A Sending Without Any Recipient," 152.
42 Cole, "Sahara Journal," 136.j.
43 Taylor, "Death of a Filmmaker," C4.
44 Miquet, "Life Without Death," 22.
45 Ibid., 22.
46 See Mikhail Bakhtin, *Art and Answerability: Early Philosophical Essays By M.M. Bakhtin*, ed. Michael Holquist and Vadim Liapunov, trans. Vadim Liapunov (Austin: University of Texas Press, 1990); and *Toward a Philosophy of the Act*, ed. Michael Holquist and Vadim Liapunov, trans. Vadim Liapunov (Austin: University of Texas Press, 1993), *passim*.
47 Taylor, "Death of a Filmmaker," C4.
48 Ibid., C4.
49 McSorley, "What Remains," In *Life Without Death*, ed. Hoolboom and McSorley, 44–49 at 44–45.
50 Geoff Pevere, "Dead Serious," in *Life Without Death*, ed. Hoolboom and McSorley, 86–91 at 88–89.
51 Cartmell, "I Come Here for the Rites of Your Unworlding," 170.
52 Wintonick, "Frank Cole (1954–2000): Life Within Death," 10.

BIBLIOGRAPHY

Abel, Elizabeth, Marianne Hirsch, and Elizabeth Langland, eds. *The Voyage in Fictions of Female Development*. Hanover: University Press of New England, 1983), 12.

Abdel-Shehid, Gamal. *Who Da Man? Black Masculinities and Sporting Cultures*. Toronto: Canadian Scholars' Press, 2005.

Adams, Rachel, and David Savran, eds. *The Masculinity Studies Reader*. Oxford: Blackwell, 2002.

Adler, Judith. "Travel as Performed Art." *American Journal of Sociology* 94, no. 6 (1989): 1366–91.

Alfred, Taiaiake. *Wasasé: Indigenous Pathways of Action and Freedom*. Peterborough: Broadview Press, 2005.

Alrich, Robert. *Colonialism and Homosexuality*. London: Routledge, 2002.

Angelides, Steven. "Feminism, Child Sexual Abuse, and the Erasure of Child Sexuality." *GLQ: A Journal of Lesbian and Gay Studies* 10, no. 2 (2004): 141–77.

Appadurai, Arun. *Modernity at Large: Cultural Dimensions of Globalization*. Minneapolis: University of Minnesota Press, 1996.

Applebaum, Louis. *John Grierson and the NFB*. Toronto: ECW Press, 1984.

Atwood, Margaret. "A Double-Bladed Knife: Subversive Laughter in Two Stories by Thomas King." *Canadian Literature* 124–25 (1990): 243–50.

———. *Survival: A Thematic Guide to Canadian Literature*. Toronto: Anansi, 1972.

———. "Writing the Male Character." *Second Words: Selected Critical Prose*. Toronto: Anansi, 1982. 412–30.

Baker, Michael Brendan. "Churchill's Island." In *24 Frames: The Cinema of Canada*. Edited by Jerry White. London: Wallflower Press, 2006. 23–32.

Bakhtin, Mikhail. *Art and Answerability: Early Philosophical Essays by M.M. Bakhtin*. Edited by Michael Holquist and Vadim Liapunov. Translated by Vadim Liapunov. Austin: University of Texas Press, 1990.

———. "Discourse in the Novel." In *The Dialogic Imagination*. Austin: University of Texas Press, 1981. 259–422.

———. *Problems of Dostoevsky's Poetics*. Edited and translated by Caryl Emerson. Minneapolis: University of Minnesota Press, 1984.

———. *Rebalais and His World*. Translated by Helene Iswolsky. Bloomington: Indiana University Press, 1984.

———. *Toward a Philosophy of the Act*. Edited by Michael Holquist and Vadim Liapunov. Translated by Vadim Liapunov. Austin: University of Texas Press, 1993.

Bal, Mieke. "Mimesis and Genre Theory in Aristotle's *Poetics*." *Poetics Today* 3, no. 1 (1982): 171–80.

Balakrishnan, Gopal, ed. *Debating Empire*. London: Verso, 2003.

Ballantyne, Tony. *Orientalism and Race: Aryanism in the British Empire*. Houndsmills: Palgrave, 2001.

Bataille, Georges. *Eroticism: Death and Sensuality*. San Francisco: City Light Books, 1986.

———. *Lascaux or the Birth of Art*. Lausanne: Skira, 1955.

———. *Visions of Excess: Selected Writings, 1927–1939*. Minneapolis: University of Minnesota Press, 1985. 171–77.

Bauman, Zygmunt. *Wasted Lives: Modernity and Its Outcasts*. Oxford: Polity, 2004.

Beauvais, Yann. "A Sending Without Any Receipt." In *Life Without Death: The Cinema of Frank Cole*. Edited by Mike Hoolboom and Tom McSorley. Ottawa: Canadian Film Institute, 2009. 152–54.

Bell, Derrick. "The Sexual Diversion: The Black Man / Black Woman Debate in Context." *Traps: African-American Men on Gender and Sexuality*. Edited by Rudolph P. Byrd and Beverly Guy-Sheftall. Bloomington: Indiana University Press, 2001.

Bennett, Andy. "Hip-Hop am Main, Rappin' on the Tyne: Hip-Hop Culture as a Local Construct in Two European Cities." In *That's the Joint! The Hip-Hop Studies Reader*. Edited by Murray Forman and Mark Anthony Neal. New York: Routledge, 2004. 177–200.

Bennett, Jason Patrick. "Apple of the Empire: Landscape and Imperial Identity in the Turn-of-the-Century British Columbia." *Journal of the Canadian Historical Association*, New Series, 9 (1998): 72.

Berger, Carl. "The True North Strong and Free." In *Nationalism in Canada*. Toronto: University of Toronto Press, 1966.

Bertram, Christopher, and Andrew Chitty, eds. *Has History Ended? Fukuyama, Marx, Modernity*. Aldershot: Avebury, 1994.

Beynon, John. *Masculinities and Culture*. Buckingham: Open University Press, 2002.

Birnie Danzker, Jo-Anne. "Foreword." In *Young Romantics*. Exhibition Catalogue. Vancouver: Vancouver Art Gallery, 1985.

Blatchford, Christie. "Judge Lashes Police for Racial Profiling." *The Globe and Mail*, 17 September 2004, A1.

Bly, Robert. *Iron John: A Book about Men*. Reading: Addison-Wesley, 1990.

Bond Stockton, Kathryn. "Cloth Wounds, or When Queers Are Martyred to Clothes: The Value of Clothing's Complex Debasements." *Women: A Cultural Review* 13, no. 3 (2002): 289–321.

Bookreporter. http://www.bookreporter.com/autors/au-gowdy-barbara.asp.

Bordo, Susan. *The Male Body: A New Look at Men in Public and in Private*. New York: Farrar, Straus and Giroux, 1999.

Borneman, Ernst. "Documentary Films: World War II." In *Canadian Film Reader*. Edited by Seth Feldman and Joyce Nelson. Toronto: Peter Martin, 1977. 48–57.

Boron, Atilio A. *Empire and Imperialism: A Critical Reading of Michael Hardt and Antonio Negri*. London: Zed, 2005.

Botting, Fred, and Scott Wilson. *Bataille*. Houndmills: Palgrave, 2001.

Bradbury, Bettina. "Colonial Comparisons: Rethinking Marriage, Civilization, and Nation in the Nineteenth Century White Settler Societies." In *Rediscovering the British World*. Edited by P. Buckner and R.D. Francis. Calgary: University of Calgary Press, 2005.

Braudy, Leo. *From Chivalry to Terrorism: War and the Changing Nature of Masculinity*. New York: Alfred A. Knopf, 2003.

Brennan, Timothy. "The Empire's New Clothes." *Critical Inquiry* 29, no. 2 (2003): 337–67.

British Colonial Office. *Information for Immigrants*. 1880.

Burns, Timothy, ed. *After History? Francis Fukuyama and His Critics*. Lanham: Rowman and Littlefield, 1994.

Burrows, Acton. *North Western Canada, Its Climate, Soil Productions, with a Sketch of Its Natural Features and Social Condition*. Winnipeg: 1880.

Butler, Judith. *Bodies That Matter: On the Discursive Limits of "Sex."* New York and London: Routledge, 1993.

———. *Gender Trouble: Feminism and the Subversion of Identity*. London: Routledge, 1990.

———. "Imitation and Gender Insubordination." *Inside/Out: Lesbian Theories, Gay Theories*. Edited by Diana Fuss. New York: Routledge, 1991. 1–31.

———. "Imitation and Gender Insubordination." In *The Lesbian and Gay Studies Reader*. Edited by Henry Abelove, Michèle Aina Barale, and David M. Halperin. New York and London: Routledge, 1993. 307–20.

Canada. *House of Commons Debates* (Monte Solberg), 10 October 1995.

"Canada's Worst Neighbourhood...Northcentral?" http://ca.youtube.com/watch?v=S2lQMZ_rc60, accessed 18 September 2008.

Canadian Pacific Railway. *Free Homes for All in Manitoba and the Canadian North West*. Winnipeg: 1886.

———. *Plain Facts about the Canadian West*. Ottawa: 1884.

———. *What Farmers Say: The Experience of Farmers Cultivating the Land of Manitoba, Assiniboia, Alberta and the Saskatchewan*. 1892.

Carr, Adrian. "On Reading Emotions and Emotionality in Organizations." In *Radical Psychology* 1, no. 1 (Summer 1999). http://radicalpsychology.org/vol1-1/Carr.html#Note1.

Carter, Sarah. *Lost Harvests: Prairie Indian Reserve Farmers and Government Policy*. Montreal and Kingston: McGill–Queen's University Press, 1990.

Cartmell, Mike. "I Come Here for the Rites of Your Unworlding." *Life Without Death: The Cinema of Frank Cole*. Edited by Mike Hoolboom and Tom McSorley. Ottawa: Canadian Film Institute, 2009. 162–76.

Case, Sue-Ellen. "Toward a Butch-Femme Aesthetic." In *The Lesbian and Gay Studies Reader*. Edited by Henry Abelove et al. New York: Routledge, 1993. 294–306.

Cavell, Richard. "Bakhtin Reads De Mille: Canadian Literature, Postmodernism, and the Theory of Dialogism." In *Future Indicative: Literary Theory and Canadian Literature*. Edited by John Moss. Ottawa: University of Ottawa Press, 1987. 205–11.

Chan, Kenneth. "The Construction of Black Male Identity in Black Action Films of the Nineties." *Cinema Journal* 37, no. 2 (1998): 35–48.

Chapman, Terry. "'An Oscar Wilde Type': 'The Abominable Crime of Buggery' in Western Canada, 1890–1920." *Criminal Justice History* 4 (1983).

———. "Male Homosexuality: Legal Restraints and Social Attitudes in Western Canada, 1890–1920." In *Law and Justice in a New Land: Essays in Western Canadian Legal History*. Edited by L. Knafla. Toronto: Carswell, 1986.

Chaput, Simone. *Les coulonneux*. Saint-Boniface: Les éditions du blé, 1998.

Chilton, Lisa. "A New Class of Women for the Colonies: *The Imperial Colonist* and the Construction of Empire." *Journal of Imperial and Commonwealth History* 31, no. 2 (2003): 36–56.

Chopra, Radhika. *South Asian Masculinities: Context of Change, Sites of Continuity*. Delhi: Women Unlimited, 2004.

Clarke, George Elliott. "Contesting a Model Blackness: A Meditation on African-Canadian African Americanism, or The Structure of African Canadianité." *Essays on Canadian Writing* 63 (Spring 1998): 1–55.

Coetzee, J.M. *Diary of a Bad Year*. Penguin: New York, 2008.

Cohan, Steve. *Masked Men: Masculinity and the Movies in the Fifties*. Bloomington: Indiana University Press, 1997.

Cole, Frank. "Sahara Journal." In *Life Without Death: The Cinema of Frank Cole*. Edited by Mike Hoolboom and Tom McSorley. Ottawa: Canadian Film Institute, 2009. 136–49.

Coleman, Daniel. *Masculine Migrations: Reading the Postcolonial in "New Canadian" Narratives*. Toronto: University of Toronto Press, 1998.

Compton, Valerie. Review of *Green Grass, Running Water*, by Thomas King. *Quill and Quire* 59, no. 3 (1993): 46.

Connell, R.W. *Masculinities*. 2nd ed. Berkeley: University of California Press, 2005.

Cooper, Frederick, and Ann Laura Stoler, eds. *Tensions of Empire: Colonial Cultures in a Bourgeois World*. Berkeley: University of California Press, 1997.

Corber, Robert. *Homosexuality in Cold War America: Resistance and the Crisis of Masculinity*. Durham: Duke University Press, 1997.

Coupland, Douglas. *Generation A*. Toronto: Vintage Canada, 2009.

———. *Generation X*. New York: St. Martin's, 1991.

———. *JPod*. Toronto: Vintage Canada, 2006.

———. *Souvenir of Canada*. Vancouver: Douglas and McIntyre, 2002.
———. *Souvenir of Canada 2*. Vancouver: Douglas and McIntyre, 2004.
Craig, Stephen, and Stephen Bennett, eds. *After the Boom: The Politics of Generation X*. Lanham: Rowman and Littlefield, 1997.
Cran, Mrs. George. *A Woman in Canada*. London: John Mile, 1910.
Creed, Barbara. *The Monstrous-Feminine: Film, Feminism, Psychoanalysis*. London and New York: Routledge, 1993.
Cumming, Peter. "Some 'Male' from Canada 'Post': Heterosexual Masculinities in Contemporary Canadian Writing." Ph.D. diss., University of Western Ontario, 2002.
Cuthand, Doug. "Less Poverty Means Less Crime." *The Leader-Post* (Regina) 25 August 2008, A3.
Cvetkovich, Ann. *An Archive of Feelings: Trauma, Sexuality, and Lesbian Public Cultures*. Durham: Duke University Press, 2003.
Daly, Coway. "Filmmaker's Duel with the Sahara." *Globe and Mail*, 11 January 2001. n.p.
Danysk, Cecilia. "'A Bachelor's Paradise': Homesteaders, Hired Hands, and the Construction of Masculinity, 1880–1930." In *Making Western Canada: Essays on European Colonization and Settlement*. Edited by Catherine Cavanaugh and Jeremy Mouat. Toronto: Garamond Press, 1996. 154–85.
Davidoff, Leonore, and Catherine Hall. *Family Fortunes: Men and Women of the English Middle Class, 1780–1850*. London: Hutchison Education, 1987.
Davies, Jon. "Imagining Intergenerationality: Representation and Rhetoric in the Pedophile Movie." *GLQ: A Journal of Lesbian and Gay Studies* 13, nos. 2–3 (2006): 369–85.
Davy, Kate. "Fe/Male Impersonation: The Discourse of Camp." In *The Politics and Poetics of Camp*. Edited by Moe Meyer. London: Routledge, 1994. 130–48.
De Lauretis, Teresa. "Eccentric Subjects: Feminist Theory and Historical Consciousness." *Feminist Studies* 16, no. 1 (1990): 115–50.
———. "Technology of Gender." In *Technologies of Gender: Essays on Theory, Film, and Fiction*. Edited by Teresa de Lauretis. Bloomington: Indiana University Press, 1997. 1–30.
De Mille, James. *A Castle in Spain: A Novel*. New York: Harper and Brothers, 1883.
———. *The Babes in the Wood*. Boston: W.F. Gill, 1875.
———. *The Cryptogram: A Novel*. New York: Harper and Brothers, 1871. Reprinted Toronto: University of Toronto Press, 1980.
———. *The Dodge Club; or, Italy in MDCCCLIX*. New York: Harper and Brothers, 1869.
———. *Old Garth: A Story of Sicily*. Seaside Library 75.1512. New York: George Munro, 1883.
Debates. House of Commons, Canada (1900), 10187.

Defraeye, Piet. "Kicking the Pricks: Attila Richard Lukacs's *E-Werk.*" *Nashwaak Review* 5 (1998): 68–74.

———. "Performances of Masculinity in Attila Richard Lukacs's *E-Werk.*" In *Queering the Canon: Defying Sights in German Literature and Culture.* Edited by Chris Lorey and John Plews. Columbia: Camden House, 1998. 420–433.

Dei, George S. "Racism in Canadian Contexts: Exploring Public and Private Issues in the Education System." In *The African Diaspora in Canada: Negotiating Identity and Belonging.* Edited by Wisdom J. Tettey and Korbla P. Puplampu. Calgary: University of Calgary Press, 2005.

Deleuze, Gilles, and Félix Guattari. *Anti-Oedipus* [1972]. Translated by Robert Hurley, Mark Seem, and Helen R. Lane. London and New York: Continuum, 2004.

———. *A Thousand Plateaus: Capitalism and Schizophrenia* [1980]. Translated by Brian Massmi. Minneapolis: University of Minnesota Press, 1987.

Dempster, Jessica. "'Aye, Daughter, and My Boys Too!' An Examination of English-Canadian Iconography of the South African War, 1899–1901." Master's research paper, McGill University, 2005.

Department of Agriculture. *Province of Manitoba and North-West Territory of the Dominion of Canada: Information for Immigrants.* Ottawa: 1878.

———. *Dominion of Canada: The Province of Manitoba and the North-West Territory, Information for Intending Immigrants.* Ottawa: 1879.

Department of the Interior. *Canada: As a Home for the Scotch Agriculturist.* Ottawa: 1898.

———. *Manitoba and the North-West Territories, Assiniboia, Alberta, Saskatchewan in Which Are Included the Newly Discovered Gold Fields of the Yukon.* Ottawa: 1897.

Derrida, Jacques. *Specters of Marx: The State of the Debt, the Work of Mourning, and the New International.* Translated by P. Kamuf. New York: Routledge, 1994.

Dickinson, Peter. *Here Is Queer: Nationalisms, Sexualities, and the Literatures of Canada.* Toronto: University of Toronto Press, 1999.

Dirlik, Arif. "The Postcolonial Aura: Third World Criticism in the Age of Global Capitalism." In *Dangerous Liaisons: Gender, Nation, and Postcolonial Perspectives.* Edited by A. McClintock et al. Minneapolis: University of Minnesota Press, 1997.

Dohla, Lloyd. "Aboriginal Gangs in Prairie Provinces in 'Crisis Proportions.'" *First Nations Drum.* http://www.firstnationsdrum.com/Fall2003/CrimeGangs.html, accessed 16 August 2008.

Dolan, Jill. "The Discourse of Feminisms: The Spectator and Representation." In *Feminist Spectator as Critic.* Edited by Jill Dolan. Ann Arbor: UMI Research Press, 1988. 1–18.

———. "'Lesbian' Subjectivity in Realism: Dragging at the Margins of Structure and Ideology." In *Performing Feminisms: Feminist Critical Theory and Theatre*. Edited by Sue-Ellen Case. Baltimore: Johns Hopkins University Press, 1990. 40–53.
Dollimore, Jonathan. "Sexual Disgust." *Oxford Literary Review* 20, nos. 1–2 (1998): 69.
———. *Sexual Dissidence: Augustine to Wilde, Freud to Foucault*. Oxford: Clarendon, 1991.
Douglas, Mary. *Purity and Danger: An Analysis of the Concepts of Pollution and Taboo*. London: Routledge, 1966.
Douglas, Susan. "In the Field of Visibility: Cadieux, Houle, Lukacs." *University of Toronto Quarterly* 71, no. 3 (June 2002): 755–664.
Down, J.W. *The Manitoban and Great North West Colony: Explanations of Its Advantages and Objects*. Bristol: Jeffries and Sons Printers, 1877.
Dickinson, Peter. *Here Is Queer: Nationalisms, Sexualities, and the Literatures of Canada*. Toronto: University of Toronto Press, 1999.
Dudink, Stefan, John Tosh, and Karen Hagermann, eds. *Masculinities in Politics and War*. Manchester: Manchester University Press, 2004.
Dummitt, Chris. *The Manly Modern: Masculinity in Postwar Canada*. Vancouver: UBC Press, 2007.
Dunae, Patrick. "Promoting the Dominion: Records and the Canadian Immigration Campaign." *Archivaria* 19 (1984–85).
Duncan, Nancy. "Introduction" and "Conclusion." In *Body Space: Destabilizing Geographies of Gender and Sexuality*. Edited by Nancy Duncan. London and New York: Routledge, 1996. 1–10 and 245–47.
Dyer, Richard. "Male Sexuality in the Media." *The Matter of Images: Essays on Representations*. London and New York: Routledge, 1993. 111–22.
———. *White*. London and New York: Routledge, 1997.
Dyson, Michael Eric. "The Culture of Hip-Hop." In *That's the Joint! The Hip-Hop Studies Reader*. Edited by Murray Forman and Mark Anthony Neal. Routledge: New York, 2004. 61–68.
Eagleton, Terry. *The Significance of Theory*. Cambridge: Blackwell, 1990.
Edmonds, Penelope. *Urbanizing Frontiers: Indigenous Peoples and Settlers in 19th-Century Pacific Rim Cities*. Vancouver: UBC Press, 2010
Edwards, Tim. *Cultures of Masculinity*. London and New York: Routledge, 2006.
Elbourne, Elizabeth. "The Sin of the Settler: The 1835–36 Select Committee on Aborigines and Debates over Virtue and Conquest in the Early-Nineteenth Century British White Settler Empire." *Journal of Colonialism and Colonial History* 4, no. 3 (2003). http://muse.jhu.edu/journals/cch.
Elder, Bruce. *Image and Identity: Reflections on Canadian Film and Culture*. Waterloo: Wilfrid Laurier University Press, 1989.

Ellis, Jack. "Grierson's First Years at the NFB." In *The Canadian Film Reader*. Edited by Seth Feldman and Joyce Nelson. Toronto: Peter Martin, 1977. 37–47.

Ennis, Nicholas Devereux. *Important Information for Intending Settlers in Manitoba: Respecting a Quarter of a Million Acres of Select Farming and Stock-Raising Land in the County of Minnedosa, Little Saskatchewan*. Liverpool: Turner and Dunnett Printers, 1882.

Evans, Dylan. *An Introductory Dictionary of Lacanian Psychoanalysis*. London and New York: Routledge, 1996.

Faludi, Susan. *Stiffed: The Betrayal of the American Man*. New York: Harper Perennial, 1999.

Fanon, Frantz. *Black Skin, White Masks*. Translated by Charles Lam Markmann. New York: Grove Press, 1982.

Faulkner, Christopher. "Affective Identities." *Canadian Journal of Film Studies* 3, no. 2 (Fall 1994): 3–23.

Fer, Briony. "Poussière/peinture. Bataille on Painting." In *Bataille: Writing the Sacred*. Edited by Carolyn Bailey Gill. London: Routledge, 1995. 154–71.

Ferguson, Kathy E. *The Man Question: Visions of Subjectivity in Feminist Theory*. Berkeley: University of California Press, 1993.

Fertile, Candace. "Novel Works on Many Levels." Review of *Green Grass, Running Water*, by Thomas King. *Calgary Herald*, 6 February 1993, section A.

Fisher, Jennifer, and Anthony Shay, eds. *When Men Dance: Choreographing Masculinities across Borders*. Oxford and New York: Oxford University Press, 2009.

"For Regina, Anger Is No Substitute for Action." *Maclean's*, 29 January 2007, 2.

Forman, Murray. "Ain't No Love in the Heart of the City: Hip-Hop, Space, and Place." In *That's the Joint! The Hip-Hop Studies Reader*. Edited by Murray Forman and Mark Anthony Neal. New York: Routledge, 2004. 155–58.

———. *The 'Hood Comes First: Race, Space, and Place in Rap and Hip-Hop*. Middletown, CT: Wesleyan University Press, 2002.

———. "'Represent': Race, Space, and Place in Rap Music." In *That's the Joint! The Hip-Hop Studies Reader*. Edited by Murray Forman and Mark Anthony Neal. Routledge: New York, 2004. 201–22.

Forth, Christopher. *Masculinity in the Modern West: Gender, Civilization, and the Body*. Hampshire: Palgrave, 2008.

Foster, Cecil. *A Place Called Heaven: The Meaning of Being Black in Canada*. Toronto: HarperCollins, 1996.

Fothergill, Robert. "Coward, Bully, or Clown: The Dream Life of a Younger Brother." In *Canadian Film Reader*. Edited by Seth Feldman and Joyce Nelson. Toronto: Peter Martin, 1977. 234–51.

Foucault, Michel. *Abnormal*. New York: Picador, 1999.

———. *The History of Sexuality*. Harmondsworth: Penguin, 1978.

———. *The History of Sexuality.* Translated by Robert Hurley. New York: Vintage, 1980.

———. *History of Sexuality: Volume 1.* New York: Random House, 1990.

Francis, Daniel. *The Imaginary Indian: The Image of the Indian in Canadian Culture.* Vancouver: Arsenal Pulp Press, 1992.

Freeman, Carla. "Is Local:Global as Feminine:Masculine? Rethinking the Gender of Globalization." *Signs: Journal of Women in Culture and Society* 26, no. 4 (2001): 1007–37.

Freud, Sigmund. "The Uncanny." In *On Creativity and the Unconscious.* New York: Harper, 1958. 122–61.

Frye, Northrop. *The Bush Garden: Essays on the Canadian Imagination.* Toronto: Anansi, 1971.

Fukuyama, Francis. *The End of History and the Last Man.* New York: HarperCollins, 1992.

Fuss, Diana. *Identification Papers.* New York: Routledge, 1995.

Gagnon, Paullette. *Attila Richard Lukacs.* Exhibition Catalogue. Montreal: Musée d'art contemporain, 1994.

Gallop, Jane. *Feminist Accused of Sexual Harassment.* Durham: Duke University Press, 1997.

Gardiner, Judith, ed. *Masculinity Studies and Feminist Theory: New Directions.* New York: Columbia University Press, 2000.

Garneau, David. "Other Men." *BlackFlash* 12, no. 4 (1994): 21–22.

Gartner, Richard B. *Betrayed as Boys: Psychodynamic Treatment of Sexually Abused Men.* New York: Guilford, 1999.

Gatehouse, Jonathon. "Canada's Worst Neighbourhood: How Did the Province Where Medicare Was Born End Up with a City This Frightening?" *Maclean's,* 15 January 2007, 20–26.

George, Nelson. "Hip-Hop's Founding Fathers Speak the Truth." In *That's the Joint! The Hip-Hop Studies Reader.* Edited by Murray Forman and Mark Anthony Neal. New York: Routledge, 2004. 45–56.

Giles, J. "Generalizations X." *Newsweek,* 6 June 1994, 63.

Gilligan, Carol. "Woman's Place in Man's Life Cycle." In *The Second Wave: A Reader in Feminist Theory.* Edited by Linda Nicholson. New York and London: Routledge, 1997. 198–215.

Gilroy, Paul. "It's a Family Affair." In *That's the Joint! The Hip-Hop Studies Reader.* Edited by Murray Forman and Mark Anthony Neal. Routledge: New York, 2004. 87–94.

Gittings, Christopher. *Canadian National Cinema: Ideology, Difference, and Representation.* London and New York: Routledge, 2002.

Gleason, Mona. "Small Bodies of Knowledge: Building the 'Healthy Child' in 20th Century Canada." Paper presented at Germs, Selves, Rules: The Gendered Body, State, and Colonialism in Western and Northern Canada, Canada Research Chair in Western Canadian Social History Colloquium, University of Manitoba, 21 November 2003.

Gledhill, Christine, ed. *Stardom: Industry of Desire*. New York: Routledge, 1991.
Goetz, William. "The Canadian Wartime Documentary: *Canada Carries On* and *The World in Action*." *Cinema Journal* 16, no. 2 (1977): 59–80.
Gopnik, Blake. "Bad-Boy Aside, Attila Richard Lukacs Is Actually Bland and Soft-Core—the Ken Danby of the Avant-Garde." *Globe and Mail*, 17 October 1998, C22
Gordon, Gisele. "*Life Without Death.*" http://hotdocs.bside.com, accessed 19 September 2008.
Gothard, Jan. *Blue China: Single Female Emigration to Colonial Australia*. Melbourne: Melbourne University Press, 2001.
Government of Canada. *Manitoba the Home of Agriculturalists*. Ottawa: 1890.
Government of Manitoba, *Manitoba. Official Information for Investors and Settlers*. Winnipeg: 1893.
Gowdy, Barbara. *Mister Sandman*. Toronto: Harper Perennial Canada, 1995.
Granatstein, J.L., and J. Mackay Hitsman. *Broken Promises: A History of Conscription in Canada*. Toronto: Oxford University Press, 1977.
Grassian, Daniel. *Hybrid Fictions: American Literature and Generation X*. Jefferson: McFarland, 2003.
Gray, Herman. "Black Masculinity and Visual Culture." *Callaloo* 18, no. 2 (1995): 401–5.
Green, Joyce. "Taking Account of Aboriginal Feminism." In *Making Space for Indigenous Feminism*. Edited by Joyce Green. Halifax: Fernwood, 2007. 20–32.
Greenson, Ralph R. *The Technique and Practice of Psychoanalysis*. New York: International Universities Press, 1967.
Greyson, John. "The Placebo Singers of Howard Stone." In *Life Without Death: The Cinema of Frank Cole*. Edited by Mike Hoolboom and Tom McSorley. Ottawa: Canadian Film Institute, 2009. 95–103.
Grierson, John. "Statement on *Inside Fighting Canada* by John Grierson, Government Film Commissioner, in answer to a statement by the Treasurer of the Province of Ontario." National Film Board of Canada Archives. Production file no. 304-1-33. *Inside Fighting Canada*. 13 April 2004.
Grossberg, Lawrence. "Postmodernity and Affect: All Dressed Up with No Place to Go." In *Dancing in Spite of Myself: Essays on Popular Culture*. Durham: Duke University Press, 1997. 45–65.
Grubisic, Brett Josef. "Review of Mr. Sandman." *The Reader*, http://collection.nlcbnc.ca/100/202/300/newreader/newreader.b03/Readers/Archive/1995.
Guerrero, Ed. "The Black Man on Our Screens and the Empty Space in Representation." *Callaloo* 18, no. 2 (1995): 395–400.
Halberstam, Judith. *Female Masculinity*. Durham: Duke University Press, 1998.
Hall, Catherine. *Civilising Subjects: Metropole and Colony in the English Imagination, 1830–1867*. Chicago: University of Chicago Press, 2002.

Hall, Stuart. "For Allon White: Metaphors of Transformation." In *Stuart Hall: Critical Dialogues in Cultural Studies*. Edited by David Morley and Kuan-Hsing Chen. London and New York: Routledge, 1996. 287–305.

Halpern Martineau, Barbara. "Before the Guerillières: Women's Films at the NFB During World War II." In *Canadian Film Reader*. Edited by Seth Feldman and Joyce Nelson. Toronto: Peter Martin, 1977. 58–67.

Harcourt, Peter. "The Innocent Eye." In *Canadian Film Reader*. Edited by Seth Feldman and Joyce Nelson. Toronto: Peter Martin, 1977. 86-94.

Harding, Sandra. "The Instability of the Analytical Categories of Feminist Theory." *Signs* 11, no. 4 (1986): 645–64.

Hardt, Michael, and Antonio Negri. *Commonwealth*. Cambridge, MA: Harvard University Press.

Hardt, Michael, and Antonio Negri. *Empire*. Cambridge, MA: Harvard University Press, 2000.

———. *Multitude: War and Democracy in the Age of Empire*. New York: Penguin, 2004.

Hardy, Forsyth, ed. *Grierson on Documentary*. London: Faber and Faber, 1946.

Hart, Lynda. "Identity and Seduction: Lesbians in the Mainstream." In *Acting Out: Feminist Performances*. Edited by Lynda Hart and Peggy Phelan. Ann Arbor: University of Michigan Press, 1993. 119–37.

Harvey, David. *The Condition of Postmodernity*. Cambridge: Blackwell, 1989.

Headlam, Bruce. "Attila Up Against the Wall." *Saturday Night*, December 1993, 87.

Healy, Murray. *Gay Skins*. London: Cassell, 1996.

Heidegger, Martin. *Being and Time* [1926]. Translated by John Macquarrie and Edward Robinson. Toronto: Harper and Row, 1962.

Henderson, Jarett. "'Most of Our Country Is Wild and Unspoiled': Advertising Gender, Race, and Empire for Western Canada, 1867–1911." M.A. thesis, University of Manitoba, 2004.

hooks, bell. *We Real Cool: Black Men and Masculinity*. New York and London: Routledge, 2004.

Hoolboom, Mike. "Frank Cole Is Dead." http://www.cfi-icf/cole_mh.html, accessed 30 January 2005.

———. "In the Theatre." *Life Without Death: The Cinema of Frank Cole*. Edited by Mike Hoolboom and Tom McSorley. Ottawa: Canadian Film Institute, 2009. 92–94.

Hoolboom, Mike, and Tom McSorley. "All Franked Out." In *Life Without Death: The Cinema of Frank Cole*. Edited by Mike Hoolboom and Tom McSorley. Ottawa: Canadian Film Institute, 2009. 4–7.

Horne, Dee. "To Know the Difference: Mimicry, Satire, and Thomas King's *Green Grass, Running Water*." *Essays on Canadian Writing* 56 (Fall 1995): 255–73.

Hutcheon, Linda. *The Politics of Postmodernism*. 2nd ed. London: Routledge, 2002.

Jameson, Fredric. *The Political Unconscious Narrative as a Socially Symbolic Act*. Ithaca, NY: Cornell University Press, 1981.

———. *Postmodernism, or, The Cultural Logic of Late Capitalism*. Durham, NC: Duke University Press, 1991.

Johnson, Barbara. *A World of Difference*. Baltimore: Johns Hopkins University Press, 1987.

Johnson, Daniel. "Robin Favel A.K.A. Burden." http://www.joybuzzard.com/danieljohnson/robinfavel.html, accessed 2 May 2011.

Jones, Malcolm, Jr. "Life Off the Reservation: A Cherokee Writer as Darkly Funny as Twain." *Newsweek*, 12 April 1993, 60.

Kaplan, E. Ann. *Feminism and Film*. Oxford: Oxford University Press, 2000.

Katz, Jonathan. *The Invention of Heterosexuality*. New York: Dutton, 1995.

Kegan Gardiner, Judith. *Masculinity Studies and Feminist Theory: New Directions*. New York: Columbia University Press, 2002.

Kelly, Raegan. "Hip-Hop Chicano: A Separate but Parallel Story." In *That's the Joint! The Hip-Hop Studies Reader*. Edited by Murray Forman and Marc Anthony Neal. New York: Routledge, 2004. 95–104.

Kelley, Robin D.G. "Looking for the 'Real' Nigga: Social Scientists Construct the Ghetto." In *That's the Joint! The Hip-Hop Studies Reader*. Edited by Murray Forman and Mark Anthony Neal. New York: Routledge, 2004. 119–36.

Kimmel, Michael S., Jeff Hearn, and R.W. Connell, eds. *Handbook of Studies on Men and Masculinities*. Thousand Oaks: Sage, 2005.

Kincaid, James. *Erotic Innocence: The Culture of Child-Molesting*. Durham: Duke University Press, 1998.

King, Lynnea. "Generation X: Searching for an Identity?" *Post Script* 19, no. 2 (2000): 8–18.

King, Thomas. *Green Grass, Running Water*. Toronto: HarperCollins, 1993.

———. "Interview with Thomas King." By Jeffrey Canton. *Paragraph* 16, no. 1 (1994): 2–6.

———. "Interview with Tom King." By Constance Rooke. *World Literature Written in English* 30, no. 2 (1990): 62–76.

———. "Introduction." In *All My Relations: An Anthology of Contemporary Canadian Native Fiction*. Edited by Thomas King. Toronto: McClelland and Stewart, 1990. ix–xvi.

———. *Medicine River* [1989]. Toronto: Penguin, 1991.

———. *The Truth about Stories: A Native Narrative*. 2003 Massey Lectures. Toronto: Anansi, 2003.

Knowles, Valerie. *Strangers at Our Gates: Canadian Immigration and Immigration Policy, 1540–1990*. Toronto: Dundurn Press, 1992.

Kranidis, Rita S., ed. *Imperial Objects: Essays on Victorian Women's Emigration and the Unauthorized Imperial Experience.* London: Twayne, 1998.
Krims, Adam. *Rap Music and the Poetics of Identity.* Cambridge: Cambridge University Press, 2001.
Kristeva, Julia, and Kelly Oliver. *The Portable Kristeva.* Updated. New York: Columbia University Press, 2002.
Laing, R.D. *The Politics of Experience and the Bird of Paradise.* Harmondsworth: Penguin, 1967.
Lainsbury, G.P. "*Generation X* and the End of History." *Essays on Canadian Writing* 58 (Spring 1996): 232.
Lamont-Stewart, Linda. "Androgyny as Resistance to Authoritarianism in Two Postmodern Canadian Novels." *Mosaic* 30, no. 3 (1997): 115–30.
Lang, Robert. *Masculine Interests: Homoerotics in Hollywood Films.* New York: Columbia University Press, 2002.
Laplanche, Jean, and J.B. Pontalis. *The Language of Psycho-Analysis.* New York: Norton, 1974.
LaRocque, Emma. "Métis and Feminist: Ethical Reflection on Feminism, Human Rights and Decolonization," In *Making Space for Indigenous Feminism.* Edited by Joyce Green. Halifax: Fernwood, 2007. 53–71.
Lehman, Peter, ed. *Masculinity: Bodies, Movies, Culture.* London and New York: Routledge, 2001.
Lester, Alan. *Imperial Networks: Creating Identities in Nineteenth-Century South Africa and Britain.* London: Routledge, 2001.
Lester, Alan, and David Lambert. "Introduction." *Colonial Lives across the British Empire: Imperial Careering in the Long Nineteenth Century.* Cambridge: Cambridge University Press, 2006.
Levine, Judith. *Harmful to Minors: The Perils of Protecting Children from Sex.* Minneapolis: University of Minnesota Press, 2002.
Littératures de l'exiguité. Ottawa: Le Nordir, 1992.
Longfellow, Brenda. "Hyperbolic Masculinity and the Ironic Gaze in *Project Grizzly.*" *Canadian Journal of Film Studies* 8, no. 1 (Spring 1999): 87–101.
Low, Denise. Review of *Green Grass, Running Water*, by Thomas King. *American Indian Quarterly* 18, no. 1 (1994): 104–6.
Lukacs, Attila Richard. "Regendering the Garden: The Very Rich Painting of Attila Richard Lukacs." Interview by Robert Enright. *Border Crossings,* Summer 1992.
MacGregor Dawson, R. *The Conscription Crisis of 1944.* Toronto: University of Toronto Press, 1961.
MacQueen, Ken, and Patricia Treeble. "Canada's Most Dangerous Cities." *Maclean's,* 24 March 2008.
Major, Robin. *Attila Richard Lukacs: Recent Work 1990.* Exhibition Catalogue. Calgary: Alberta College of Art, 1991.

Makin, Kirk. "Police Engage in Profiling, Chief Counsel Tells Court." *Globe and Mail,* 18 January 2003, A1.

———. "Police Use Racial Profiling, Appeal Court Concludes." *Globe and Mail,* 17 April 2003, A1.

Malinowski, Sharon, ed. *Notable Native Americans.* New York: Gale Research, 1995.

Marsh, Charity. "'Bits and Pieces of Truth': Storytelling, Identity, and Hip Hop in Saskatchewan," Forthcoming 2011 in *Perspectives on Contemporary Aboriginal Music in Canada.* Edited by A. Hoefnagels and B. Diamond. Montreal and Kingston: McGill–Queen's University Press, 2009.

———. "(Indigenous) Hip Hop Culture in Western and Northern Canada. http://www.charitymarsh.com/Dr._Charity_Marsh/Indigenous_Hip_Hop.html, accessed 2 May 2011.

———. "Understand Us before You End Us: Regulation, Governmentality, and the Confessional Practices of Raving Bodies." *Popular Music* 25, no. 3 (2006): 415–30.

Marshall, Bill. *Quebec National Cinema.* Montreal and Kingston: McGill–Queen's University Press, 2001.

Martin, Sandra. "This Land Is Whose Land?" *Quill and Quire* 60, no. 5 (1994): 24.

Martindale, Kathleen. *The Making of an Un/popular Culture: From Lesbian Feminism to Lesbian Postmodernism.* Albany: SUNY Press, 1996.

Massood, Paula J. "Mapping the Hood: The Geneology of City Space in *Boyz N the Hood* and *Menace II Society.*" *Cinema Journal* 35, no. 2 (1996): 85–95.

Matchie, Thomas, and Brett Larson. "Coyote Fixes the World: The Power of Myth in Thomas King's *Green Grass, Running Water.*" *North Dakota Quarterly* 63, no. 2 (1996): 153–68.

McClintock, Anne. *Imperial Leather: Race, Gender, and Sexuality in the Colonial Conquest.* London: Routledge, 1995.

McCullough, John. "*Rude*; or the Elision of Class in Canadian Movies." *CineAction* 49 (1999): 19–25.

McGill, Robert. "The Sublime Simulacrum: Vancouver in Douglas Coupland's Geography of the Apocalypse." *Essays on Canadian Writing* 70 (2000): 258.

McKenzie, Kirsten. *Scandal in the Colonies: Sydney and Cape Town, 1820–1850.* Melbourne: Melbourne University Press, 2004.

McPherson, Kathryn. "Domesticity and Disease: Disciplining Healthy Bodies in the Colonization of the Canadian West." Paper presented at Germs, Selves, Rules: The Gendered Body, State, and Colonialism in Western and Northern Canada, Canada Research Chair in Western Canadian Social History Colloquium, University of Manitoba, 21 November 2003.

McPherson, Kathryn, Cecilia Morgan, and Nancy M. Forestell, eds. *Gendered Pasts: Historical Essays in Femininity and Masculinity in Canada.* Toronto: Oxford University Press, 1999.

McRuer, Robert. "Compulsory Able-Bodiedness and Queer/Disabled Existence." In *Disability Studies: Enabling the Humanities.* Edited by Sharon L. Snyder, Brenda Jo-Brueggemann, and Rosemarie Garland-Thomson. New York: Modern Language Association of America, 2002.

McSorley, Tom. "What Remains." In *Life Without Death: The Cinema of Frank Cole.* Edited by Mike Hoolboom and Tom McSorley. Ottawa: Canadian Film Institute, 2009. 44–49.

Miki, Roy. *Broken Entries: Race, Subjectivity, Writing.* Toronto: Mercury, 1998.

Miquet, Francis with Peter Wintonick. "'Frank Cole (1954–2000): Life Within Death." *Point of View* 44 (Fall 2001): 20–23.

Minister of the Interior. *Letters from Settlers in Canada: Official and Other Information for Intending Settlers in Manitoba, the North-West Territories, British Columbia, and the Other Provinces of Canada.* Euston: McCorquodale and Co., 1896.

———. *Western Canada: Manitoba, Assiniboia, Alberta, Saskatchewan, and Northern Ontario.* Ottawa: 1899.

Mitchell, David, and Sharon Snyder. *Narrative Prosthesis: Disability and the Dependencies of Discourse.* Ann Arbor: University of Michigan Press, 2000.

Mitchell, Tony. "Another Root: Hip-Hop Outside the U.S.A." In *Global Noise: Rap and Hip-Hop Outside the U.S.A.* Edited by Tony Mitchell. Middletown: Wesleyan University Press, 2001. 1–38.

Modleski, Tania. *Feminism Without Women: Culture and Criticism in a "Postfeminist" Age.* New York: Routledge, 1991.

Morris, Peter. "In Our Own Eyes: The Canonizing of Canadian Film." *Canadian Journal of Film Studies* 3, no. 1 (Spring 1994): 27–44.

———. "Re-thinking Grierson: The Ideology of John Grierson." In *History on/and/in Film.* Edited by T. O'Regan and B. Shoesmith. Perth: History and Film Association of Australia, 1987. 20–30.

Morris, Peter, ed. *The National Film Board of Canada: The War Years.* Ottawa: Canadian Film Institute, 1971.

National Film Board of Canada Archives. Production file no. 0122–*Letter From Aldershot.* 13 April 2004.

National Film Board of Canada Archives. Production file no. 0180–*Inside Fighting Canada.* 13 April 2004.

National Film Board of Canada Archives. Production file no. 1012–*Quebec Path of Conquest.* 13 April 2004.

National Film Board of Canada Archives. Production file no. 7029–*Proudly She Marches.* 13 April 2004.

Neal, Mark Anthony. "No Time for Fake Niggas: Hip-Hop Culture and the Authenticity Debates." In *That's the Joint! The Hip-Hop Studies Reader*. Edited by Murray Forman and Mark Anthony Neal. New York: Routledge, 2004. 57–60.

Neale, Steve. "Masculinity as Spectacle: Reflections on Men and Mainstream Cinema." *Feminism and Film*. Edited by E. Ann Kaplan. Oxford: Oxford University Press, 2000.

Nelson, Joyce. *The Colonized Eye: Rethinking the Grierson Legend*. Toronto: Between the Lines, 1988.

Noble, Jean Bobby. *Sons of the Movement: FtMs Risking Incoherence in a Post-Queer Cultural Landscape*. Toronto: Women's Press, 2006.

Nonnekes, Paul. *Northern Love: An Exploration of Canadian Masculinity*. Edmonton: AU Press, 2008.

Nustak, Alan. "Sudden Acclaim Is a Surprise for Aboriginal Writer." *The Gazette* (Montreal), 11 April 1993, section F.

Offe, Claus. *Disorganized Capitalism: Contemporary Transformations of Work and Politics*. Cambridge, MA: MIT Press, 1985.

O'Shea, Anthony. "Desiring Desire: How Desire Makes us Human, All Too Human." *Sociology* 36, no. 4 (2002): 925–40.

Paré, François. *La distance habitée*. Ottawa: le Nordir, 2003.

———. *Littératures de l'exiguité*. Ottawa: Le Nordir, 1992.

Parker, Andrew, and Eve Kosofsky Sedgwick, eds. *Performativity and Performance*. New York: Routledge, 1995.

Parpart, Lee. "The Nation and the Nude: Colonial Masculinity and the Spectacle of the Body in Recent Canadian Cinema(s)." *Masculinity: Bodies, Movies, Cultures*. Edited by Peter Lehman. New York and London: Routledge, 2001. 167–92.

———. "Pit(iful) Male Bodies: Colonial Masculinity, Class and Folk Innocence in *Margaret's Museum*." *Canadian Journal of Film Studies* 8, no. 1 (Spring 1999): 63-86.

Parr, Joy. *Gender and History in Canada*. Toronto: Copp Clark, 1996.

Passavant, Pal, and Jodi Dean, eds. *Empire's New Clothes: Reading Hardt and Negri*. New York: Routledge, 2004.

Perry, Adele. "From 'the Hot-Bed of Vice' to the 'Good and Well-Ordered Christian Home': First Nations Housing and Reform in Nineteenth-Century British Columbia." *Ethnohistory* 50, no. 4 (Fall 2003): 593.

———. *On the Edge of Empire: Gender, Race, and the Making of British Columbia, 1849–1871*. Toronto: University of Toronto Press, 2001.

Persky, Stan, and John Dixon. *On Kiddie Porn: Sexual Representation, Free Speech, and the Robin Sharpe Case*. Vancouver: New Star, 2001.

Pevere, Geoff. "Dead Serious." In *Life Without Death: The Cinema of Frank Cole*. Edited by Mike Hoolboom and Tom McSorley. Ottawa: Canadian Film Institute, 2009. 86–91.

Pevere, Geoff, and Greig Dymond. *Mondo Canuck: A Canadian Pop Culture Odyssey.* Toronto: Prentice-Hall, 1996.
Phelan, Peggy. "Reciting the Citation of Others; or, a Second Introduction." *Acting Out: Feminist Performances.* Edited by Lynda Hart and Peggy Phelan. Ann Arbor: University of Michigan Press, 1993. 13–31.
———. *Unmarked: The Politics of Performance.* New York: Routledge, 1993.
Plummer, Ken. *Telling Sexual Stories: Power, Change and Social Worlds.* London and New York: Routledge, 1995.
Pomerance, Murray, and Frances Gateward, eds. *Where the Boys Are: Cinemas of Masculinity and Youth.* Detroit: Wayne State University Press, 2005.
Powrie, Phil, Ann Davies, and Bruce Babington, eds. *The Trouble with Men: Masculinities in European and Hollywood Cinema.* London and New York: Wallflower, 2004.
Probyn, Elspeth. "Lesbians in Space: Gender, Sex, and the Structure of Missing." *Gender, Place, and Culture* 2, no. 1 (1995): 77–84.
Pronger, Brian. *The Arena of Masculinity: Sports, Homosexuality, and the Meaning of Sex.* New York: St. Martin's, 1990.
The Province of Manitoba. *Dominion of Canada.* 1879.
Quan, Douglas. "Filmmaker 'Thrived on Adversity': DNA Tests Confirm Body Discovered Bound and Bludgeoned in Sahara Desert Was That of Ottawa's Frank Cole." *Ottawa Citizen,* 11 February 2001, A1.
Ramsay, Christine. "Canadian Narrative Cinema from the Margins: The Nation and Masculinity in *Goin' Down the Road.*" *Canadian Journal of Film Studies* 2, nos. 2–3 (1993): 27–49.
———. "Leo Who?: Questions of Identity and Culture in Jean-Claude Lauzon's *Léolo.*" *Post Script* 15, no. 1 (Fall 1995): 23–37.
———. "Regina's *Moccasin Flats*: A Landmark in the Mapping of Urban Aboriginal Culture and Identity." In *Indigenous Screen Cultures in Canada.* Edited by Sigurjón Baldur Hafsteinsson and Marian Bredin. Winnipeg: University of Manitoba Press, 2010. 105–26.
———. "Social Surfaces and Psychic Depths in David Wellington's *I Love a Man in Uniform.*" *Canadian Journal of Film Studies* 4, no. 1 (1995): 3–26.
Reber, Susanne, and Robert Renaud. "A Cold and Desperate Walk." *Maclean's,* 15 November 2005, 94–100.
"Regina, One Year Later." *Maclean's,* January 17, 2008, 2–3.
Restivo, Angelo. "Lacan According to Žižek." *Quarterly Review of Film and Video* 16, no. 2 (1997): 193–206.
Rhodes, Veronica. "Arrested on Camera." *The Leader-Post* (Regina), 18 August 2007, A1.
Rich, Adrienne. "Compulsory Heterosexuality and Lesbian Existence." *Blood, Bread, and Poetry.* New York: Norton, 1986. 23–74.

Robin, Régine Robin. *La Québécoite: Roman*. Vol. 88. Montreal: Typo, 1993.

Robinson, Margaret. "Making and Breaking Manhood: Masochistic Masculinity in *The Passion of the Christ* and in *Fight Club*." *Socialist Studies Bulletin* 75 (Winter 2005): 25–28.

Roman, Karin. "Life and Death in the Desert." *Ottawa Citizen*, 15 February 2001, A4.

Rosen, Bernard. *Masks and Mirrors: Generation X and the Chameleon Personality*. Westport: Praeger, 2001.

Rubin, Gayle. "Thinking Sex." In *The Lesbian and Gay Studies Reader*. Edited by Henry Abelove, Michèle Aina Barale, and David M. Halperin. New York and London: Routledge, 1993. 3–44.

Rutherdale, Myra. "'If Only We Had Some Sort of Communal Wash and Bathhouse': Southern Nurses and Northern Bodies, 1945–1970." Paper presented at Germs, Selves, Rules: The Gendered Body, State, and Colonialism in Western and Northern Canada, Canada Research Chair in Western Canadian Social History Colloquium, University of Manitoba, 21 November 2003.

Said, Edward. "Culture and Imperialism." Lecture delivered at York University, Toronto. 10 February 1993.

———. *Culture and Imperialism*. New York: Vintage, 1993.

Salée, Daniel. "Quebec Sovereignty and the Challenge of Linguistic and Ethnocultural Minorities: Identity, Difference, and the Politics of Ressentiment." *Quebec Studies* 24 (Fall 1997): 6–23.

Salih, Sara, with Judith Butler, eds. *The Judith Butler Reader*. Oxford: Blackwell, 2004.

Sarup, Madan. *An Introductory Guide to Post-Structuralism and Postmodernism*. 2nd ed. Athens: University of Georgia Press, 1993.

Sassen, Saskia. "Women's Burden: Counter-Geographies of Globalization and the Feminization of Survival." *Journal of International Affairs* 53, no. 2 (2000): 503–24.

Savoy, Eric. "Queer Apocalypse: Attila Richard Lukacs at the End." *Torquere* 3 (2001): 2–5.

Savran, David. *Taking It Like a Man: White Masculinity, Masochism, and Contemporary American Culture*. Princeton: Princeton University Press, 1998.

Scholes, Robert. "Reading Like a Man." In *Men in Feminism*. Edited by Alice Jardine and Paul Smith. New York: Routledge, 1989. 204–18.

Scott, David B. *The Home Front in the Second World War*. Ottawa: Canadian Heritage, 1995.

Scott, Melanie. "Life Without Frank." *Take One: Film and Television in Canada* 11, no. 37 (May–June 2002): 18–21.

Sedgwick, Eve Kosofsky. *Between Men: English Literature and Male Homosexual Desire*. New York: Columbia University Press, 1985.

———. *Epistemology of the Closet*. Berkeley: University of California Press, 1990.

———. "How to Bring Your Kids Up Gay: The War on Effeminate Boys." *Tendencies*. Durham: Duke University Press, 1993. 154–66.

———. "Queer Performativity: Henry James's *Art of the Novel*." *GLQ: A Journal of Lesbian and Gay Studies* 1, no. 1 (1993): 1–16.

Segal, Lynne. *Is the Future Female? Troubled Thoughts on Contemporary Feminism*. London: Virago, 1987.

Sharp, Joanne P. "Gendering Nationhood: A Feminist Engagement with National Identity." In *Body Space: Destabilizing Geographies of Gender and Sexuality*. Edited by Nancy Duncan. London and New York: Routledge, 1996.

Sharrett, Christopher. "Introduction." In *Mythologies of Violence in Postmodern Media*. Edited by Christopher Sharrett. Detroit: Wayne State University Press, 1999. 9–20.

Shogun, Debra. "Queering 'Pervert City." *Torquere: Journal of the Canadian Lesbian and Gay Studies Association* 4–5 (2002–3): 110–24.

Shugart, Helene. "Isn't It Ironic? The Intersection of Third-Wave Feminism and Generation X." *Women's Studies in Communication* 24, no. 2 (2001): 162.

Simon, Sherry. "The Intimate Other: Representations of Cultural Diversity on Quebec Film and Video (1985–1995)." In *Textualizing the Immigrant Experience in Contemporary Quebec*. Edited by Susan Ireland and Patrice J. Proulx. Westport: Praeger, 2004.

Simpson, Mark. *Male Impersonators: Men Performing Masculinity*. New York and London: Routledge, 1994.

Sinfield, Alan. *Faultlines: Cultural Materialism and the Politics of Dissident Reading*. Oxford: Clarendon, 1992.

Sloniowski, Jeannette. "Violations: The Boys of St. Vincent." *Canadian Journal of Communications* 21, no. 3 (1996): 1–10.

Smith, Neil. *The Endgame of Globalization*. New York: Routledge, 2005.

Sokolowsi, Thomas. "Attila Richard Lukacs," *Attila Richard Lukacs*. Exhibition Catalogue. New York: 49th Parallel, 1989.

Spence, Thomas. *Useful and Practical Hints for the Settler on Canadian Prairie Lands and for the Guidance of Intending British Emigrants to Manitoba and the North-West of Canada*. Manitoba: 1878.

Spender, Dale. *Man Made Language*. London: Routledge and Kegan Paul, 1980.

Spillius, Elizabeth Bott. *Melanie Klein Today: Developments in Theory and Practice*. London and New York: Routledge, 1988.

Spivak, Gayatri. "Displacement and the Discourse of Woman." *Displacement: Derrida and After*. Edited by Mark Krupnick. Bloomington: Indiana University Press, 1983. 169–95.

Stack, Peter. "Painful Look at Pedophilia: *Boys* Based on True Story of Abuse in Orphanage." *San Francisco Chronicle*, 3 February 1995, C3.

Steinbachs, John. "A Long, Slow Trek to Justice: More Than Two Years after an Ottawa Filmmaker's Murder in the Desert, Mali Officials Claim They Have 2 Suspects in Custody." *Ottawa Sun*, 23 February 2003, 4.

Stephens, John. *Ways of Being Male: Representing Masculinities in Children's Literature*. London and New York: Routledge, 2002.

Stevenson, Michael D. *Canada's Greatest Wartime Muddle: National Selective Service and the Mobilization of Human Resources During World War II*. Montreal and Kingston: McGill–Queen's University Press, 2001.

Stoler, Ann Laura. "Making Empire Respectable: The Politics of Race and Sexual Morality in 20th Century Colonial Cultures." *American Ethnologist* 16, no. 3 (1989): 634–60.

Stringer, Julian. "'Your Tender Smiles Give Me Strength': Paradigms of Masculinity in John Woo's *A Better Tomorrow* and *The Killer*." *Screen* 38, no. 1 (1997): 25–41.

Studies in Gender and History Series. Toronto: University of Toronto Press.

Stukator, Angela, ed. "Cinemas, Nations, Masculinities." *Canadian Journal of Film Studies* 8, no. 1 (Spring 1999).

Tate, Andrew. *Douglas Coupland*. Manchester: Manchester University Press. 2001.

Taylor, Richard. "Death of a Filmmaker." *Ottawa Citizen*, 28 January 2001, C4.

Thomson, Rachel. "'An Adult Thing'?: Young People's Perspectives on the Heterosexual Age of Consent." *Sexualities* 7, no. 2 (2004): 133–49.

Toles, George. "Drowning for Love: Jean-Claude Lauzon's *Léolo*." In *Canada's Best Features: Critical Essays on 15 Canadian Films*. Edited by Eugene P. Walz. Amsterdam: Rodopi, 2002. 291–322.

Tosh, John. *Manful Assertions: Masculinities in Britain since 1800*. Edited by Michael Roper and John Tosh. London: Routledge, 1991.

———. *Manliness and Masculinities in Nineteenth-Century Britain: Essays on Gender, Family, and Empire*. London: Longman, 2005.

Traister, Bryce. 2000. "Academic Viagra: The Rise of American Masculinity Studies." *American Quarterly* 52, no. 2 (2000): 274–304.

———. "North Central Regina Through Our Eyes." http://ca.youtube.com/watch?v=9UmEv-I1Q-k&feature=related, accessed 18 September 2008.

Tunnacliffe, Catherine. "True-Life Tales of the Unexpected: Hot Docs." http://www.Eye.note/eye/issue/issue-5.04.00/film/hotdocs.html, accessed 28 June 2005.

Turbide, Diane. "A Literary Trickster: Thomas King Conjures Up Comic Worlds." *Maclean's*, 3 May 1993, 43, 45.

"2005 Intelligence Trends: Aboriginal-Based Gangs in Saskatchewan." *Criminal Intelligence Service Saskatchewan* 1, no. 1 (Winter 2005). http://www.csgv.ca/counselor/assets/AboriginalGangsSask.pdf, accessed 18 September 2008.

Vaisbord, David. *Drawing Out the Demons*. Vancouver: Screen Siren Pictures, 2004.
Valverde, Mariana. *The Age of Light, Soap, and Water: Moral Reform in English Canada, 1885–1925*. Toronto: McClelland and Stewart, 1991.
van Hoven, Bettina, and Kathrin Hörschelmann, eds. *Spaces of Masculinities*. London and New York: Routledge, 2005.
Vettel-Becker, Patricia. *Shooting from the Hip: Photography, Masculinity, and Postwar America*. Minneapolis: University of Minnesota Press, 2005.
Vibert, Elizabeth. *Traders Tales: Narratives of Cultural Encounters on the Columbia Plateau*. Norman: University of Oklahoma Press, 1997.
Vizenor, Gerald. "A Postmodern Introduction." *Narrative Chance: Postmodern Discourse on Native American Indian Literatures*. Edited by Gerald Vizenor. Albuquerque: University of New Mexico Press, 1989.
Walcott, Rinaldo. *Black Like Who?* Toronto: Insomniac Press, 1997.
Walcott, Rinaldo, ed. *Rude: Contemporary Black Canadian Cultural Criticism*. Toronto: Insomniac Press, 2000.
Wallace, Robert. "Performance Anxiety: 'Identity,' 'Community,' and Tim Miller's *My Queer Body*." *Modern Drama* 39 (1996): 97–116.
Waugh, Thomas. "Cinemas, Nations, Masculinities: The Martin Walsh Memorial Lecture (1998)." *Canadian Journal of Film Studies* 8, no. 1 (Spring 1999): 8–44.
———. *The Romance of Transgression in Canada: Queering Sexualities, Nations, Cinemas*. Montreal and Kingston: McGill–Queen's University Press, 2006.
Waugh, Thomas, and Jason Garrison. *Montreal Main*. Vancouver: Arsenal Pulp Press, 2010.
Weaver, Jace. "Thomas King." *Publishers Weekly*, 8 March 1993, 56–57.
Wendell, Susan. *The Rejected Body: Feminist Philosophical Reflections on Disability*. New York: Routledge, 1996.
Wertheim, Margaret. *The Pearly Gates of Cyberspace: A History of Space from Dante to the Internet*. New York: Norton, 1999.
"Which Have You Read?" *University Affairs* 43, no. 1 (2002): 8.
Whitehead, Stephen. *Men and Masculinities: Key Themes and New Directions*. Cambridge: Polity, 2002.
Whyte, William. *The Organization Man*. New York: Simon and Schuster, 1956.
Winston, Brian. *Claiming the Real: The Griersonian Documentary and Its Legitimations*. London: British Film Institute, 1995.
Wintonick, Peter, with Francis Miquet. "Frank Cole (1954–2000): Life Within Death." *Point of View* 44 (Fall 2001): 20–23.
Wise, Wyndham. "History of Ontario's Film Industry, 1896 to 1985." *Take One* 9, no. 28 (Summer 2000): 20.
Woollacott, Angela. *Gender and Empire*. Houndsmills: Palgrave, 2006.

———. *To Try Her Fortune in London: Australian Women, Colonialism, and Modernity.* London: Oxford University Press, 2001.

Wyatt, G.H. *Dominion of Canada. Manitoba, The Canadian North-West, and Ontario.* Toronto: 1880.

Young, Katherine, and Paul Nathanson. *Spreading Misandry: The Teaching of Contempt for Men in Popular Culture.* Montreal and Kingston: McGill–Queen's University Press, 2001.

Žižek, Slavoj. *Cogito and the Unconscious.* Vol. 2. Durham: Duke University Press, 1998.

———. *The Fright of Real Tears: Krzysztof Kieslowski between Theory and Post-Theory.* London: British Film Institute, 2001.

———. *The Parallax View.* Cambridge, MA: MIT Press, 2006.

———. *The Ticklish Subject: The Absent Centre of Political Ontology.* London: Verso, 1999.

BIOGRAPHICAL NOTES

Michael Brendan Baker

Michael Baker (Ph.D., McGill University) is the FQRSC Postdoctoral Fellow in the Centre for Cinema Studies, Department of Theatre and Film, at the University of British Columbia. He is co-editor of *Challenge for Change: Activist Documentary at the National Film Board of Canada* (with Thomas Waugh and Ezra Winton) and author of numerous book chapters and journal articles on film and media.

Nicole Côté

Nicole Côté is Associate Professor at the Department of Literature and Communication, University of Sherbrooke. She has published a number of articles and chapters on Quebec and on Franco- and Anglo-Canadian literatures. She has translated several Canadian authors and has edited two volumes of short stories, which she also translated: *Nouvelles du Canada anglais* (1999), an anthology; and *Vers le rivage* (2004), stories from Mavis Gallant ranging from the 1950s to the 1990s. She also co-edited *Varieties of Exiles: New Essays on Mavis Gallant* (2002), and *Expressions culturelles de la francophonie mondiale* (2008). She is French book review editor for *Journal of Canadian Studies* and is an editorial board member of *Analyses*. Her research centres on questions of identity, gender, and minorities, as well as on questions of cultural transfers.

Peter Cumming

Peter E. Cumming is Associate Professor of Children's Literature and Culture and is Coordinator of the Children's Studies Program at York University. His M.A. thesis, "Life After Man: 'New' Men in Canadian Fiction," and his Ph.D. dissertation, "Some 'Male' from Canada 'Post': Heterosexual Masculinities in Contemporary Canadian Writing," focus on constructions of masculinities in contemporary Canadian writing, including in the works of Robert Kroetsch, Guy Vanderhaeghe, Leon Rooke, Leonard Cohen, Brian Fawcett, Thomas King, and Michael Ondaatje. As a teacher, consultant, and writer, Peter worked for six years in Inuit communities in Nunavut. Peter has taught Children's Literature, Canadian Literature, First Nations Literature, Creative and Expository Writing, Theatre, and Film at Guelph and York Universities as well as the University of Western Ontario. He is also a children's author (*A Horse Called Farmer*, *Mogul and Me*, *Out on the Ice in the Middle of the Bay*) and playwright in theatre for young audiences (including the bilingual plays *Ti-Jean* and *Snowdreams*). Peter is President of the Association for Research in Cultures of Young People (ARCYP).

Piet Defraeye
Piet Defraeye is Associate Professor and Graduate Program Coordinator in the Department of Drama at the University of Alberta. He is a drama critic, theorist, director, and dramaturge. Before coming to the University of Alberta, he taught and directed in Belgium, Toronto, and Fredericton. Recent directing credits include Arnold Wesker's *The Kitchen* (1999) and Von Kleist's *Amphitryon* (2002). His areas of specialization include dramaturgy, performance studies, theatre theory and modern drama, theatre of provocation, audience reception, Quebec theatre, and European theatre practices.

Kit Dobson
Kit Dobson is Assistant Professor in the Department of English at Calgary's Mount Royal University, where he works in Canadian Literature, Globalization Studies, and Film. His first book, *Transnational Canadas: Anglo-Canadian Literature and Globalization,* was published by Wilfrid Laurier University Press in 2009.

David Garneau
David Garneau is Associate Professor of Visual Arts at the University of Regina. He was born and raised in Edmonton, received most of his post-secondary education (B.F.A. Painting and Drawing, M.A. English Literature) at the University of Calgary, and taught at the Alberta College of Art and Design for five years before moving to Regina in 1999. His practice includes painting, drawing, curation, and critical writing. His solo exhibition, *Cowboys and Indians (and Métis?)*, toured Canada, 2003–7. His work often engages issues of nature, history, masculinity, and Métis identity. His artworks are in the collections of the Canadian Museum of Civilization, the Canadian Parliament, the Indian and Inuit Art Centre, the Glenbow Museum, the MacKenzie Art Gallery, and many other public and private collections. He has curated several large group exhibitions: *The End of the World (as we know it), Picture Windows: New Abstraction, Transcendent Squares, Sophisticated Folk, Contested Histories,* and *Making It Like a Man!* Garneau has written numerous catalogue essays and reviews and was a co-founder and co-editor of *Artichoke* and *Cameo* magazines. He is currently exploring the Carlton Trail and roadkill as landscape subjects and working on curatorial projects featuring contemporary Aboriginal art exchanges between Canada and Australia.

Sally Hayward
Sally Hayward received her Ph.D. in 2006 from the Department of English and Film Studies at the University of Alberta. Since 2007 she has worked as an instructor in the Academic Writing Program at the University of Lethbridge.

Her research focuses on the rhetorical and narrative construction of disability in literature, medicine, the law, and the media. More specifically, she analyzes how and why people with disabilities are either appropriated by or occluded from the national imaginary. Her interest in disability and masculinity is reflected in the work she has done on the Robert Latimer case as well as in "'Those Who Cannot Work': An Exploration of Disabled Men and Masculinity in Henry Mayhew's London Labour and the London Poor," which was published in *Prose Studies*, and in "(Dis)Enabling Masculinities: The Word and the Body, Class Politics, and Male Sexuality in El Saadawi's God Dies by the Nile," which was published in *African Masculinities*.

Jarett Henderson
Jarett Henderson completed his M.A. in Western Canadian social history at the University of Manitoba in 2004 and his Ph.D. in Canadian history at York University in 2010. His research interests include, but are not limited to, the intimate intersection of domestic and political life, the conflict between colonial and imperial states, and how the lived history of nineteenth-century imperialism was affected by notions of gender, race, status, and sexuality. He has taught Canadian history in Winnipeg, Toronto, and Oshawa and is currently completing a manuscript on Lord Durham's 1838 administration.

Charity Marsh
Charity Marsh holds the Canada Research Chair in Interactive Media and Performance in the Department of Media Production and Studies at the University of Regina. She completed her Ph.D. in Popular Studies and Ethnomusicology at York University. Her thesis was titled "Raving Cyborgs, Queering Practices, and Discourses of Freedom: The Search for Meaning in Toronto's Rave Culture." Her current research focuses on interactive media and performance and how cultures and practices associated with this broad category contribute to dialogues concerning regionalism, cultural identity, and community specifically in western and northern Canada, and more generally on a global scale. In 2007 she was awarded a Canadian Foundation for Innovation Grant and a Saskatchewan Fund for Innovation and Science grant to develop the Interactive Media and Performance Labs as a way to support her ongoing research in the following areas: (1) Canadian (Indigenous) Hip-Hop Cultures; (2) DJ Cultures, including EDM, Club Culture, Rave Culture, Techno, Psy-Trance, and online, community, and pirate radio; and (3) Isolation, Identity, and Space: Production and Performance of Popular Music in Western and Northern Canada. In her artistic practices, she incorporates interdisciplinary approaches and multiple media, including turntables, video, radio broadcasting, text, and soundscape composition.

Donna-Lynne McGregor

Donna-Lynne McGregor is an independent screenwriter who focuses on film, television, and digital media screenwriting as an artistic practice that contributes to the development of discourse and theory in popular media. She received her M.F.A. in Film and Video Production from the University of Regina in 2007 and was the recipient of the University of Regina Governor General's Academic Gold Medal in 2008. In partnership with co-writer Chris Cunningham, she has written several half-hour comedies, TV series pilots, and feature-length thrillers and dramas, several of which have garnered awards.

Bobby Noble

Bobby Noble is an Associate Professor of Sexuality and Gender Studies at the School of Women's Studies at York University. He completed his Ph.D. at York University in 2000 and, after teaching on the west coast at the University of Victoria, returned to join the School of Women's Studies at York University in July 2006. His research focuses on sexuality, gender, anti-racist whiteness, and feminist cultural studies. In particular, his work looks at the intersections of masculinity, embodiment, and sexuality in the fields of trans-sexual/transgender studies, queer theory, and cultural studies.

Sheila Petty

Sheila Petty is Professor of Media Studies at the University of Regina. She has written extensively on issues of cultural representation, identity, and nation in African and African diasporic cinema and new media, and has curated film, television, and new media exhibitions for galleries across Canada. She is author of *Contact Zones: Memory, Origin and Discourses in Black Diasporic Cinema*. She is leader of an interdisciplinary research group and New Media Studio Laboratory that spans computer science, engineering, and fine arts.

Christine Ramsay

Christine Ramsay is Associate Professor of Film and Media Studies at the University of Regina. She is a member of the editorial boards of *Topia: Canadian Journal of Cultural Studies* and *Imaginations: Journal of Cross-Cultural Image Studies*. Her research is in the areas of Canadian and Saskatchewan cinemas, masculinities in contemporary cinemas, the culture of cities, and philosophies of identity. She has published in several anthologies and journals, including *Indigenous Screen Cultures in Canada, Expressions culturelles de la francophonie mondiale, Self Portrait II: Cinema in Canada, Boys: Masculinities in Contemporary Culture, North of Everything: English Canadian Cinema since 1980, Canada's Greatest Films, The Canadian Journal of Film Studies*, and *Post Script*. She is currently editing an anthology with Randal Rogers entitled *Mind the Gap! Saskatchewan Cultural Spaces* (Canadian Plains Research Center, forthcoming 2012).

Christina Stojanova
Christina Stojanova is Assistant Professor of Film and Media Studies at the University of Regina. Her areas of research include cultural semiotics of ethnic and immigrant representation; philosophical, psychoanalytical, and religious sources of identity formation; and theories of propaganda and persuasion in media and visual arts. Among her major publications are chapters in *Traditions in World Cinema, Horror International*, and *The Cinema of Eastern Europe*. She is co-editor, with Bela Szabados, of the critical anthology *Wittgenstein at the Movies: Cinematic Investigations*. She is co-editor of the anthology *The Legacies of Jean-Luc Godard* (Wilfrid Laurier University Press, forthcoming 2012) and is currently at work on her book *New Romanian Cinema* for University of Edinburgh Press.

Thomas Waugh
Thomas Waugh has since 1976 taught Film Studies at Concordia University, where he has also developed curriculum in Queer Studies and on AIDS. He has lectured, programmed, and published extensively on documentary, queer media, and sexual representation, as well as on the national cinemas of Canada and India. Among his books are *"Show Us Life": Towards a History and Aesthetics of the Committed Documentary; Hard to Imagine: Gay Male Eroticism in Photography and Film from Their Beginnings to Stonewall; The Fruit Machine: Twenty Years of Writings on Queer Cinema; The Romance of Transgression in Canada: Queering Sexualities, Nations, Cinemas;* and (forthcoming) *The Right to Play Oneself: Essays on Documentary by Thomas Waugh 1976–2001* and *Challenge for Change / Société nouvelle: The Collection* (co-edited with Ezra Winton and Michael Baker).

Ken Wilson
Ken Wilson lectures in English and Film Studies at the University of Regina. He has worked as a freelance writer for Saskatchewan Communications Network's series *Prairie Night at the Movies* and *Prairie Eye*. A past president of the Saskatchewan Filmpool Cooperative, he has served as editor of the Filmpool's *Splice Magazine* and has made experimental and site-specific films for several Saskatchewan-based arts events, including Crossfiring / Mama Wetotan, and, most recently, Windblown / Rafales.

INDEX

Abduction of Europa (Rubens), 94, 100
Aboriginal: cultures in Canada, 152; gang activity, 158; gang culture, 150; men, young, 153–54, 159, 168; minority cultures, xxiv; people in the North West, 29–30, 33; women, 153, 165, 168, 170; youth, 72, 149, 151, 154, 158–59, 161, 166
Aboriginal Women and Gangs, 158
abuse: industry, 243–52; scandals in Catholic church, 244; at Maple Leaf Gardens, 244
abuser, demonization of, 247
"Academic Viagra" (Traister), 238, 255
adolescent: masculine fantasy of infinite ongoing being, 291; preoccupation with fighting, partying, and crime, 60; sexual agency, 250, 256
African American: blackness, 136; communities, 155; cultures, 135; political and social issues, 136; societies, racial inequality in, 139
African-Canadian: 'hood, 137; identities, 135; masculinity, 139
Afrocentric nationalists, 134
alcoholism, 158
Alexis Tremblay: Habitant (Marsh), 49
Alfred, Taiaiake, 151, 165–66
all-male: households, 23, 25; public spheres, 46
androgynous characters, 180
L'Ange de goudron (Tar Angel) (Chouinard), 113–14, 121
animal passion and unruliness, 85
Annau, Catherine, 121
anti-heteronormative orientation, 275
anus(es), 88, 242, 253
apartheid, South African, 157
Appadurai, Arjun, 204, 213
The Apprenticeship of Duddy Kravitz (Richler), 115
Aquin, Hubert, 241

Arbor Vitae (Lukacs), 97
An Archive of Feeling: Trauma, Sexuality, and Lesbian Public Cultures (Cvetkovich), 275, 279
"Arrested on Camera," 163
Artaud, Antonin, 88
artificial insemination, 176
assimilation, 186
ass-men, 91–92
ass-skin leaders, 93
atomic bomb, 207
Atwood, Margaret, 174, 178, 201–2
autistic ("brain damaged"), 221
autoerotic hair dryer, 176
aversive behaviour, 224

The Babes in the Wood (De Mille), 6
bachelor identity in prairie West, 23
"back door boyfriends," 217
Bailey, Norma, xxvi, 243, 251
Bal, Mieke, 97, 100
Bass Acwards (Friedrich), 71–72
Bataille, Georges, 79, 81–86, 89, 91–93, 95, 97
battered wife syndrome, 243
Battle of the Harvests (Beveridge), 49
Bauman, Zygmunt, 101–2, 123–25
B-boying, 156
Beauvais, Yann, 286, 290, 295
Before They Are Six (Parker), 49, 240
Begg, Alexander: *Free Homes for All in Manitoba*, 28, 36
Being Different (Murphy and Parker), 240
Bennett, Andy, 150, 167–68
Berger, Carl, 31, 37
Berger, John, 9
bestiality, 253
La Bête de foire (Beast of the Fair) (Hayeur), 107–9
Beveridge, James, 49
Bhabha, Homi, 102–3, 261

Big Daddy Kings (drag kings), 260
bigotry, 112
Bigras, Dan, 238, 242
Billy Elliott (Daldry), 242–43
bio-boy, 275
biological determinism, 264
bisexual, xxvi, 217, 223, 226, 275
black: action film, 135–37, 139–40, 142, 145; artists, 134–39, 146, 317; Canadian masculinities, 137, 145; Canadians, xxiv, 134–38, 145; diasporic peoples, 138; identities, 136; male gangster, xxiv; male identities, 134; male identity, 134; male oppression, 144; man, 133–34, 138, 144, 154; masculinities, 134, 138; masculinity, xxiii, 134–39, 143–45, 269; subjectivity, 134; urban gangster, 136
black-on-black violence, 144
Blut und Ehre Skins (Pure Blood and Pride), 90
Bly, Robert, 238
Bodies That Matter (Butler), 264, 278–79
bodybuilding, xxvii, 287
body image, 69
Bois Will Be Boys (drag kings), 260, 274–77
Bollywood, Hollywood (Mehta), 118–19
bomb anxiety, 207
bomber jackets, 91, 94
Bondage Television (Hall), 236–37
Bordo, Susan, 239
Les "Borges" (Malet), 105
Boschman, Lorna, 244
boudoir photograph, 67
Les Boys I, II, and III (Saia), 239
The Boys of St. Vincent (Smith), xxvi, 244, 247–48
Boyz n the Hood (Singleton), 136
"brain-damaged," 217, 220–21
Brault, Jacques, 192
Brault, Michael, 106–7, 126
breast reconstruction, 277
Brennan, Blair, 73–75
Breughel, Pieter, 93

British Colonial Office immigration handbook, 20
British imperial ideals, 18
"bros before hoes" attitude, 152
Browne, Colin, 240
butch body, 277
butch bois, 274
butch-femme: about, 262–63, 267; couple, 263–64, 266–67; as parody of lesbian signifying system and heterosexual gender roles, 264; performances, 264; sexual identities and female masculinity, 271; subjectivities, 262, 267
Butler, Judith, 179, 186, 189–91, 195, 236, 264, 277–78

Cadieu, Tom, 104
Caffe Italia Montréal (Tana), 120
Canada Arts Council, 104
Canada Carries On series (NFB), 39–50
Canadian identity, 102
Canadian Landscape (Crawley), 49
Canadian North West. *See under* North West
capitalism, 203–12; alienation and, 210
Carceri d'Innenzione (Piranesi), 82
Carter, Sarah, 30, 36
Cartmell, Mike, 286–87, 293, 295
Case, Sue-Ellen, 259–61, 263–64, 266–68, 277–78
A Castle in Spain (De Mille), 7–8
castration: dread of, 223; father's symbolic, 116; fear for, 94; symbolic, 110, 116; symbolic linguistic, 111
Catholic Church, 103, 244, 249; nuns in convent, 194
Charter of Rights and Freedoms, 103
Chère Amérique (Malet), 105
childhood narratives, early, 207
child molester, 252
child sexual abuse, 247, 249, 251–52
Chouinard, Denis, 111
Clapp, J.B., 22–23
Clarke, George Elliott, 134, 146, 300
class: antagonism, 157; hierarchy, 19;

struggle, 124; values, 139; of white males, 206
codes of manliness, 12
Cole, Frank, 281–85, 287, 292–94
colonialism, 134, 143, 151–58, 165–67
colonial society, 20
The Colonized Eye (Nelson), 44, 50, 312
Colville, Alex, 287
comic book superheroes, 69
comic fiction, 4
coming of age, 252
coming-out: as abuse survivor, 249; appropriation of, 248–49; drama of a common right of passage, 116; of a hitherto unmentionable issue, 246; in Montreal's Little Italy, 119; stories, 120
"Compulsory Able-Bodiedness and Queer/Disabled Existence" (McRuer), 215, 228
"Compulsory Heterosexuality and Lesbian Existence" (Rich), 215, 228
Connell, R.W., xii–xv, xx, xxviii
Conscription Act (Canada), 44–45
copulation, 88
Côté, Denis, 122
Le coulonneux (Paré), 186–87, 194–95
Coupland, Douglas, 199–200, 202–3, 206, 209, 211–12
Cowards Bend the Knee (Maddin), 292
Crawley, F.R., 40, 49
C.R.A.Z.Y. (Vallée), 120
criminal: acts with steel baseball bat, 58; assaults, 172
Criminal Intelligence Service Saskatchewan, 154, 158, 168
cross-dressing, 6–9
cross-gendered ways, 173
cross-gendering (gender transitivity), 267
cryogenics, 289
The Cryptogram (De Mille), 6
cultural: dominance and normativity, 211; hetero-normative, 55; stereotypes, 12; survival, 72
culture: of abuse survivors, 249; of accumulation and learning, 121; of disengagement, discontinuity and forgetting, 121; of drag kings, 273; of masculinity, xxviii; of urban poverty, 158; of violence, 70
Curing the Male Homosexual, 219
cyber-disembodiment, 289

Daldry, Stephen, 242–43
Danysk, Cecelia, 23, 35–36
Davidoff, Leonore, 21–22, 35
Davy, Kate, 261–62, 264–66, 268, 277–78
Dead Ringers (Cronenberg), 292
death wish, 284, 286
debauchery, 191
Deep Cover (Duke), 136
Degas, Edgar, 88
De Lauretis, Teresa, 263, 277
De Mille, James, 4–8, 13–14
democracy, 95, 207
Demonology and Homosexuality, 219
Department of the Interior (Canada): *Manitoba and the North-West Territories*, 31–32, 34; *Western Canada*, 18–19, 22, 27–28
Derrida, Jacques, 203, 208, 213
desire(s): "abnormal" sexual, 217; about, 85–86; for an elusive mystery man, 223; to be heterosexual male, 218; of black male bodies, 136; of the body, 292; conflict between conflict and, 8; contradictions of male, xxvi; Darwinistic conceptions of, 85; to delete (heterosexual) decency, 223; diasporic, 135; to disappear into oblivion, 193; to eliminate people threatening "normal" social order, 227; "enduring animality" notions of, 85; for erasure, 194; erotics of, 82; of escape, 188; to escape the body, 289; to espouse his minority condition, 192; for expenditure, 93; of the exploited and the repressed, 82; exploration and communication of, 86; "feminized" by woman-identification,

263; femme, 267; flesh alive with, 97; forbidden, xxvi, 217; hazardous exploration of, 82; hegemonic gender and, 267; of heteromasculinity, 254; homosexual, 98, 222; homosocial, xxii; homosocial and homosexual, xxiii; to inhabit a perpetual present, 199; for invisibility, 186; to join the hegemonic culture, 192; lesbian, 263, 268; male, 98; male–male, 82; masculinist heterosexual organization of, 95; between men, sexual, 218, 222, 266, 271; of the minoritized, 190; narcissistic, 124; for normality, 218; objects of displaced, 124; for obliteration, 186–87, 192; for other men, 218; to perennially re-enact that shame, 254; to perfect and control the body, 289; physical, 82; post-queer, 268; pursuit of some elusive, 186; Québécois projective object of, 109; queer/post-queer, xx; repressed, 109, 226; to retain position of hegemony, 211; sacred and, 93; same-sex, 267; sexual, 9, 28, 84, 124; sexual diversity and "outer limit," 252; sexual yearning, 84; for simple "truths" of ontological plenitude and social significance, 207; social and historical constructions of, 82; soul's, 287; "stardom" as technology of, 261; transgressive sexual, 263; urban diasporic, xxiv; for variety of men, 218; woman as passive object of male subject's active, 263; world of flesh and, 83
deviant, 218, 225–27, 229
deviant disabilities, 227, 229
dialogue of the deaf, 124
Dickerson, Ernest, 136
Dion, Yves, 240
Dirk Diggler (drag king), 268, 278. See also Pearce, Deb
"The Discourse of Feminisms: The Spectator and Representation" (Dolan), 263, 277

discrimination, 154
disenfranchised: Western subjects, 205; workers, 204; young people, 149
disenfranchisement, 210
disgust, 84, 189
displaced persons, 101
The Dodge Club (De Mille), 4–5, 8–14
Dogz Lyfe: Burdens of a Gangster Rapper (Generoux), 155, 161–67
Dolan, Jill, 259–64, 267–68, 277
Dollimore, Jonathan, 81–82, 98
domestic: abuser, 58; family politics, xxv; life, 321; patriarchy, xxi, xxii, 21; politics, xii, xxvi; relations, 22; violence, 158
domesticity, xxviii, 22–23, 47–48, 141
Dominion of Canada (Wyatt), 20, 22, 34
Double Happiness (Shum), 118–19
Down, John W., 26, 36
drag king: bois, 275; performances, xxvii, 259, 273; show, 259, 261–62, 264–76, 278
drag kinging, xxvii, 259, 273–74
Drag King Invasion I, 259, 261, 268
Drawing Out the Demons (Vaisbord), 79, 98
Drever, Dean, 58–59
drug: addiction, 158; dealer, 135, 137–40, 161; economy, 139; trade, 139–40, 158
Dudiak, Mark, 60
Dudiak CAN (After the Alkaholiks) (Dudiak), 60
Duke, Bill, 136
Dunae, Patrick A., 27–28, 34, 36
Dunlop, Derek, 64–66
"The Dust of Ages" (De Mille), 5
Dyer, Richard, 235, 239, 255

economic disparity, 210, 212
Egoyan, Atom, 102, 243, 283, 292
Elder, Bruce, 49, 51
emotional disaffection, 192
Empire (Hardt and Negri), 205, 213
Emporte-moi (Set Me Free) (Pool), 112–13, 115–16
Ennis, Nicholas D., 29–30, 36
entrepreneurial capitalism, 212

ephebophilia, 250
Epistemology of the Closet (Sedgwick), 267, 278
erotic experiments, 122
Erotic Innocence (Kincaid), 242, 256
eroticization of the political, 94
erotics of desire, 82–83
eschatology, 212
ethnic identity, 28, 122
ethnicity, 4, 107, 152, 172, 175, 195, 276
ethnocentrism, 12
ethnolinguistic minority, 190
Eurocentric histories, 133
Europa's abduction by Zeus, 94
Everybody Wants the Same Thing (Lukacs), 96–98
Evo-Blaster 2000 (Little), 69–70
E-Werk cycle (Lukacs), 80–81, 84–85, 90–91, 96–98
excess of life, baroque, 193
Exotica (Egoyan), 292

La Fabrication d'un meurtrier (The Fabrication of a Murderer) (Poisannt), 107, 109–10
The Fabulous Toronto Drag Kings, 260, 268–74
Falling Down (Schumacher), 239
Fall of Icarus (Breughel), 93
Family Fortunes: Men and Women of the English Middle Class, 1780–1850 (Davidoff and Hall), 21–22, 35
Family Secrets (Boschman), 244
Fanon, Frantz, 133, 145, 165
fascist, 80; imagery, 90; leaders, 91; posse, 95; symbols, 91
Fathers and Sons (Browne), 240
Faulkner, Christopher, 283, 293–94
Favel, Robin (a.k.a. Burden), 149–51, 155–56, 160–62, 164–67
fear: of castration, 94; of "feminization," 266; of the flesh, 194; of moral choice, 123
female: body, 191, 264; centred society, 180; gender identity, 174; masculinists, 239; masculinity, 266–67, 271–72; masculinity, dis-

avowed, 272; superiority, 176; trans masculinities and, 275
"Fe/Male Impersonation" (Davy), 262, 277–78
female-to-male cross-dressing, 262
feminine foil, 189
feminism(s): about, 60, 259, 263–64, 273; indigenous, 153; lesbian, 264, 273; second-wave, 267
feminist theory, 95, 262–64
fertility symbol, phallic male, 73
Fiacco, Pat, 159, 169
Fight Club (Fincher), 239
Fincher, David, 239
Fisher, Daniel, 72–73
Flowers (Lukacs), 97
Forman, Murray, 150, 155–56, 167, 169
Foster, Cecil, 134, 146
Foucault, Michel, 46, 50, 219
Fox, Terry, 292
Francis B. Sim Gallery, 56–63
francophone filmmakers, 102
Free Homes for All in Manitoba (Begg), 28, 36
Freidrich, Kevin, 71–72
Frye, Northrop, xvi, 44
FtM body, 277
FtM boi, 274
Fukuyama, Francis, 207–8, 214

gang: culture, 149–51, 153–54, 158, 164; lifestyles, 149; violence, 160
gangsta: archetype, 154; culture, 139, 154; hip-hop culture, 152; hip-hop lifestyle, 152; identity, 151–52; image, 144; lifestyle, stereotypical, 154; rap, xxiii, 58, 136, 150, 155, 166–67; rap cultures, xxiv, 149, 151, 153; rapper culture, 150; rapper masculinity, 151, 165; rapper's life, 156; rapper violence, 166; stereotype, 140
gangster: black male, xxiv; black urban, 136; culture, 155; life, hip-hop, 166; life of a, 161; lifestyle, 154–55; masculinity, 154; persona, stereotypical, 161; rapper, commercial, 162

Gardiner, Judith, 239
Gatehouse, Jonathan, 157–59, 169
Gaudreault, Émile, 118–19
gay(s), 275. *See also* homosexuality; bashing, 90, 135; boi, 274–75; camp, 262, 266; masculinity, 260, 270, 272; sexualities, 217
gender: ambiguity of names, 8; as assignment, 266; -based conflict, 153; -bending characters, 172; carnivalized treatment of, 4; codes, 64; complex historical constructions of, 3; construction, re-evaluating, 56; constructions of, 4; cultural scripts of, 260; divide, 188; division, 56; equality, 145; formation, 125; hegemonic, 186, 195, 267; hegemonic concepts of, 23; hegemony through queer exclusion, 46; identities off known gender maps, 260; maps, 264, 274; politics, 199, 273; roles, carnivalization of, 6; roles, fixed, 152; separatism, 267; as social construction of sex, 264; as social construction *vs.* biological phenomenon, 3; stereotypical, 72
gendered: male subject, 134; narratives, 149; performances of settler men, 23; physicality, socialized, 65
Gendered Pasts: Historical Essays in Femininity and Masculinity in Canada, 3–4, 14, 311
gender identity: female, 174; normalization of, 14; parodic hyperbolization of, 265–66
Gender Trouble (Butler), 264, 277–78
Generation A (Coupland), 199, 203, 212
Generation X (Coupland), 199–203, 206–12
Generoux, Cory, 155, 161–67
genitalia fixation, 83
German concentration camps, 91
Gilligan, Carol, 174, 182
Gilroy, Paul, 151–53, 165
Girlfriend in a Coma (Coupland), 212

Glamour Crew (Lukacs), 80, 82, 92, 98
global domination and exploitation, 210
globalization, 101, 125, 150, 204–5, 207–8, 211
Golden Gloves (Groulx), 241
Gopnik, Blake, 80, 98
Gowdy, Barbara, 215–16, 223, 228
Greater Toronto Drag King Society, 259
Greene, Lorne, 41, 46, 48–49
Green Grass, Running Water (King), 171–81
Grierson, John, 39–40, 42–44, 47, 49
Gross, Paul, 239
Grossberg, Lawrence, xxvii, 283, 293–94
Gross Misconduct (Egoyan), 243
Groulx, Gilles, 241

Haïti (Quebec) (Rached), 105
Haldane, Don, 45–46
Hall, Catherine, 21–22, 35
Hall, Stev'nn, 236–37
Hands for the Harvest (Jackson), 49
Hardt, Michael, 205, 213
Harper, Ray, 240
Hart, Lynda, 268, 278
Harvey, David, 204, 213
Hayeur, Isabelle, 107–9
hegemonic: concepts of gender, 23; culture, 189–90, 192; gender, 186, 195, 267; gender and desire, 267; masculine culture, 187; masculinities, xxiv, 171, 180
Heidegger, Martin, 57, 77
hetero-erotic painting, 82
heterogeneity: subversive practice of, 81
heterogeneous reality, 89
hetero-masculine: anuses, 242; sport mythologies, 241
hetero-masculinity, 55, 186, 238–39, 241, 244, 253–54
hetero-normative: cultural, 55; femininity, failed, 272; masculinity, 266, 270; sensibilities, 155
hetero-normativity, 261, 268
hetero-patriarchal vengeance, 236
heterosexist cleavage of sexual difference, 264

heterosexual. *See also* macho; "normal": black masculinity, 145; culture, 216; family, institutionalized, 223; family, traditional, 216–18, 222–26, 228, 240; "fiction," 225; gender roles, 264; identified white male bodies, 200; identities, "reality" of, 236; identity, interruption of, 275; marriage, 106; masculine power, 9; masculinity, "normal" family-oriented, 218; masculinity studies, 238; men and erotic and virgin lands to gratify sexual desires, 28; norm, monogamous, 217; "normal" or "natural," 227; normativity demands "tremendous lies," 226; norms, 65; "queer" aspects of "normal," 216; relationships, "normal," 218; romance, 223; socialization, 243; universe, 223; vision of a "normal" family, 223
heterosexuality: compulsory, xxvi, 215; contradictions of, 234; dysfunctional consequences of insistence on, 228
heterosexualization of the abused, 247–48
heterosexually defined "white lies," 223
hierarchization of the sexes, 180
hip hop: culture, 150–52, 154–56, 159, 161–62, 167; gangsta lifestyle, 151; gangster life, 166
hockey culture, 243, 247, 250, 253–54, 256; violence and sexual abuse, 249
Hoe, Hunt, 240
Home (Katrapani), 117–18
home instinct, 22
Homeric *kalos kagathos*, 83
L'homme renversé (Dion), 240
homoerotic: art, 82; nuances, 241; panic, 58
homogeneic: masculinity, 92; principle of commensurability, 82; structuring of behaviour, actions, and ideas, 81

homogenous: citizenry, 44; ferociousness of the, 85; group, xviii; pressures and prohibitions, 85; society, 89
homophobia, xiii, xxvi, 250, 273
homophobic: agenda of the media, 61; man, 273; national game figure (Kennedy), xxvi; reaction to emotion, 12
homosexual. *See also* same-sex: desire, 98, 222; desires, xxiii, 98, 222; images, 219; love affair, 119; masculinities, xxvi, 223, 229; nature of love, 7; panic, 241; Presbyterian minister, 226; subjectivities, 227
homosexuality. *See also* gay(s): about, 216, 218–20, 223, 226–27, 236; in Canadian military during Second World War, 43, 47; of Jordan in *Rude*, 135; male, 216; metaphorical and metonymical conflation of, 219; repressed, 223; "unacceptable," 223
homosocial: behaviour in the Canada Carries On films, 46–47; desires, xxii; home of male settlers, 26; love, 242; masculine Canadian North West, 28; narratives on homosexuality and women, 61; settler societies, 23; space, 25; world, 92
housing projects, subsidised, 156
Howard (Haldane), 46
human decay and transience, 191
human rights protest, 114
hustlers, 64, 139, 142
Hutcheon, Linda, 203, 213
hyperconsciousness of the minority, 194
hyper-masculine star, parody of, 261
hypermasculinity, 151, 190

Icarus, 93
Iceland on the Prairies (Crawley), 49
identity (identities): black male, 134; Canadian, 102; delegation of, 186; ethnic, 28, 122; female gender,

174; gangsta, 151–52; heterosexual, interruption of, 275; heterosexual, "reality" of, 236; left uncollected, 187; male, 216; national, xvi, xx, 44, 46, 104; personal, 154, 293; politics, 202, 264, 274
I Don't Play (Le Blanc), 61–63
I Love a Man in Uniform (Wellington), 239
"IMITAT," 97
immigrant: identities, 118; males, 108, 111, 113, 116, 127; masculinities, xxiii, 102, 105, 111
immigration handbooks: Aboriginal people aspire to tenets of transimperial manliness, 29–30, 33; agriculture fostered virtue, independence, and hard work, 30; appealed to imperial imaginations of male British subjects, 18; climate was agent of masculinization, 31–32; gendered performances of settler men in homosocial space, 25; manliness and all-male households, 25; manliness on Canada's colonial frontier, 17; manly characteristics for settlers and Aboriginals to practise, 33; normative ideas of "family" and "home," 22; North West as colonial society, 20; North West as racially pure white society, 23; North West climate improved physical health and robustness, 30–31; sexualized descriptions of land, 26–29; transimperial manliness, 18–19, 21, 25–26; virgin soil of Canadian North West, 27
imperialism (US), 205
Important Information for Immigrants (Ennis), 29, 36
Improper Channels (Till), 244
Indian Act of 1876, 29
Indian culture, traditional, 174
indigenous: feminisms, 153; man, 154; warrior, 151, 165–66

Information for Immigrants (Province of Manitoba), 20–21, 34
In My Father's House (Lukacs), 84–85
inner-city communities, 155
Inside Fighting Canada (Marsh), 40–42, 45
Instructional Bat Series #2 (Drever), 58–59
International Drag King Extravaganza, 269
The Invention of Heterosexuality, 235–36, 255
inversion, 6
Iron John (Bly), 238
Is It a Woman's World? (Haldane), 45–46
Italian Canadian filmmakers, 120
Ithaca (Katrapani), 117
ithyphallic men, 91, 95. *See also* phallic

Jackson, Stanley, 49
Jackson, Thomas E., 22–23
James, Graham, 244
Jameson, Fredric, 105, 120–21, 126, 203
Jennings, Humphrey, 49
Johnson, Barbara, 272, 278
Jong, Erica, 235
JPod (Coupland), 200, 212
Juice (Dickerson), 136
Just Watch Me: Trudeau and the 70s Generation (Frenchkiss – La génération du rêve Trudeau) (Annau), 121

karmic retribution, 221
Karmina I (Pelletier), 121
Karmina II (Pelletier), 121
Katrapani, Phyllis, 117
Kemp, John, 32
Kennedy, Sheldon, 244, 247–48, 250
Kincaid, James, 242, 256
King, Thomas, 171, 181
KingSize Kings (drag kings), 260, 276
Knockout (May), 56–58
knuckle-dusters, 58
Kristeva, Julia, 102, 106, 111–13, 118–19, 122

Labonté, François, 113
Lainsbury, G.P., 207, 209, 214
Lanctot, Micheline, 107
Land of Hope (Cadieu), 104
language of marginalization, 203
Lascaux, prehistoric paintings of, 85
Lauzon, Jean-Claude, 107, 239, 252–55
Law of the Father, 113, 121
Le Blanc, Craig, 60–63
Legg, Stuart, 39–40, 50
Léolo (Lauzon), 107, 252–55
Les Amoureuses (The Enamoured) (Prégent), 107–8, 110
lesbian: aesthetic, 262; affairs, 217; boi, 274–75; bois, 274; cultures, 260; desire, 263, 268; desires, 263, 268; drag, 265; existence, 215; feminism, 264, 273; performance theorists, 259, 264; practices and identifiers, 272; yearning for women, 217
lesbianism, 116, 224, 263, 272
"Lesbians in Space" (Probyn), 267–68, 278
"'Lesbian' Subjectivity in Realism: Dragging at the Margins of Structure and Ideology" (Dolan), 262–63, 277
Les Clandestins (Stowaways) (Chouinard), 111, 113
Les Noces de papier (Paper Wedding) (Brault), 106–7, 110
Letter from Aldershot (Legg), 40–41, 43, 47–48
Letter from Overseas (Marsh), 40–41, 48
LGBTQ people, 235
Life with Dad (Harper), 240
Life Without Death (Cole), 281–85, 287–88, 292–94
Life Without Death: The Cinema of Frank Cole (Hoolboom and McSorley), 281–82, 294
linguistic minority, 195
Little, Jefferson, 69–70
Little Mosque on the Prairie (CBC), 102
Long Life, Happiness, and Prosperity (Shum), 118
Lost Harvests (Carter), 30, 36

Loyalties (Pittman), 244
La lutte (Wrestling) (Groulx), 241

macho: bully and a, 115; posturing, 49; potboilers, 238; rhetoric and knife brandishing, 112; self-confidence, 123; sexism, 145; sexism of white counterparts, 145; sexuality and sinister gun culture, 66. *See also* heterosexual
MacKenzie Art Gallery (Regina, Saskatchewan), ix, xxii, 55, 76, 161, 320
mail-order Third World brides, 240
Major, Robin, 80, 98
Making It Like a Man! exhibition, xxii, 55, 73, 76
male(s): bodies, privileged white, 206; body, 191, 239, 242, 264, 286–88; body, performative, 97; body of muscle and brawn fetish, 98; classes of white oppressive, 206; desires, 98; hero, Western, 177–78; heterosexual, 76; heterosexual fantasy of hyperbolic submission and impotence, 236–37; homosexuality, 216; identity, 216; identity, black, 134; immigrants, xxiii, 105, 110, 124; impersonation, 265–67, 272; incompetence, 176; masochism, 237; mystique, 80; socialization, shame of, 254
The Male Body: A New Look at Men in Public and in Private (Bordo), 239
male–female intimacy, 174
male–male: desires, 82; kiss in Tour de France, 241; sexuality, 95
Malet, Marilu, 105
male-to-female drag queen, 271
male-victim melodramas, 244
Malinowski, Sharon, 178, 183, 310
Mambo Italiano (Gaudreault), 118–20
man bashing, 60
manhood, 18, 33, 69, 139, 275
man–house relationship, 25
Manitoba and the Great North West, 24–25

Manitoba and the North-West Territories (Canadian Department of the Interior), 31–32, 34
manliness, 3, 12; physical prowess, 9; sex, 218; trans-imperial, 17, 19–23, 25–31, 33
Man Murray (drag king), 260, 268–69, 271–72, 278. *See also* Pearce, Deb
Manuel le fils emprunté (Manuel, the Awkward Son) (Labonté), 113–15
Manitoba, Province of, 20–21, 34
The Man Who Crossed the Sahara (Matthews), 281, 293
Maple Leaf Gardens abuse scandal, 244
marginalization, 188, 202–3, 206, 210–11, 239, 254
marginalized: from American culture, 207; anxiety about passive dispersal of Western privilege, 208; Canadian males and the war effort, xxii; communities and the inner city, 155; by contemporary society, 206; disenfranchised young people, 149; in economic terms, 206; ethnic minorities in Central and Eastern Europe, 112; as fluid state, 133; generation X ignores the, 209; high school dropout, xxv; male figure, 46; masculinities on outside of protector–producer paradigm during war era, 46; minoritized Aboriginal youth in North Central, 166; people living in diaspora, exile, or poverty, 209; people without jobs, 204; queer studies in academe, 239; social groups articulating violence done to them, 202; by structures of late capitalism, 210; urban Aboriginal warrior, xxiv; women in patriarchal culture, 211
marginal status, 185
Marsh, Jane, 40–42, 45, 48–49
masculine: adolescent fantasy of infinite ongoing being, 291; fetishism, neurotic, 286; identities, affective, 283; power and physicality, 94; pursuit of land, 26; "stardom," 265; stereotypes, 108
masculine-feminine hetero-gendering, 262
The Masculine Mystique (Smith and Walker), 235, 240, 244
masculinist heterosexual organization of desire, 95
masculinity (masculinities): "acceptable" practices of, 216; African Canadian, 139; alternative, 154, 165, 171, 211; as anathema to masculine condition, 76; asocial, 283; black, xxiii, 135–39, 143–45, 269; Black Canadian, 137, 145; in broadcast sports, 60; Canada Carries On and NFB's constructed, 48–49; in Canadian arts and culture, 199; Canadian man fit to conquer nature and enemies alike, 41; carnivalized treatment of, 4; concept, 133; conflicted, 9; constructed and delimited notion of, 39; cultural constructions of, 44; dangerous, 216, 225, 227, 229; dead-end, 173; decorporalized, 192; defined by separation, 174; defined by protector/producer dichotomy, 41; defined by war effort involvement, 43; destructive, 172; family-oriented "normal" heterosexual, 218; female and trans, 275; female or trans, 274; gangsta rapper, 151, 165; gangster, 154; as girl-crazy, bar-hopping soldiers, 44; hegemonic, xxiv, 171, 180; hetero, 55, 186, 238–39, 241, 244, 253–54; heteronormative, 266, 270; as heteronormative discourse, 265; heterosexual black, 145; heterosexual/homosexual, 225; homosexual, xxvi, 223, 229; hyper, 151, 190; hysterical fear of "feminization," 266; images of, produced and endorsed by government, 40; immigrant, xxiii, 102, 105,

110–12; industry, 237–43; male protagonists and crypto homoeroticism, 47; masculine power and, 97; middle-class, 21; minority, 185; mythology of, 152; normative, 171, 180; Ontario Board of Censors and, 42; ontology of, 133; parody of heteronormative, 266; patriarchal, xiii; performance of, 80; performative deconstructions of, 272; popular comic book, 69; progressive, 173, 180; protector–producer paradigm, 44–46; queer, 48, 255; queered gay, 272; send-off of heterosexual, 265; settler, 21; as socialization of boys into culture of violence, 70; as soldier on warfront or labourer at home, 45; stereotyped, 70; straight, 255; traditional, 177; violence of normative, 180; youthful worship of celluloid, 67
Masculinity Studies and Feminist Theory (Gardiner), 239
masquerade, 6, 8–9, 11–12, 266
master–slave relationship, 141
material wealth, 143, 145
Matiabi, Afshin, 66–67
Matthews, Korbett, 281, 293
May, Walter, 56–58
McClintock, Anne, 32, 34
McGill, Robert, 212, 214
McInnes, Graham, 49
McKenzie, Kirsten, 20, 35
McRuer, Robert, 215, 228
Medicine River (King), 171–74, 177–81
Mehta, Deepa, 118
men (men's): "act like a man," 55; club on Wall Street, 154; dubious possession of penises, 177; fighting each other, 234; in war, 4; ithyphallic, 91, 95; mainstream Canadian, 206; "real," 218; should not behave like women, 55; shower scene with men, 47; struggle to reassert power, 283; "take it like a man," 55

mental alienation, 188, 191
"mental defectives," 219
Men with Brooms (Gross), 239
"metamorphosing flesh," 289
Michelangelo, 93
Middleton, Frank, 22
minorities, 185–86
minoritization, 133, 185–86, 188, 191, 194–95
minoritized: gender, 190; masculine, 191; Native male, 171; self-hatred of, 193
minority: cultures, xxiv, 185–86, 190, 195; ethnolinguistic, 190; group, 190, 195, 201–2; hyperconsciousness of, 194; linguistic, 195; masculinities, 185; status, 186–89
Miquet, Francis, 284–88, 290, 293–95
misandry, 173, 175, 177, 238
misogynistic implications, 94
misogyny, 94, 152, 168, 173, 177, 262
Mister Sandman (Gowdy), 215–16, 223, 228
Moccasin Flats (APTN), 151, 155, 158, 161
Modleski, Tania, 105, 126
moral codes, 81
Morin, Robert, 121
multiculturalism, 102, 104, 111, 121
Multiculturalism and Citizenship Canada, 135–36
Mulvey, Laura, 110, 127
Murphy, Julia, 240
Murray, Ann, 271
muscleboys, lovestruck angelic, 93
My Big Fat Greek Wedding (Zwick), 119

Nachtigall, Jeff, 67–69
narcissism, 110, 123, 286
narcissistic: ascetic fantasy of infinite consciousness, 290; cocoon of Imaginary, 111; desires, 124; desires of filmmakers, 124; identification, 106–7; nihilistic masculine subjectivity, xxvii, 287; nostalgia for lost hegemony, xxv; obsession with "beating death,"

284; personality, transnational, transcultural type of, 121; projective identification, 105; subjectivity, 293; superego figures, 121
narcotics trade, 141–42, 145
National Aboriginal Achievement Foundation, 161
National Aboriginal Women's Summit, 158
National Film Board (NFB), xxii, xxvi, 39–40, 42–49
national identity, xvi, xx, 44, 46, 104
Native Syndicate, 164
Native Women's Association of Canada, 158
nature, abhorrence of, 84
Nazi salute of skinhead, 94–95
Neale, Steve, 110, 127
Le Nèg (The Negro) (Morin), 121
Negri, Antonio, 205, 213
neo-Nazi movement, 90
New Cocks on the Block, 274, 276–77
New Jack City (Van Peebles), 136
NFB. *See* National Film Board (NFB)
Noble, Bobby, xxviiin1, 259–79
Noelle, Christopher, 272
"normal": family, queer sexuality as threat to health of, 224; heterosexual, able-bodied existence, 216; heterosexual and "uprightly" promiscuous, 217; heterosexual family, 217, 226; heterosexual masculinity, family-oriented, 218; heterosexual relationships, "uprightness" of privileged, 218; heterosexual vision of, 223; male head of household and heterosexual family, 226; "natural" heterosexual with family central, 227; patriarchal family structure, xxvi; sense of self as man, 223; social order, 227; social order, desire to eliminate people who threaten the, 227. *See also* heterosexual
normative: ethical and moral standards, 225; male, 202–3; male sexuality, 270; masculinities, 171, 180

North Central, Regina, xxiv, 149–51, 153–62, 164–67
Northern Canadian Oils Gallery, 64–67
North West Canada, 17–19, 21–23, 26–28, 30, 33
Nos vies privées (Our Private Lives) (Côté), 122–23
nuclear family: Canadian, xxvi; heterosexual, xi; traditional, 65

object: of obsessive nostalgia for flesh, 189; of attention of "bevy of masked beauties," 11; of [female] gaze, 110; of gaze of others, 9; of grandfather's ashes, 287; of intergenerational sexual exchange, 245–46; of male subject's active desire, 263; of masculine gaze, 267; of projected desires and fears, 108
occupational slumming, 206
Oedipal phases, 113
Old Garth (De Mille), 6–7, 13–14
"One Good Story, That One" (King), 174
Ontario Board of Censors, 42
On Technologies of Man's Sensuality (Matlabi), 66–67
Open Secrets (Torrealba), 43, 47
oral storytelling, 172
L'Orchestre de l'opéra (Degas), 88
orgasm with queer men, 226
orifice fascination, 83
O'Shea, Anthony, 86, 93, 99
out-of-body experiences, 292

Painters of Quebec (Crawley), 49
The Parallax View (Žižek), 124
Paré, François, 185–87, 192, 195
Pariser Platz (Berlin), 95–96
Parker, Gudrun Bjerring, 49, 240
parody: of drag kings, 261, 264, 266, 270–71; of failed heteronormative masculinity, 270; of fascist imagery in *Wild Kingdom,* 90–92; of gay masculinity, 270; of heteronormative masculinity, 266; of Pete and Joey in *Goin' Down the Road* (Shebib), xvi; of sexual

desire between men, 266, 271; as universal mode of operation, 86–87; of white notions of queer diversity, 270
Passion of the Christ (Gibson), 234, 237
paternity of children, 179
Paterson, Dr. James, 31
patriarchal: culture, 211; doctrine, 56; family structure, "normal," xxvi; family values, 108; logic, 204; masculinity, xiii; norms, 152; oppression, colonial and, 153; power and privilege, 165; privilege, 152, 166; sensibilities, 155; tradition, 56; vengeance, hetero, 236
patriarchy: authoritarian pastoral, 152; domestic, xxi, xxii, 21
Pearce, Deb, 260, 268, 271. *See also* Dirk Diggler; Man Murray
The Pearly Gates of Cyberspace (Wertheim), 281, 294
pedophilia, 250
Peggy Wakeling Gallery, 67–75
Pelletier, Gabriel, 121
Perry, Adele, 22, 33, 35
personal identity, 154, 293
phallic. *See also* ithyphallic men: discourse, 172; discourse, hysterocentric counter to, 172; fertility symbol, 73; men vs. powerlessness of woman, 91; noses, hieroglyphic profiles with, 67; position, threat to, 76; power, 275; pride and conquest, 94; queue of hammers, 56; shapes of men, 97; weapon, 9
phalluses, 72, 91, 175, 271
Phelan, Peggy, 265, 276, 278–79
physical: abuse, parental, 249; desire, 82; space, 288
Pilon, Benoit, 110, 127
Piranesi, Giovanni, 82
Pittman, Bruce, 244
Playgirl centrefold, 66
Please Use Me (Le Blanc), 63
pleasure-seeking postmodern society, 101

"Ploughing on William Hamilton's Farm near Hamiota, Manitoba, 1905–1909," 27
Plummer, Ken, 249, 256
Podeswa, Jeremy, 245, 256
Poisannt, Isabelle, 107, 109
polyvocality, 194
Pomerance, Murray, 242, 256
Pool, Lea, 112–13
La Position de l'escargot (The Snail Position) (Saal), 115
position of privilege, 211
post-Oedipal: phases, 113; universe, 116; wasteland, 122
poverty, 26, 136, 139, 149, 154–55, 157–58, 160, 209
power dynamics, unequal, 179
Prégent, Joanne, 107–8
pre-Oedipal: chora, 122; films, 106; male subject formation, 105
Privates' Lives (A Film of the First Canadian Division in Britain), 43–44
Probyn, Elspeth, 267–68, 278
promiscuous, the, 217, 219
propaganda, Nazi and fascist, 80
prostitute, 81, 151–52; prostitution, 157, 160, 248
public/heteronormative languages, 276
Pumping Iron (Nachtigall), 68–69

Quebec Arts Council, 104
Quebec Path of Conquest (Spottiswoode and Crawley), 40
queer: academics and theoreticians, 235; allegorical response, 95–96; bashing, 251; countercultural publics, 275; cultures, 252, 276; disabled existence, 215; eye for straight guy, 241; gender-dissident supporting player, 243; masculinity, 255; men, orgasms with, 226; outsider artists, 235; sexualities, 218; sexualities, shame of, 217–20; sexuality, 224; theory, xiv, 260, 264, 272–73, 275; voices, marginalization of, 239
queered gay masculinity, 272

queerness (sexual minorities), 215, 220, 235
queer/post-queer desire, xx

race antagonism, 157
Rached, Tahani, 105
racialized humiliation, 142
racism, 121, 133, 261; antiracist potential, 208
racist: narratives, 149; social matrix, 144; tensions of Québécois, 105
Ramsay, Christine, 151, 155–58, 161, 167
Rape of Ganymede (Michelangelo), 93
rap music, xxiv, 136, 149–50, 155, 167
Rastafarian symbolism, 137
Reinke, Steve, 233–36
religious universalist integration, 122
Requirements of Monumentality (Lukacs), 79
Rich, Adrienne, 215, 228
Rich, Matty, 136
Richler, Mordecai, 115
Riddle, William, 19
Rien qu'un jeu (Pittman), 244
right-wing politics, 91
Le ring intérieur (The Ring Within) (Bigras), 238, 242
Robin, Regine, 101
Roffman, Julian, 47, 51
Roman, Karin, 284, 294
The Romance of Transgression in Canada: Queering Sexualities, Nations, Cinemas (Waugh), 46, 50, 119
Rubens, Peter Paul, 82, 94, 100
Rude (Virgo), 135–39, 146
rules of gender and sexuality, 261
rural xenophobia, 102

Saal, Michka, 115
sadomasochism, 287
Saia, Louis, 239
Salée, Daniel, 103, 106, 111, 114, 125
same-sex. *See also* homosexual: desires, 267; incest, 253; marriage, 234; monadic twosome-ness, 95

Saskatchewan First Nations, 159
satyrs, 92
Schumacher, Joel, 239
Schwarzenegger Shrine (Nachtigall), 67–69
secret(s): diaries, 109; dirty little, 160; of epic proportions, xxvi; family's darkest, 217; "fantasy-land" lives, 225; of female masculinity, 271; "forbidden desires" and, xxvi; homosexuality, repressed, 223, 227; homosexual love affair, 119; men and carnal exhalations, 191; sexual identities, 226; sexual life, 220; shameful jouissance and, 108; shame of queer sexualities, 217–20
Sedgwick, Eve Kosofsky, 243, 267, 278
self-hatred, 144, 193
self-identified femme, 272
self-loathing, 191
self-marginalization, 211
self-mockery, 200
"A Sending Without Any Recipient" (Beauvais), 286, 295
settler: femininity, 21; masculinity, 21
"Settlers' Opinions of the Country," 19
sex for money, 235
sexism, 145, 150, 152, 168
sex toys, 264
sexual: braggadocio, 172; contact among males, 250; desire, transgressive, 263; desire between men, 266, 271; desires, 9, 28, 84, 124; desires, "abnormal," 217; desires, transgressive, 263; desires between men, 266, 271; disgust, 82; dissidence, 82; encounters, 191, 217; fantasies, savage, 80; favours, 217; liberation of heterosexual family, 227; yearning, 84
sexual abuse, 246; adult heterosexual survivors of, 248; of boys, 234; child, 247; of girls, 234; mythology of, 247; of boys in orphanage, 248; survivor "coming out," 248–49

sexualities, "outer limit," 235
sexuality: authentic, 152; coming out and, 115; dissident boys', 242; disturbing blend of macho, 66; experienced honestly and openly, 220; of gender dissonant and stigmatized childhood, 243; in immigration handbooks, 29; of Italian immigrant male, 108; male–male, 95; multiple identities of, 4; normative male, 270; "peaches and cream," 223; *Please Use Me*, 63; political power exercised through, 219; as precondition for lesbianism, 263; queer, 224; queering of heteronormative male, 270; of "real" men, men who have "manly sex," 218; rules of gender and, 261; threat to homogeneous, 85; without ethical and/or normative mores, rules, and standards, 223
sexual orientation, 226–27, 235, 248, 273
Shabbat Shalom (Brault), 107
shame, 225, 234, 236, 243, 247, 254–55
SHARPs. *See* Skinheads Against Racial Prejudice (SHARPs)
The Sheldon Kennedy Story (Bailey), xxvi, 243–44, 246–51
Shirts and Skins (Brennan), 74–75
Shum, Mina, 118
Silence of the Lambs (Demme), 247
Simon, Sherry, 106–7, 126
Singleton, John, 136
skin-ass: gang, 92; sports, 90
skin boys, 90
skinheads: about, 83, 86, 90–95; over endowed donkey, 93–94; violent gangs of Nazi, 90
Skinheads Against Racial Prejudice (SHARPs), 90
slavery, 134, 138, 140, 143–44
slaves, servile or pseudo, 81
Slump (Le Blanc), 63
smelter workers, nude, 81
Smith, John N., xxvi, 104, 235, 240, 244, 247
Smyth, Clare ("Flare"), 268

social: barriers, 133; justice and equality, 157; mobility for whites, 157
social collapse, 199
Sokolowski, Thomas, 83
"The Solar Anus" (Bataille), 88, 99
Sonatine (Lanctot), 107
Sons of the Movement (Noble), 269
Souvenir of Canada (Coupland), 200, 212
Spence, Thomas, 17–18, 21, 26–27, 31–32, 34
spiritual space, 288
Split Britches, 260, 262, 268
Le Sport et les hommes (Of Sport and Men) (Aquin), 241
Spottiswoode, Raymond, 40
spousal abuse, 172
Steiner, George, 121
Stolen Glances (Pilon), 110, 127
Stoler, Ann Laura, 23, 27, 32–33, 35
Straight Out of Brooklyn (Rich), 136
A Strange Manuscript Found in a Copper Cylinder (De Mille), 4
Street Hustlers (Szatmari), 64
St. Urbain's Horseman (Richler), 115
suicide, 107, 158, 258, 291
Sun Dance, 175–76, 178, 181
Survival (Atwood), 201–2, 212
swastika ensigns, 80, 90, 94, 269
Swingers News, 234–35
Symbolic Law, 116
symbolic order, 116
symbolic prohibitive norms, 121
systemic: poverty and racism, 149; racism, 133
Szatmari, Andrew, 64

taboo violation, 115
Tales of Hoffman (Offenbach), 223
Tana, Paul, 120
Tarkovsky, Andrei, 122
Taylor, Richard, 283–84, 290–92, 294
"The Technology of Gender" (de Lauretis), 263, 277
Telefilm Canada, 104
Telling Sexual Stories (Plummer), 249, 256

That's It (Lukacs), 92
13th Platoon (Roffman), 47, 51
Till, Eric, 244
"Toccata and Fugue for the Foreigner" (Kristeva), 102
tools of adulthood, 69
Torrealba, Jose, 43, 47
Tosh, John, 3, 9, 14, 18, 21, 23, 34–35
Touch (Podeswa), 245, 256
"Toward a Butch-Femme Aesthetic" (Case), 263, 278
toys of childhood, 69
Traister, Bryce, 238, 255
trannyfag-boi, 275
trans: bois, 274; folks, 275; gendered, 273, 275, 277; person, 276–77; sexual boi, 275
trans-imperial: ideal, 17, 25–26, 30; immigration handbook, 17; manhood, 33; manliness, 17, 19–23, 25–31, 33
tricksters, 179; feminized male, 172
The Truth about Stories: A Native Narrative: (King), 171, 181
Truth and Bright Water (King), 172
Turbide, Diane, 177–78, 183
turf rivalries, 150
Tyler, Stephen, 177, 183

Understanding Heterosexuality (Reinke), 233–36
United Kingdom (drag king), 260
Untitled (Dunlop), 65–66
Useful and Practical Hints for the Settler (Spence), 17–18, 21, 26–27, 31–32, 34

Vaisbord, David, 79, 98
Vallée, Jean-Marc, 120
Van Peebles, Mario, 136
Venus and Adonis (Rubens), 82
Vibert, Elizabeth, 26, 36
violence of normative masculinities, 180
violent crime, 160; black-on-black, 144
Virgo, Clement, 135
Les Voleurs de job (Rached), 105
voyeuristic gaze, 83

Walcott, Rinaldo, 134–36, 138, 146
Walker, Giles, 235, 240, 244
Wasáse: Indigenous Pathways of Action and Freedom (Alfred), 151, 165–66
WASP Canadians, 201
Waugh, Thomas, 46, 50–51, 119–20
wealth symbols, 151
Welcome to Canada (Smith), 104
Wellington, David, 239
Wertheim, Margaret, 281, 294
Western Canada (Canadian Department of the Interior), 18–19, 22, 27–28
Western imperialisms, 205
Western privilege, 205, 208
West Wind (McInnes), 49
"What do gay men want?", 235
"What do heterosexual men want?", 235
"What do heterosexual women want?", 235
"What do lesbians want?", 235
"What do men want?", 235
"What do women want?", 235
What Do Women Want? (Jong), 235
Where the Boys Are (Pomerance), 242, 256
Where the Spirit Lives (Pittman), 244
White: -boy persona, 270; imperative privileges, 133; masculinity, 268–70; racist gaze, 269; supremacy, 269–70, 274; universalisms, 133
Whitehead, Stephen M., 3, 133, 145
"white lies," "heterosexually defined," 223
Who Is Albert Woo? (Hoe), 240
Wild Kingdom (Lukacs), 81–82, 86–98
Wings on Her Shoulder and Proudly She Marches (Marsh), 40
Wintonick, Peter, 284–85, 294
Within Reach (Katrapani), 117
women dressing as men, 8
women's bodies: hetero-male projecting on, 189; interests and feminism, xvii; liberation, 108; low-heeled shoes, 271; movement,

246; power predicated on men's weakness, 180; reproductive rights, 234; studies, xvii, 238
Wounded War Pony (Fisher), 72–73
WOW ("Women's One World") Café, 260, 268
Wyatt, G.H., 20, 22, 34

xenophobic attitudes, 105

youth: Aboriginal, 72, 149, 151, 154, 158–59, 161, 166; cultures, xxiv; displaced, 81; in neo-Nazi movement, 90; non-operative transgendered, 277; recruited into gangs, 154; revolt, 240; training programs, 160; worship of celluloid masculinity, 67
Youth Forum Symposium on Sustainability, 161

Žižek, Slavoj, 113, 124
Un zoo la nuit (Lauzon), 239

Books in the Cultural Studies Series
Published by Wilfrid Laurier University Press

Slippery Pastimes: Reading the Popular in Canadian Culture edited by Joan Nicks and Jeannette Sloniowski 2002 / viii + 347 pp. / ISBN 0-88920-388-1

The Politics of Enchantment: Romanticism, Media and Cultural Studies by J. David Black 2002 / x + 200 pp. / ISBN 0-88920-400-4

Dancing Fear and Desire: Race, Sexuality, and Imperial Politics in Middle Eastern Dance by Stavros Stavrou Karayanni 2004 / xv + 244 pp. / ISBN 0-88920-454-3

Auto/Biography in Canada: Critical Directions edited by Julie Rak 2005 / viii + 280 pp. / ISBN 0-88920-478-0

Canadian Cultural Poesis: Essays on Canadian Culture edited by Garry Sherbert, Annie Gérin, and Sheila Petty 2006 / xvi + 530 pp. / ISBN 0-88920-486-1

Killing Women: The Visual Culture of Gender and Violence edited by Annette Burfoot and Susan Lord 2006 / xxii + 332 pp. / ISBN-13: 978-0-88920-497-3 / ISBN-10: 0-88920-497-7

Animal Subjects: An Ethical Reader in a Posthuman World edited by Jodey Castricano 2008 / x + 314 pp. / ISBN 978-0-88920-512-3

Covering Niagara: Studies in Local Popular Culture edited by Joan Nicks and Barry Keith Grant 2010 / xxx + 378 pp. / ISBN 978-1-55458-221-1

Imagining Resistance: Visual Culture and Activism in Canada edited by J. Keri Cronin and Kirsty Robertson / x + 282 pp. / ISBN 978-1-55458-257-0

Making It Like a Man: Canadian Masculinities in Practice edited by Christine Ramsay / xxx + 342 pp. / ISBN 978-1-55458-327-0